# Europe 1992

# EUROPE 1992

## An American Perspective

GARY CLYDE HUFBAUER

*editor*

THE BROOKINGS INSTITUTION
*Washington, D.C.*

*Copyright © 1990 by*
THE BROOKINGS INSTITUTION
*1775 Massachusetts Avenue, N.W., Washington, D.C. 20036*

*Library of Congress Cataloging-in-Publication data:*

Europe 1992 : an American perspective / Gary Clyde Hufbauer,
editor.

   p.    cm.
  Includes bibliographical references.
  ISBN 0-8157-3810-2 (alk. paper).—ISBN 0-8157-3809-9 (pbk.)
  1. Europe 1992.  2. European Economic Community
countries—Commercial policy.  3. United States—Commercial
policy. 4. European Economic Community countries—Foreign
economic relations—United States.  5. United States—Foreign
economic relations—European Economic Community countries.
  I. Hufbauer, Gary Clyde.
HC241.2.E81285  1990                      90-35041
337.4—dc20                                  CIP

9  8  7  6  5  4  3  2  1

## THE BROOKINGS INSTITUTION

The Brookings Institution is an independent organization devoted to nonpartisan research, education, and publication in economics, government, foreign policy, and the social sciences generally. Its principal purposes are to aid in the development of sound public policies and to promote public understanding of issues of national importance.

The Institution was founded on December 8, 1927, to merge the activities of the Institute for Government Research, founded in 1916, the Institute of Economics, founded in 1922, and the Robert Brookings Graduate School of Economics and Government, founded in 1924.

The Board of Trustees is responsible for the general administration of the Institution, while the immediate direction of the policies, program, and staff is vested in the President, assisted by an advisory committee of the officers and staff. The by-laws of the Institution state: "It is the function of the Trustees to make possible the conduct of scientific research, and publication, under the most favorable conditions, and to safeguard the independence of the research staff in the pursuit of their studies and in the publication of the results of such studies. It is not a part of their function to determine, control, or influence the conduct of particular investigations or the conclusions reached."

The President bears final responsibility for the decision to publish a manuscript as a Brookings book. In reaching his judgment on the competence, accuracy, and objectivity of each study, the President is advised by the director of the appropriate research program and weighs the views of a panel of expert outside readers who report to him in confidence on the quality of the work. Publication of a work signifies that it is deemed a competent treatment worthy of public consideration but does not imply endorsement of conclusions or recommendations.

The Institution maintains its position of neutrality on issues of public policy in order to safeguard the intellectual freedom of the staff. Hence interpretations or conclusions in Brookings publications should be understood to be solely those of the authors and should not be attributed to the Institution, to its trustees, officers, or other staff members, or to the organizations that support its research.

# Foreword

THE END of the cold war brings into sharp focus the shifting balance between military and economic power. As national security alliances recede (NATO) or collapse (Warsaw Pact), new economic alliances gather strength. Japan is forging special economic ties with China and its other Asian neighbors; the United States is creating a North American free trade area that could extend from Canada to Mexico; and the European Community is moving aggressively to complete its internal market—the Europe 1992 process—and establish stronger links with the nations of the European Free Trade Association and Eastern Europe.

The emergence of a unified Europe promises to affect the United States in several ways, some immediate and obvious, others long-term and subtle. Accordingly, the Brookings Institution commissioned a study of the Europe 1992 process at its midway point, while important issues are still being debated within Europe and across the Atlantic. This book provides a close look at the economic consequences of that process in four important sectors: banking and securities, automobiles, telecommunications, and semiconductors. It explores the ramifications of the Community's newly energized approach to competition policy. Finally, it examines the negotiating strategy that will best serve U.S. economic interests in Europe.

The authors suggest that U.S. companies established in Europe will prosper with the completion of the internal market: they are adept at operating on a continental scale. More problematic is the position of U.S. firms that export their goods and services to the European market, although the negotiating record suggests that potential barriers can be reduced or eliminated. Finally, the successful unification of Europe may very well prompt the United States to reexamine its own economic institutions, ranging from the Glass-Steagall and McFadden acts that preclude universal banking, to the role of government-assisted research consortia in promoting high technology.

Gary Clyde Hufbauer, the editor, is the Marcus Wallenberg Professor of International Financial Diplomacy at Georgetown University. He wishes to thank Claudia Schmitz, Joanna van Rooij, and Constance Rotival for their assistance in coordination and research; Jeanette Morrison, Nancy D. Davidson, Vicky Macintyre, and Brenda B. Szittya for editing the manuscript; and Roshna M. Kapadia and Pamela Plehn for verifying its factual content. Susan L. Woollen prepared it for typesetting and Fred L. Kepler compiled the index.

The views expressed in this book are those of the authors and should not be attributed to the trustees, officers, or staff members of the Brookings Institution.

BRUCE K. MACLAURY
*President*

*May 1990*
*Washington, D.C.*

# Contents

# Appendixes

# Tables

# Figures

# Introduction

## CHARLES L. SCHULTZE

THE CONCEPT of a united Western Europe has been a major force shaping events on that continent throughout the postwar era. In the economic sphere important progress had already been made by 1985. Early on, agreement was reached and steps gradually taken to remove virtually all the tariffs on commodity trade among the countries of the European Community (EC), initially six, then expanded to nine, and now including twelve Western European nations. In 1979 the EC nations, excepting the United Kingdom, adopted an arrangement to stabilize exchange rates among themselves, and as an indirect consequence gave to the most conservative central bank of the group—the German Bundesbank—a dominant influence over the monetary policy of the member states.

Despite the progress, economic integration in 1985 was far from complete. While tariffs on intra-Community trade in commodities had been eliminated, merchandise imports and exports within the Community still faced complex and time-consuming border controls. More important, trade in services of all kinds was still protected, firms in one country were not fully free to set up shop in others, and each country had its own set of complex technical standards—for purposes of financial regulation, consumer protection, and compliance with health, safety, and environmental objectives—that had to be met. At the same time, the first half of the 1980s had been a period of stagnation for most European economies. From 1979 to 1986 GNP growth averaged only 1.6 percent a year. And although the inflation of the late 1970s had lessened, the European unemployment rate rose steadily, reaching 11 percent of the labor force. While observers differed on the specifics, most agreed that the European economies had become encrusted with all kinds of rigidities and impediments to dynamic growth from which they needed to be set free.

In this environment, when a 1985 White Paper of the European Community proposed to put in place by 1992 the radical institutional reforms required to complete European economic integration, it struck a responsive chord, not only as a means to make European firms more efficient, but also as a politically acceptable device to open the European economies to the stiff breeze of additional competition. And well before the reforms got under way, Europe 1992 began to have a beneficial effect on European economies. In an effort to position themselves to compete better in the hugely enlarged arena of an integrated European market, German, French, British, and other European—and non-European— firms stepped up their investment activities sharply. As a result, Europe in the last three years has enjoyed a mini-boom, which has begun to put a noticeable dent in its high unemployment rate without, so far, seriously heating up inflation.

A few of the most ambitious aspects of the broader European integration program will not be completed quickly; for example, tax harmonization and the achievement of a common currency with a common central bank. But difficult and politically sensitive steps to formulate and approve the 279 legal and regulatory reforms needed to achieve most of the Europe 1992 objectives have been taken with surprising speed. This book examines the program of European integration from the standpoint of how it will affect American interests. The authors look at two interrelated aspects of the question:

1. How will the *specific nuts and bolts* of the far-ranging legal and regulatory changes now in prospect for Europe affect the economic interests of the United States? This investigation concentrates on six specific areas of concern, and these studies make up the bulk of the book. Four deal with industries that are likely to be particularly affected— banking and securities, automobiles, telecommunications, and semiconductors. The remaining two represent crosscutting areas of special interest to U.S. firms and trade negotiators, namely, the emerging European competition policy and the question of U.S. negotiating strategy.

2. Relying on both the results of the six specific studies and a more general examination of economic consequences, the overview chapter reflects more broadly on how a successful completion of European economic integration is likely to affect *international economic relationships* (mainly in terms of speeding up changes already under way) and, in turn, what changes those effects may require in U.S. economic policies. Here Gary Hufbauer looks not only at what Europe 1992 implies for the U.S.

role in the world economy but also at the less obvious but nevertheless important question of how Europe 1992 may challenge the way Americans manage their domestic affairs.

Most of the research for this book was completed before the revolution that is sweeping through Eastern Europe got well under way. The individual chapters do not reflect the consequences of that development. In his Overview, however, editor Gary Hufbauer does assess how the progress toward Europe 1992 is likely to be affected. While he foresees some major consequences for the Western European economy arising from the Eastern European revolution, he concludes that the core of Europe 1992—the 279 directives in the formal program—is not at risk. Hence the essential conclusions of the chapters that follow remain valid.

## The Web of Europe-U.S. Economic Connections

On first glance the major issue for U.S. policymakers and business leaders seems to be how the economic integration of Europe is likely to affect the $160 billion worth of trade merchandise between the United States and Europe. What Europe 1992 portends for American exports is indeed a most important subject. But a more careful look at the economic connections between the two areas reveals a wider web of economic relationships. While U.S. exporters sold and shipped $75 billion worth of American goods across the Atlantic to the European Community in 1988, the affiliates of U.S. multinational firms in Europe sold some $620 billion worth, principally but by no means exclusively, to European customers. (Affiliates of European firms located in the United States had sales of $600 billion in the same year.) To be sure, almost all the $75 billion in exports represented income for U.S. workers and profits for U.S. firms, while most of the $620 billion in U.S. multinational sales represented income paid to European workers and firms. But even the relatively modest fraction of U.S. multinational sales in Europe that went to purchase American-made components, some $23 billion, when added to the fraction that was earned as profits, another $23 billion, represents a sizable total, approaching $50 billion annually.

There are other connections. Even in an era of large American trade deficits financed by net U.S. receipts of capital from abroad, U.S. firms continued to make substantial direct investments in their European affiliates, some $18 billion in 1989. And European firms directly invested some $39 billion here. The more U.S. and European firms invest and operate in each other's territory, the more there is a subtle but effective exchange of technological ideas and managerial techniques. And as U.S. multinational firms press to have their affiliates treated as equal to German, French, and British firms, with respect to satisfying the streamlined financial and technical standards of an integrated Europe, so the European Community will surely press the United States to change some of its regulatory standards where those are more restrictive than their European counterparts.

Thus the United States has a wide variety of connections and many different interests in the outcome of the legal, regulatory, and economic changes that are being set in motion by Europe 1992. Sometimes the most interesting but also the most difficult issues are those that arise when different American interests conflict with each other.

## Preview: The Major Issues Explored

From the standpoint of its likely effects on the United States, European economic integration raises five major classes of issues, which are explored throughout this volume. *First*, the successful dismantling of barriers to trade and commerce within the European Community will have direct effects on American exports to Europe and will indirectly affect American exports to the rest of the world. Firms located in a Community country will gain improved access and increased competitive advantage for sales in other Community countries relative to firms now exporting into Europe from the outside. Consequently, there will be some *trade diversion* from U.S. exporters to firms located in Europe (some firms benefiting from diversion will, of course, be the European affiliates of U.S. multinationals). On the other hand, market integration will raise European national income and expand overall demand for goods and services; hence there will be some *trade creation*. To the extent that unification reinvigorates the European economies, which seemed to flag in the early 1980s, European national income will not merely be higher but will grow faster. In short, American exporters are likely to have a smaller share of a bigger and more rapidly expanding market. Finally, after a shakeout period, many German, French, and other European firms will grow. As they successfully expand into the much larger market of a unified Europe, and to the extent there are efficiencies to be gained from larger scale, these firms will become more effective competitors against the United

States in world markets. The overall effect on U.S. exports on a global basis will depend on the net balance among these conflicting forces.

A *second* major area of concern for the United States is the extent to which the European Community, through unification, hastens a trend— already in evidence around the world—to subsidize, protect, and otherwise pursue policies designed to expand its *high-technology industries* at the expense of those based in other countries. So far Europe has lagged behind Japan and the United States in many aspects of the computer and information technology industries. In formulating policies and practices that will govern the flow of trade within and into a unified Europe, EC policymakers may be tempted to increase their use of various devices—including antidumping and local content rules—to boost home-grown European high-technology firms. Several European countries have been moving in this direction in recent years. And, in resisting this development, the United States does not enter the negotiations with completely clean hands, given the recent semiconductor chip agreement through which it imposed a cartel-like arrangement on Japanese chip manufacturers, guaranteeing a minimum price umbrella to cover U.S. producers.

The *third* category includes an array of highly specific issues that have arisen or are likely to arise between the United States and the European Community about the effect on one or more American industries of the particular rules that are adopted under the Europe 1992 Program. The chapters that follow identify and examine a number of such issues, among which five stand out. (a) *Reciprocity:* to what extent will the European Community insist, as a condition for U.S. firms to operate freely in a unified Europe, that European firms be given the same rights in the United States? That insistence could prove very troubling in a few cases— banking being the most prominent—where our laws will not let any firms, including American banks, set up branches in all the states and otherwise operate as freely as banks will be allowed to do throughout the various countries of a unified Europe. (b) *National quotas:* many individual European countries now have import quotas on some goods— autos and textiles being the prime examples. Individual country quotas would be impossible in a unified Europe, given the easy transshipment among countries that goes with a unified market. What will happen to the current quota system? (c) *Technical standards:* under Europe 1992 the major technique for handling disparate national standards will be the practice of "mutual recognition"—if a particular good meets the standards of one member state it will be deemed to meet the standards of other member states, and may be sold there. But for a limited range of products affecting health, safety, and the environment, and for some products with strong interoperability features (notably telecommunications), the EC will lay down minimum standards or enforce harmonization. The dual approach of mutual recognition and selected minimum standards raises several questions. How soon and for what products will the mutual recognition approach be adopted between the United States and the Community? Under what circumstances will the Community accept product testing and certification performed in the United States, and vice versa? And what level of consultation and coordination will take place between the Community and the United States in setting minimum standards? (d) The Europe 1992 process contemplates opening *govern- ment procurement* to firms from other European countries: to what extent will this liberalization also apply to imports? This question is particularly important to American exporters of telecommunications equipment. (e) The final specific issue concerns *competition policy:* how will the European Community carry out its antitrust policy? In particular, what will be the policy regarding mergers and acquistions, especially when the acquiring firm is non-European?

A *fourth* broad area involves the negotiating strategy for the United States in dealing with the European Community on the specific issues reviewed above, as well as on other issues that will inevitably arise. One fascinating but difficult problem that will surface time and again has already been noted. Because U.S. economic connections with Europe are so diverse and wide ranging, there will often be conflicts among various American interests, especially between large U.S. multinationals already producing in Europe and small and medium-sized American firms and their workers who are exporting to Europe. Another strategic question that has to be addressed by U.S. trade negotiators is how to mesh the particular bilateral concerns with the Community on Europe 1992 issues with the current round of multilateral negotiations (the Uruguay Round), now reaching a conclusion under GATT auspices.

The *final two* major issues transcend the particulars of European unification and relate to the longer-run implications of an economically united Europe for the American business community and for American economic policy. Over time the unification of the European market will promote the growth of numerous large multinational firms headquartered in Europe but with worldwide markets and production facilities in many countries. Adding a large crop of multinationals to the current group will expose U.S. multinationals to increased competition around the world, but cross-national alliances and acquisitions may also increase. The domain of competition policy is becoming increasingly international, suggesting the need for coordination of such policy between Brussels and Washington. Even more important, a new crop of multinationals will accelerate a process that has been under way for some time, namely, an increasing disassociation between many of the world's major producers and the national interests of particular countries, raising in turn a host of questions for policymakers in all the industrial countries. Last, a successful transition to a highly integrated European economy, with a population and GNP larger than those of the United States, will challenge the postwar status of America as the acknowledged leader in the formulation of international economic policy. How Americans will adjust to the new circumstances is beyond the scope of this book, but it does raise some of the relevant questions.

# Chapter 1

# An Overview

GARY CLYDE HUFBAUER

IN MARCH 1957, six nations signed the historic Treaty of Rome, setting in motion the economic and political integration of Western Europe (milestones in this process are detailed in appendix 1-1). When the Treaty of Rome entered into force on January 1, 1958, it established the European Economic Community (EEC), which—together with the European Coal and Steel Community (ECSC) and the European Atomic Energy Community (Euratom)—came to be known as the European Community (EC) or the Common Market.[1] The basic institutions of the EC are depicted in appendixes 1-2 and 1-3. The Treaty of Rome envisaged the ultimate goal of an integrated market for the free movement of goods, services, capital, and people. These are known as the "four freedoms"; Europe 1992 will turn them into reality.

## A Brief History

The United States publicly applauded the EC at its formation—and for good reason.[2] Europe grew into a strong political and military ally; American business invested and prospered in the Common Market; and Atlantic trade relations were accented more often by harmony than acrimony. Yet, over the past three decades, the United States has questioned certain economic aspects of the emerging European state. Questions continue during the present leap toward an integrated market,

Gary Clyde Hufbauer is the Marcus Wallenberg Professor of International Financial Diplomacy at Georgetown University. Claudia Schmitz and Joanna van Rooij, both graduates of the School of Foreign Service at Georgetown University, provided valuable research assistance.

1. The ECSC was established by the Treaty of Paris (April 1951). Euratom was created by a second Treaty of Rome, also signed in March 1957. The separate councils and commissions of the ECSC, EEC, and Euratom were merged in July 1967.

2. See Stanley Hoffman, "The European Community and 1992," *Foreign Affairs*, vol. 68 (Fall 1989), pp. 27–47.

TABLE 1–1. Economic Profile of the European Community,
North America, and Japan, 1987[a]

| Country or region | GNP (billions of dollars) | Population (millions) | GNP per capita | Merchandise trade (billions of dollars) | | Services and factor income[b] (billions of dollars) | |
|---|---|---|---|---|---|---|---|
| | | | | Exports | Imports | Credits | Debits |
| Belgium | 138 | 10 | 14,000 | 84 | 83 | 34 | 32 |
| Denmark | 97 | 5 | 19,000 | 26 | 26 | 9 | 11 |
| France | 877 | 56 | 15,700 | 148 | 159 | 75 | 67 |
| Germany, West | 1,124 | 61 | 18,400 | 294 | 228 | 49 | 54 |
| Greece | 47 | 10 | 4,700 | 7 | 13 | 3 | 3 |
| Ireland | 26 | 4 | 7,400 | 16 | 14 | 2 | 4 |
| Italy | 751 | 57 | 13,200 | 116 | 125 | 28 | 26 |
| Luxembourg | 8 | c | 20,000 | c | c | c | c |
| Netherlands | 213 | 15 | 14,200 | 92 | 91 | 24 | 23 |
| Portugal | 36 | 10 | 3,600 | 9 | 13 | 2 | 3 |
| Spain | 287 | 39 | 7,400 | 34 | 49 | 15 | 9 |
| United Kingdom | 671 | 57 | 11,800 | 131 | 154 | 99 | 87 |
| TOTAL, EC-12 | 4,274 | 323 | 13,200 | 958 | 956 | 340 | 319 |
| United States | 4,502 | 244 | 18,500 | 250 | 422 | 144 | 122 |
| Canada | 398 | 26 | 15,300 | 98 | 90 | 17 | 31 |
| TOTAL, NORTH AMERICA | 4,900 | 270 | 18,100 | 348 | 513 | 161 | 152 |
| Japan | 2,387 | 122 | 19,600 | 231 | 151 | 46 | 51 |

SOURCES: International Monetary Fund, *Direction of Trade Statistics, 1981–1987; Yearbook 1988* (Washington, D.C., 1988); Organization for Economic Cooperation and Development, *Historical Statistics 1960–1987* (Paris, 1989), and *OECD Member Countries' Data on Trade in Services* (Paris, October 1987); and Arthur Andersen and Co., *1992: Guide for Clients* (Brussels, March 1989).
a. Totals may not add because of rounding.
b. 1985 data.
c. Luxembourg population is 0.4 million; Luxembourg trade is grouped with Belgian trade.

the Europe 1992 Program. (For reference, table 1-1 provides an economic profile of the European Community, North America, and Japan.)

In the years immediately after the Second World War, the United States enthusiastically supported the integration of Western Europe. U.S. policy in those years was dominated by strategic considerations: the initial instruments of policy were the Marshall Plan (1947) and the North Atlantic Treaty Organization (1949), backed by European leaders such as Aneurin Bevan of Britain, Jean Monnet of France, and Konrad Adenauer of Germany. An economically strong and politically unified Western Europe would further enhance the Atlantic ability to withstand Soviet expansion. European cooperation would provide an excellent starting point for Franco-German rapprochement and diminish the danger of a third European war. These were not fanciful aspirations. Soviet expansion came to an abrupt halt, and Europe has now enjoyed four decades without a land war—the longest uninterrupted peace in European history. Revolutionary change in Eastern Europe and the Soviet Union now promise additional decades of peace and prosperity.

U.S. economic power dominated the world of the 1950s and 1960s. A prosperous Europe would hardly threaten U.S. business leadership, and it would assuredly provide larger markets for U.S. products. The American business community saw great opportunities in the rapid removal of tariffs among the original six Common Market members—Belgium, the Federal Republic of Germany, France, Italy, Luxembourg, and the Netherlands. U.S. firms began to plan and organize on a continental basis—by the 1960s both Ford and GM had continental operations—while most European business leaders continued to think in terms of national markets.

In the economic framework of the day, conceptualized by Jacob Viner as early as 1950, U.S. government officials believed that the "trade-creating" effects of a unified Europe would far offset any "trade-diverting" effects from intra-European preferences.[3] Within U.S. business circles, trade diversion was not even regarded as a problem: through their plants in Europe, U.S. firms could take advantage of new intra-European trade patterns. Such considerations prompted the United States to regard the adverse commercial implications of European economic integration as a manageable matter within the transatlantic dialogue.

As a first step, the Treaty of Rome committed the six member states to eliminate trade barriers within the Community and to establish a Common Commercial Policy, thereby creating a customs union. Over the next decade, the Common External Tariff (CET) was put in place by averaging the member state duty rates, and tariffs on intra-EC trade were progressively reduced and then totally eliminated in July 1968, eighteen months ahead of schedule. Meanwhile the Six moved forward with the Common Agricultural Policy (CAP), which entailed freer trade within Europe but greater insulation of European agricultural markets from external competition.

## President Kennedy's Approach

American economic and political attitudes toward these developments were reflected in President John F. Kennedy's January 1962 message to the U.S. Congress. The Kennedy administration realized that the elim-

---

3. Jacob Viner, *The Customs Unions Issue* (New York: Carnegie Endowment for International Peace, 1950).

ination of tariffs among the Six, coupled with the erection of the Common External Tariff, would put U.S. manufactured exports at a disadvantage relative to manufactured exports among the member states. The Kennedy administration also harbored serious misgivings about the Common Agricultural Policy, fearing an erosion of U.S. agricultural exports, though it must be noted that exclusion of agriculture from the disciplines of the General Agreement on Tariffs and Trade (GATT) was an American policy initiative, dating from 1955. The U.S. response to these concerns set the pattern for much of postwar U.S. trade policy (extending down to the Omnibus Trade and Competitiveness Act of 1988): meet the challenge by opening foreign markets to U.S. exports, not by closing U.S. markets to foreign imports. The main way to do this was to negotiate a lower Common External Tariff. And the way to persuade Europe to cut the CET was to offer the prospect of lower U.S. tariffs in return.

President Kennedy thus asked Congress for authority to cut U.S. tariffs by 50 percent in the GATT negotiations that came to be known as the Kennedy Round of multilateral trade negotiations. In his prophetic 1962 message to Congress, Kennedy declared:

There is arising across the Atlantic a single economic community which may soon have a population half again as big as our own, working and competing together with no more barriers to commerce and investment than exist among our 50 states—in an economy which has been growing roughly twice as fast as ours—representing a purchasing power which will some day equal our own and a living standard growing faster than our own.

. . . For the first time, as the world's greatest trading nation, we can welcome a single partner whose trade is even larger than our own—a partner no longer divided and dependent, but strong enough to share with us the responsibilities and initiatives of the free world.

. . . The success of our foreign policy depends in large measure upon the success of our foreign trade, and our maintenance of western political unity depends in equally large measure upon the degree of western economic unity. An integrated Western Europe, joined in trading partnership with the United States, will further shift the world balance of power to the side of freedom.[4]

4. "Special Message to the Congress on Foreign Trade Policy," *Public Papers of the Presidents: John F. Kennedy, 1962* (Government Printing Office, 1962), pp. 68–77.

As it turned out, the Kennedy Round (1963–68) was a great success in terms of reducing the Common External Tariff, but it did little to restrain the irritating Common Agricultural Policy. An important but less-noticed point is that, without the prior formation of the EC, there would not have been a Kennedy Round at all. France and Italy, for example, would have strongly resisted making any trade concessions in the 1960s, and Germany would not have made concessions in isolation from its continental partners. Similar political arithmetic was responsible for the success of the Tokyo Round (1973–79), and it will decide the outcome of the Uruguay Round (1986–90). In all cases, the most vital commercial policy dialogue has taken place between Brussels and Washington.

## Europe at Low Tide

After the initial flush of activity and excitement stimulated by the Treaty of Rome and the Kennedy Round, Europe fell into a period of doubt, accented by Jean Jacques Servan-Schreiber's Le Défi Americain (1967).[5] In the late 1960s the Japanese challenge was not yet apparent.

During the late 1960s and early 1970s, EC diplomacy was preoccupied with geographic expansion and completion of the customs union. On January 22, 1972, after difficult negotiations, the United Kingdom, along with Ireland, Denmark, and Norway, signed the Treaty of Accession with the European Community. In a subsequent referendum, the Norwegian electorate rejected membership, and Norway remains to this day a member only of the European Free Trade Association (EFTA). Accession of the other three countries turned the original Six into the Nine.

The United States had strongly encouraged the United Kingdom and other EFTA countries to become full members of the Community. In the hopes of U.S. policy planners, a Community that included Britain would increase Atlantic solidarity. British political traditions would strengthen the democratic dimensions of the European Community, and British membership would help prevent the EC from becoming a protectionist economic bloc.

By expanding from Six to Nine, the EC was broadened but not deepened. U.S. hopes for a character change were disappointed, to the

---

5. Jean Jacques Servan-Schreiber, Le Défi Americain (Paris: Denoel, 1967), trans., The American Challenge (New York: Atheneum, 1968).

relief of France and certain other members of the original Six. The economic climate of the 1970s, with two oil shocks and high inflation, reinforced the tendency of many member states to pursue dirigiste policies. Stanley Hoffman has called the period between 1973 and 1984 the Community's dark age.[6] The only important milestone toward European unification during the 1970s was the creation, in 1979, of the European Monetary System (EMS), with its companions, the European currency unit (ECU) and the Exchange Rate Mechanism (ERM). Internal trade liberalization slowed during the decade, as the elimination of tariffs and quotas exposed the protective effect of numerous, seemingly immutable, behind-the-border barriers. Meanwhile the Common Agricultural Policy, which became an object of EC financing in the early 1970s, escalated transatlantic frictions. When Greece, Spain, and Portugal joined the EC in the mid-1980s, thereby enlarging the Nine to the Twelve, agricultural disputes with the United States again came to the fore.

By the mid-1980s the combination of slow European growth, high unemployment, internal barriers, and policy drift added up to a picture of "Eurosclerosis" and "Europessimism." To cite one type of internal barrier, the European Community suffers an array of differing technical standards, which diminish competition, erode efficiency, and annoy consumers. A German who wants to register his car in France must first change headlights, wiring, and windshield. Philips N.V. produces seven types of TV sets equipped with different tuners, semiconductors, and plugs to meet differing national standards. Such examples can be multiplied endlessly.

### The 1985 White Paper

By 1985 the distasteful metaphor of Eurosclerosis, reinforced by fears of U.S. and now Japanese competition on a global scale, prompted bold action. The European Council discussed and agreed with a Commission White Paper, drafted by the Commission under the leadership of Lord Cockfield, entitled *Completing the Internal Market*.[7] The 1985 White Paper attempted to identify all existing barriers to the "four freedoms," the free movement of goods, services, capital, and people; and listed some 300 legislative proposals necessary to create a unified market (the

6. Hoffman, "European Community," p. 29.

7. EC Commission, *Completing the Internal Market: White Paper from the Commission to the European Council* (Luxembourg, 1985). An EC white paper establishes policy themes; an EC green paper sets forth technical details.

TABLE 1–2. Estimated Macroeconomic Consequences of EC Market Integration for the Community in the Medium Term[a]

| Category | Customs formalities | Public procurement | Financial services | Supply-side effect[b] | Total effect |
|---|---|---|---|---|---|
| GDP (percent) | 0.4 | 0.5 | 1.5 | 2.1 | 4.5 |
| Consumer prices (percent) | −1.0 | −1.4 | −1.4 | −2.3 | −6.1 |
| Employment (thousands of workers) | 200 | 350 | 400 | 850 | 1,800 |
| Budgetary balance (percent of GDP) | 0.2 | 0.3 | 1.1 | 0.6 | 2.2 |
| External balance (percent of GDP) | 0.2 | 0.1 | 0.3 | 0.4 | 1.0 |

SOURCE: HERMES (EC Commission and national teams) and INTERLINK (OECD) economic models, reproduced in Paolo Cecchini, The European Challenge 1992: The Benefits of a Single Market (Aldershot, Eng.: Wildwood House for the EC Commission, 1988), p. 98.

a. These estimates do not include an allowance for the additional stimulus that might be derived from using the fiscal surplus or external surplus generated by the EC-1992 Program to stimulate the European economy. See Cecchini, European Challenge, pp. 99–102.

b. Based on a scenario that includes supply-side effects, greater economies of scale in manufacturing, and enhanced competition.

agenda of proposed directives was later reduced to 279; for an outline of topical coverage, see appendix 1-4). Even cautious scholars, such as Horst Siebert of the Kiel Institute, see in Europe 1992 the promise of a "Schumpeterian Event"—an economic change of landmark significance.[8]

According to estimates made in the official Cecchini report (sponsored by the Commission to demonstrate the benefits that could accrue to the Community from removing barriers), welding together the twelve individual markets into one single market could, over the medium term, boost EC gross domestic product (GDP) by 4.3 to 6.4 percent. This jump amounts to some $270 billion and would lead to the creation of millions of new jobs, the reduction of inflation, and the harvest of large budgetary gains (table 1-2).[9]

8. Horst Siebert, "The Single European Market—A Schumpeterian Event?" Kiel Discussion Paper 157 (FRG: Kiel Institute of World Economics, November 1989). The reference is to Joseph A. Schumpeter, The Theory of Economic Development: An Inquiry into Profits, Capital, Credit, Interest and the Business Cycle (Harvard University Press, 1934), p. 74.

9. Paolo Cecchini and others, The European Challenge 1992: The Benefits of a Single Market (Aldershot, Eng.: Wildwood House for the EC Commission, 1988), table 9.2; and Organization for Economic Cooperation and Development, Historical Statistics, 1960–1987 (Paris, 1989), p. 17. The present book does not explore the macroeconomic consequences of Europe 1992. A good survey, however, is offered by Rudiger Dornbusch, "Europe 92: Macroeconomic Implications," Brookings Papers on Economic Activity, 2:1989, pp. 341–62 (hereafter BPEA).

To be sure, the projections in the Cecchini report were drafted in part to mobilize political support for European unification. It would surprise no one if foot-dragging slowed the removal of internal barriers in such areas as opening government procurement and removing fiscal barriers. Alternative estimates, based on business surveys and sectoral studies, reach more subdued conclusions as to the macroeconomic gains from the 1992 program. While the official Cecchini report projects an increase of 4.3 to 6.4 percent of GDP, some unofficial studies suggest a GDP gain of only 1.5 to 2.5 percent.[10] On the other hand, Richard Baldwin has calculated that the boost in EC capital stock resulting from the Europe 1992 Program would add another 1.7 to 2.6 percent to the GDP gains estimated by Cecchini. Baldwin argues that further gains may be realized on account of economywide returns to scale.[11] It is premature to say whether the optimists or the pessimists in the EC-1992 growth debate have the better case, but so far Community growth has been remarkably buoyant.[12]

The 1985 White Paper classified existing barriers under three categories: physical, technical, and fiscal. The most obvious obstacles to cross-border movements are physical barriers—customs controls and immigration restrictions. Tariffs and most quantitative restrictions on intra-EC trade were eliminated in the 1960s. But intra-EC border controls remain in place for various reasons inspired by economic considerations: differing value-added-tax (VAT) rates and excise duties; statistical formalities; adjustments at the border of farm prices in order to offset currency fluctuations; and checks at the border to prevent intra-EC transshipments that would undermine residual national quotas aimed at non-EC suppliers. The Cecchini report estimates the costs of border delays alone at almost $10 billion annually (this figure does not include the much larger cost of underlying market segregation).[13] The introduction of the Single Administrative Document in January 1988 has already reduced the paperwork on EC cross-border trade. Further progress now depends on eliminating the underlying conditions that give rise to border controls.

10. Merton J. Peck, "Industrial Organization and the Gains from 1992," *BPEA 2:1989*, pp. 277–99.

11. Richard Baldwin, "The Growth Effects of 1992," *Economic Policy* (October 1989), pp. 248–81.

12. Steve Prokesch, "Europe Taking a Lead in Growth," *New York Times*, January 15, 1990, p. D5; "EC Economies Perform Strongly in 1989, but Face Major Policy Challenges," *IMF Survey*, vol. 19 (January 22, 1990), p. 17.

13. Cecchini and others, *European Challenge*, table 9.2.

Differing national technical and licensing regimes create major obstacles to a unified market. These are by far the most important barriers, for they restrict market entry on a grand scale. The Cecchini report puts the gains from opening market entry, and the consequent intensification of competition and realization of scale economies, at about $240 billion.[14]

Differing product standards and certification procedures hamper the Europe-wide acceptance of numerous items ranging from autos to pharmaceuticals to packaged cereals. Public procurement markets are practically closed in four sectors that are now exempt from EC public procurement procedures—energy, telecommunications, transportation, and water supply. Even in areas that are covered by EC rules, cross-border government procurement has been minimal: less than 2 percent of awards are made to non-national suppliers. In the service sector, extensive licensing and rate-setting practices by the member states impede trans-European competition in financial services, telecommunications services, road haulage, and air transport. A typical result: labor productivity in Lufthansa is only half the average of U.S. airlines.[15] Beyond that, different educational approaches and professional qualifications hinder the ability of many people to seek jobs throughout the Common Market.

Fiscal differences also create underlying obstacles. Member states fear that—if not redressed at the border—large national differences in VAT and excise tax rates could entice people to make extensive purchases in other EC states. The fiscal authorities in high-tax jurisdictions would then lose revenue on a large scale. Equally important, producers in high-tax jurisdictions would be disadvantaged, even if they were more efficient than their competitors in low-tax jurisdictions. To address the underlying problem, the White Paper calls for three steps: approximate harmonization of VAT and excise tax rates;[16] imposition of indirect taxes only by the country of origin (that is, the state where the goods are produced); and establishment of a clearinghouse among member states to divide up

14. Ibid. See also Siebert, "Single European Market."

15. "Europe's 1992 Labour Pains," *Economist*, December 9, 1989, p. 71. Other European airlines show about the same productivity levels as Lufthansa.

16. The original proposal was to group all goods into two VAT bands, 14 percent to 20 percent and 4 percent to 9 percent. The current proposal is to set a target range of 14 percent to 20 percent for VAT rates. VAT rates that fall outside this range cannot be pushed further, but there is no obligation on member states to change their rates. Martin DuBois, "EC Clinches Accord to Open Banking Markets," *Wall Street Journal*, December 19, 1989, p. A10.

tax receipts on the basis of trade statistics, so that the revenue is eventually collected by the country of destination (that is, the state where the goods are consumed). Whether or not approximate harmonization and the other steps are achieved, adjustments at the border for differences in national tax rates will supposedly not be permitted after December 31, 1992.[17] However, this is one deadline that may slip by two or three years.

Absent from the White Paper agenda was action on several collateral fronts: monetary union, fiscal policies of member states, common defense procurement, common norms for working conditions and social services, and the Common Agricultural Policy. Broadly, these matters can be viewed as the "outer wrapping" of the commercial integration sought in the core Europe 1992 Program. They are the subject of parallel, less-structured, negotiations.

### The Single European Act and Companion Measures

The critical step in implementing the White Paper proposals was the adoption of the Single European Act, which revised the Treaty of Rome in important ways (appendix 1-5). The Single Act, drafted in conjunction with the White Paper, took effect on July 1, 1987. It extended the use of qualified majority voting to most internal market issues; unanimity is now required only in sensitive matters such as taxation, the movement of persons, the rights of employees, and the environment. The act also enhanced the role of the European Parliament in the legislative process. Under the "new cooperation procedure" (see appendix 1-6), Parliament now has two formal opportunities to consider Commission proposals: once when it submits comments on Commission proposals, and again when Parliament may amend proposals with a two-thirds majority. Finally, the act sets a distinct deadline: "The Community shall adopt measures with the aim of progressively establishing the internal market over a period expiring on 31 December 1992." While this deadline will not be met on all subjects, it has galvanized European business and political leaders to concentrate the European mind on unification.

Apart from the driving force of the Single Act, and the singularly strong personality of Jacques Delors (president of the Commission since

---

17. In October 1989 member state finance ministers put forward a plan that retains the destination principle for the imposition of taxes but assigns to companies the burden of ensuring that the right amount of tax is paid to the right authority. See "EC Ministers Agree to Keep Tax Borders after 1992," *Europe-1992*, vol. 1 (October 10, 1989), p. 361.

1985), two other measures have contributed to the Europe 1992 Program. In February 1989 the European Council agreed that, by 1992, the amount of EC "structural funds" should be doubled to compensate depressed regions for intensified competition resulting from a unified market. As a result, the EC structural contribution will reach 5 percent of GNP in Portugal and Greece, a figure comparable to the postwar Marshall Plan contribution to the Netherlands.[18] Generous structural assistance has dampened fears that completion of the internal market would worsen regional disparities.

The second measure was a "new approach" to the harmonization of technical standards. The Council no longer intends to adopt detailed product standards for every good (the "old approach"). Rather, the basic principle is that, once a product has been lawfully manufactured and distributed in one member state, it may be sold throughout the Community. In other words, each member state will be required to accept the goods that meet the standards of other members (the mutual recognition approach).[19] The principle of mutual recognition also applies to testing and certification procedures, which enable a manufacturer to sell throughout the Community by demonstrating acceptability to the authorities of one member state.

Common EC standards—implemented through EC "essential requirements" that member states must meet in setting their own national standards—will be limited to areas of fundamental importance, notably goods and services that affect health, safety, the environment, and essential interoperability (especially in telecommunications).[20] Where

18. In 1987 structural funds totaled ECU 8.1 billion, about 19 percent of the EC budget and about 0.2 percent of Community GDP. Arthur Andersen and Co., *1992: Guide for Clients* (Brussels, March 1989), p. 19. This figure will double by 1992. The comparison with the Marshall Plan was supplied by EC Director-General Corrado Pirzio-Biroli in a speech to the Global Interdependance Center, Philadelphia, Pennsylvania, October 20, 1989.

19. The mutual recognition approach may require a higher degree of comity among member states than the commerce clause of the U.S. Constitution requires among individual states. The commerce clause has been interpreted by the U.S. Supreme Court to allow each state to insist on its own product quality standards—unless the subject matter has been preempted by federal legislation, or unless the state standards would unduly burden interstate commerce.

20. Before the advent of the mutual recognition approach, the EC adopted about 1,000 Community standards a year, but about 2,000 to 3,000 new standards were created annually by the member states. Enforced harmonization thus became a losing battle. The EC will continue to adopt "essential requirements" for pharmaceuticals, auto emissions, potentially hazardous products, and some but not all products falling under the health, safety, and

common standards are required—perhaps 10 to 20 percent of products—the Commission gives a mandate to the appropriate European body to spell out the details.[21]

The general principle of mutual recognition expands upon a decision issued by the European Court of Justice in 1979, based on Article 30 of the Treaty of Rome and dealing with cassis de Dijon, a French alcoholic beverage. The German "Branntweinmonopolgesetz" statute of 1922 required 32 percent alcohol content, whereas the French liqueur contained only 17 percent alcohol; hence cassis de Dijon was excluded from the German market. The Court ruled that Germany could no longer exclude the French liqueur, even though it failed German consumer protection standards, inasmuch as the beverage was legally produced and sold in France.[22]

Mutual recognition opens the door, not only for competition between firms, but also for competition between governments. This will have sweeping consequences. For example, if Dutch TV standards are less onerous than German standards, but Dutch TV sets are practically interchangeable with more costly German sets in the eyes of consumers, German television producers will lose business to their Dutch competitors. They will then bring pressure on Bonn to revamp German standards.[23]

After the Hannover Summit in 1988, which agreed on the structural funds initiative, public attention rapidly turned to Europe 1992. In this

environment rubric. The Commission hopes that, for the most part, interoperability will be achieved either through moral suasion of the quasi-official EC standard-setting bodies—CEN, CENELEC, and ETSI—or by Darwinian survival of the best standards under the mutual recognition approach.

21. Under the new approach, the EC adopts directives that establish the "essential requirements" that products must meet in order to be marketed within the Community. The drafting of detailed standards is left to quasi-official organizations (CEN, CENELEC, ETSI). An example of a mandatory standard: the EC has issued a directive setting Community standards for the transmission of data over public telecommunications networks.

22. The *Cassis de Dijon* rationale has been applied by the European Court of Justice to other products, for example, beer in Germany and pasta in Italy. But the court has also created exceptions: Denmark, for example, is permitted to exclude throwaway bottles and cans, in order to promote its environmental policy of returnable containers. As of 1990 the court had not ruled whether the principle of *Cassis de Dijon* applies to, for example, U.S.-made goods that meet Dutch standards, in terms of their acceptability throughout the Community. Many observers think the principle would apply, but I have heard skeptics in the Commission. The skeptics believe that mutual recognition, vis-à-vis foreign products, should be an object of bilateral negotiation, not a court decision.

23. Horst Siebert, "The Harmonization Issue in Europe: Prior Agreement or a Competitive Process?" Working Paper 377 (FRG: Kiel Institute of World Economics, June 1989).

drama the role of the European business community should not be underestimated. At first, skepticism was rampant, but business leaders soon convinced themselves that the internal market program would provide the framework for economic expansion. They embarked on an anticipatory wave of investment, merger, and rationalization. European stock markets boomed. As Giovanni Agnelli, the Italian industrialist and chairman of Fiat, wrote: "Ironically, it was politicians who in 1957 first conceived the idea of a common market—often over objections from the business community. Now the situation has been reversed; it is the entrepreneurs and corporations who are keeping the pressure on politicians to transcend considerations of local and national interest."[24]

Unlike negotiations within GATT, where every part of a multilateral round hinges on acceptance of all the other parts—so the dimensions of the final package remain unknown until the last days—the internal market program was accepted in total at the outset. Subsequent negotiations were concerned with details, not the size of the package. In fact, roughly 85 percent (some 236) of the planned 279 directives were placed on the agenda by the Commission by September 1989.[25]

The Council of Ministers has not done as well—so far it has adopted 143 measures—but its pace is quickening as the prospect of qualified majority voting prompts recalcitrant member states to join the consensus. Progress was fast on minor matters, such as common rules for price labels, but headway has also been made on difficult issues, such as public contract procedures and liberalization of capital movements. Still, the most controversial proposals have been left to last; for example, tax harmonization and company law issues.

The incorporation of decisions taken at the EC level into national law is taking time and effort. Of the eighty-eight directives that should have been carried out by early 1990, fifty or more had become national legislation in France, Denmark, the Netherlands, and the United Kingdom. At the other extreme, Spain, Italy, and Portugal had enacted fewer than thirty-five directives.[26]

The "outer wrapping" of European unification has not proceeded so

24. Giovanni Agnelli, "The Europe of 1992," *Foreign Affairs*, vol. 68 (Fall 1989), p. 62.

25. U.S. General Accounting Office, unpublished data.

26. "Europe's Rhetoric and Reality," *Economist*, September 23, 1989, p. 64; and Peter Brimelow, "The Dark Side of 1992," *Forbes*, January 22, 1990, p. 88. Apart from their failure to enact directives in a timely fashion, the member states have ignored some forty-four rulings of the European Court of Justice (Italy alone is in violation of twenty rulings).

smoothly, and it is in this realm that revolutionary change in Eastern Europe will have the greatest impact. To begin with, the United Kingdom from the start has balked at European unification in areas outside the core Europe 1992 commercial program. Broadly speaking, Prime Minister Margaret Thatcher believes that unification beyond the core program should evolve from enlightened national self-interest and market competition, not be imposed top-down by Brussels.[27]

Thus in April 1989 the Schengen Group (Benelux, France, and West Germany) agreed in principle to abolish their internal frontiers and to adopt common immigration and visa policies, but the United Kingdom declared that it was not yet prepared to accept these sweeping changes. Implementation of the Schengen accord has been delayed while the implications of East German immigration are being sorted out. Quite apart from events in Eastern Europe, Britain does not want to abandon the power to detain drug dealers and to ferret out terrorists at the border.

The United Kingdom also resists monetary integration. At a philosophical level, Thatcher believes in competition between currencies; at a pragmatic level, she wants to retain the power to appreciate or depreciate the pound sterling to suit British circumstances. Britain enthusiastically supported Directive 88/361, which will sweep away nearly all barriers to capital flows on July 1, 1990, but Britain remains strongly opposed to monetary union. Nevertheless a common currency, like a common passport, is seen by most Europeans as a key ingredient and high symbol of European unification. In April 1989 the Delors Committee—a group of seventeen monetary experts led by Jacques Delors, who sees monetary union as the central objective of his second term as president—published its *Report on Economic and Monetary Union in the European Community*, proposing a three-stage process to economic and monetary union (EMU).[28] Only reluctantly, at the Madrid Summit of June 1989, did Prime Minister

27. Stanley Hoffman characterizes Jacques Delors as the new Jean Monnet of Europe, and Margaret Thatcher, with her view of retained member state sovereignty, as the new Charles de Gaulle. Hoffman, "European Community," p. 34.

28. In sympathy with the Delors report, the European Parliament has called for the creation of a European central bank by 1995 and a European currency by 1997. For a diagrammatic portrayal of the Delors plan, see David Buchan, "Building from a Distorted Blueprint," *Financial Times*, July 10, 1989, p. 10. Also see Niels Thygesen, "Fiscal Constraints and EMU," *Amex Bank Review*, September 1989; and David Folkerts-Landau and Donald J. Mathieson, "The European Monetary System in the Context of the Integration of European Financial Markets," International Monetary Fund Occasional Paper 66 (Washington, October 1989).

Thatcher conditionally agree to implement the first of the three proposed stages of the EMU.

Stage one entails closer coordination of national monetary policies and the inclusion of all currencies in the Exchange Rate Mechanism.[29] While Delors stressed that adoption of stage one "will [irreversibly] lead to economic and monetary union," Thatcher asserted that "there's absolutely nothing automatic about going beyond phase one"—that is, into the realm of a single currency, a European central bank, and fiscal coordination.[30] At the Strasbourg Summit in December 1989, agreement was reached (with Britain dissenting) to call an intergovernmental conference in December 1990 to consider stages two and three of monetary integration. The clear impression is that all member states, save Britain, wish to adopt a common currency with deliberate speed.[31]

Another item on the Madrid Summit agenda met equal British resistance: the social aspects of the single market. Thatcher refused to accept a European Charter of Fundamental Social Rights enshrining "old" rights such as social security, fair wages, and sexual equality, and advancing "new" rights, such as union representation on company boards. The prime minister fears that the EC social agenda would reconstruct, at the European level, all the evils of welfare statism and trade unionism that she credits herself for dismantling within the United Kingdom.[32] Nevertheless, the Social Charter was endorsed by the Commission, and accepted as a political commitment by all member states, save Britain, at the Strasbourg Summit in December 1989. Some parts of the implementing legislation can be adopted by qualified majority voting, but other parts may require unanimity, which, of course, Britain can block.

29. The ERM indirectly establishes a grid of bilateral exchange rates between participating member states. Each participating state's currency may fluctuate no more than 2.25 percent up or down from the central exchange rate expressed in terms of ECU (European currency units). (The permitted fluctuation for the Italian lira is plus or minus 6 percent.) The ECU is a basket currency made up of specific amounts of member state currencies (including the pound sterling).

30. Tim Carrington and others, "European Lenders Take Big Step on Monetary Union and Currency," *Wall Street Journal*, June 28, 1989, p. A2. Thatcher further argues that going beyond stage one would entail "the biggest transfer of sovereignty we've ever had." Buchan, "Building from a Distorted Blueprint."

31. Alan Riding, "European Leaders Give Their Backing to Monetary Plan," *New York Times*, December 9, 1989, p. A1.

32. "We have not successfully rolled back the frontiers of the state in Britain only to see them reimposed at a European level with a European superstate exercising a new dominance from Brussels." Margaret Thatcher, Bruges, September 20, 1988.

### Revolution in Eastern Europe

The democratic revolution that swept Eastern Europe in 1989 and 1990 will profoundly affect the Europe 1992 process. The basic questions are to what extent will developments in Eastern Europe preoccupy EC leaders so as to delay economic integration, and to what extent will those developments propel even faster unification?

Since the White Paper was issued in 1985, the Community has resolutely pursued deeper integration in preference to wider geographic expansion. European leaders have accorded first priority to the core 1992 program; the most dedicated Europeans have, additionally, pushed for the outer wrapping of the Economic and Monetary Union, generous structural adjustment funds, the Social Charter, and a common European approach to political and security questions. Meanwhile the EC has greeted Austria's application with a lukewarm response, it has delayed consideration of Turkey's application until after 1992, it has proposed a slow timetable for EC-EFTA talks on creating a European Economic Space, and it has paid less-than-total attention to the Uruguay Round. These priorities reflect the vision of Jacques Delors: first ensure deep internal integration; only then respond to new opportunities offered by closer ties with nonmember states.[33] Revolution in Eastern Europe now threatens the Delors vision.[34]

To start with the economics: the combination of democratic governments and market economics in the East spells macroeconomic stimulus for Western Europe, even as it creates policy tension for the 1992 process. Macroeconomic stimulus will have both demand-side and supply-side components. On the demand side, the Community promises to finance a huge rebuilding program in Eastern Europe. Taking public and private outlays together, it is possible that EC exports to Eastern Europe, financed by public aid and private investment, could double over the next several years, to reach $35 billion to $40 billion annually, entailing new demand of nearly one-half of 1 percent of Community GDP. On the supply side, Eastern Europe offers a large pool of labor at wage rates less than a third of those prevailing in the West. If this labor can be

33. Delors has argued that any further enlargement should be accompanied by greater supranational powers for Brussels. See *Financial Times*, January 12, 1989, p. 3.

34. See, for example, "Westward Ho," *Economist*, November 25, 1989, p. 58; and John Templeman and others, "German Unity: A Threat to Europe 1992?" *Business Week*, January 22, 1990, pp. 40–41.

organized by Western firms, and if Eastern Europe can successfully practice market economics, rapid productivity gains will significantly boost the supply of goods made and sold throughout Europe.

Turning to areas of policy tension, at stake is not the core of Europe 1992—the 279 directives in the formal program. The timetable for those proposals will not be derailed by events in the East. Indeed, to preserve the momentum of Europe 1992, national leaders may compromise more quickly on contentious directives—for example, directives to narrow the range of value-added taxes, to harmonize company law, and to open government procurement in a meaningful fashion.[35] At risk from revolution in the East is the outer wrapping of the Europe 1992 process: monetary union, structural adjustment, the Social Charter, political cohesion, and security integration.

Reunification of Germany has captured center stage attention.[36] As the former deputy editor of the *Economist* put the matter: "The economic integration of Europe will now have to take a back seat to the age-old German question. Until the two Germanys are inevitably united—probably sometime in the mid-1990s—Bonn cannot pursue the planned economic integration with its 11 partners in the European Community."[37] To cite one example: the problems of monetary union with East Germany will surely take precedence over the European monetary union. But even here there is a silver lining. With the adoption of the deutsche mark as the legal currency of East Germany, and the widespread use of the mark as a parallel currency throughout Eastern Europe (much as the dollar is used in Latin America), the Bundesbank will occupy an even more powerful role in European monetary affairs. This development will

35. For example, see President François Mitterrand's call for faster integration, in Karen Elliot House and E. S. Browning, "Mitterrand Sees Europe at the Crossroads," *Wall Street Journal*, November 22, 1989, p. A6.

36. The headlong rush of events started with the opening of the Berlin Wall on November 9, 1989, followed by the December 9, 1989, Strasbourg Summit blessing that Germany could "regain its unity through free self-determination"; Chancellor Kohl's call for monetary union on February 7, 1989; and agreement, on February 13, 1990, that East and West Germany would first decide the terms of internal arrangements, and then the four Second World War allies (the United States, Great Britain, France, and the Soviet Union) would address external security. Paul Lewis, "West and Soviets Agree with Two Germanys on Rapid Schedule for Unification Talks," *New York Times*, February 14, 1990, p. A1; see also "United Germany" *Economist*, January 27, 1990, pp. 49–52.

37. Norman Macrae, "One Germany before One Europe," *Business Month*, February 1990, pp. 16–18.

ease the way for the eventual European monetary union organized around the Bundesbank.[38]

European resources will be taxed by the reconstruction of the East, and this too will slow the pace of EC integration. At the Strasbourg Summit the Community established a European Bank for Reconstruction and Development, with authorized capital of $10 billion (to be 51 percent controlled by the twelve member states). This is the first, but by no means the last, installment of large-scale financial assistance from West to East. West Germany will spend massive amounts to revive the East German economy.[39] France, Italy, and Britain will extend large sums through their private banks, through their export credit agencies, and through Community institutions. This spending will curtail northern European enthusiasm for financing the modernization of southern Europe. Spain, Portugal, and Greece will find themselves faced with new competition from Hungary, Czechoslovakia, and Poland—not only in export markets, but also in the search for new investment—and in competition for European aid funds. Accordingly the upward harmonization of living standards within the Community will be delayed.

In fact, the prospect of closer ties with Eastern Europe draws into question whether the EC Social Charter can soon move beyond the realm of political rhetoric. Fast economic growth in southern and eastern Europe is vital to retard the unwanted migration of millions of workers to northern Europe. Bureaucratic fiat—a Social Charter with teeth—cannot be used to harmonize wages, working conditions, and social benefits throughout Europe without destroying the possibility of rapid economic advance in the poorer states.

The final casualty of revolution in the East is likely to be the emergence of a single European voice on political and security questions. Now that the Soviet Union looks far less fearsome, what themes can unify European opinion? Surely not the "threat" of a single Germany. The search for common ground on political and security issues will become even more problematic if full or associate membership is extended to such "neutral" nations as Austria and Hungary ("neutrality" is rapidly losing its historic meaning but will no doubt acquire new connotations).

Apart from its impact on European unification, the revolution will

38. David Buchan, "Bonn Links May Speed EC Monetary Union," *Financial Times*, February 8, 1990, p. 2.

39. In February 1990 the Federal Republic approved a supplementary budget of $4.1 billion to shore up East Germany. *Financial Times*, February 15, 1990, p. 7.

indirectly affect relations between the Community and the rest of the world, especially the United States. Most important, this drama has underscored the shifting center of gravity of the Atlantic alliance, from shared security interests to shared economic interests. With this shift, U.S. attention will increasingly focus on Bonn and the EC, rather than London and NATO.

Greater competition for intra-European aid resources, together with increased imports from the East, will inevitably put pressure on the Commission to find new means of addressing economic dislocation. The Commission could respond with a more leisurely pace of EC trade liberalization relative to the outside world, especially in agriculture and low-technology products such as textiles and apparel, footwear, and consumer durables. A response of this sort would make it harder for the United States to pursue its own agenda of freer trade on a multilateral basis.

On the other hand, Western Europe has mounted a major campaign, both in political and economic terms, to open Eastern Europe to high-technology exports. EC members have vigorously urged the seventeen-nation Coordinating Committee on Multilateral Export Controls (CO-COM) to relax its limits on exports to Eastern Europe and the Soviet Union.[40] Success in this campaign is all but assured. New markets in the East will boost Europe's position in the world ranks of high-technology exporters.

Finally, time demands on Community leaders will have their own impact. Eastern Europe is regarded as a historic opportunity, not only to spread democratic values and free markets, but also to reestablish Europe at the center of world affairs. Trade and investment links between East and West Europe are far smaller than U.S.-European links across the Atlantic, but Eastern questions will surely command disproportionately long hours on the Brussels calendar. The corollary is clear: issues of interest to the United States will inevitably be addressed at a slower pace.

## U.S.–Community Economic Relations

When the White Paper was first presented, no explicit consideration was given to the external impact of the proposed unification program. Voices inside and outside the Community soon raised the question, and

40. *New York Times,* February 17, 1990, p. 9.

the EC started a step-by-step process of defining the external dimensions of its 1992 program.

In the first round, fears were expressed within the Community that the benefits of the internal market would unduly accrue to powerful and well-prepared third-country firms—especially those based in Japan and the United States. Such firms, it was said, would be better able than their European counterparts to operate on a continental scale.[41] To take the edge off this concern, the Commission pronounced that EC firms, not outsiders, would be the main beneficiaries of internal liberalization.[42]

These pronouncements provoked concern outside Europe, especially in the United States: it was feared that the internal market process might be rigged to disadvantage third-country interests. The phrase "Fortress Europe" gained currency. In an attempt to quiet such fears, the Commission restated its position in a news release in October 1988:

•The abolition of physical and technical frontiers, coupled with faster economic growth, will benefit both the EC and its trading partners.
•The Community will respect all international commitments, multi-lateral and bilateral. However, in areas where international obligations do not presently exist, the EC will not unilaterally extend the benefits of internal liberalization to third countries. Instead, the EC will seek comparable liberalization on the part of its major trading partners.

The first argument recalled Viner's classic dichotomy between trade creation and trade diversion, with a strong emphasis on creation, while

41. As one small example, Rorer International Pharmaceuticals, based in the United States, has already closed or sold four of its fourteen European manufacturing plants and is specializing production in the surviving ten plants. See Richard P. Storm, Rorer Group, "EC Manufacturing in 1992: Myth, Mirage or Manageable Opportunities?" speech delivered in Philadelphia, Pennsylvania, October 13, 1989. For a similar account of American International Group's consolidation in Europe, see Stuart Emmrich, "Consolidation Isn't Easy," *Business Month*, August 1989, p. 34. These cases illustrate the ability of U.S. firms to consolidate production in the cheapest locations throughout Europe.

42. In August 1988 Willy De Clercq, then EC Commissioner for External Relations (DG-1), stated: "Where international obligations do not exist . . . we see no reason why the benefits of our internal liberalization should be extended unilaterally to third countries. We shall be ready and willing to negotiate reciprocal concessions with third countries." See "1992: The Impact on the Outside World," speech by EC Commissioner Willy De Clercq, Europaeisches Forum, Ansprach, August 29, 1988, in Michael Calingaert, *The 1992 Challenge from Europe: Development of the European Community's Internal Market*, NPA 237 (Washington: National Planning Association, 1988), p. 120. Informed sources say that De Clercq was speaking extemporaneously, with the Commission's blessing, when he made this famous remark.

the second echoed a major theme of recent U.S. trade policy—the call to negotiate "level playing fields."[43] Still, these pronouncements, even with their tone of "Not Fortress Europe, but Partnership Europe," did not end debate over the external dimensions of Europe 1992.[44] But attention was shifted to ramparts, moats, and drawbridges, rather than the large fortress on the hill.

The EC maintains an exceedingly wide variety of trading relations with the outside world (appendix 1-7). Quite apart from Europe 1992, these relations are constantly undergoing realignment. The EFTA and the EC are talking economic marriage, to be consummated after 1992. Meanwhile, upheavals in Eastern Europe promise to redraw the economic map. As the Community adjusts its relations with one set of partners, others—especially the United States—will demand better treatment.

## Trade Creation and Trade Diversion

The European Community is now America's largest market for exports. In 1988 it bought 24 percent of U.S. exports, more than the 22 percent share going to Canada, and substantially more than the 12 percent share destined for Japan. Moreover, the EC buys high-technology exports: in 1988 some 45 percent of U.S. exports to Europe were classified as high-technology goods, whereas only 29 percent of U.S. exports to Japan were in that category.[45]

In terms of textbook price and income mechanisms, the EC offers a resilient market for U.S. products: a more competitive dollar sells significantly more American exports to Europe, and higher European income results in significantly larger purchases from America. According to one set of estimates, the European market is more responsive to price and income mechanisms than the Japanese market, although considerably less responsive than the Canadian (table 1-3). Since the dollar volume of U.S. exports to the EC greatly exceeds the dollar volume to Japan, the European price and income elasticity parameters operate on a much larger base. Thus, between 1985 and 1988, U.S. exports to the EC-12 rose from $49 billion to $76 billion, an increase of $27 billion. Over the

43. EC Commission, "Europe 1992—Europe World Partner," European Community News Release 28188 (EC Office of Press and Public Affairs, October 19, 1988).

44. "Survey of Europe's Internal Market," Economist, July 8, 1989, p. 6.

45. U.S. International Trade Administration, United States Trade: Performance in 1988 (Washington: Department of Commerce, September 1989), tables B.2, B.6.

TABLE 1–3. Price and Income Elasticities of U.S. Exports
to Europe and Japan, 1989

| U.S. exports to: | Price elasticity | Income elasticity |
|---|---|---|
| Europe[a] | −0.65 | 1.9 |
| Canada | −3.00 | 2.1 |
| Japan | −0.55 | 1.2 |

SOURCE: William R. Cline, *United States External Adjustments and the World Economy* (Washington: Institute for International Economics, 1989), pp. 172–74, tables 4A.2, 4A.3.
a. Unweighted average of France, Germany, Italy, and United Kingdom.

same period of time, U.S. exports to Japan rose from $23 billion to $38 billion, an increase of only $15 billion.

Past U.S. experience with the formation and enlargement of the EC has not been notably adverse to U.S. export interests. To be sure, between 1958 and 1986, intra-EC trade grew by a factor of 36 in nominal terms, while EC trade with the outside world grew by only a factor of 16.[46] But more rapid growth of internal European trade was to be expected. And, overall, the EC remains the most trade-oriented region: its external imports in 1987 amounted to 9.3 percent of Community GNP, compared with 7.8 percent for North America and 6.2 percent for Japan.[47]

Estimates made by one scholar (table 1-4) suggest that, vis-à-vis the United States, the formation of the original Common Market of Six led to trade creation in excess of trade diversion to the extent of $18.5 billion (in 1988 prices); again, in the enlargement from Six to Nine, the positive balance was about $0.8 billion; while the subsequent enlargement to Twelve slightly reduced U.S. exports.

If, as the Cecchini report suggests, internal liberalization facilitates an additional 4.5 percent of real European GNP over the medium term, then the trade-creating effects of Europe 1992 would raise the level of U.S. exports by a further $6.4 billion.[48] A companion Commission document estimated merchandise trade diversion ranging up to 2.6 percent of EC imports, which in the case of the United States would

46. Arthur Andersen and Co., *1992*, p. 36.
47. Siebert, "Single European Market," table A4.
48. Calculated as follows: (1988 U.S. exports to the EC, $76 billion) times (income elasticity of European demand for U.S. exports, 1.9) times (Cecchini medium-term macroeconomic gains, 4.5 percent) equals $6.4 billion.

TABLE 1–4. Estimated Effects of the Formation and Enlargement of the European Community on U.S. Trade, 1960–86[a]

Billions of dollars

| Item | U.S. gains | U.S. losses | Net balance |
|---|---|---|---|
| *Original Common Market (EC-6; c. 1960)* | | | |
| External trade creation in manufactures | 28.1 | . . . | . . . |
| Trade diversion against manufacturing exports | . . . | 6.3 | . . . |
| Net trade diversion in agricultural exports | . . . | 3.3 | . . . |
| Net trade effect | . . . | . . . | 18.5 |
| *First Enlargement (EC-9; 1973)* | | | |
| External trade creation in manufactures | 16.6 | . . . | . . . |
| Trade diversion against manufacturing exports | . . . | 12.2 | . . . |
| Net trade diversion in agricultural exports | . . . | 3.6 | . . . |
| Net trade effect | . . . | . . . | 0.8 |
| *Second Enlargement (EC-12; 1986)* | | | |
| External trade creation in manufactures | 0.3 | . . . | . . . |
| Trade diversion against manufacturing exports | . . . | 0.0 | . . . |
| Net trade diversion in agricultural exports | . . . | 0.6 | . . . |
| Net trade effect | . . . | . . . | −0.3 |

SOURCE: Adapted from G. N. Yannopoulos, *Customs Unions and Trade Conflicts* (London: Routledge, 1988), p. 128.
a. Estimates reported by Yannopoulos are adjusted to 1988 prices by using the producer price indexes for "foods and feeds" and "industrial commodities" reported in *Economic Report of the President, January 1989*, tables B-63, B-64.

amount to $2.0 billion.[49] Thus if EC-1992 generates its promised growth, trade creation will exceed trade diversion by a comfortable $4.4 billion. If the growth stimulus of the 1992 program does not materialize, the trade diversion effects would loom larger in the overall balance, but if the growth stimulus lives up to Richard Baldwin's optimistic calculations, the trade diversion effects would be swamped by trade creation.

## U.S. Investment in Europe

Europe is also a major destination for U.S. investment abroad. In fact, the share of U.S. direct foreign investment stock placed in the EC-12

49. Michael Emerson and others, "The Economics of 1992," *European Economy*, no 35 (Luxembourg: European Communities Directorate-General for Economic and Financial Affairs, March 1988), table A.5.

TABLE 1–5. U.S. Direct Investment Position in the EC-12, 1960–88
Billions of dollars unless otherwise specified

| Item | 1960 | 1970 | 1980 | 1985 | 1988 |
|---|---|---|---|---|---|
| Petroleum industry | 1.6 | 4.7 | 17.2 | 16.4 | 15.7 |
| Manufacturing | 3.6 | 12.6 | 43.4 | 43.7 | 65.4 |
| Banking, finance, insurance, and real estate | n.a. | n.a. | 8.9 | 14.2 | 27.5 |
| Other industries | 0.8 | 3.5 | 10.3 | 9.8 | 17.9 |
| All industries in EC-12 | 6.0 | 20.9 | 79.9 | 84.0 | 126.5[a] |
| Total U.S. direct investment position abroad | 32.7 | 78.1 | 213.4 | 229.7 | 326.9 |
| U.S. direct investment in EC-12 as a percentage of total U.S. direct investment abroad | 18.3 | 26.7 | 37.4 | 36.4 | 38.7 |
| Estimated sales of U.S.-owned affiliates in EC-12[b] | 29.0 | 102.0 | 392.0 | 412.0 | 620.0 |

SOURCE: U.S. Department of Commerce, *Survey of Current Business*, various issues.
n.a. Not available.
a. U.S. direct investment in 1988 in major EC countries was as follows: France, $12.5 billion; Germany, $21.7 billion; Italy, $9.1 billion; the Netherlands, $15.4 billion; United Kingdom, $48.0 billion.
b. For 1985, estimated as 94 percent of sales reported by non-bank foreign affiliates of U.S. firms operating in Europe. The 94 percent factor represents the proportion of U.S. affiliate employment in Europe accounted for by employment in the EC-12. See *Survey of Current Business*, June 1988, pp. 90–91. For other years, estimated as 4.9 times the direct investment position in EC-12 (based on 1985 ratio).

has risen from about 18 percent in 1960 to nearly 40 percent in 1988 (table 1-5). The stock of U.S. direct investment in EC-12 has grown substantially faster than the value of exports: between 1960 and 1988 by a factor of 21 versus a factor of 12 for exports (compare tables 1-5 and 1-7). In 1988 sales of U.S.-owned affiliates in the Community totaled $620 billion, compared with just $76 billion for U.S. exports to the EC-12.

Out of such comparisons emerges a simple but compelling observation: for the great majority of large American firms, the business climate inside Europe, and their place in the European economic scheme, have become far more important than their exports to Europe. This is true not only in manufacturing, but also in financial services, where business presence is far more critical than trade links.

From all this follows the proposition that, to the extent the U.S. government responds to the interests of the U.S. business community, it will be more concerned about operating conditions within Europe than export opportunities to Europe. Seen from an investment perspective, EC-1992 is highly attractive to American firms. It is "Opportunity Europe," not "Fortress Europe." European nations almost unanimously

TABLE 1–6.  EC Direct Investment Position in the United States, 1965–88ᵃ

Millions of dollars unless otherwise specified

| Item | 1965 | 1975 | 1980 | 1985 | 1988 |
|---|---|---|---|---|---|
| Petroleum industry | 0.9 | 5.4 | 9.6 | 25.3 | 31.2 |
| Manufacturing | 1.9 | 5.0 | 13.0 | 37.5 | 79.5 |
| Finance, insurance, and real estate | 1.2 | 1.1 | 7.9 | 22.7 | 34.1 |
| Other industries | 0.9 | 4.1 | 9.5 | 21.6 | 49.1 |
| All industries | 4.9 | 15.6 | 40.0 | 107.1 | 193.9 |
| Total foreign direct investment in the United States | 8.8 | 27.7 | 68.4 | 184.6 | 328.8 |
| EC direct investment in the United States as a percentage of total foreign direct investment in the United States | 55.6 | 56.3 | 58.5 | 58.0 | 59.0 |
| Sales of EC-owned affiliates in the United States | n.a. | n.a. | 230 | 336 | 606 |

SOURCE: *Survey of Current Business* (U.S. Department of Commerce), October 1968, October 1977, August 1982, October 1983, May 1987, August 1989.

n.a. Not available.

a. For consistency, the figures comprise data from all twelve current EC member states, though only six were members in 1965, nine in 1975 and 1980, and ten in 1988.

welcome foreign investors; EC competition policy is favorable to newcomers; and foreign firms established within Europe enjoy numerous opportunities to participate in shaping the internal market (see appendix 1-8).[50] Whatever EC-1992 may hold for U.S. exports, it basically holds great promise for General Motors, International Business Machines, Merck, American Telephone and Telegraph, and a long list of other U.S. firms with a strong presence in Europe.[51] Not surprisingly, the principal organizations that speak for U.S. business—the Business Roundtable, the U.S. Council for International Business, the National Association of Manufacturers, and the U.S. Chamber of Commerce—are enthusiastic about Europe 1992.

In any event, export concerns do not necessarily conflict with invest-

50. See Phillip Revzin, "Brussels Babel," *Wall Street Journal*, May 17, 1989, p. A1, for an account of U.S. business efforts at lobbying within the EC.

51. Among other advantages of the 1992 program, multinational firms will be able to simplify corporate legal life by organizing all their EC subsidiaries into a single European Economic Interest Grouping (EEIG). See *Business Month*, August 1989, for a series of articles on U.S. corporate activity in Europe 1992.

TABLE 1–7. U.S.-Community Merchandise Trade, 1960–88[a]

| | U.S. exports to EC-12 | | U.S. imports from EC-12 | | Trade balance (billions of dollars) |
|---|---|---|---|---|---|
| Year | Billions of dollars | Percent of U.S. exports | Billions of dollars | Percent of U.S. imports | |
| 1960 | 6.0 | 29.2 | 3.5 | 24.1 | 2.5 |
| 1965 | 7.9 | 28.8 | 5.2 | 24.2 | 2.7 |
| 1970 | 12.3 | 28.5 | 9.7 | 24.3 | 2.6 |
| 1975 | 25.9 | 24.1 | 17.8 | 18.4 | 8.1 |
| 1980 | 58.7 | 26.2 | 37.9 | 15.2 | 20.8 |
| 1985 | 49.0 | 22.7 | 67.8 | 20.1 | −18.8 |
| 1988 | 75.9 | 23.6 | 84.9 | 19.2 | −9.0 |

SOURCES: *Economic Report of the President, January 1989*, table B-102, p. 424; U.S. Bureau of the Census, *Statistical Abstract of the United States* (Department of Commerce), various issues; and U.S. International Trade Administration, *United States Trade Performance in 1988* (Department of Commerce), September 1989, p. 83.

a. For consistency, the figures comprise data from all twelve current EC member states for all years. Exports are valued f.a.s.; imports are valued on a customs value basis.

ment opportunities. In some cases, totally new U.S. exports may follow from an expansion of investment ties. In more cases, investment abroad enables the U.S. parent to sell components and earn royalties from its foreign affiliate, in circumstances where the market for the final product would have been lost to a local competitor if the U.S. firm had not established a plant.[52] But, in some cases, U.S. corporations will be faced with a clear choice between locating highly desirable R&D centers in, for example, Grenoble or Rochester, or between expanding semiconductor capacity in Dublin or San Jose.[53]

## Nagging Export Questions

As a consequence of such choices, export issues will not quietly fade into a glow of trade creation effects or a sunset of investment opportunities.

52. Some 33 percent of U.S. exports to Europe are shipped to European affiliates of U.S. companies. See *Survey of Current Business*, vol. 69 (June 1989), p. 32; and International Monetary Fund, *Direction of Trade Statistics: Yearbook 1989* (Washington, 1989), p. 402.

53. A large literature on the relation between direct foreign investment and U.S. exports blossomed in the 1960s and 1970s, but the question faded in the 1980s as macroeconomic forces (budget deficits and exchange rates) clearly became the dominant force in the growing U.S. deficit. One of the best books written in the 1970s on the investment-trade link concluded: "The general thrust of our cross-sectional evidence seems consistent with inferences drawn from product cycle studies. The initial investments of an American manufacturer tend to promote exports by developing foreign markets for U.S. products. Over time, however, foreign investment becomes less and less the complement of, and more and more the substitute for, U.S. exports." C. Fred Bergsten, Thomas Horst, and Theodore H. Moran, *American Multinationals and American Interests* (Brookings, 1978), p. 97.

American leaders will continue to be concerned about the vitality of the United States as a geographical base for high-technology exports for several reasons:

—Economic nationalism is well served when leading-edge corporations locate their headquarters and their R&D facilities on national soil, manned by national citizens.

—High-technology manufacturing often generates skilled work and high wages. These are the politicians' "good jobs at good wages."

—High-technology manufacturing is strongly linked with national security. In turn, national security calculations traditionally emphasize the geographic location of production.

—High technology is also linked with strategic trade analysis. Strategic trade theory argues the possibility (or probability, depending on the author) of one nation capturing learning curve and economy of scale advantages, and extracting monopolistic prices from its trading partners.

The Europe 1992 process, coming in the wake of Japanese industrial triumphs, is bound to heighten American anxieties about the U.S. position in the high-technology world of the twenty-first century. How well-founded are such anxieties? Will a unified Europe prove to be a honey pot for U.S. and Japanese high-technology investment, attracting the jewels of the manufacturing and service sectors, and limiting U.S. growth in one of America's best markets for high-technology wares?

The political arithmetic underlying U.S. fears of European moats and drawbridges is easy to understand. The internal market program will progressively expose thousands of EC firms to the hot breath of competition from other EC firms. New supplies from Eastern Europe could intensify competition in low-technology products. Protected market niches will disappear and economic rents will evaporate. The Brussels bureaucracy might cope with the inevitable political pressures by slowing the pace of EC liberalization toward the outside world—however inconsistent this course of action might be with the announced objectives of Europe 1992 or the Uruguay Round.

Those inclined to dwell on downside risks will find it worthwhile to reflect on the history of U.S.-Community agricultural trade, historically the sector of greatest contention between Europe and the United States. Soon after it was created, the Common Agricultural Policy came to entail far higher agricultural prices within Europe than on world markets. The higher price structure was buttressed by EC import barriers, export subsidies, and stockpile schemes. The European Agricultural Guidance

TABLE 1–8. U.S. Agricultural Exports to the EC and EC Agricultural Exports to the World Market, 1960–87[a]

Billions of dollars unless otherwise specified

| Category | 1960 | 1970 | 1980 | 1985 | 1987 |
|---|---|---|---|---|---|
| OECD exports | 16.4 | 23.7 | 126.9 | 109.6 | 147.9 |
| U.S. exports | 4.7 | 5.1 | 30.3 | 22.0 | 22.7 |
| As percentage of OECD exports | 29 | 22 | 24 | 20 | 15 |
| EC-12 exports | 5.0 | 12.6 | 72.3 | 65.0 | 97.9 |
| As percentage of OECD exports | 31 | 53 | 57 | 59 | 66 |
| EC-12 imports | 9.9 | 19.3 | 84.2 | 72.2 | 108.2 |
| EC-12 imports from U.S.[b] | 1.6 | 2.3 | 11.0 | 6.5 | 6.8 |
| As percentage of U.S. exports | 34 | 45 | 36 | 30 | 30 |
| As percentage of EC imports | 16 | 12 | 13 | 9 | 6 |

SOURCES: OECD, *Foreign Trade by Commodities—Historical Outlook, 1965–80* (Paris 1987), *Historical Statistics 1960–1987* (Paris, 1989), and *Commodity Trade: Exports Detailed Analysis by Products,* series C (January–December 1965); Census Bureau, *Statistical Abstract of the United States* (1989), and U.S. Department of Commerce, *Foreign Commerce and Navigation of the United States, 1946–1964* (Washington, 1964); United Nations, *Yearbook of International Trade Statistics, 1962* (New York 1964); and General Agreement on Tariffs and Trade, *Trends in U.S. Merchandise Trade, 1953–1970* (Geneva, July 1972).

a. Agricultural exports are here defined as SITC categories 0 and 1 (food, beverages, and tobacco).

b. In 1960, EC-6 plus United Kingdom; thereafter EC-12.

and Guarantee Fund (EAGGF) now entails annual expenditures of $20–25 billion and consumes 60 to 70 percent of the total EC budget.[54]

All this translated into a massive loss of export opportunities for U.S. farmers. Over the period 1960 to 1988, U.S. agricultural exports to the EC-12 declined from 16 percent of EC imports to 6 percent of EC imports (table 1-8). One analyst offers the following estimates: the loss of U.S. agricultural exports resulting from the original Common Market (measured in 1988 prices) was $3.3 billion; the loss from the first

54. See Dale E. Hathaway, *Agriculture and the GATT: Rewriting the Rules,* Policy Analyses in International Economics 20 (Washington: Institute for International Economics, September 1987), pp. 72–78; and P. C. van den Noort, "Agricultural Policy," in Peter Coffey, ed., *Main Economic Policy Areas of the EEC–Towards 1992,* 2d rev. ed. (Dordrecht, Neth.: Kluwer Academic Publishers, 1988), pp. 31–51.

The United States, like the EC, also subsidizes its farmers to a very high degree. A major difference between EC and U.S. agricultural programs is that the EC imposes a far greater share of costs on agricultural consumers, and a far smaller share on taxpayers, than does the United States. For example, in 1986–87 the cost to consumers in the United States was only $6.0 billion versus $32.6 billion in the EC, but the cost to U.S. taxpayers was a whopping $30.6 billion versus only $13.6 billion to EC taxpayers. The greater share of consumer costs in Europe means, of course, higher internal prices and attendant restrictive trade policies in Europe. See Vernon O. Roningen and Praveen M. Dixit, "Economic Implications of Agricultural Policy Reform in Industrial Market Economies," Staff Report AGES 89-36 (Washington: U.S. Department of Agriculture, Economic Research Service, May 1989).

TABLE 1–9. U.S.-Community GATT Litigation, 1960–85[a]

| | U.S. versus EC[b] | | EC versus U.S. | |
| --- | --- | --- | --- | --- |
| Category of dispute | Number | Percent | Number | Percent |
| Sector | | | | |
| Agriculture and fisheries | 17 | 81 | 4 | 45 |
| Industry and mining | 1 | 5 | 3 | 33 |
| General | 3 | 14 | 2 | 22 |
| TOTAL | 21 | 100 | 9 | 100 |
| Policy measure | | | | |
| Tariffs | 3 | 14 | 3 | 33 |
| Nontariff barriers | 11 | 53 | 4 | 45 |
| Subsidies | 7 | 33 | 2 | 22 |
| TOTAL | 21 | 100 | 9 | 100 |

SOURCE: Robert E. Hudec, "Legal Issues in US-EC Trade Policy: GATT Litigation 1960–1985," in Robert E. Baldwin, Carl B. Hamilton, and André Sapir, eds., *Issues in US-EC Trade Relations*, National Bureau of Economic Research (University of Chicago Press, 1988), pp. 45–51.

a. The term *litigation* is used to denote any GATT proceeding in which one GATT member has attempted to obtain an authoritative legal ruling that another member's action is either in violation of GATT law, or has "impaired" the value of GATT rights (a special kind of GATT legal claim). The term is limited to legal claims against specified governments; it does not include requests for general legal rulings. It includes all cases in which the complaining government *began* a lawsuit on the public record, that is, took at least the first step in pursuit of such a legal ruling in a formal GATT proceeding or document.

b. Suits against EC member states are treated as EC litigation only when the defendant was a member state at the time of the suit. One case submitted jointly by the U.S. and the EC is listed both under U.S. v. EC and EC v. U.S.

enlargement (Six to Nine) was $3.6 billion; and the loss from the second enlargement (Nine to Twelve) was $0.6 billion (table 1-4).

Moreover, as the EC disposed of its agricultural surpluses on world markets and expanded its share of agricultural exports from the Organization for Economic Cooperation and Development from 31 percent to 66 percent (table 1-8), it put considerable downward pressure on the world price structure and diminished the quantity of U.S. exports to third-country markets.

With this history in mind, it is not surprising that some 80 percent of GATT actions initiated by the United States against the EC have concerned agriculture and fisheries, and that the great majority of actions were triggered by nontariff barriers and subsidies (table 1-9).

Agricultural battles are largely yesterday's story in the transatlantic dialogue. European disenchantment with ever-escalating CAP costs, coupled with current talks in the Uruguay Round, point toward a lasting settlement of U.S.-Community agricultural disputes in the 1990s. The main concern—for those who worry about downside risks—is whether the agricultural experience of the past foreshadows the high-technology experience of the future. Clearly there are important differences between agriculture and high technology:

—Farmers have a strong emotional claim on the pocketbooks of innocent consumers and naive taxpayers;

—While agricultural self-sufficiency was part of the explicit political glue of the early Common Market, high-technology self-sufficiency remains an implicit item on the internal market agenda; and

—In the manufacturing realm, high technology or low technology, multinational firms often resist costly nationalistic schemes. Comparable countervailing pressures do not exist in agriculture.

Still, set against these differences is the simple fact that high-technology civilian and defense goods are widely seen as the hallmark of economic competitiveness and military security. The joint challenge of high-technology Japanese and U.S. firms was a key force behind political acceptance of the 1985 White Paper agenda. Many high-technology European firms are gearing up for the challenge. As one example, Siemens spends 10 percent of its sales on R&D, far more than its U.S. competitors, General Electric and IBM; as another example, erstwhile rivals Compagnie Générale d'Electricité (CGE) of France and General Electric of Britain have formed a $6.3 billion joint venture.[55]

The EC has already committed itself to a great many ambitious high-technology research projects and research consortia that collectively could claim as much as $16 billion over the next six years (appendix 1-9). The Community alone has committed nearly $7 billion to research over the next five years; additional funds will come from member state governments and private firms.[56] The Joint European Submicron Silicon Initiative (JESSI) program is illustrative. Funded at $5 billion, a quarter of JESSI costs will be paid by the EC, a quarter by member states, and the rest by individual companies.[57] Total JESSI funds are many times the proposed U.S. financial commitment to Sematech ($500 million). Further accentuating the contrast, a proposed U.S. private sector research consortium,

55. Thane Peterson, "Can Europe Catch Up in the High Tech Race?" *Business Week*, October 23, 1989, p. 146.

56. Lucy Kellaway, "EC Research Budget Confined to £4 Billion," *Financial Times*, December 18, 1989, p. 4.

57. Steven Greenhouse, "Europeans Unite to Compete with Japan and U.S.," *New York Times*, August 21, 1989, p. A1. To be sure, it is not self-evident that the EC will be able to keep the benefits of publicly supported R&D within Europe, even if it tries. Good R&D findings tend to leak rather quickly outside corporate and national boundaries. The United States, and U.S. firms that are not part of European research consortia, could still end up as major beneficiaries of European research.

U.S. Memories (with a planned budget of $1 billion), collapsed in December 1989.

From a political standpoint, it would not be surprising to find the EC pursuing five complementary policies to further its excursion into the world of high technology:

—Protect EC firms in the old-fashioned way by maintaining external tariff barriers and by resisting common international technical standards (there is little evidence of such behavior);

—Stall the admission of "foreign" firms into European consortia (however, IBM was admitted to JESSI in early 1990, even though the United States still excludes foreign firms from Sematech and other research consortia);

—Favor European firms in public procurement of high-technology products;

—Subsidize high-technology production (as has already happened on a very large scale with Airbus) to capture an "equitable share of world export trade";[58] and

—Subordinate competition policy to strategic trade policy; that is, nourish EC champion firms in world markets by permitting anticompetitive behavior within the EC.

Such policies are no strangers to Europe. Their antecedents were espoused by Friedrich List 150 years ago.[59] Today member state industrial subsidies total $98 billion a year, Community subsidies amount to $26 billion a year, and the combined amount adds up to 3 percent of Community GDP, more than the direct tax payments of all EC industrial companies.[60] As a result of high-technology market fragmentation and entry barriers, Europeans today buy only half as many personal computers and consumer electronic items as Americans, often at prices two to three times as high.[61]

As this book is published in 1990, such policies belong to the realm of future dangers. Commissioner Leon Brittan has launched a crusade

58. The phrase "equitable share of world export trade" originates in the GATT standard applied to the discipline of agricultural subsidies; it has often been used by the EC to defeat complaints in GATT about subsidized EC agricultural exports.

59. Friedrich List, *The National System of Political Economy* (J. B. Lippincott and Co., 1856).

60. EC Commission, *First Survey on State Aids in the European Communities* (Brussels, 1988), tables I, II.

61. Peterson, "Can Europe Catch Up?" p. 154.

TABLE 1-10.  U.S. Exports of High-Technology Manufactured Goods
to the European Community, 1980 and 1987[a]

Billions of dollars unless otherwise specified

| Category | 1980 (EC = 10) | 1987 (EC = 12) |
|---|---|---|
| OECD exports | 355.3 | 522.8 |
| U.S. exports | 77.1 | 100.9 |
| As percent of OECD exports | 22 | 19 |
| EC exports | 177.9 | 266.7 |
| As percent of OECD exports | 52 | 50 |
| EC imports | 124.3 | 219.2 |
| EC imports from U.S. | 19.6 | 27.6 |
| As percent of U.S. exports | 25 | 27 |
| As percent of EC imports | 16 | 13 |

SOURCES: GATT, *International Trade 1983/84* (Geneva, 1984), tables A23–A26, and *International Trade 1987/88* (1988), vol. 2, tables AB5–AB8.

a. High-technology products are here defined, in terms of GATT categories, as "engineering products" minus "road motor vehicles" and minus "household appliances."

against state aid to assist declining industries (see chapter 6). Nearly all the EC research consortia are open to U.S. firms operating in Europe and several U.S. firms such as AT&T, IBM, and General Motors have joined EC research consortia.[62] EC authorities are talking privately about negotiations with the United States that would extend the mutual recognition approach, in the realm of technical standards, on a reciprocal basis. Coming to the bottom line, the United States is almost holding its own in the EC high-technology market. In 1980, the EC bought 25 percent of U.S. high-technology exports; in 1988, 27 percent (table 1-10). To be sure, the U.S. share of the EC high-technology market slipped from 16 percent to 13 percent, but little of this share loss can be attributed to EC public sponsorship of high technology in the 1980s.

Yet, despite the comfort of past statistics, the overarching trade question for the 1990s is whether a European drive for high-technology self-sufficiency will emerge from a series of piecemeal decisions, and whether the outcome will be a shrinking share of U.S. high-technology exports, not only to Europe but also to third-country markets.

62. For membership of U.S. firms in EC research consortia, see Hearing before the Subcommittee on Science, Research and Technology, and the Subcommittee on International Science Cooperation of the House Committee on Science, Space, and Technology, 100 Cong. 1 sess., November 2, 1989, p. 91.

## Specific Issues

The next four chapters in this book are organized along industry lines: banking and securities, automobiles, telecommunications, and semiconductors. A sixth chapter deals with competition policy, and the last chapter looks at negotiating strategy. Rather than summarize the chapter findings here, it might be useful to outline common themes.

Four large questions emerge from the industry-by-industry and subject-by-subject analyses:

—How will U.S. firms operating in Europe fare?

—Do the details of EC-1992 add up to bad news for U.S. exports?

—What challenges will a powerful and unified Europe pose for the United States in world markets?

—How will a unified Europe shape American attitudes toward our own economic institutions and our role in shaping international economic policy?

The first two questions constitute the bread-and-butter of transatlantic trade and investment negotiations. To anticipate the findings of later chapters: specific issues, such as the definition of local content and rules of origin, or the procedures for setting technical standards, will in fact get resolved on a rolling basis between Brussels and Washington. Moreover, U.S. firms operating within Europe will fare at least as well as their European competitors, and sometimes better. But it remains to be seen whether U.S. high-technology exports are gradually eroded as European firms gain technological prowess and as American and Japanese firms erect new facilities in Europe, and whether competitive processes in the high-technology arena are materially altered by EC policy.

The second two questions add up to broader challenges that European unification poses for the United States. These questions have little historical precedent. They are not traditionally the subject of economic negotiation. The U.S. response must largely entail reexamination of our economic institutions and our role in the world economy.

Five major specific EC-1992 issues are now part of the U.S.-Community negotiating agenda: reciprocity, national quotas, technical standards, local content coupled with rules of origin, and government procurement. The sections that follow briefly impart the flavor of these issues. The broad thesis of this book is that, through hard bargaining, loud rhetoric, and occasional retaliation, these specific issues and others will indeed be resolved. Europe and the United States will emerge from the 1992 process as stronger economic allies than they are today.

### Reciprocity

The EC insists that it will not automatically extend the benefits of the internal market to outsiders unless required to do so by existing international agreements. No GATT or other agreements presently compel the EC to extend unilaterally the benefits of the single banking license, open procurement, mutual recognition of technical standards, or pan-European TV programming. In these areas the EC will ask third countries for "reciprocity."[63]

What does reciprocity mean? In the context of GATT negotiations, reciprocity has historically meant that each trading partner extends concessions that ensure *new* access to its markets equivalent to the new access its exports gain in foreign markets. The EC challenges this traditional formulation of reciprocity, especially in the financial service and high-technology sectors where Japanese firms are prominent. The EC is not prepared to allow Japanese banks, for example, to increase their share of the European banking market from a base of 10 percent to a new level of 12 percent, if EC banks gain just 2 percent of the Tokyo market starting from zero. Nor is the EC prepared to buy unlimited quantities of Japanese semiconductors when Philips N.V. and Siemens can gain barely a foothold in the Japanese market.

In the context of the 1992 program, the EC has reinterpreted reciprocity to mean that an EC firm should enjoy both national treatment—the same treatment that a government accords to its domestic firms—plus effective access to the foreign market. The test of meaningful reciprocity comes down to an ad hoc combination of rules and performance. The rules are usually phrased in terms of permissible tariff and quota barriers, plus agreed implementation of the national treatment standard; performance is often defined in terms of the market share acquired by EC firms in the foreign country, whether through exports or investment. The EC

63. See, generally, Karl M. Meessen, "Europe en Route to 1992: The Completion of the Internal Market and Its Impact on Non-Europeans," *International Lawyer*, vol. 23 (Summer 1989), pp. 359–71. For a glossary of possible definitions of reciprocity, see "Survey of Europe's Internal Market," *Economist*, p. 35. While it is true that the EC presently has no legal obligations in a great many areas, the Community has agreed to support the Uruguay Round initiatives in services, and it has signed the Tokyo Round Codes on Government Procurement and Technical Standards.

position in these matters calls to mind American enthusiasm for a "level playing field," forcefully voiced by Congressman Richard A. Gephardt (Democrat-Missouri) in the 1988 presidential campaign and expressed in various provisions of the Omnibus Trade and Competitiveness Act of 1988.[64]

The reciprocity issue has surfaced in several EC directives. Proposals on the access of third-country firms into banking and life insurance markets, the benefits of liberalized capital flows, exchange of credit information, and public procurement have all incorporated reciprocity clauses.

So far the greatest stir about reciprocity requirements has been created by those envisaged in the first version of the Second Banking Directive. This episode is explored in chapter 2. It was feared, perhaps wrongly, that the EC would require "mirror image" reciprocity and that the mirror image test would have indirectly blocked the access of U.S. banks to the enlarged EC financial market.[65] The traditional U.S. separation between banking and commerce, embodied in the Glass-Steagall Act, together with the geographic restrictions on banking embodied in the McFadden Act, prohibit banks operating in the United States from providing the full range and geographic scope of financial services that banks operating in Europe can offer. Given congressional resistance to amending Glass-Steagall and especially McFadden, the United States was in no position to grant mirror image reciprocity to European banks. Eventually, however, the Commission declared that it is not, in fact, seeking mirror image reciprocity from the United States, but instead wants European firms to enjoy "market access and competition opportunities comparable to those granted by the Community." The EC has not lost sight of Glass-

64. For a summary of level playing field provisions (also known as market access provisions) in the 1988 Trade Act, see U.S. Chamber of Commerce, *The Omnibus Trade and Competitiveness Act of 1988* (1988), chap. 3.

65. Article 58 in the Treaty of Rome requires member states to accord the right of establishment and national treatment to firms incorporated in other member states. There is an old debate whether Article 58 applies only to "genuine" EC companies (that is, EC-owned firms) or also to European subsidiaries of, for example, U.S. multinational firms. The Commission has long regarded all European companies, regardless of ownership, as "genuine" EC firms, entitled to Article 58 rights. However, a definitive ruling by the European Court of Justice has never been made on this question. The Commission also takes the view that the first establishment of a foreign-owned firm within a member state can be subject to EC reciprocity tests. The Second Banking Directive concerns the appropriate content of such first establishment tests.

Steagall or McFadden, but Community officials have all but publicly said that their immediate target is Japan, not the United States.[66]

As this episode suggests, the EC reciprocity principle will be pragmatically adapted to the circumstances of each sector. For example, in high-technology sectors, reciprocity will probably come to mean that EC subsidiaries of U.S. companies will be excluded from EC-sponsored research consortia, such as RACE, Esprit, and JESSI, if EC companies continue to be excluded from U.S. consortia such as Sematech, or from research sponsored by the U.S. Department of Defense.[67] In a recent test case, practically at the same moment that IBM announced a joint memory chip program with Siemens, IBM was also admitted to JESSI, possibly with the expectation that the United States would reconsider its own restrictions on Sematech.[68] In the end, Japan is likely to become the target of EC high-technology reciprocity requirements: Japan will be called upon to open private and public procurement of high-technology goods and services, to facilitate European investment in Japan, and to ensure the transfer of Japanese technology to Europe.[69]

## National Quotas

Quotas against products shipped from other member states are obviously inconsistent with the principles of an integrated single market. Thus a critical question is how will the EC phase out the 700-odd national quantitative restrictions (QRs) that limit third-country suppliers and that are backed up, both for foreign imports and for intra-EC shipments, by national border controls authorized under Article 115 of the Treaty of Rome. Of these quotas, about 70 percent limit textile and apparel imports under the Multifiber Arrangement (most cover imports from developing countries), and about 26 percent limit other industrial goods (most cover imports from Eastern Europe and the Soviet Union; with

66. William Dullforce, "Brussels Stands Firm on Banking Access," *Financial Times,* September 21, 1989, p. 6.

67. Alan Cane, "IBM Applies to Join European Semiconductor Research Project," *Financial Times,* October 5, 1989, p. 1.

68. John Markoff, "I.B.M. Joins Siemens in Developing Chips," *New York Times,* January 25, 1990, p. D1.

69. The "Group of 12" European technology firms (Alcatel, Philips N.V., Thomson, Siemens, AEG, and others) have called for the EC to block entry by Japanese and U.S. telecommunications firms to European procurement unless reciprocal access is guaranteed by those states. "Europe's Telecom Giants Urge No Free Entry for Japan, U.S.," *Europe-1992,* vol. 1 (October 10, 1989), p. 363. The United States and the Community will probably reach an accommodation more quickly than the Community and Japan.

recent developments, these are likely to be liberalized). France and Italy account for the great majority of Article 115 actions against textiles, apparel, and other industrial goods.[70] It should be noted that some member state auto quotas are grey area measures, not authorized under Article 115.

Various policy options are available: transformation of national quantitative restrictions into EC-wide quotas; unilateral abandonment of quantitative restrictions; or abandonment of quantitative restrictions coupled with the mobilization of alternative trade policy measures designed to "safeguard" ailing industries and to thwart "unfair" foreign practices. The policy choice will largely depend on the sensitivity of the protected industries. The automobile industry, and the textile and apparel industry, are strong candidates for, respectively, EC-wide "soft" monitoring and "hard" quotas. Other industries are likely to find their quotas abandoned entirely or replaced with less-sweeping trade policy measures.

Chapter 3 examines the interesting case of automobiles. Various member states limit Japanese imports (to under 3 percent of the market in France and Italy, up to 11 percent in Britain), but there are no restrictions in Germany, the Benelux nations, and several smaller countries (where the Japanese market share ranges up to 40 percent). Italy, Spain, and Portugal can appeal to Article 115 as justification for restricting intra-EC auto shipments, but the restrictions imposed by other member states are grey area measures with no legal sanction. European motor industry leaders from Germany, Italy, and France, together with Ford of Europe, have demanded transitional EC-wide controls on the sale of Japanese cars through the mid-1990s, and relaxation only in the context of true reciprocity from Japan.[71]

Consistent with these views, it seems that auto restrictions will initially be transformed into EC-wide monitoring of Japanese market penetration over the period 1992 to 1997 (see chapter 3).[72] Progressive relaxation would require parallel liberalization by Japan. The sales of Japanese auto transplant firms located in Europe would be taken into account in the

70. Siebert, "Single European Market," table A3.

71. Kevin Done, "EC Car Makers Urge Controls on Japanese Imports after 1992," *Financial Times*, September 14, 1989, p. 1; and Agnelli, "Europe of 1992," pp. 65–66.

72. Also see Bruce Barnard, "EC to Ask Japan to Curb Car Sales," *Journal of Commerce*, September 29, 1989, p. 1A (citing current Japanese market share data), and *Journal of Commerce*, November 13, 1989, p. 1A; *Financial Times*, December 5, 1989, p. 2, and *Financial Times*, February 2, 1990, p. 5; and Steven Greenhouse, "Europeans Press Japan on Autos," *New York Times*, December 29, 1989, p. D1.

monitoring exercise but not actually included under the import column—a distinction without a difference. This whole approach, with the implied foundation of understandings between Japanese producers and the Community, could endanger the potential growth of U.S. automobile exports to Europe shipped from Japanese transplant firms in Ohio (Honda) and Tennessee (Nissan). In fact, the proposed EC monitoring program assumes that exports to Europe from Japanese transplant firms in the United States will remain small—a forecast that has the quality of self-fulfilling prophecy.

The policy challenge for the United States is to become a vigorous and effective voice for Nissan and Honda as exporters of autos from the United States to Europe. The United States has the law on its side: EC limitations of U.S.-made Hondas would be illegal under GATT. But legal niceties can quickly dissolve in the face of Community understandings with Japanese producers. U.S. commercial diplomacy must engage not only Brussels but also Tokyo and the parent auto companies in Japan. Further, the United States will have to make its own concessions. Is the United States prepared, for example, to reconsider its discriminatory fleet mileage regulations—which bear heavily on European luxury car imports—in order to boost Japanese transplant exports to the European market?

## Technical Standards

The eventual harmonization of European technical standards, backed by common testing and certification procedures, is a key ingredient in creating an integrated European market. Technical standards play a major role in two of the industries examined in this book: automobiles (chapter 3) and telecommunications (chapter 4).

Harmonization of standards will be accomplished in two ways: through the adoption of directives that lay down essential requirements in critical areas related to public health, safety, and the environment, and through Darwinian selection mechanisms growing out of the mutual recognition approach. To be effective, harmonization of standards must also be supported by EC-wide testing and certification procedures (as in pharmaceuticals), or by mutual recognition of national testing and certification procedures.

At one time it was thought that technical harmonization would offer pluses and minuses for U.S. companies. On the one hand, large U.S. firms established in Europe might enjoy a competitive advantage under harmonized conditions, since they are accustomed to operating on a continental scale. This is particularly true of automobile, telecommunications, and pharmaceutical firms. In addition, all U.S. firms would enjoy cost savings, because they could now market their products throughout Europe by meeting one set of standards rather than twelve. On the other hand, it was feared that exclusion from EC standard-setting procedures could work to the disadvantage of U.S. companies, particularly those exporting high-technology products to Europe.

U.S.-Community talks, prompted by U.S. Commerce Secretary Robert Mosbacher, have already blunted the downside concerns. The American National Standards Institute (ANSI) will exercise a voice in the EC standards boards—the European Committee for Standardization (CEN) and the European Committee for Electrotechnical Standardization (CENELEC)—and vice versa.[73] In addition, individual U.S. companies— especially larger companies—already enjoy a variety of access routes to the EC process (appendix 1-8). For now, the technical standards issue is relatively calm.

A new technical standards issue is looming over the horizon. The *Cassis de Dijon* decision does not require acceptance of U.S. products by, for example, Italy without testing and certification in Italy, even though the products may meet Italian quality standards. The United States and the Community have not yet agreed on mutual recognition of testing and certification. In fact, such an agreement would put the cart before the horse: mutual recognition of standards should precede mutual recognition of testing and certification. Until there is transatlantic acceptance of the mutual recognition principle (see chapter 7), or on harmonized standards, national testing and certification procedures will continue to hamper trade.

## Rules of Origin and Local Content

Rules of origin and local content are two mind-numbing concepts that, when linked in certain ways, can create almost impenetrable trade barriers. "Local content" refers to the percentage of value embodied in a good or service made within a geographic area, for example, the EC or EFTA.[74] "Rules of origin" define the patrimony of individual compo-

---

73. "European Standards Bodies to Accept U.S. Comments," *Europe-1992*, vol. 1 (August 16, 1989), p. 294. U.S. firms and U.S. associations can participate as observers in the European Telecommunications Standards Institute (ETSI).

74. The EC applies a variety of local content standards, depending on the context: for

nents.[75] Together these rules determine, in some circumstances, eligibility for the following benefits of the unified EC market: exemption from residual national quotas, eligibility for government procurement (including TV programming), acceptability of the product under EC-EFTA and other preference schemes, and avoidance of certain antidumping duties. These issues arise with some force in chapter 3 (Automobiles), chapter 4 (Telecommunications), and chapter 5 (Semiconductors).

The coupling of stringent local content requirements with tight rules of origin can essentially exclude products made outside the Community. The local content issue has created a transatlantic melodrama in television programming, where the EC Broadcast Directive gives national authorities permission to require 50 percent European content.[76] Rules of origin coupled with local content requirements have been hotly debated in the context of Community antidumping laws applied to semiconductors.

To illustrate with the case of semiconductors, the EC has insisted that the process of diffusion (laying the circuit on the chip) must take place within Europe to meet the EC rule of origin. (This particular rule represents a new interpretation of the general EC rule that assigns a component EC patrimony if the "last substantial transformation occurred in a member state.") The diffusion rule was originally aimed at dumping by Japanese firms—more particularly at so-called screwdriver plants, Japanese-owned assembly plants located in Europe and designed to avoid EC antidumping duties on the final product simply by importing and assembling the components.[77]

---

example, 60 percent for EFTA autos in order to be imported duty free; 35–45 percent for goods to escape Article 115 national quotas. See Siebert, "Single European Market," p. 18.

75. The Kyoto Customs Convention of 1973 sets forth internationally agreed rules of origin. The United States, however, has not signed Annex D.1 of the convention, which entered into force in 1977 and which lays out the substantial transformation rule.

76. Phillip Revzin, "The Battle for Europe's TV Future," Wall Street Journal, October 6, 1989, p. B1; "La Boob Tube: Europe Complains about U.S. Shows," Wall Street Journal, October 16, 1989, p. A1; and Nancy Dunne, "EC Rule to Be Taken to GATT," Financial Times, October 10, 1989, p. 10. One result of European TV content rules is to spur the production of more knock-off series, such as "Eurocop" to replace "Miami Vice," and "Chateaurallon" to replace "Dallas." The United States will take up the Broadcast Directive in GATT.

77. In technical terms EC antidumping anticircumvention rules ("screwdriver plant" rules) require that no more than 60 percent of components assembled in the EC screwdriver plant come from the producer found to be dumping products in the Community. The screwdriver rules were adopted in February 1989, pursuant to EC Council Regulation

But the diffusion rule, coupled with the agreement by Japanese firms to ensure at least 40 percent content from non-Japanese sources, quickly affected U.S. semiconductor exporters: downstream computer manufacturers replaced U.S.-made semiconductors with European-made semiconductors, supposedly because of the diffusion rule.[78] For example, NEC Corporation stopped buying U.S.-made computer chips for the circuit boards it puts into its computer printers assembled in Great Britain. The impact on investment has been equally dramatic: Intel is building a $400 million semiconductor plant near Dublin, almost entirely to meet the new EC rule of origin.[79] The map of Europe is already dotted with Japanese semiconductor facilities, in large part for the same reason.[80] This is the outstanding example of a seemingly small change in technical rules triggering significant investment that, in time, will very likely shift the balance of semiconductor trade.

## Government Procurement

The multibillion-dollar EC procurement market—some 15 percent of GDP, about $600 billion, including the purchases of state-owned enterprises—has traditionally been closed, not only to U.S. suppliers, but also to suppliers from other member states.[81] Member states have a long tradition of favoring national champion firms through explicit and implicit

---

802/68, which entered into force in June 1988 and was designed to avert circumvention of EC antidumping rules. In March 1990 the EC antidumping anticircumvention rules were found to be inconsistent with GATT by a GATT panel. See *Inside U.S. Trade*, Special Report, March 30, 1990.

78. Clyde H. Farnsworth, "U.S. Cautions Europe on Protectionism," *New York Times*, October 6, 1989, p. D6.

79. "Intel to Manufacture Chips in Ireland," *Europe-1992*, vol. 1 (October 10, 1989), p. 367. It is also worth noting that the EC imposes a 14 percent duty on semiconductor chips, compared with zero duties imposed by the United States and Japan. The EC duty can be avoided, in an integrated circuit, only if the wafer is fabricated in the EC. Europe may drop its duty in the context of the Uruguay Round. See Terry Dodsworth, "Brussels May Reduce Tariff on Imports of Semiconductors," *Financial Times*, October 2, 1989, p. 1.

80. Terry Dodsworth and Hazel Duffy, "Fujitsu Plans Chips in Britain to Supply EC Market," *Financial Times*, February 2, 1989, p. 1; and "Chip Makers Begin to Conform with EC Policy on Full Manufacturing in Europe," *Japan Economic Journal*, August 26, 1989, p. 6.

81. U.S. International Trade Commission, *The Effects of Greater Economic Integration within the European Community on the United States*, USITC Publication 2204 (Washington, July 1989), p. 4–7. Also see Guy de Jonquières, "Hurdles Too High," *Financial Times*, November 13, 1989, p. 20.

"Buy National" policies. Between 1984 and 1988 the Deutsche Bundespost awarded 99.5 percent of its contracts to German firms; while France, the United Kingdom, the Netherlands, and Portugal awarded 100 percent of their telecommunications contracts to their own national firms. Overall, less than 2 percent of government contracts go to firms in other member states.[82] In light of this tradition, it is not surprising that previous EC efforts to harmonize government procurement regulations, and to open procurement markets, have failed. This is a central issue in chapter 4 on telecommunications.

Since the AT&T break-up decree was issued by U.S. District Court Judge Harold Greene in 1982, the United States has had an increasingly open telecommunications market; correspondingly, the closed EC procurement market has seemed more and more anomalous to the U.S. Congress and to U.S. trade officials.[83] The Trade Act of 1988 instructed the U.S. Trade Representative to open foreign telecommunications markets, with a special view toward Europe and Japan.

Meanwhile, the Commission has formulated a directive that would do two things when public procurement is opened to the four excluded sectors (energy, telecommunications, transportation, and water supply): enable public authorities to reject outright any bid that does not meet a 50 percent EC content requirement, and impose a 3 percent Buy European preference margin on bids that do not meet the local content requirement but, at the option of the public authority, are not rejected.[84]

82. "Survey of Europe's Internal Market," *Economist*, p. 16.

83. The telecommunications provisions of the 1988 Trade Act particularly illuminate both U.S. and EC trade strategies. U.S. telephone deregulation, coupled with the 1982 court decree that divested American Telephone and Telegraph (AT&T) of its regional operating companies (the so-called Baby Bells), created a huge market for foreign suppliers of telecommunications equipment to the U.S. market. This happened because the Baby Bells were freed from their purchasing ties to Western Electric, the manufacturing arm of the old AT&T system. Meanwhile, other nations, including the EC member states, kept their strong links to private suppliers. As a result, in part, the U.S. trade deficit in telecommunications products deteriorated from $5.0 billion in 1981 to $15.6 billion in 1987. See International Trade Administration, *United States Trade: Performance in 1987* (Washington: U.S. Department of Commerce, 1988), tables 10, 11. On the one hand, the EC is determined not to experience a similar unilateral deterioration in its own high-technology trade balances as an unintended result of the EC-1992 Program; on the other hand, the United States is attempting to recoup its telecommunications trade losses through the market access provision of the 1988 Trade Act.

84. Under the U.S. federal Buy American provisions, all bids are considered, regardless of local content. However, bids with more than 50 percent foreign content are subject to

The 3 percent margin was deliberately set at one-half the U.S. federal Buy American preference margin and will self-destruct on a bilateral basis when another country (say the United States) eliminates its own Buy National preference at all levels of government, or on a multinational basis if preferences are negotiated away in the Uruguay Round.

The European market is already the biggest export market for U.S. suppliers. In 1988 the United States exported $1.3 billion of telecommunications apparatus to the EC, compared with $0.6 billion to Japan and $0.8 billion to Canada.[85] But U.S. exports to Europe could be far larger. The EC telecommunications equipment market, which amounted to $17.5 billion in 1986, is expected to grow 67 percent by 1995 (by comparison, the U.S. market is expected to grow only 23 percent).[86] Even more dramatic is the prospective growth in telecommunications services, an area of decided U.S. strength (see chapter 4). If European growth is coupled with the abolition of preferential government procurement, and genuine national treatment of foreign firms, the market potential for U.S. suppliers of telecommunications goods and services would be enormous.

Will the United States override its Buy American provisions—both at the federal and at the state and local levels—by subjecting a wide range of public purchases to the GATT Code on Government Procurement, in order to gain access to the EC telecommunications market?[87] Will the United States extend the GATT Code to its regulated monopolies such as the Baby Bells (the regional Bell operating companies)? Will the United States open its own TV and radio broadcast systems to foreign

a 6 percent reference margin. State and local Buy American procedures may, however, exclude bids with foreign content.

85. U.S. International Trade Commission, *Effects of Greater Economic Integration*, p. 4-43.

86. EC Commission, *The Benefits of Completing the Internal Market for Telecommunication* (Luxembourg, 1988), p. 16; and U.S. Chamber of Commerce, *Europe 1992: A Practical Guide for American Business* (Washington, 1989), p. 53.

87. The U.S. Defense Department has already laid the analytic groundwork for curbing the scope of Buy American provisions in defense procurement. See Office of the Secretary of Defense, *The Impact of Buy American Restrictions Affecting Defense Procurement* (Washington, July 1989). As a political matter, it will prove harder to override state and local Buy American provisions, even though, as a constitutional matter, an override is fully within the power of Congress. Note that the GATT Code on Government Procurement permits local content requirements, such as the 50 percent test proposed by the EC for the excluded sectors, provided they can be met by goods or services furnished by any code signatory.

ownership? This dialogue contains the makings of a transatlantic trade bargain of immense commercial dimensions.

## Resolution of Specific Issues

The history of U.S.-Community trade and investment disputes is a history of issues getting resolved. The resolution process is neither quiet nor painless. Quite the opposite: disputes flare up; ministers bluster; retaliation is often threatened and sometimes inflicted; and then ingenious technical solutions emerge, or the matter is consigned to a transatlantic study group. A sampler of U.S.-Community trade disputes appears in appendix 1-10. Apart from agriculture, most issues have been satisfactorily addressed in a fashion that results in more open markets.

In this respect, U.S.-Community relations differ markedly from U.S.-Japanese relations. Since the early 1970s, U.S.-Japan trade relations have been acrimonious and, in the view of many U.S. business firms, unproductive. Recently, Edward L. Hennessy, Jr., chairman of Allied-Signal, wrote an op-ed piece titled "Japan's Market Is Closed Drum Tight."[88] In the same cheerful spirit, Professor Rudiger Dornbusch wrote an op-ed piece titled "Give Japan a Target and Say 'Import'!"[89] Such declarations are rare in the dialogue between Washington and Brussels.

Recognizing that the United States and the EC have a history of sorting out their differences, America still needs a well-articulated strategy to address the challenges of EC-1992. Should talks take place bilaterally or only within GATT? What is the right priority of agenda items? What concessions should the United States make? Those questions are addressed in chapter 7 on Negotiating Strategy.

# Broader Challenges

Apart from the specific issues that will inevitably arise issue-by-issue and industry-by-industry, the EC-1992 Program raises broader questions for the United States. Broad questions seldom lend themselves to negotiation, but they often pose major challenges for U.S. public policy.

## U.S. Position in the League of Top Firms

The EC-1992 Program could well spawn a new generation of European industrial and banking giants and put renewed pressure on U.S. mem-

88. New York Times, October 1, 1989, sec. 3, p. 2.
89. New York Times, September 24, 1989, sec. 3, p. 2.

bership in the league of top firms. Should this be a matter of concern? Not to those who believe wholeheartedly in atomistic competition and small entrepreneurs. But most observers would agree that top firms enjoy a decided advantage in financing the huge R&D costs associated with leading-edge technology, in carrying the losses incurred in bringing new products to market, in reaping economies of scale, and in financing industrial restructuring. In a similar vein, giant banks can take on greater risks. Indeed, within Europe and Japan, giant banks underwrite entire corporate groups. Seen in this light, the prospective decline of U.S. business in the ranks of the world's top 100 industrial firms and top 50 banks cannot be dismissed as an inconsequential scene in the larger drama of international competition.

Between 1970 and 1988 the share of sales of the world's top 100 industrial firms accounted for by U.S.-based firms dropped from 69 percent to 45 percent; EC-12 firms rose from 24 to 33 percent; and Japanese firms rose from 6 to 15 percent (table 1-11). The Japanese rise in automobiles, and in telecommunications, computers, and semiconductors, was especially pronounced. Likewise, the U.S. share of assets of the top fifty banks plummeted from 38 percent to 6 percent; the EC-12 also lost ground, from 31 to 29 percent, while Japan rose, from 18 to 59 percent (table 1-12).

It seems highly likely that European firms will now join Japanese firms in pushing U.S.-based firms further down in the rankings of industrial and financial giants. And it is all but certain that European direct investment in the United States, now $149 billion at book value, will grow much faster than U.S. direct investment in Europe, now $127 billion at book value (compare tables 1-5 and 1-6). As a consequence, the sales of European firms operating in the U.S. market, which already exceed $600 billion, will expand rapidly.[90] All in all, in the 1990s European giants will vigorously compete with their U.S. counterparts, not only in the American market, but also on a world scale.

The follow-on policy question is this: should the United States further relax its antitrust policy, and revamp its banking policy, so that top U.S. firms can combine and better compete in world markets? The economic rise of Japan and Europe has clearly furnished both the occasion and

90. For comparison, the top 200 U.S. manufacturing companies had sales of about $980 billion in 1987. See Gary Hufbauer and Andreas Bender, *The Revenue Impact of Proposed Changes in Tax Rules Determining Source of Export Income*, report to the Export Source Coalition (Washington, May 1989), table 5.

TABLE 1–11. Country and Industry Distribution of the Top 100
Industrial Corporations, 1970 and 1988

| Home country or area | Total sales (billions of dollars) | | Number of firms | | Percent of top 100 sales | |
|---|---|---|---|---|---|---|
| | 1970 | 1988 | 1970 | 1988 | 1970 | 1988 |
| *All industries* | | | | | | |
| EC-12 | 82 | 768 | 26 | 33 | 24 | 33 |
| United States | 236 | 1,044 | 64 | 42 | 69 | 45 |
| Japan | 21 | 336 | 8 | 15 | 6 | 15 |
| Other[a] | 4 | 169 | 2 | 10 | 1 | 7 |
| TOTAL | 343 | 2,317 | 100 | 100 | 100 | 100 |
| *Automobiles* | | | | | | |
| EC-12 | 15 | 181 | 5 | 7 | 25 | 27 |
| United States[b] | 41 | 309 | 3 | 8 | 67 | 47 |
| Japan | 5 | 158 | 2 | 4 | 8 | 24 |
| Other[c] | n.a. | 16 | n.a. | 1 | n.a. | 2 |
| TOTAL | 60 | 664 | 10 | 20 | 100 | 100 |
| *Telecommunications, computers, and semiconductors* | | | | | | |
| EC-12 | 12 | 96 | 4 | 4 | 26 | 25 |
| United States | 25 | 81 | 5 | 3 | 56 | 21 |
| Japan | 8 | 152 | 3 | 6 | 18 | 39 |
| Other[d] | n.a. | 57 | n.a. | 3 | n.a. | 15 |
| TOTAL | 45 | 386 | 12 | 16 | 100 | 100 |

SOURCES: *Fortune*, May 1971, August 1971, April 24, 1989, and July 31, 1989.
n.a. Not available.
a. In 1970: Switzerland, 1; Australia, 1. In 1988: Brazil, 1; Kuwait, 1; Mexico, 1; South Korea, 2; Sweden, 2; Switzerland, 3.
b. The Canadian and European subsidiaries of certain U.S. firms are here classified under the United States, for example, General Motors of Canada, Ford Motor of Canada, Ford-Werke (West Germany), and Ford Motor (United Kingdom). As a consequence, Canada is not credited as the home country of any of the top 100 industrial corporations.
c. In 1988: Sweden, 1.
d. In 1988: South Korea, 2; Sweden, 1.

inspiration for a fundamental reconsideration of U.S. attitudes toward giant corporations. It is often said that, with the globalization of world markets, U.S. firms will be forced to behave as competitors by their foreign rivals. In the new world of global competition, the Sherman Act and the Glass-Steagall Act, it is said, only serve to handicap U.S. firms.

As chapter 6 points out, the irony of this argument is that EC policies are now generally as pro-competitive as those of the United States and at least as likely to remain that way as are U.S. policies. In most industries, European giants are significantly smaller than their U.S. rivals (the one conspicuous exception is banking). Repeal of the Glass-Steagall and McFadden Acts, the first and critical step toward a nationwide banking

TABLE 1-12. Distribution by Home Country of the Top Fifty Banks, 1970 and 1988

| Home country or area | Total assets (billions of dollars) | | Number of banks | | Percent of top fifty assets | |
|---|---|---|---|---|---|---|
| | 1970 | 1988 | 1970 | 1988 | 1970 | 1988 |
| EC-12 | 156 | 2,258 | 16 | 17 | 31 | 29 |
| North America | 223 | 566 | 19 | 5 | 45 | 7 |
| United States | 188 | 484 | 15 | 4 | 38 | 6 |
| Canada | 35 | 82 | 4 | 1 | 7 | 1 |
| Japan | 89 | 4,662 | 11 | 24 | 18 | 59 |
| Other[a] | 28 | 422 | 4 | 4 | 6 | 5 |
| TOTAL | 496 | 7,908 | 50 | 50 | 100 | 100 |

SOURCES: "Fifty Largest Banks outside the U.S.," *Fortune*, August 1971, pp. 154–55; and William Glasgall, "The World's Biggest Banks Enjoyed a Bountiful Year," *Business Week*, June 26, 1989, pp. 114–15.
a. In 1970: Switzerland, 3; Brazil, 1. In 1988: Switzerland, 2; China, 1; Hong Kong, 1.

system in the United States, may be long overdue, and may even be accelerated by EC-1992 (see chapter 2). But it is doubtful that either the United States or Europe wants to promote industrial groups on a scale to match the Japanese *keiretsu*.

Indeed, in the mid- to late 1990s, the Community and the United States could conceivably agree to coordinate their antitrust policies, and to jointly evaluate transatlantic corporations engaged in merger or strategic alliances (chapter 6). American and European authorities may come to the view that competition policy must acquire a global dimension, as General Motors, Siemens, Hitachi, and many other firms criss-cross the world with acquisitions and alliances. Otherwise the consumer gains from free trade could easily be lost as giant firms engage in informal market sharing on a global basis.

## Weakening Ties between Firms and States

Nearly twenty years ago, in his classic book *Sovereignty at Bay*, Raymond Vernon wrote of a world of attenuated identification between multinational firms and their home states.[91] Although Vernon's title remains to be realized, a significant offshoot of the European state will be further disassociation between firms and nations, as transatlantic and transpacific mergers and alliances redraw the map of global business. When Charles E. Wilson, president of General Motors, was appointed

91. Raymond Vernon, *Sovereignty at Bay: The Multinational Spread of U.S. Enterprises* (Basic Books, 1971).

secretary of defense by President Dwight D. Eisenhower in 1953, he uttered his epitaph: "What's good for the country is good for General Motors, and vice versa." Wilson's words were, of course, never entirely accurate; but they were far more accurate in 1953 when nearly all of GM profits originated in North America, than in 1988, when North America accounted for 44 percent of GM's net income, Europe for 37 percent, and other areas 19 percent.[92]

The disassociation between giant firms and their mother countries raises new questions for policymakers. Already Du Pont is regarded by statisticians as a Canadian company, since Seagrams holds 20 percent of Du Pont common shares. But is Du Pont really Canadian? After all, Seagrams exercises little management control in practice. Similar confusion of national patrimony will beset many large firms by the year 2000. It will then be harder to call Siemens a European company, Honda a Japanese company, or IBM an American company.

The disassociation between firms and states calls into question the wisdom of a national champion firm strategy. Like baseball teams of today, national champions of tomorrow may prove surprisingly "disloyal" to their local supporters.

The disassociation trend raises other questions. U.S. automotive export interests are now more strongly linked to the welfare of Japanese transplants than the welfare of Ford or GM (chapter 3). In the face of such changes, how quickly will U.S. policy officials come to evaluate a range of economic measures—trade policy, tax proposals, environmental measures—on a strictly geographic criterion? Will the public policy pendulum swing so far that multinational enterprises with global interests lose their clout as a major integrating force in the world economy? Or will the temptations of geographic nationalism quickly yield to transatlantic (and perhaps transpacific) consultation on a range of economic policies previously thought to fall squarely within the domain of sovereign economic decisions?

## Management of the Domestic Economy

The United States has always regarded Japan as an exotic country, separated by great cultural and linguistic differences from North America. Japanese successes in industry, education, and other aspects of life have

92. Standard and Poor's Corporation, "General Motors," *Standard NYSE Stock Reports*, vol. 56, September 19, 1989.

prompted little U.S. emulation. The same cultural and linguistic gap simply does not exist between the United States and Europe. Instead, the United States has often imitated European experiments in economic management, and vice versa. To cite just two examples: Bismarck's system of mandatory health and old age pensions eventually became part of the fabric not only of all Europe but also of the United States; Reagan's supply-side tax policy was quickly and widely adopted within Europe. Thus if European research consortia succeed, or if Europe manages its pharmaceutical testing program or worker retraining system decisively better than the United States manages its version, Washington will probably become an attentive audience.

In broad terms, the direction of a successful European experiment can be foretold. Led by Prime Minister Thatcher, Europe is still on a cycle of deregulation and disintervention. But however hard Prime Minister Thatcher tries to rewrite the story—and her nationalistic "us versus them" rhetoric has harmed her cause—Europe is likely to remain more interventionist than the United States across a range of economic policies: greater resistance to hostile takeover bids, more security of worker tenure, more health care, wider environmental controls, and a much larger public sector. This disparity follows from the fact that the EC governance represents a permanent coalition of socialists, liberals, and conservatives. If Europe prospers under such conditions—whether because of, or in spite of, state intervention—the tendency to duplicate aspects of European social and economic legislation will be very strong in the United States. On the other hand, if Europe turns in a sluggish economic performance, it is likely that Brussels will pay more attention to U.S. policy innovations.

## Custodian of the International System

Between the 1940s and the 1980s the United States regarded itself as the custodian of the international economic system. It is now shedding its patriarchal role, as the burdens of external and internal deficits have been coupled with lagging productivity and weakening technological leadership. In this era of changing roles, the real questions for the 1990s are whether Brussels will become the titular custodian of the international economic system, whether a Washington-Brussels alliance will emerge, or whether a true U.S.-EC-Japan triumvirate will be formed.

In financial matters, a triumvirate seems likely, given Japanese financial strength and the already close coordination between the United States,

Japan, and West Germany on macroeconomic questions. But in trade and competition policy, it is not out of the question that Brussels could become the titular leader. Already Europe is the most outward-looking of the major blocs in trade terms, and it could adopt the most pro-competitive policies. In many product lines, European technical standards could become the world norm. The Community has seized the initiative in restructuring Eastern Europe. Based on British experience after the Napoleonic Wars, and American experience after the Second World War, one can predict that the strongest and most market-oriented nation is typically the most dedicated internationalist. So Brussels could take the lead in shaping international commercial policy.

But my own guess is that the United States will not quietly accept a secondary role, and that, since America and Europe share a common outlook on the design and direction of the world trading and competition systems, a Washington-Brussels duumvirate will emerge. Washington policymakers enjoy one great advantage over their Brussels counterparts: they are able to design policy initiatives with far greater speed and flexibility, because they are not constrained by the consensus system that dominates policy formation in the Community.

In 1956 Richard Gardner wrote of "sterling-dollar diplomacy."[93] The implied alliance was far clearer after the event, and especially after Gardner documented it episode by episode, than at the time. Perhaps a similar relationship will characterize Washington-Brussels commercial diplomacy of the 1990s. A transatlantic alliance will work best behind the scenes, and its successes will be enhanced if they are channeled into commitments within the framework of international institutions, especially GATT and the OECD.

93. Richard N. Gardner, *Sterling-Dollar Diplomacy* (Clarendon Press, 1956).

APPENDIX 1–1. Key Events in the Evolution of the
European Community

Post–World War II

The aftermath of the Second World War furnished the driving force for a united Europe: the United States contributed hope; the USSR provided fear. The Benelux (Belgium-Netherlands-Luxembourg) customs union of 1944, and the Organization for European Economic Cooperation (OEEC, the predecessor to the OECD) created for Marshall Aid distribution in 1947, pointed to formation of the European Communities.

May 9, 1950

Robert Schuman, French minister of foreign affairs, proposes that France and the Federal Republic of Germany pool their coal and steel production under the auspices of a European organization.

April 18, 1951

Belgium, France, the Federal Republic of Germany, Italy, Luxembourg, and the Netherlands (known as the Six) sign the Treaty of Paris establishing the European Coal and Steel Community (ECSC).

March 25, 1957

The Six sign the Treaties of Rome establishing the European Economic Community (EEC) and the European Atomic Energy Community (Euratom). The Treaties of Rome together with the Treaty of Paris form the Constitution of the European Community. Jean Monnet is credited as a leading force behind the Treaties of Rome.

January 1, 1958

The EEC and Euratom treaties enter into force.

January 1, 1959

The first step is taken toward eliminating customs duties between member states and toward establishing a common external tariff.

January 1962

The Common Agricultural Policy (CAP) is adopted.

July 1, 1964

The European Agricultural Guidance and Guarantee Fund (EAGGF) begins operating to implement the CAP.

June 30, 1965

France rejects the Commission's Initiative 1964, which sought to make the EC financially autonomous, extend the powers of the European Parliament, and widen the application of qualified majority voting in the Council; thereafter it boycotts Community meetings.

January 28–29, 1966

The 1965 crisis is solved by the Luxembourg Compromise, which states that the other EC

|  | member states will not overrule a country that opposes a piece of draft EC legislation on the ground that a vital national interest is at stake. |
|---|---|
| July 1, 1967 | The treaty provisions enter into force establishing a single Council and a single Commission to administer the EEC, the ECSC, and Euratom. |
| July 1, 1968 | The customs union is completed. All customs duties are eliminated in trade between member states and a common external tariff is established. |
| December 1–2, 1969 | At the Hague summit, the heads of state declare that the Community has reached the final stage provided for in the Rome treaties; they call for an economic and monetary union, strengthened EC institutions, and closer political cooperation. |
| January 1, 1973 | Denmark, Ireland, and the United Kingdom become members of the EC; the Six become the Nine. |
| December 9–10, 1974 | The European Council is created, comprising the heads of state, their foreign ministers, and key Commission officials, superseding the earlier summits. |
| February 20, 1979 | The European Court of Justice issues the *Cassis de Dijon* decision, based on Article 30 of the Treaty of Rome, pointing the way toward member state "mutual recognition" of other member state standards. |
| March 9–10, 1979 | The European Council launches the European Monetary System (EMS) with four main components: a European currency unit (ECU), an Exchange Rate Mechanism (ERM), credit facilities, and transfer arrangements. |
| June 7–10, 1979 | First direct elections to the European Parliament. |
| January 1, 1981 | Greece joins the EC; the Nine become the Ten. |
| June 14, 1985 | The Commission sends the Council of Ministers a White Paper (drafted under the leadership of Lord Cockfield) on the completion of the internal market by December 31, 1992. |
| January 1, 1986 | Portugal and Spain become members of the European Community; the Ten become the Twelve. |
| February 17–28, 1986 | The Single European Act is signed, to take effect July 1, 1987, amending the Treaties of Rome, to improve EC functioning both by allowing for the adoption of legislation by less than unanimous vote of the member states, and by expanding EC powers (see appendix 1-5). |

SOURCE: EC Commission, *Steps to European Unity—Community Progress to Date: A Chronology*, 6th ed. (Luxembourg, 1987).

## APPENDIX 1–2. Institutions of the European Community, January 1990

### European Commission

The European Commission is the executive body of the EC. Like the Council of Ministers, it meets in Brussels, Belgium, the executive center of the EC. There are twenty-three directorates-general overseen by seventeen commissioners (two from each of the five larger EC member states and one from each of the seven smaller members; see appendix 1–3). The commissioners are appointed by the member states, but they act independently of their national governments. The current president of the Commission is Jacques Delors. Each commissioner has particular responsibilities, but the Commission's decisions are collegiate. The Commission has a four-year term; the current Commission's term expires at the end of 1992. The EC-1992 Program was deliberately planned to occupy the terms of two Commissions. The main tasks of the Commission are: (1) ensuring that the founding EC treaties and their amendments are carried out; (2) drawing up the budget; (3) exercising its sole power to initiate Community legislation (directives and regulations) and power to amend legislation at any stage; and (4) implementing decisions reached by the Council of Ministers.

### Council of Ministers

The Council of Ministers is the decisionmaking body of the EC. It is composed of appropriate ministers from the twelve member states, depending on the subject under discussion. Under the Single European Act, the Council decides on EC policy by "qualified majority" voting, except in matters concerning taxation, the free movement of people, and workers' rights; in these subjects, unanimity is still required. Policy is expressed through directives (which must be enacted in national law before they are binding) and regulations (which are self-enforcing). The presidency of the Council rotates among the member states (in alphabetical order), with each president serving a six-month term. The total number of votes in the Council is 76, distributed as follows:

| | |
|---|---|
| France, Germany, Italy, United Kingdom | 10 each |
| Spain | 8 |
| Belgium, Greece, Netherlands, Portugal | 5 each |
| Denmark, Ireland | 3 each |
| Luxembourg | 2 |

It takes 54 votes to pass a directive or regulation by "qualified majority." Thus a coalition of the seven smaller members cannot outvote the five larger ones. Nor can the big five impose their will on a reluctant seven. Any coalition of 23 votes is sufficient to block a proposed directive or regulation.

### Committee of Permanent Representatives (COREPER)

The COREPER comprises the ambassadors of the member states to the EC, together with their advisers. The COREPER prepares the work of the Council of Ministers and serves as the key link between the governments of the member states and the Commission.

### European Council

The European Council comprises the heads of state or government, their foreign ministers, and the president and one of the vice-presidents of the Commission. The European Council meets at least twice a year and sets the broad guidelines for EC policy in areas of prime importance such as the accession of new members, the European Monetary System, and the reform of the agricultural policy.

### European Parliament

The European Parliament comprises 518 members elected from the twelve member states by a system that takes account of relative population. The parliament meets alternately in Luxembourg and in Strasbourg, France. Members of the EP form political rather than national groups. The EP is largely an advisory body; it does not have legislative powers like those of national parliaments. The EP makes proposals to the Commission, watches over the Commission's work, and can even require (with a two-thirds majority) the resignation of the Commission. It has limited budgetary powers. The 1987 Single European Act gave the EP the power of assent in issues concerning the expansion of the EC; it has also introduced a cooperative procedure that gives the EP a direct influence on qualified majority decisions having a bearing on the internal market, social policy, economic and social cohesion, and research.

### Court of Justice

The court comprises thirteen judges and six advocates-general appointed for six years by agreement of the member states. The court meets in Luxembourg. The EC Court of Justice interprets the European constitution and other European enactments in disputes brought by the Commission, by member states, or by private parties, and in advisory opinions on matters referred by national courts. The court's judgments are binding on all courts in all member states. An inferior Court of First Instance was created in 1989 to hear competition cases; judgments may be appealed on legal grounds to the Court of Justice.

### Economic and Social Committee

The Economic and Social Committee, organized in nine subject-matter specialties, is made up of representatives of trade unions and professional bodies. It gives its advisory opinions on the proposals made by the Commission.

SOURCE: European Communities Eurostat, *Europe in Figures* (Luxembourg, 1982); and Arthur Andersen and Co., *1992: Guide for Clients* (Brussels, March 1989), pp. 4–7.

## APPENDIX 1–3. The EC Commission's Directorates

| | |
|---|---|
| DG-1 | External Relations and Trade Negotiations |
| DG-2 | Macroeconomic and Monetary Affairs |
| DG-3 | Internal Market and Industrial Affairs |
| DG-4 | Competition, Cartels, and State Aids |
| DG-5 | Employment, Education, and Social Affairs |
| DG-6 | Agriculture |
| DG-7 | Transport |
| DG-8 | Aid to Developing Countries |
| DG-9 | Personnel and Administration |
| DG-10 | Information and Communication |
| DG-11 | Environment, Consumer Protection, and Nuclear Safety |
| DG-12 | Research and Development |
| DG-13 | Telecommunications |
| DG-14 | Fisheries |
| DG-15 | Financial Services, Company Law, and Tax |
| DG-16 | Regional Development |
| DG-17 | Energy |
| DG-18 | EC Borrowing and Lending |
| DG-19 | EC Budget |
| DG-20 | Internal Financial Control |
| DG-21 | Customs Union and Indirect Tax |
| DG-22 | Coordination of Structural Instruments |
| DG-23 | Small and Medium-sized Enterprises |

SOURCE: U.S. Chamber of Commerce, *Europe 1992: A Practical Guide for American Business* (Washington, 1989), pp. 128–29.

| Measure | Goods markets | Services markets | Capital markets | Labor markets |
|---|---|---|---|---|
| Market access | Abolition of intra-EC frontier controls<br><br>Approximate harmonization of: technical regulations; VAT rates; and excise taxes<br><br>Unspecified implications for external trade policy, e.g., Italian regime of strict quotas on Japanese auto imports, compared with German regime of no quotas | Mutual recognition of national regulatory standards<br><br>Removal of licensing restrictions (especially in banking and insurance)<br><br>Freedom of road haulage under EC permit<br><br>Greater access to intra-EC air transport routes and facilities | Abolition of exchange controls<br><br>Admission of securities listed in one member state to trading in other states<br><br>Measures to facilitate industrial cooperation and migration of firms | Abolition of intra-EC frontier checks on persons<br><br>Relaxation of residence requirements for access to social services<br><br>Right of establishment for highly educated workers, e.g., doctors, lawyers |
| Competitive conditions | Renewed discipline on state aid to industry | Introduction of competition policy in air transport<br><br>Liberalization of public procurement<br><br>Merger control at the EC level | EC surveillance of takeovers and large corporate groups<br><br>Approximation of tax and regulatory conditions in various service markets | European "vocational training card" to facilitate EC-wide recognition of skills<br><br>Fiscal approximation on: double taxation as between corporations and share holders; security transfer taxes; parent-subsidiary links |

| | | | | |
|---|---|---|---|---|
| Market functioning | Specific proposals on R&D in telecommunications and information technology<br><br>Proposals on standards, trade marks, corporate law, and so forth | Approximate harmonization of: banking regulation (solvency ratios, deposit insurance, etc.); consumer protection in insurance<br><br>EC standards for credit cards | European company statute Harmonization of industrial and commercial property laws<br><br>Common bankruptcy provisions | Approximation of: income tax on migrant workers; training provisions<br><br>Mutual recognition of diplomas |
| Sectoral policy | Agriculture (CAP): abolition of frontier restrictions; approximation of veterinary and phytosanitary standards<br><br>Reduction of steel subsidies | Common crisis regime in road transport<br><br>Common air transport policy on access capacity and prices<br><br>Common rules on insurance of mass risks | Call to strengthen European Monetary System | |

SOURCE: J. Pelkmans and A. Winters, *Europe's Domestic Market* (London: Routledge, 1988), reproduced in Xavier Pintardo and others, *Economic Aspects of the European Economic Space*, European Free Trade Association Occasional Paper 25 (Geneva, November 1988), p. 4.

APPENDIX 1–5. Key Provisions of the Single European Act, Effective July 1, 1987

A. Institutional provisions
    (1) Changes in legislative process:
        —qualified majority voting in the Council of Ministers
        —"cooperation procedure" to increase role of European Parliament
        —assent procedure for new EEC membership applications
        —implementing powers for rulemaking by Commission
    (2) Establishment of Court of First Instance under European Court of Justice

B. Internal market provisions
    (1) 1992 deadline for completion of the internal market
    (2) Qualified majority voting for most "1992" measures, replacing Luxembourg Compromise requirement of unanimity; exceptions for measures affecting taxes, free movement of persons, rights of employed persons

C. Other amendments to EEC Treaties
    (1) *Economic and monetary policy:* increase in cooperation efforts; member state conference required for institutional changes
    (2) *Social policy:* new measures for health and safety of workers; Commission role in labor relations; emphasis on reduction of regional disparities and increase in structural funds for social and regional aid
    (3) *Research and technological development:* new goals for competitiveness, common standards, and R&D "framework programs"
    (4) *Environmental policy:* environmental, health, and natural resource objectives; principles for legislative action and for liability; action at Community level secondary to action at member state level

D. Foreign policy provisions
    (1) Note: European Political Cooperation (EPC) lies outside the institutional framework of EEC
    (2) Undertakings:
        —member states endeavor to achieve joint formulation and implementation of European foreign policy
        —prior consultation and consideration of other member state views
        —external policies of EEC and EPC "must be consistent"
        —cooperation between EEC and EPC delegations to third countries and international organizations
        —possible coordination on national security issues
        —establish foreign policy secretariat in Brussels

SOURCE: Linda F. Powers, "The Single European Act and '1992,' " *1992—New Opportunities for U.S. Banks and Business in Europe* (New York: American Bar Association, 1989), pp. 15, 16.

APPENDIX 1–6. The New Cooperation Procedure for Enacting EC Legislation, Effective July 1, 1987

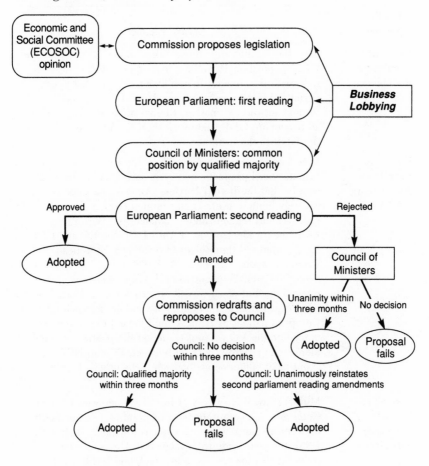

SOURCE: U.S. Chamber of Commerce, *Europe 1992*, p. 23.

APPENDIX 1–7. Trade Regimes between the EC and Non-EC Countries, January 1990

| Trading partner | Trade regime |
|---|---|
| German Democratic Republic | Sometimes called the "thirteenth member" of the EC. The GDR (population 16 million) has long enjoyed close trade links with the Federal Republic of Germany that have permitted GDR goods to circulate (with limitations) throughout the EC market. Reunification will soon eliminate all barriers to GDR trade with the EC and effectively add the GDR to the Community. |
| European Free Trade Association (EFTA)[a] | Free trade agreement: no tariffs or quotas are applied to manufactured products; however, each area maintains its own behind-the-border barriers. Agricultural trade is severely limited; there is no common tariff; and government procurement remains highly nationalistic. With the Luxembourg Declaration of April 1984, the EC and EFTA have committed themselves to creating a "European Economic Space." In December 1989 the EC and EFTA agreed to intensify negotiations leading to economic integration, but no deals will be struck before 1992. EFTA is now regarded as a potential "soft window" for such Eastern European nations as Hungary and Poland to gain economic entry into the EC without taking on the political burdens of membership. Two-way trade between EC and EFTA is about $220 billion annually (each is the other's largest partner). |
| Council on Mutual Economic Assistance (Comecon)[b] | Mutual recognition treaty of June 1988 between EC and Comecon, and comprehensive bilateral trade agreements between EC and individual Comecon nations. (Latest EC-USSR ten-year trade treaty signed in December 1989 covering all goods except coal, steel, and textiles, with a promise to remove EC quotas in 1995.) Industrial imports by EC from Comecon are limited by numerous ad hoc quantitative restrictions; high-technology exports from EC to Comecon are limited by COCOM restraints, now being reevaluated. Two-way trade between EC and Comecon is about $60 billion annually. |
| United States | Most-favored-nation status, as established in GATT. Two-way trade is about $160 billion annually. |
| Japan | Most-favored-nation status, with many "extra-GATT" quantitative restrictions applied against Japanese exports. Two-way trade is about $70 billion annually. |

| African, Caribbean, and Pacific countries | Various trade and aid arrangements extending preferences and benefits to those ACP nations covered by the Lome Convention (currently 68). Lome III (about $8.3 billion of aid over the period 1986 to 1990) expires in February 1990; Lome IV is under negotiation (the aid figure now under discussion is $12.8 billion). Note: the Yaounde Convention was precursor to the wider Lome Convention. |
| Mediterranean countries[c] | Various association, cooperation, and preferential agreements. |
| Generalized System of Preferences | Duty-free treatment of imports from all developing countries, with product exclusions and competitive need limitations. |
| Gulf Cooperation Council[d] | Negotiations in process for an industrial free trade agreement between the EC and the GCC. |

SOURCE: Thomas D. Gallagher, *European Unification: An Inward-Looking Europe?* (Shearson Lehman Hutton Inc., March 1989), p. 5; and "A New Treaty Eludes E.C., Third World," *Europe-1992*, vol. 1 (November 8, 1989), p. 415.

a. Austria, Switzerland, Iceland, Norway, Sweden, and Finland; total population approximately 30 million. For EC-EFTA agreements, see Steven Prokesch, "A New Trade Zone for Europe," *New York Times*, December 8, 1989, p. A1; *Europe-1992*, vol. 2 (February 7, 1990), p. 535.

b. Also called CMEA, Comecon comprises the USSR, Bulgaria, Czechoslovakia, East Germany, Hungary, Poland, and Romania; total population, USSR about 290 million, Eastern Europe about 110 million. With the democratic revolution in Eastern Europe Comecon is rapidly losing its institutional vitality. For EC-USSR agreement, see Paul L. Montgomery, "Trade Pact for Soviets and Europe," *New York Times*, November 28, 1989, p. D1.

c. For example, Morocco, Tunisia, and Algeria.

d. Bahrain, Kuwait, Oman, Qatar, Saudi Arabia, and the United Arab Emirates.

APPENDIX 1–8. Points of Access for U.S. Companies To Voice Opinions on EC-1992 Proposals, January 1990

Specialists within the relevant directorate of the European Commission.

Member state trade and industry associations, as well as the EC-wide employers' association (UNICE), headquartered in Brussels.

Functional ministries of national governments in sympathetic member states.

Member state permanent delegations to the EC, which, through the Committee of Permanent Representatives (COREPER), do most of the background work for meetings of the Council of Ministers.

Members of the European Parliament who may be sympathetic to the position of the U.S. company.

National EC member state legislatures, which must enact all EC-1992 directives into specific laws.

SOURCE: Stephen Cooney, *EC-92 and U.S. Industry: An NAM Report on the Major Issues for U.S. Manufacturers in the European Community's Internal Market Program* (Washington: National Association of Manufacturers, February 1989), p. 14.

APPENDIX 1–9. European High-Technology Projects,
January 1990

**Airbus:** A consortium of aerospace companies from France, Britain, Spain, and West Germany that has become the world's second-largest manufacturer of passenger aircraft (after Boeing and in front of McDonnell Douglas).

**Arianespace:** An 11-nation European launch consortium that has put 58 satellites into orbit.

**CERN:** The European Laboratory for Particle Physics is a 14-nation research project that has built the world's largest atom smasher, the 17-mile-long Large Electron-Positron Collider.

**Comett:** An EC-sponsored program for links between universities and business, projected to cost $258 million through 1995.

**Esprit:** The European Strategic Program for Research and Development in Information Technology is a $5 billion EC program under which nearly 450 cooperative projects seek to improve microelectronics technology in such areas as integrated circuit design and computer-aided manufacturing.

**Eureka:** A group of 302 research projects in which some 1,600 firms cooperate to develop, for example, high-definition television standards and external automobile guidance systems. Governments have so far provided $6.3 billion.

**Eurofighter:** A production program in which British, German, Italian, and Spanish companies are set to build 800 new fighter aircraft at a cost of more than $30 billion.

**Euromissile:** A French-German consortium to build antitank and antiaircraft missiles.

**European Space Agency:** A 13-nation program that has built 28 satellites for weather, telecommunications, and research and is building the $4.8 billion Hermes space shuttle and part of the planned International Space Station.

**JESSI:** The Joint European Submicron Silicon Initiative is a $5 billion program to develop new generations of semiconductors and the machines to manufacture them. A direct competitor to Sematech, with about twice the funding.

**JET:** Joint European Torus is a 14-nation project to develop a prototype nuclear fusion reactor.

**RACE:** A $1.5 billion EC program, involving dozens of projects and companies, to further Europe's telecommunications technologies for a Europe-wide high-speed data telecommunications network.

SOURCES: Steven Greenhouse, "Europeans Unite to Compete with Japan and U.S.," *New York Times*, August 21, 1989, p. D8; and Thane Peterson, "Can Europe Catch Up in the High-Tech Race?" *Business Week*, October 23, 1989, pp. 142–54.

APPENDIX 1–10. A Sampler of U.S.-Community Trade
Disputes, 1960–89

| Date and issue | Dispute | Resolution |
| --- | --- | --- |
| Chicken war, 1962–63 | U.S. chicken exports were hurt when West Germany raised duties on poultry as part of its obligations under the CAP. | The U.S. withdrew tariff concessions on EC exports of trucks and related items; although the chicken war is forgotten, the concessions are still withheld. |
| U.S. wine-gallon-tax system, 1963–79 | Tax discriminated against foreign bottled spirits and indirectly protected the U.S. alcoholic beverage industry. | In the Tokyo Round, the EC granted concessions on agricultural products in exchange for revision of the wine-gallon tax. |
| Steel voluntary restraint agreements, 1982 | EC shipments of subsidized and dumped steel to the U.S. market added to the woes of U.S. steel producers. | Instead of countervailing and antidumping duties, the U.S. and EC negotiated a VRA that effectively curbed EC steel exports to the U.S. |
| U.S. farm exports to Portugal and Spain, 1986–87 | The U.S. sought compensation for its lost trade when Portugal and Spain entered the EC. | The EC agreed to a compensation plan that increased U.S. exports, in exchange for removal of U.S. retaliatory tariffs. |
| Hormone-treated beef, 1987–89 | The EC banned imports of beef containing growth hormones. | The EC will accept imports from U.S. packagers that certify their meat as hormone free. |
| Second Banking Directive, January 1988–June 1989 | The EC initially asserted it would not license third-country banks if those countries failed to give EC banks reciprocal access. | The EC will accept national treatment reciprocity provided that it results in equivalent market access. |
| Technical standards, January 1988–August 1989 | The U.S. expressed concern about the exclusion of U.S. firms from the EC standard-setting process. | CEN and CENELEC, two quasi-public standards boards, will accept comments from ANSI, the U.S. counterpart. |

SOURCES: Robert E. Baldwin, Carl B. Hamilton, and André Sapir, eds., *Issues in U.S.–EC Trade Relations*, National Bureau of Economic Research (University of Chicago Press, 1988); Bradley B. Billings, "The Trade Dispute between the United States and the European Community upon the Accession of Spain and Portugal," Pew Foundation Case Study, Georgetown University, 1988; "EC Confirms Partial Solution to Hormone Row," *Europe-1992*, vol. 1 (May 10, 1989), pp. 157–58; "EC Reaches Outline Accord on Banking Directive," *Europe-1992*, vol. 1 (June 21, 1989); and "European Standards Bodies to Accept U.S. Comments," *Europe-1992*, vol. 1 (August 16, 1989).

Chapter 2

# Banking and Securities

## CARTER H. GOLEMBE & DAVID S. HOLLAND

IF EUROPE 1992 is realized, the European Community will soon be lowering its barriers to interstate financial services. Understandably, the immediate concern of most analysts has been to predict how the twelve member states will react to the competitive opportunities and threats that financial unification will undoubtedly bring if it goes through as planned. But some thought should also be given to the possible effect on the financial organizations and markets of countries outside this sphere. Although only a small percentage of U.S. firms are currently operating in the European Community, Europe 1992, in combination with forces already under way in the United States, may have long-term implications for U.S. financial services.

To assess the possible repercussions of Europe 1992 from an American perspective, one must look closely at the legal and institutional details of the financial services portion of the proposed 1992 program actions in the European Community prior to the inauguration of Europe 1992, and differences in the structure of the U.S. and European banking and securities industries. That is the approach taken in this chapter. The discussion concentrates on banking and securities and only touches on the insurance industry, tax matters, and monetary integration.

The single banking market that is scheduled to come into existence at the end of 1992 will provide for universal banking in the sense that it will include a full range of investment banking activities. At this point, no one can say precisely what impact this will have in the United States. It may well be so attenuated that only a handful of scholars will be interested in the results. At the other extreme, if the United States decides to follow the European Community's lead in financial services,

Carter H. Golembe is chairman of the Secura Group in Washington, D.C. David S. Holland was formerly editor of *Banking Expansion Reporter*. The authors wish to thank Nancy Gelson for her research help.

U.S. banks may soon be establishing branches nationwide and underwriting and dealing in securities.

For those U.S. financial institutions now doing significant business in Community nations, completion of the internal market and the creation of a single banking market will do little to increase their range of services or the places at which they may be offered. Such services are primarily wholesale banking products and investment banking services, and U.S. financial institutions may provide them without regard to the distinctions applicable to business done in the United States under the Glass-Steagall Act of 1933. At present, at least, these firms seem to have a competitive edge over their European counterparts in servicing the increasing mergers and acquisitions that are accompanying European economic integration.

The developments in Europe are obviously important to these multinational U.S. firms, as they provide an opportunity to develop and distribute retail financial services over a broad new market. But the vast majority of U.S. firms are not engaged in that business in Europe, and the availability of this new market is a matter of little interest. Nonetheless, it is the conclusion of this chapter that all financial institutions in the United States will feel the effects of Europe 1992 in the long run, primarily because of the legislative and regulatory changes that are bound to ensue in the United States. If such changes occur, they are likely to alter the structure of the American financial system.

## What Does Europe 1992 Mean for Banking and Securities?

Amid all the enthusiasm for the 1992 program, it is easy to lose sight of what came before the White Paper of 1985. The details of the capital movement, banking, and securities aspects of the 1992 program cannot be fully understood without some idea of the actions leading up to the White Paper and its implementing legislation, the 1986 Single European Act.

### Pre–1985 White Paper Actions

A number of actions before 1985 promoted the integration of financial markets in the European Community. These, along with the directives and recommendations for implementing the 1992 program, are outlined in appendixes 2-1, 2-2, and 2-3.[1] The authority for all actions taken both

1. *Directives* are binding upon European Community member nations but only with respect to the results to be achieved. The implementation of directives depends upon

before and after 1985 can be traced back to the 1957 Treaty of Rome. The directive of May 11, 1960, particularly as amended in 1963, relaxed capital restrictions in a number of ways.[2] Although safeguard clauses enabled member states to delay implementation, the barriers to capital continued to weaken over the next twenty-five years. One important event was the lifting, by the United Kingdom, of all exchange controls in 1979. As of early 1989, four countries had fully liberalized capital movements: the United Kingdom, Germany, the Netherlands, and Denmark.[3]

The First Banking Directive of 1977 marked the beginning of EC efforts to establish Community-wide standards for the banking business.[4] The directive dealt with credit institutions, which it defined as undertakings "whose business is to receive deposits or other repayable funds from the public and to grant credits for their own account." It called for minimum capital requirements, suggested various financial ratios, and urged member states to supervise trans-European credit institutions through cooperative efforts.

A 1983 directive addressed the question of consolidated supervision.[5] Under its terms, the supervisor of a credit institution is required to review the accounts, exposure, and management of the institution on a consolidated basis at least yearly.

In the securities field, the European Community focused on securities listed on official stock exchanges. Three directives were promulgated before 1985: the Admissions Directive, the Listing Particulars Directive, and the Interim Reports Directive.[6]

---

legislation by the individual states. *Recommendations* are nonbinding, being invitations to the member nations to take certain actions. Article 189 of the Treaty of Rome also provides for regulations, decisions, and opinions. *Regulations* are binding as promulgated by the European Commission and require no implementing legislation by member nations. *Decisions* and *opinions* are issued regarding particular factual or legal situations.

2. *Official Journal of the European Communities*, no. P921 (Luxembourg: EC Commission, July 12, 1960) [hereafter *O.J. Eur. Comm.*]; and 64/21/EEC, *O.J. Eur. Comm.*, no. P9 (1963), p. 62.

3. Sidney J. Key, *Financial Integration in the European Community*, International Finance Discussion Paper 349 (Washington: Board of Governors of the Federal Reserve System, April 1989), p. 18.

4. 77/780/EEC, *O.J. Eur. Comm.*, no. L322 (December 17, 1977), p. 30.

5. 83/350/EEC, *O.J. Eur. Comm.*, no. L193 (July 18, 1983), p. 18.

6. 79/279/EEC, *O.J. Eur. Comm.*, no. L66 (March 16, 1979), p. 21; 80/390/EEC, *O.J. Eur. Comm.*, no. L100 (April 17, 1980), p. 1; and 82/121/EEC, *O.J. Eur. Comm.*, no. L48 (February 20, 1982), p. 26.

The Admissions Directive established minimum conditions for the admission of securities to official listing on stock exchanges. The Listing Particulars Directive—"disclosure" would be the U.S. synonym for "listing particulars"—specified the requirements for drawing up, scrutinizing, and distributing information to be published by companies seeking admission for their securities on stock exchanges. And the Interim Reports Directive required companies whose securities are listed on stock exchanges to supply investors with adequate periodic information. Originally, the Listing Particulars Directive did not insist on mutual recognition of home country disclosure requirements. It merely set forth minimal information requirements and called upon national authorities to try to coordinate any further disclosure items. In 1987, however, an amendment added the principle of mutual recognition in the disclosure area.[7] European Community host countries must recognize the listing particulars requirements of the company's home country.

## Principles of the 1985 White Paper

Before 1985, a guiding concept of European integration was harmonization. Thus each EC member nation was expected to accept identical rules and regulations. The difficulty was that these nations found it extremely difficult to reach complete agreement on any particular matter. In the words of the White Paper, a Community-wide uniform market constructed only through harmonization "would be over-regulatory, would take a long time to implement, would be inflexible and could stifle innovation."[8]

The White Paper replaced this concept with that of mutual recognition, which means there will be no attempt to impose Community-wide rules beyond a core of essential regulations and standards. Instead, the EC nations will be required to recognize the validity of each other's rules and regulations.

Mutual recognition will not be an end in itself. The assumption is that mutual recognition will lead to regulatory convergence. Member states that hope to limit the permissible activity of financial institutions will likely lose business to states with more expansive views. In theory, this could prompt a "race to the bottom" as each supervisory authority strives to attract business to its country through more relaxed regulation. The

7. 87/345/EEC, *O.J Eur. Comm.*, no. L185 (July 4, 1987), p. 81.
8. EC Commission, *Completing the Internal Market: White Paper from the Commission to the European Council* (Luxembourg, 1985), para. 64.

core of essential regulations and standards, if adopted throughout the Community, should both forestall an unmitigated "race to the bottom" and provide a target for regulatory convergence.

The White Paper's program for achieving a unified financial market calls for three types of action. First, member states are expected to harmonize essential standards for the supervision of financial institutions and the protection of investors, depositors, and consumers. Second, there is to be mutual recognition of laws and regulations beyond those required for essential harmonization. Third, home countries must be able to control and supervise EC financial institutions that operate in more than one EC member nation.

The White Paper contained a list of 300, later reduced to 279, specific measures for implementing its general principles. Some 15 of these proposals dealt with capital movements and the banking and securities industries.

In 1986 the Single European Act was adopted to implement the White Paper program. Although the Single European Act did not specifically refer to mutual recognition, it did say that the Council "may decide that the provisions in force in a Member State must be recognized as being equivalent to those applied by another Member State."[9]

A topic not dealt with in the White Paper or the Single European Act was the external dimension of the 1992 program. How the 1992 program will affect non-EC nations only gradually became an issue as various individual directives were developed. In the financial services sector, the principal external issue has come to be reciprocity. The directives concerned with banking and investment services require non-EC nations to agree to "reciprocity" before business firms from those nations can establish subsidiaries in an EC member state.

The meaning of reciprocity in the context of Europe 1992 is by no means certain, however. If reciprocity was interpreted in a strict mirror-image sense, non-EC nations would have to grant European firms the same powers that they possess in their EC home states. In the context of the U.S. banking industry, strict reciprocity would mean that EC banking organizations would have to be able to underwrite and deal in securities in the United States and to set up branches throughout the country before a U.S. banking organization could establish a subsidiary in an EC member state.

9. Single European Act, Art. 19, adding Art. 100B to the EEC Treaty of Rome.

An alternative, much looser, reciprocity approach would require only national treatment comparable to that practiced by the EC and its commercial partners. Under a national treatment standard, each nation would treat foreign firms operating within its borders in the same way that it treats domestic firms,[10] by applying the same establishment criteria, the same limitations on the scope of activity, and the same prudential and supervisory approaches. Under a policy of reciprocal national treatment, if a non-EC nation offered national treatment to organizations from EC states, the European Community would offer national treatment to an organization from that nation.

In elaborating the reciprocity requirement, the European Commission seems to have settled on the national treatment standard, with an important qualification: "effective market access" must be available. Otherwise, countries that impose stringent controls on a particular industry—say, the banking industry in Japan—might not grant "effective market access" to EC banks trying to enter the Japanese market. In this instance, the Commission would not regard national treatment by the Japanese authorities as appropriate recompense for giving Japanese banks access to the more open EC banking market. Japan would be asked to provide further concessions, beyond national treatment, to come up with a package of effective market access for EC banks.

## Capital Movements in Europe 1992

A basic characteristic of an integrated financial market is the freedom of movement given to capital. If pan-EC competition is to be created in the financial services industry, funds must be free to move across borders. Exchange controls must be abolished. Firms and individuals must be able to hold foreign currencies and to place deposits in foreign banks.

The process of liberalizing capital movements began early in the history of the European Community. The directive of May 11, 1960, reduced some of the barriers to the cross-border movement of funds and securities. With the amendments to the 1960 directive and unilateral action by some EC member states, the process continued, although a number of restrictions still remained at the time of the White Paper. A 1986 amendment to the 1960 directive removed restrictions on capital movements ancillary to trade and direct investment.[11]

10. The United States follows a national treatment policy regarding foreign banking organizations. See International Banking Act, P.L. 95-369.

11. 86/566/EEC, *O.J. Eur. Comm.*, no. L332 (November 26, 1986), p. 22.

Complete liberalization is the goal of Directive 88/361, adopted in 1988 and scheduled to come into effect by July 1, 1990.[12] This directive seeks to remove all remaining restrictions on capital movements within the EC. Capital transfers are to be made at the same exchange rates that apply to current transactions. Safeguards can be applied only in exceptional situations and must be temporary.

By early 1989 the United Kingdom, Germany, the Netherlands, and Denmark had removed all restrictions on capital movements.[13] Belgium, Luxembourg, France, and Italy needed to take only minor steps to meet the July 1, 1990, deadline: Belgium and Luxembourg still had a dual exchange rate system that applied official rates to trade and direct investment transactions and market rates to other capital movements; France restricted the foreign accounts that could be held by residents; and Italy maintained a variety of small limitations. The 1990 deadline for the complete removal of limitations on capital movements does not apply to Ireland, Spain, Portugal, or Greece. The deadline for these countries is 1992, but an additional extension is possible for Portugal and Greece.

The 1988 directive also specifies that member states should "endeavor to obtain the same degree of liberalization" of capital movements to non-EC nations as is to be achieved within the Community.

As of mid-1989 an unresolved problem concerning capital movements was what to do about differing tax structures. The member states handle taxes on interest and dividend payments in a variety of ways. At one end of the spectrum, Luxembourg does not impose any withholding tax on interest or dividend payments. Withholding tax rates in other countries can be as high as 35 percent (10 to 15 percent is most common). These divergent rates could produce substantial tax-inspired capital flows once restrictions are lifted.

To forestall such flows, the Community has considered a minimum withholding tax of 15 percent on interest income paid to European Community residents. The EC proposal has aroused considerable opposition, led by Luxembourg and the United Kingdom. A Community-wide withholding tax proposal may be some years off, since the Single European Act did not relax the requirement for unanimity on decisions regarding tax and other fiscal matters. In the meantime, tax competition may force all member states toward zero rates, to match Luxembourg and the United Kingdom.

12. 88/361/EEC, *O.J. Eur. Comm.*, no. L178 (July 8, 1988), p. 5.
13. Key, *Financial Integration*, p. 18.

## Banking under Europe 1992

The centerpiece of the 1992 program in the banking field is the Second Banking Directive, which will take effect January 1, 1993.[14] Other 1992 decrees concerned with banking are the Own Funds and Solvency Ratios directives. The Second Banking Directive does not replace pre–1985 White Paper actions but instead builds on the First Banking Directive of 1977 and the Consolidated Supervision Directive of 1983. In fact, the First Banking Directive's definition of "credit institution" is carried over to the Second Banking Directive. The emphasis in this directive is on the concept of a single banking license and a list of permissible banking activities.

If its home nation permits, a credit institution licensed in one EC member nation will be able to engage in all activities on the EC list in other member states, either directly by establishing branches or indirectly by marketing and advertising its services. For the most part, the credit institution will be supervised by its home country authorities. Host countries will retain primary responsibility for supervising liquidity, "until further coordination" measures are adopted by the EC member states. Host countries will have the authority to require credit institutions engaging in securities operations to provide sufficient protection against market risk, again until further coordination measures are adopted. In addition, host countries will retain responsibility for their own monetary policy.[15]

Not only is the EC list of permissible banking activities broad (see appendix 2-4), but it can be updated by the Commission to reflect the emergence of new banking services. The list contains two items that in the United States would be called dealing in and underwriting securities. Item seven allows a credit institution to trade in securities. Item eight allows a credit institution to participate in issuing securities. In short, credit institutions in the European Community will not be prevented from entering into the securities field by restrictions of the Glass-Steagall type.

Securities are also covered in item nine, which allows a credit institution to provide various types of financial advice, and item eleven, which allows a credit institution to engage in portfolio management activities.

14. 89/646/EEC, *O.J. Eur. Comm.*, no. L386 (December 30, 1989), p. 1.

15. A European Community nation's ability to maintain an independent monetary policy may be curtailed if the monetary union measures called for in the Delors report are adopted.

Absent from the list of permissible activities are insurance activities (with the exception of item six), guarantees, and commitments.

If an institution engages in activities on the list but is not authorized and supervised as a credit institution by an EC member state, it will not benefit from the Second Banking Directive's policy of mutual recognition. Therefore, it will not be able to operate throughout the European Community with a single license from one member state.

A significant change under the single license concept is that a host state will no longer be able to require initial endowment capital for the establishment of a branch (a branch is an office with the same corporate identity as that of the parent credit institution). Before a parent credit institution can be established, it must have initial capital of at least ECU 5 million, or approximately $6 million. Once a parent institution is established, however, no further capital will be required to open branches.

Credit institutions will be able to acquire or maintain noncredit and nonfinancial businesses, subject to two limits. The credit institution must not hold a participation exceeding 10 percent of its own funds, or capital, in any one business that is neither a credit nor a financial institution. And the total value of all such participations must not exceed 50 percent of a credit institution's own funds.

Although the Second Banking Directive covers a broad area, it does not control the activities of what in the United States are called bank holding companies. In the European Community setting, these would be companies that own credit institutions. To be sure, companies contemplating the acquisition of a credit institution must inform the appropriate supervisory authorities, who "shall assess the suitability" of the acquiring company. And credit institutions must furnish the appropriate authorities with the names of major shareholders every year. But other than having the power to terminate control situations that pose a threat to the prudent and sound management of a credit institution, supervisory authorities are given no explicit guidance concerning the kinds of organizations that may not own credit institutions.

Nor does the Second Banking Directive give credit institutions any guidelines on establishing financial subsidiaries (including other credit institution subsidiaries), with the exception of certain subsidiaries that are substantially integrated with their parent credit institutions.[16] Prior

16. Financial subsidiaries of credit institutions are controlled to some extent by the Consolidated Supervision Directive, 83/350/EEC, which requires that regulators review the accounts, exposures, and managements of institutions on a consolidated basis.

consultation is the only other requirement pertaining to the establishment or acquisition of financial subsidiaries in the Second Banking Directive. By default, such subsidiaries would be subject to host country control. In addition, the acquisition by a credit institution of another credit institution or some other type of financial institution would be subject to EC provisions concerning mergers and acquisitions in general.

The Second Banking Directive does not cover branches of banks headquartered outside the EC. Thus branches of third-country banks will not benefit from the single banking license and the mutual recognition of permissible banking activities. The establishment of direct branches of third-country credit institutions remains subject to the First Banking Directive of 1977 and under the control of individual EC member states.

To take advantage of the single banking license concept and the mutual recognition of permissible banking activities, a bank from a nation outside the Community must possess or establish a subsidiary (a firm with its own corporate identity) in an EC member state. Foreign-owned subsidiaries already established there are grandfathered and will enjoy the full benefits of the Second Banking Directive. However, foreign banks will only be able to establish or acquire a new EC subsidiary if the laws of the non-EC nation meet the reciprocity requirement of the Second Banking Directive.

The reciprocity provision in the original draft of the Second Banking Directive drew loud complaints from foreign banks and bank supervisors. As a result, the Commission issued a revised reciprocity proposal in April 1989, and the Council approved a version of the revised proposal when it adopted the Second Banking Directive on June 19, 1989. Non-EC banking organizations consider the final version more favorable than the original proposal, but they still have a few concerns.

Procedurally, the final version eliminates a cumbersome review process designed to assess the quality of reciprocity in a non-EC bank's home country. The application of a non-EC banking organization will not be automatically suspended while the treatment of EC banks in the foreign country is reviewed. Such a suspension was called for in the original proposal. Moreover, the Commission itself will not be the final judge of whether a non-EC nation is granting sufficient reciprocity to banking organizations from EC member nations. The final decision will be made by the Council of Ministers, which may be attuned to broader policy considerations.

One of the more substantive changes in the final reciprocity provision concerns equivalent treatment, which is defined as market access and competitive opportunities comparable to those granted by the Community to non-EC banks. If a non-EC nation fails to grant *national* treatment to EC credit institutions, a subsidiary of an institution from that nation may be denied an EC banking license. However, the lack of *equivalent* treatment by a non-EC nation will apparently not provide grounds for denying an EC banking license. In such circumstances, the Commission will ask the Council to hold negotiations with the third country. The vagueness of the equivalent treatment concept may lead to problems in the years ahead.

Note that the reciprocity provision of the Second Banking Directive does not apply to direct branches of non-EC banks. Thus a banking organization in a country that does not provide EC banks with comparable market access could still establish a branch in any EC state that so permitted, but could not establish a subsidiary with banking powers throughout the European Community.

The principal goal of the other 1992 banking directives is to harmonize essential regulations. The Second Banking Directive will take effect only when the Own Funds Directive (*own funds* being the EC term for bank capital) and the Solvency Ratios Directive become effective. The Own Funds Directive establishes a standard definition of bank capital compatible with the definition promulgated by the Basle Committee.[17] The Solvency Ratios Directive calls for a minimum ratio of 8 percent between bank capital and risk-weighted assets.[18]

A 1986 directive on the Accounts of Banks specifies the format and the content of financial reports.[19] Under the 1989 Branch Accounts Directive, EC member states no longer have the power to require branches to publish separate accounts.[20] Instead, branches of EC banks are to provide the consolidated accounts of their parent banks. Branches of non-EC parents can be asked to provide branch accounts if the accounts of their parents do not conform with EC standards.

A Winding Up Directive establishes measures for the reorganization and winding up of institutions in trouble.[21] The directive would make the authorities of the home country responsible for the institution's

17. 89/299/EEC, *O.J. Eur. Comm.*, no. L124 (May 5, 1989), p. 16.
18. 89/647/EEC, *O.J. Eur. Comm.*, no. L386 (December 30, 1989), p. 14.
19. 86/635/EEC, *O.J. Eur. Comm.*, no. L372 (December 31, 1986), p. 1.
20. 89/117/EEC, *O.J. Eur. Comm.*, no. L44 (February 16, 1989), p. 40.
21. COM (88) 4 Final (Brussels, January 4, 1988).

reorganization or winding up. The Council has made recommendations instead of enacting directives in three areas: large exposure reporting, deposit guarantee programs, and electronic payments procedures.[22]

### Securities in Europe 1992

In the securities field, the counterpart to the Second Banking Directive is the proposed Investment Services Directive.[23] This directive will allow investment firms established in one EC member state to set up branches and to provide services in other member states. Investment firms are defined as institutions engaged in the activities listed in appendix 2-5. Briefly, the activities are brokerage, dealing as principal, market making, portfolio management, arranging or offering underwriting services, giving professional investment advice, and securities safekeeping.

Credit institutions that provide investment services would, for the most part, not be covered by the directive. These institutions will come under the Second Banking Directive.

A reciprocity condition similar to that in the Second Banking Directive would apply if an organization from a non-EC nation tried to establish a subsidiary in an EC member state. Like the Second Banking Directive, however, the Investment Services Directive will not cover direct branches of non-EC investment firms. The establishment of such branches will still fall under the rules of individual EC states.

In essence, the Investment Services Directive provides a home country with control over an investment firm's branches located in other EC states. Business rules governing the relationship between an investment firm and its customers would, for the time being, be subject to host country control. Another matter subject to host country rules is compensation to customers in the event of default. The host country's compensation fund for the protection of investors would serve the in-country branches of businesses chartered in other member nations.

The proposed directive also contains rules aimed at giving investment firms greater access to stock exchanges and financial futures and options exchanges. However, the firms must comply with regulations relating to the structure and organization of the host exchange. The proposed rules

22. 87/62/EEC, *O.J. Eur. Comm.*, no. L33 (February 4, 1987), p. 10; 87/63/EEC, *O.J. Eur. Comm.*, no. L33 (February 4, 1987), p. 16; and 87/598/EEC, *O.J. Eur. Comm.*, no. L365 (December 24, 1987), p. 72.

23. COM (89) 629, *O.J. Eur. Comm.*, no. C42 (1990), p. 7.

regarding access to exchanges do not cover credit institutions engaged in securities activities.

The Commission is formulating legislation for investment firms that is comparable to the Own Funds Directive and the Solvency Ratios Directive developed for credit institutions. The new directive will focus on adequate protection against market risk incurred by investment firms.

As already mentioned, three directives adopted before 1985 (the Admissions Directive, the Listing Particulars Directive, and the Interim Reports Directive) applied to companies with shares listed on stock exchanges. Firms wanting to sell newly issued shares that are not yet listed on a stock exchange come under the Prospectus Directive adopted in December 1988.[24] It sets forth minimum requirements concerning the publication, scrutiny, and distribution of prospectuses for public offerings. It also provides for mutual recognition of prospectuses. The directive exempts a broad range of securities classified as those that are not connected with a generalized campaign of advertising or canvassing aimed at the public. These exempt securities are termed Eurosecurities.

Another directive adopted in December 1988 concerns large shareholdings.[25] Persons acquiring or disposing of large holdings in the equity of a company are required to make public the changes. The threshold reporting levels are 10, 20, 33.3, 50, and 66.6 percent. An insider-trading directive has also been adopted.

The UCITS Directive became effective in October 1989.[26] The acronym UCITS stands for undertakings for collective investment in transferable securities, and it takes in securities similar to mutual fund shares in the United States. The directive permits UCITS to be marketed throughout the European Community on the basis of a license from one member nation.

## A Survey of the Financial Industry

The structure of the financial industry is extremely complex. Most of its products are intangibles. They are not easy-to-count physical items such as automobiles or refrigerators. Instead, a substantial portion of the industry's output consists of rights and obligations, the purposes of which

24. 89/298/EEC, *O.J. Eur. Comm.*, no. L124 (May 5, 1989), p. 8.

25. 88/627/EEC, *O.J. Eur. Comm.*, no. L348 (December 17, 1988), p. 62.

26. 85/611/EEC, *O.J. Eur. Comm.*, no. L375 (December 31, 1985), p. 3, as amended by 88/220/EEC, *O.J. Eur. Comm.*, no. L100 (April 19, 1988), p. 31.

are often difficult to discern. Moreover, their details are often daunting. One observer has identified in excess of fifty "more or less distinct financial services available to various client segments in various markets."[27]

The variety of institutions that provide these services are often placed into two categories: banks and securities firms. Indeed, these classifications are so entrenched that commentators and observers speak of the "banking industry" and the "securities industry." The activities of institutions within the two so-called industries overlap considerably, however, particularly at the international level.

### Banking and Securities—Definition and Overlap

The principal characteristic of institutions in the banking industry is that they take deposits. Also, in most countries banks are legally defined entities: operating as a bank requires a license from the appropriate governmental authority.

Few banks attempt to provide all possible products for all potential customers. Banks specialize both in their products and in their customers. A distinction is often drawn between retail and wholesale banks, but these are not legal terms. Moreover, there is no sharp dividing line: when a bank stops being a retail bank and becomes a wholesale bank is not all that clear.

A retail institution can be defined as a bank that relies primarily on deposits from individuals or small businesses for its funds and that confines its lending by and large to the same groups. In contrast, the wholesale bank serves primarily medium-sized and large businesses, as well as other banking organizations. The types of services rendered by the wholesale bank range from the provision of funds in a variety of forms to the giving of different types of advice, to the provision of payment services. To obtain their funds, wholesale banks rely less on deposits from customers and more on buying funds in the money markets.

Because of the way it operates, a large retail banking business requires more physical offices than does a large wholesale banking business. The convenience afforded by a nearby banking office is important to the individual and small business customers of the retail bank. In contrast, the customers of a wholesale bank can easily conduct most of their transactions over the telephone and through other forms of electronic communication.

27. Ingo Walter, *Global Competition in Financial Services: Market Structure, Protection and Trade Liberalization* (American Enterprise Institute/Ballinger, 1988), p. 22.

The divisions within the securities industry are even more ill-defined. A principal reason is that, in some countries, entry into the securities business is far less regulated than entry into the banking business. Another reason is that the structure of capital markets varies considerably among nations: some countries raise funds by issuing securities much more than others do. The securities industry is said to have four functional areas:[28]

*Primary markets*—Primary markets are concerned with the creation and issuance of new debt and equity securities. "Related operations include underwriting, syndication and marketing of new securities issues through public offerings or private placement." The term "investment banking" is often applied to the activities that securities firms perform in the primary markets. Note that success in investment banking depends a great deal on client relationships and financial advice about such matters as restructurings, mergers, and acquisitions. Fees from merger and acquisition work are likely to be substantial in the European Community as industrial restructuring takes place in response to the 1992 program.

*Secondary markets*—In the secondary markets, existing securities are bought and sold. Securities firms may buy and sell for themselves; that is, they may "deal as principals." Securities firms may also engage in market making, an activity that consists of standing ready to buy and sell a security both to provide a market for the security and to stabilize that market. In addition, securities firms may engage in brokerage activities, which consist of accepting buy and sell orders from customers and executing those orders.

*Collective investments*—Securities firms engaged in the collective investment business combine individual securities into a single legal entity and sell shares in that entity to the public. Collective investments are known by different names, such as mutual funds, unit trusts, and investment trusts.

*Portfolio management and counseling*—Securities firms that perform these functions manage portfolios for individuals and institutional investors. The management is done for a fee. Insurance companies and pension funds are common institutional investors.

As already mentioned, the activities of the banking and securities industries overlap considerably. This overlap is more pronounced in some

28. Organization for Economic Cooperation and Development, *International Trade in Services: Securities* (Washington, 1987).

countries than in others. Three general types of relationships appear to exist between the banking and securities industries.

First, the banking industry and the securities industry have been separated in some countries, notably the United States, Canada, and Japan. In the United States, the separation was mandated by the Glass-Steagall Act, which was passed in 1933 in response to the financial troubles of the Great Depression. Parallel legislation was adopted in Japan after the Second World War (Article 65 of Japan's Securities and Exchange Law). The Glass-Steagall Act by no means constitutes an absolute barrier between the banking and securities industries. Its main effect is to curtail the ability of banking organizations to perform the investment banking functions of underwriting and dealing in securities.

Second, at the other extreme is universal banking, a system that permits banks to engage both in deposit taking and in the full range of securities activities. European Community countries that have universal banking systems are Denmark, West Germany, Luxembourg, and the Netherlands. As a consequence of the 1986 "Big Bang," the United Kingdom should probably be added to the universal banking roster.

Universal banking systems may differ from country to country. For example, a bank in this system may or may not be allowed to conduct all financial activities itself, and some activities, such as certain securities transactions, may have to be performed by bank affiliates. Germany provides an example of a universal banking system in which banks themselves can engage in the full range of financial activities. In contrast, banks in the United Kingdom cannot perform certain securities activities themselves, but they can own or be associated with companies performing those activities.

Third, some countries try to separate secondary market activities from other securities functions. In most such countries, securities must be bought and sold on recognized exchanges through independent brokers. Banks may be able to take orders from customers, but the orders have to be executed through the independent brokers. In essence, brokers in these countries have a monopoly on secondary market activities. Brokers in such systems are often individuals or small partnerships. European Community countries with some form of separation between secondary market activities and other securities functions are Belgium, France, Greece, Ireland, Italy, Portugal, and Spain. Prior to the "Big Bang," the United Kingdom's financial industry had this type of a separation.

The overlap between the banking and securities industries can also

FIGURE 2–1. The Retail-Wholesale Spectrum, Banking and Securities Business

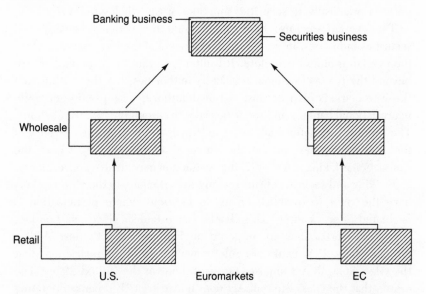

be described in terms of the retail-wholesale distinction. Retail securities activities would be those in which the main customers served are individuals and small businesses. In this analysis, the secondary market function and the collective investment function would be categorized as securities activities with a strong retail bent. Primary market functions would be classified as wholesale activities. Providing portfolio management and advice would be a wholesale activity if provided for institutional investors and retail if provided for individuals.

Although it takes some effort to portray both the banking and securities industries in a retail-wholesale framework graphically, the result does highlight differences between the United States and the European Community (figure 2-1).

In the United States at the retail level, the banking and securities industries are by and large separate. In contrast, in the European Community the two industries overlap to a far greater extent. A degree of separation still exists, however, mainly because several EC countries prohibit banks from executing securities orders on exchanges. The overlap between the industries in both the United States and the European Community increases as one moves across the spectrum from retail banking to wholesale banking. Nevertheless, there is still a significant lack of overlap in the United States in the area of securities underwriting and dealing. In the European Community, banks or bank affiliates can perform practically all securities functions at the wholesale level.

The overlap can also be found beyond the national banking and securities industries, in the international realm of the Euromarkets. Here the overlap is almost complete. It is often said that the Euromarkets are beyond the reach of national regulatory authorities, but the truth is that the Euromarkets exist because national authorities simply do not apply many national banking and securities laws to certain types of transactions. The exempt transactions fall into two principal types: (1) the currency of the transaction may not be the currency of the country where the transaction is taking place, or (2) the transaction may involve nonresidents.

Banking and securities firms seeking to participate in the Euromarkets have the right to establish offices in locations where participation is facilitated. For example, U.S. banks can establish offices in London, where few restrictions are imposed on Euromarket activities. With a London office, U.S. banks are able to avoid most of the restrictions that the Glass-Steagall Act imposes on institutions in the United States. The reason that the Glass-Steagall Act does not restrict U.S. banks operating in London is simply that, at some point in the distant past, the Federal Reserve Board determined it did not do so.

This ability of financial institutions to establish offices in jurisdictions that put few restrictions on the provision of services to international customers has fueled the growth of the Euromarkets. Banks in these hospitable jurisdictions can provide most of the services that securities firms provide. Similarly, securities firms can provide most of the services that banks provide. The result is that "it is often nearly impossible to distinguish between a bank and a securities firm in the Euromarkets."[29]

## Banking and Securities—Some Numbers

As mentioned earlier, the 1977 First Banking Directive defined credit institutions as undertakings in the business of receiving deposits or other repayable funds from the public and granting credits for their own accounts. Each year the European Commission draws up and publishes a list of all credit institutions authorized to do business within the Community. In compiling the annual list, the Commission has had to cope with differing national financial structures and a variety of institutions

29. Ibid., p. 20.

that are not full-fledged banks but that do take deposits and make various types of loans.

Despite the variety of financial structures in the nations of the European Community, their credit institutions can be classified into four broad types:

*Commercial banks*—This group includes credit institutions that cover the entire range of commercial banking activities. They have varied funding bases and engage in wide-ranging lending and off-balance-sheet activities. They often have an international business.

*Savings banks*—The funding base for this group is exclusively savings deposits from the general public. The lending activities are generally less wide-ranging than those of commercial banks, and the international business is limited. Savings banks often have a more pronounced local or regional identity than do commercial banks.

*Cooperative banks*—Mutual ownership is the characteristic feature of this group. Otherwise, cooperative banks are similar to savings banks in their source and use of funds and in organizational structure. Their activities are tailored to the needs of small business, the agricultural sector, and self-employed individuals. Some of the cooperative organizations can be quite large, however. For example, Credit Agricole of France was the largest bank in Europe at the end of 1988.

*Specialized institutions*—This category includes specialized credit institutions engaged mainly in long-term lending. Mortgage providers and finance companies are the principal subtypes.

The different types of credit institutions in the EC member states, together with approximate figures for total credit institution assets, are presented in table 2-1. The numbers and assets of depository institutions in the United States are given in table 2-2. Like most European countries, the United States has a variety of depository institutions, banks being the most important. A unique feature of the U.S. banking industry is that regulatory authority over banks is divided among three primary agencies: the Office of the Comptroller of the Currency, the Federal Reserve Board, and the Federal Deposit Insurance Corporation. Corporate owners of banks, called bank holding companies, are also subject to regulation, the primary regulator being the Federal Reserve Board.

At the end of 1987, there were 14,207 banks in the United States, and 6,503 bank holding companies. The banks comprised three main types: national banks regulated by the Office of the Comptroller of the Currency; state-chartered banks regulated by state agencies and the

**TABLE 2–1.** EC Credit Institutions, Year-end 1986

Number of institutions unless otherwise specified

| Country | Commercial banks[a] | | Savings banks | Cooperative banks | Other institutions | Total institutions | Assets[b] (billion ECU) |
|---|---|---|---|---|---|---|---|
| | Total | Foreign branches | | | | | |
| Belgium | 88 | 29 | 34 | ... | 53 | 175 | 219 |
| Denmark | 79 | 6 | 147 | n.a. | 18 | 244 | 69 |
| Germany, West | 277 | 61 | 600 | 3,604 | 77 | 4,558 | 1,286 |
| Greece | 35 | 16 | ... | ... | 9 | 44 | 33 |
| France | 386 | 56 | 422 | 192 | 1,080 | 2,080 | n.a. |
| Ireland | 39 | 6 | ... | 16 | 2 | 57 | 21 |
| Italy | 268 | 39 | 90 | 717 | 96 | 1,171 | 373 |
| Luxembourg | 115 | 17 | ... | 58 | 28 | 201 | 174 |
| Netherlands | 83 | 19 | 62 | 1 | 29 | 175 | 260 |
| Portugal | 19 | 9 | 1 | ... | 3 | 23 | n.a. |
| Spain | 135 | 38 | 79 | 142 | 260 | 616 | 255 |
| United Kingdom | 588 | 254 | n.a. | n.a. | 164 | 752 | 1,032 |
| TOTAL | 2,112 | 550 | 1,435 | 4,730 | 1,819 | 10,096 | 3,722 |

SOURCE: EC Commission, *Panorama of EC Industry—1989* (Brussels, 1989), pp. 29-3, 29-7, 29-8.

n.a. Not available.

a. The totals for commercial banks include branches of both EC banks and non-EC foreign banks. Foreign branches are also stated separately.

b. June 1987.

TABLE 2-2. U.S. Depository Institutions, Year-end 1987

| Type of institution | Number of institutions | Assets (billions of dollars) |
|---|---|---|
| Banks, total[a] | 14,207 | 3,263 |
| Of which: holding company banks[b] | (9,322) | . . . |
| Savings institutions[c] | 3,147 | 1,251 |
| Credit unions[d] | 14,335 | 163 |
| TOTAL | 31,689 | 4,676 |

SOURCES: Board of Governors of the Federal Reserve System, *Annual Statistical Digest, 1987*, table 76; Federal Deposit Insurance Corporation, *Statistics on Banking, 1987*, tables 101, RC-1; Federal Home Loan Bank Board, *Combined Financial Statements, FSLIC-Insured Institutions, 1987*, table 1; and U.S. Department of Commerce, *Statistical Abstract of the United States, 1989*, table 804. Figures are rounded.
n.a. Not available.
a. FDIC-insured commercial banks, savings banks, and trust companies; includes Puerto Rico and outlying areas.
b. Held by 5,904 holding company groups.
c. FSLIC-insured savings and loan institutions and savings banks.
d. Federally insured credit unions.

Federal Deposit Insurance Corporation; and state-chartered Federal Reserve member banks regulated by the Federal Reserve System.

In addition to banks, there were 3,147 state and federally chartered savings and loan institutions and federally chartered savings banks regulated by the Federal Home Loan Bank Board—which, as a result of the Financial Institutions Reform, Recovery, and Enforcement Act of 1989 (FIRREA), has become the Office of Thrift Supervision.[30] In addition, there were 14,335 state and federally chartered credit unions regulated by the National Credit Union Administration.

One reason for the relatively large number of banks in the United States is that interstate banking has been subject to severe restrictions. Banks are unable to open branches across state lines. The McFadden Act imposed this restriction on national banks a half century ago. Although there is no comparable federal legislation restricting interstate branching by most state-chartered banks, the states themselves have not permitted such branching.

Interstate banking through corporate subsidiaries is also limited. Until the early 1980s, bank holding companies were generally unable to establish or acquire banks outside their home states. This situation has changed considerably because a majority of the states have since enacted some form of interstate banking law. Many of them allow interstate banking within certain geographically defined regions. Some of them allow interstate banking nationwide. In many instances, a reciprocity require-

30. P.L. 101-73.

TABLE 2–3. Comparisons of Bank Concentration, Mid–1980s

| Country | Date | Concentration |
|---|---|---|
| United States | 1985 | Out of 13,739 commercial banks, the largest 5 control 12.8 percent of total assets, the largest 10 control 20.3 percent, and the largest 100 control 57.5 percent |
| Japan | 1986 | Out of 87 commercial banks, 13 city banks control 56.7 percent of total assets |
| West Germany | 1987 | Out of 316 commercial banks, the largest 6 control 37.9 percent of total assets |
| France | 1986 | Out of 367 banks, 3 control 41.7 percent of total assets |
| Italy | 1984 | Out of some 250 banks, the largest 5 control 34.4 percent and the largest 10 control 52.3 percent of total deposits |
| United Kingdom | 1986 | Out of 588 banks, the largest 5 control 45.6 percent of total assets |
| Canada | 1985 | The 4 largest banks control 51.2 percent of all deposits, and 7 banks account for over 80 percent of all deposits. |

SOURCE: Organization for Economic Cooperation and Development, *Economies in Transition: Structural Adjustment in OECD Countries* (Paris, 1989), p. 97.

ment exists—that is, an out-of-state banking organization can enter a target state only if the home state grants similar privileges to banking organizations based in the target state. As a result of the restrictions on interstate banking, the U.S. banking industry is relatively fragmented. By international standards, the United States exhibits the least concentrated structure among the industrial countries (table 2-3).

Further complicating the regulatory picture for the U.S. financial industry is the Securities and Exchange Commission (SEC). That body is responsible for implementing and enforcing a wide variety of securities laws, which can apply to commercial companies, securities firms, and banking organizations. In some instances, the banking regulators take the place of the SEC in applying securities laws to banks.

The principal trade association for securities firms in the United States is the Securities Industry Association, which had 554 members as of January 1988. The trade association for the collective investment securities function is the Investment Company Institute; in 1987, there were 2,324 mutual funds in the United States.[31]

As a source of funds for businesses, the securities industry is more

31. Investment Company Institute, *1988 Mutual Fund Fact Book: Industry Trends and Statistics for 1987* (Washington, 1988), p. 13.

TABLE 2–4. Relative Importance of Securities Industries, Mid-1980s

| Country | Issues of securities | |
| | Percent of domestic credit, 1983–85[a] | Percent of fixed investment, 1985[b] |
| --- | --- | --- |
| United States | 50 | 20 |
| Japan | 38 | 9 |
| Germany | 36 | 6 |
| France | 41 | 17 |
| United Kingdom | 35 | 11 |
| Canada | 52 | 19 |

SOURCE: OECD, *Economies in Transition*, p. 91.
a. Value of net bond and share issues as percentage of total domestic credit.
b. Value of gross securities issues as percentage of private nonresidential gross fixed investment.

important in the United States than in most other countries. In the late 1980s, securities issues accounted for 50 percent of total domestic credit in the United States (table 2-4). Of five other major countries, the closest one to this level was France at 41 percent. Similarly, securities accounted for a higher percentage of total investment in the United States than in France, West Germany, and the United Kingdom. The U.S. percentage was 20.3 percent. The closest EC country was France, at 16.8 percent.

## Financial Market Consequences for the United States

The central conclusion of this chapter is that Europe 1992 will probably have little effect on the U.S. financial system over the short term but a significant effect over the long term.

By "short term," we mean the period over the next three or four years, say until 1994. By "long term," we mean the decade or so that will follow, as the new twelve-nation market works its effects on the U.S. financial system. While it would be convenient to think of December 1992 as a thunderclap event giving birth to a single market, this is not realistic. Part of the structure for Europe 1992 is already in place, much more is expected to be in place by the end of 1992, and other pieces will come later, a few probably never. An irreversible process is under way, fueled now in large part not by the bureaucrats in Brussels but by business firms making decisions in anticipation of new market opportunities and problems.

The "financial system," in this context, comprises commercial banks and securities firms (especially investment banking firms), to which we would add the government agencies that supervise them. Admittedly, the U.S. financial system encompasses many more institutions with many different specialties—insurance companies, finance companies, and mortgage banking companies, among others, plus more than 17,000 nonbank depository institutions, along with a cluster of government agencies that have bits and pieces of regulatory authority. But our central conclusion would be much the same even if we included all these institutions in our definition.

## The Run-up to 1992

For the vast majority of U.S. financial institutions, the completion of the internal market in the European Community is a retail phenomenon that is producing, at best, a large yawn. It is "retail" in the sense that, as far as banking institutions in the EC are concerned, 1992 means that they will be able to deliver a broad variety of financial services or products in a relatively unrestricted manner over a larger market. But all that this means for most U.S. financial institutions, particularly for the overwhelming majority of commercial banks, is that a part of the world in which they do no business or do not contemplate doing any business, and in which few if any of their customers do any business, is changing the form of its market. Today, 1992 has about as much relevance to most U.S. financial institutions as a coup d'état in Argentina.

At the same time, a small number of U.S. financial institutions are engaged in doing business in the Community. These multinational financial firms are quite large. Probably there are no more than 20 commercial banks in the United States (out of a total of some 14,000 commercial banks) that do a multinational financial business of any significance. (This at least is the number tracked by the Federal Reserve Board in overseeing country risk exposure.) But these 20 banks account for about 45 percent of the total assets of all U.S. banking organizations. Similarly, the handful of securities firms—out of more than 500—doing a multinational business (for example, Goldman Sachs, Morgan Stanley, and Salomon Brothers) account for a large proportion of the securities business.

These multinational U.S. financial firms are keeping a close watch on 1992. But Europe 1992 will not appreciably widen the scope of services that they are already engaged in providing, such as mergers and acquisition work, financial advisory services, and a range of other investment banking activities—virtually all of which are directed at large or medium-sized

TABLE 2–5. World's Twenty-five Largest Securities Firms by Capital, Year-end 1987

| Firm | Home country | Capital (billions of dollars)[a] |
|---|---|---|
| Nomura Securities | Japan | 10.3 |
| Salomon Brothers | United States | 8.9 |
| Merrill Lynch | United States | 8.6 |
| Daiwa Securities | Japan | 6.4 |
| Nikko Securities | Japan | 5.6 |
| Yamaichi Securities | Japan | 5.4 |
| Shearson Lehman Hutton | United States | 5.4 |
| Credit Suisse First Boston | United Kingdom | 2.6 |
| Goldman Sachs | United States | 2.4 |
| Drexel Burnham Lambert | United States | 2.2 |
| Morgan Stanley | United States | 1.7 |
| Kleinwort Benson | United Kingdom | 1.6 |
| First Boston | United States | 1.5 |
| Paine Webber | United States | 1.4 |
| Bear Stearns | United States | 1.3 |
| Prudential-Bache | United States | 1.3 |
| Nippon Kangyo Kakumaru | Japan | 1.2 |
| Wako Securities | Japan | 1.2 |
| New Japan Securities | Japan | 1.2 |
| Morgan Grenfell | United Kingdom | 1.0 |
| Smith Barney | United States | 1.0 |
| S.G. Warburg | United Kingdom | 0.9 |
| Sanyo Securities | Japan | 0.9 |
| Hill Samuel Group | United Kingdom | 0.6 |
| Cosmo Securities | Japan | 0.6 |

SOURCE: *Wall Street Journal*, September 23, 1988, p. 22R.
a. Capital includes owner's equity, reserves, minority interest, preferred stock, and long-term debt.

business firms. With one or two exceptions, these multinational U.S. financial institutions are not doing a retail banking or securities business in the EC, nor is there much indication that they plan to do so. Only Merrill Lynch and Salomon Brothers have a substantial presence in the European securities market (see table 2-5).

As the twelve-state market comes together—as nonfinancial companies begin to plan for or implement strategic moves—the implications for the multinational U.S. financial industry are obvious: it will experience considerably more wholesale business. Virtually everyone we met in the course of our study commented on this prospect, and on the fact that U.S.-based financial institutions are better situated to compete than their

European counterparts. The U.S. financial houses are known to be objective (they are unaffiliated with industrial groups in Europe) and have a reputation for aggressiveness and expertise (for example, in the realm of leveraged buy-outs). A recent *Wall Street Journal* article (August 23, 1989) characterized the situation as a "boom" for "U.S. deal makers."

How long this "window of opportunity" will last—how long the present objectivity and technical superiority of U.S. organizations will prevail— is another question. In the short term, however, it means more business, and while this has caught the attention of the press, it is not of particular significance for this discussion.

There is, however, another by-product of Europe 1992 that is even now affecting all U.S. commercial banks: the adoption of risk-based capital requirements for banks in the United States. Actually, this important innovation in supervision and regulation is not a direct result of developments within the Community. It came from the Basle Committee on Banking Regulations and Supervisory Practices (better known as the Cooke Committee, or the "Group of Twelve"), which agreed upon this regulatory initiative at the end of 1987.

However, the adoption of the Basle Committee rules depended on a prior consensus within Europe, and those rules were incorporated by the European Commission into its Solvency Ratios Directive. The risk-based capital regulations are scheduled to take effect at the same time as the Second Banking Directive, on December 31, 1992; they are viewed as a necessary part of the harmonization the Community nations are required to achieve in order to make feasible a single banking market.

The idea of regulating risk-based capital—that is, of subjecting capital adequacy to rules having the force of law—represents a major innovation for the United States, which, for about 175 years prior to 1983, had never even regulated bank capital, opting instead to supervise capital adequacy. However, risk factors might have been introduced into regulation even if there had never been a 1992 program. The Federal Reserve Board in the United States has long championed this approach to capital adequacy, and it had already found a willing partner in the Bank of England. When this approach was adopted by the Basle Committee, which includes seven members of the EC, the Federal Reserve Board achieved a major coup. The drive by the European Community toward a unified market accelerated the implementation of the Basle Committee rules.

Once the risk-based rules were in place, U.S. regulatory authorities decided that they should apply them to all U.S. institutions and not just to those engaged in multinational banking. Thus, to some degree, the events leading up to 1992 have already had their effect on all U.S. commercial banks (and indirectly, therefore, on all U.S. depository institutions, for which the new rules are taken as a guide). Few U.S. banks realize that, but for the internationalization of banking and Europe 1992, it might have taken the Federal Reserve Board much longer to succeed in its thirty-year campaign to apply risk-based capital rules to U.S. banks and bank holding companies.

## The U.S. Financial Structure

The structure of the financial industry in the United States is a product of federal and state statutes more than market forces. The statutes are legislative expressions of two, somewhat incompatible, public policy objectives dating back to the founding of the Republic: first, that banking power (the so-called money power) shall be dispersed and, second, that banks shall be operated in a safe and sound fashion. Legislation to achieve these objectives defines not only the businesses in which banks can engage but also the businesses in which nonbank financial institutions cannot engage.

The cornerstone statutes are the McFadden Act of 1927, the Glass-Steagall Act of 1933, and the Bank Holding Company Act of 1956, all of which have been amended on several occasions since they were passed. These acts can be briefly summarized as follows:

The *McFadden Act* prohibits a national bank from branching outside of its home state, and permits it to branch within its home state only to the extent that banks chartered by that state may branch. Thus interstate branching is expressly prohibited for all national banks regardless of what state law may say, and is virtually a nonevent for state-chartered banks because (with only a few ineffectual exceptions) no state permits its chartered banks to branch beyond state boundaries, or permits banks located in other states to open branch offices in the host state.

The *Glass-Steagall Act* attempts to separate the commercial banking business from the investment banking business by, first, prohibiting any institution from conducting at the same time a deposit-taking business and an investment banking business (essentially defined as underwriting, dealing in, and distributing securities). There are exceptions to this prohibition: for example, a deposit-taking institution may also underwrite or deal in U.S. government obligations or the general obligations of states and their subdivisions. In addition, the Glass-Steagall Act prohibits member banks of the Federal Reserve System from affiliating with securities firms, unless, depending on the nature of the affiliation, the securities firm is not engaged "primarily" or "principally" in the defined investment banking activities.

The *Bank Holding Company Act* states that any corporation owning at least one bank cannot have affiliates that engage in a business that is not "so closely related to banking as to be a proper incident thereto." Also, a corporation owning banks cannot acquire banks in other states unless the host state has explicitly permitted such action by statute. However, a bank holding company may acquire nonbank financial firms outside its home state if they are properly incidental to banking.

Under these three statutes, the financial system in the United States has evolved into a structure with the following characteristics: a very large number of commercial banks, the overwhelming proportion of which are small; distinctly separate commercial banks and securities firms, with different federal authorities to regulate them (the three so-called banking agencies for commercial banks and the Securities and Exchange Commission for securities firms); and virtually no interstate branching by commercial banks but almost unrestricted branching by securities firms (which probably accounts for the much smaller number of securities firms in comparison with commercial banks).

Important changes are now under way in the U.S. financial system. For example, restrictions on interstate banking are being erased as individual states act to permit other states to enter their markets (usually on a reciprocal basis), but through bank subsidiaries rather than branching. Securities firms (as well as other financial firms) have found ways to offer financial services and products once thought to be solely within the province of commercial banking (for example, checking or transaction accounts). Commercial banks are beginning to exploit a number of the exceptions in the Glass-Steagall Act in order to expand their activities in the investment banking business. Still, the fact remains that the United States does not permit universal banking and it does not permit unrestricted branching throughout the fifty states.

There is a fourth factor that has played an equally important role in the structuring of the U.S. financial system: the federal government has not prohibited the states from chartering banks. Indeed, at one time, only the states chartered banks, but in 1863 the federal government provided for the federal chartering of commercial banks. Two years later, it attempted to drive state-chartered banks out of existence through the use of the tax power. This effort failed, and ever since, the United States has had a so-called dual banking system: bank organizers may obtain a charter from either the federal or the state government, and thenceforth operate under the laws and supervision of the chartering entity. The same dual system applies to savings and loan associations and credit unions. As far as we are aware, the United States is unique in this regard.

The question is, What effect, if any, will Europe 1992 have on this structure? The answer seems to be that, over the next several years, there will be no effect. A different answer might have been given in 1988, or even early in 1989. At that time, many analysts speculated that the Second Banking Directive would require "mirror-image" reciprocity. It was feared that U.S. financial institutions might not be able to take advantage of the new EC single banking market, because the United States could not meet a mirror-image test, owing to the limitations of the Glass-Steagall and the McFadden acts.

If the European Community had persisted in its mirror-image position, it is possible that this would have been enough, finally, to tilt the congressional balance in favor of repeal (or significant modification) of the Glass-Steagall Act. But, as it happened, the EC modified its position on reciprocity in April 1989.

In any event, the long controversy over the Glass-Steagall Act seems to be approaching its end. On March 30, 1988, the Senate voted to repeal the Glass-Steagall Act by an overwhelming margin of 94 to 2. The congressional session ended before the House of Representatives could take action, but in the election that followed the principal opponent of House action, Congressman Fernand J. St Germain of Rhode Island, was defeated. In response to these and other indications of the growing sentiment for repeal, the securities industry itself has begun to back away from its long-time adamant opposition to change. EC influence was more than hinted at in the statement of a Securities Industry Association official who noted that his organization's new proposal for reform of Glass-Steagall "readies the nation, its banks, and its securities firms for the global competition of the 1990s."[32]

Meanwhile, commercial banks continue to make progress in entering certain investment banking activities through Federal Reserve Board rulings that involve Section 20 of the Glass-Steagall Act (which permits

32. *Banking Expansion Reporter*, vol. 9 (January 1, 1990), p. 2; see also pp. 4–5.

the affiliation of commercial banks with investment banking firms where the latter are not "engaged principally" in the prohibited activities).

If the savings and loan crisis had not erupted to dominate all other financial market issues, the end of the Glass-Steagall controversy would be near. In the current regulatory climate, an additional push coming out of reciprocity demands from the EC might have been the deciding factor in amending the Glass-Steagall Act in 1988 or 1989. But the McFadden Act would have remained, and the possibility for changing that piece of legislation appeared remote, even as late as 1990.

When the European Council adopted the Second Banking Directive in June 1989, it was "national treatment" reciprocity that was called for, coupled with an equivalent market access test. This appeared to eliminate the reciprocity issue as a factor in early passage of legislation to alter the Glass-Steagall Act.

If we look at the long term, however, the issue seems very much alive. One of the important consequences of Europe 1992 for the U.S. financial system will undoubtedly be the removal of the present barriers that limit the powers banks may exercise and the form these powers may take over broad geographic areas. Several of the most thoughtful and knowledgeable observers we interviewed in the United States and in Europe did not hesitate to suggest that in the long run Europe 1992 would set the stage for a "complete restructuring" of the U.S. financial system. What they had in mind was the disappearance of the restrictions now imposed by the McFadden Act and the Glass-Steagall Act, together with the other changes that would inevitably follow. The most drastic change would be an acceleration in the bank consolidation movement, already under way in the United States, which would lead to a substantial decline in the number of U.S. banking organizations and the adoption of universal banking.

We tend to agree with this view for a number of reasons. In the first place, pressure from the EC is not likely to end simply because the European Council adopts national treatment reciprocity. The Commission is empowered to recommend to the Council at any time that negotiations be conducted with any third country that does not provide equivalent treatment to institutions in EC nations, and equivalent treatment in this instance means effective market access and competitive opportunities comparable to those granted by the Community to non-EC banks. As the *Economist* put it recently (July 8, 1989): "A demand for effective access remains a demand for a bending of local rules in favor of foreigners—and thus applies some pressure to liberalize local rules."

To be sure, some of the harsh provisions of the original Second Banking Directive proposal, such as automatic suspension of an application while treatment of EC banks was being investigated, have been dropped, and it is not the Commission but the Council that will now make the final decision. Still, the tools are there for pressure to be brought. As one knowledgeable commentator (Michael Gruson of the law firm of Shearman & Sterling in New York) observed in a note to clients, even the revised language "is broad enough to allow the EEC to take aggressive positions against third country discriminatory or non-reciprocal treatment of EC credit institutions if the political climate in the EEC requires such an approach."

Quite apart from future Commission actions with respect to reciprocity, there is every reason to expect that Europe will continue its efforts to persuade the United States to liberalize Glass-Steagall and McFadden restrictions. We were explicitly told as much by a high official in Brussels who, when asked for an illustrative forum, mentioned the GATT negotiations. Financial services are a big item in the Uruguay Round. The lessons that the Community brings to those negotiations will be most influential, particularly with respect to acceptance of the notion of mutual recognition by foreign nations, the underlying principle of the Second Banking Directive. The mutual recognition approach, applied to banking, would require the United States to permit European banks to carry on the same scope of business in the United States as their home country permits them to practice in Europe.

More generally, it is contrary to common sense to think that the United States can remain aloof forever from the influence of the Community when it comes to walls that determine what financial organizations may do, and to limits on where they may do it. To us, this is the most persuasive and yet the least demonstrable of the reasons that developments in the European Community will hasten changes in the U.S. banking structure, at least over the longer term.

It is well to keep in mind that the European Community is the largest trading partner of the United States and that EC banks already have a considerable presence in this country. Similarly, U.S. banks and securities firms have a significant presence in the European Community. EC banking institutions located in the United States already number 79, with 214 offices (as of August 1989)—and more are certain to come. Their weight will be increasingly felt in various trade group discussions and in their contacts with legislators. Foreign banks in the United States already employ more than 100,000 persons. This is reason enough for some congressmen to pay close attention to foreign banks that complain they are being discriminated against by certain state laws.[33]

Moreover, even if "national treatment" reciprocity remains the position of the EC, the activities of U.S. banking organizations in the Community will be affected by how closely each member state conforms to the generally accepted policy of the Community as a whole. One observer in Brussels reminded us that the Commission, at present at least, has relatively little information on, let alone control over, the extent to which each member state conforms to a particular policy or directive. If multinational U.S. financial firms should capture the cream of the European mergers and acquisitions business, U.S. banks could well face administrative harassment of various kinds in different member states, especially if the United States persists in maintaining its present restrictions on bank powers and branching.

Moreover, there is hovering on the horizon the possibility, even the likelihood, that Japan will drop its equivalent of the Glass-Steagall Act (Article 65 of Japan's Securities and Exchange Law). This matter is already being studied by officials in Japan. If Article 65 is abandoned, the United States will be even further out of step with the rest of the world and will likely experience considerable pressure from the European Community to provide "equivalent treatment."

There remains the matter of the McFadden Act. Even though change in that act seems much further out on the horizon than repeal of the Glass-Steagall Act, McFadden will also be affected by what is occurring in the European Community. In public policy discussions, a question just beginning to surface is whether it is prudent for the United States to prohibit branching between states when the European Community does not seem to have suffered from permitting virtually unrestricted branching between countries. The example of the European Community may seem a small thing; yet, for those who have long regarded the McFadden Act as indestructible, the current discussion of its possible

33. Lawrence R. Uhlick, executive director and counsel, Institute of International Bankers, testimony before the Subcommittee on Financial Institutions Supervision, Regulation, and Insurance of the House Committee on Banking, Finance and Urban Affairs, September 28, 1989.

change in banking circles, and even in congressional hearings, suggests that the seeds of a new policy are being sown.

Indeed, as we write, various pieces of legislation are being prepared to permit interstate branching among selected states on a regional basis. In other words, we can see the beginnings of the same kind of movement that started about a decade ago and that led to interstate expansion through bank holding companies. The economics of the situation are fairly clear. As banking organizations in the United States establish themselves in multistate regions or across the nation, they will be impressed by the efficiency of operating through branches rather than through numerous bank subsidiaries.

The precise effect that an internal market in the European Community, particularly a single banking market with universal banking, will have on the U.S. banking structure is impossible for us or for anyone to predict. There will be many new pressures to contend with, possibly as a result of the enhanced activity and legislative clout of Community banking organizations now in the United States, or the fact that the United States will henceforth be dealing with one entity in Europe rather than twelve, or the possibility that the EC Commission may in the next several years revert to a position that resembles more closely its initial mirror-image reciprocity position. There will also probably be continued pressure exerted on U.S. banking organizations attempting to do business in the Community when only the United States is out of step with the rest of the world. In sum, those who argue that one of the most important consequences of Europe 1992 will be the restructuring of the U.S. financial system seem to us to be correct. To be sure, one might also argue that, as the internationalization of banking and finance progresses, restructuring in the United States would be inevitable, in any case, and probably this is true. What Europe 1992 will do is hasten that event.

## The Supervision of U.S. Financial Institutions

The nature and thrust of the supervision of financial institutions in the United States depends heavily on the balance of power among federal agencies and between federal and state agencies. This balance is not fixed; rather, it is continually shifting. Europe 1992 can and probably will have a strong influence on that process. Efforts to achieve an international level playing field will have an important overall effect. The principal vehicle will likely be capital regulation. The Community nations, speaking with one voice rather than twelve, will obviously exert greater influence in international deliberations, and thus on the evolution of prudential capital standards and other supervisory policies.

Precisely this possibility was discussed by Manuel H. Johnson, vice-chairman of the Federal Reserve Board, in recent congressional testimony. After noting the importance of EC-1992 for U.S. bank supervision, Governor Johnson suggested that the Community will likely seek "further harmonization of bank supervisory and regulatory practices" and that, when it does, its prior decisions will have considerable influence because "various issues discussed in the Basle Committee will have already been discussed by an EC body and . . . there will be greater unity of positions taken by representatives of EC countries in meeting of the Basle Supervisors Committee."[34]

Although this is not the place for a lengthy discussion of the supervision and regulation of U.S. financial institutions, we need to go over the principal elements of the U.S. supervisory system before we can identify the specific features that may be affected by Europe 1992. In the main, four federal agencies are responsible for supervising and regulating securities firms and banks: the Securities and Exchange Commission for securities firms, the Office of the Comptroller of the Currency, the Federal Reserve Board, and the Federal Deposit Insurance Corporation for commercial banks.

Just as there is not an impenetrable wall between commercial banking and investment banking in the United States, so too there is not a clear division between the responsibilities of the SEC and the three federal banking agencies. Banks do engage in securities activities, and they do come into contact with the SEC (or with SEC rules enforced by the banking agencies) in the areas of disclosure and permissible activities.

This overlap may be substantially altered if universal banking takes root in the United States. If there is a merger of the separate regulatory systems, how will the quite different regulatory styles of the SEC and the banking agencies be coordinated? The SEC depends heavily (though not entirely) on disclosure and market punishment of transgressors; the banking agencies depend on regulatory enforcement and shield the public as much as possible from distressing information about troubled institutions. There is already pressure on the banking agencies to rely more heavily on market enforcement: for example, "mark-to-market" proposals

34. Manuel H. Johnson, testimony before the Subcommittee on Financial Institutions Supervision, Regulation, and Insurance of the House Committee on Banking, Finance and Urban Affairs, September 26, 1989.

have been put forth for bank assets, and FIRREA regulations now require banking agencies to disclose enforcement actions, such as cease-and-desist and officer removal orders. Europe 1992 may give added impetus to this trend.

Europe 1992 is likely to exert an even more direct impact on the three banking agencies. Of the three, only the Office of the Comptroller of the Currency (OCC) is a true regulatory agency. It charters banks, which then operate in accordance with a federal banking code and are supervised by the OCC. In the other two federal agencies, the task of supervising and regulating banks is ancillary to their other responsibilities.

The Federal Deposit Insurance Corporation regularly examines and supervises the majority of banks in the United States, primarily those of small size, which are chartered by the states but are not members of the Federal Reserve System. (These banks are also supervised and regulated by their respective state agencies.)

The Federal Reserve Board supervises those state-chartered banks that have opted to join the Federal Reserve System (membership is mandatory for national banks but optional for state banks). These banks are relatively few in number but include some very large institutions (such as Morgan Guaranty, Chemical, and Bankers Trust in New York City). More important, however, the Federal Reserve Board has the sole authority to regulate bank holding companies, which have approximately 9,400 bank subsidiaries, most of which are also supervised and regulated by the OCC (national banks) or by the Federal Deposit Insurance Corporation (FDIC) and the various states (state banks).

If the policies of the three banking agencies were identical, it would make little difference how supervisory and regulatory power was divided among them. However, their policies differ in important ways.

The OCC is concerned with the safety and soundness of the banks under its jurisdiction and, in addition, with the ability of its banks to operate profitably and without competitive disadvantage when compared with state-chartered banks. The FDIC must give first priority to its deposit insurance responsibilities, including protecting the deposit insurance fund. As the central bank, the Federal Reserve accords first priority to monetary policy and maintaining its position of "independence within government," a goal that creates its own special effects on the board's approach to bank supervision and regulation.

In a broad sense, the most conservative regulatory approach over the years has been taken by the Federal Reserve Board, whereas the most liberal approach, in terms of providing opportunities for banks to do business, has been advocated by the Comptroller of the Currency. (However, OCC examiners approach asset valuation in traditional conservative fashion, unencumbered by such policy considerations as the ongoing negotiations over third world debt.) The FDIC position has usually fallen somewhere between the two extremes, although in recent years it has tended to lean toward the philosophy of the OCC rather than the Board of Governors. It is dangerous to generalize about the fifty state agencies, but they are probably closer to the OCC position on most matters, espousing new business opportunities for the state-chartered banks.

Although the reasons for the regulatory approach traditionally taken by the Comptroller of the Currency seem fairly obvious from the nature of the responsibilities assigned to that office, the reasons for the approaches taken by the FDIC and the Federal Reserve Board are less transparent.

The FDIC has traditionally been, and by and large continues to be, a "strict" regulator since its deposit insurance fund is immediately affected whenever regulation has been conducted loosely and losses from bank failure are high. At the same time, the FDIC came into being in 1933 over the opposition of major banks in the United States but with the enthusiastic support of the thousands of small, community banks, who saw deposit insurance as a way of preventing the enactment of branch banking legislation on a regional or national basis. At the federal level, the FDIC has, over the years, acted as the champion of the state banking system. Accordingly, while tending to be strict in its approach to examining and adhering to regulations, the FDIC has also taken much the same position as the Comptroller of the Currency in providing freedom for state-chartered banks to conduct a reasonably wide range of profitable banking activities.

The Board of Governors, on the other hand, is faced with entirely different considerations in its bank regulatory responsibilities. In the first place, the board has long been convinced that supervisory and regulatory authority is necessary for the intelligent conduct of monetary policy. But, of the three banking agencies, the board directly supervises and regulates the smallest number of banks. It can occupy a significant position in the regulatory business only as long as it has sole authority over bank holding companies. It is not surprising, therefore, that the Federal Reserve advocates the use of the holding company as the proper vehicle for bank expansion, nor is it surprising that both the present and immediate past chairmen of the FDIC have advocated repeal of the Bank Holding Company Act, claiming that it is unnecessary.

Probably the most important component of the Federal Reserve's regulatory philosophy is the concept that it must be free to conduct monetary policy without undue influence from the Treasury, Congress, or any other branch of government. This means that the board will rarely take a regulatory position or adopt a regulatory initiative that is expected to draw significant political opposition from the Congress. To illustrate, when the savings and loan industry had strong support in Congress, the Federal Reserve Board, for obviously political reasons, maintained that bank holding companies could not acquire savings and loan associations.

Similarly, while continually urging Congress to take action, the board delayed as long as possible the inevitable move by commercial banks into the investment banking business, through new interpretations of the Glass-Steagall Act. Even so, the board has proceeded cautiously by placing severe restrictions on this activity and only grudgingly easing them. The point, of course, is that as long as the Federal Reserve Board's highest priority is to maintain "independence within government," its regulatory policy will remain essentially conservative and will tend to avoid innovative ideas.

With the increasing internationalization of finance, all industrial nations will be pressed to harmonize fundamental regulatory principles. This is precisely what the EC Commission is attempting to do among its twelve member states and what the Basle Committee has done with respect to risk-based capital regulations. The linkage between U.S. regulation and developments in the rest of the world will become more important in the future.

The question of the moment is how Europe 1992 will affect the evolution of the existing bank regulatory structure in the United States. What, if anything, will happen to the balance of authority at the federal level? How might the federal-state relationship be changed?

A likely answer to the first question is that, once Europe 1992 takes effect, the Federal Reserve Board will move into a "first-among-equals" position within the federal structure, possibly even to a dominant position, with the other two agencies playing subsidiary roles. The OCC and FDIC could even become part of the Federal Reserve itself. This would be the logical course of events if the board takes on central bank responsibilities and an EC central bank plays an important role in the future.

The recently completed *Report on Economic and Monetary Union in the European Community*, also known as the Delors report, notes that management of the economic and monetary union would call for a "new monetary institution" in order to implement a single monetary policy (p. 21). This new institution, tentatively referred to as the European System of Central Banks (ESCB), would have four functions. Three of these are traditional for central banks (issuer of bank notes, implementer of monetary policy, lender of last resort), but the fourth is of utmost interest: "The System would participate in the coordination of banking supervision policies of the supervisory authorities." This wording reads much as if it had been provided by the Federal Reserve Board.

If Europe 1992 does establish an ESCB with responsibility for the coordination of the banking supervision policies, the Federal Reserve Board would seem to be the obvious candidate for the same job in the United States. The board could remind the U.S. Congress that it does not now have full control over U.S. banking supervision policies and, accordingly, would have "one hand tied behind its back" in international negotiations. Indeed, the Federal Reserve Board might remind Congress that a number of prestigious studies conducted in the past (such as that by the Commission on Money and Credit in 1961) have urged that all banking supervision be placed under the wing of the Federal Reserve Board.

If Congress were to agree, the Federal Reserve philosophy would likely shape the future of U.S. bank supervision and regulation, probably steering it in the direction of a more conservative attitude toward banking powers, an emphasis on holding company regulation, and continued separation of "banking and commerce." A large segment of the U.S. banking system would react favorably to such a prospect, which also runs counter to the universal banking spirit emanating from Europe. Such an expansion of Federal Reserve authority would likely add fuel to the persistent view, recently restated by Congressman Lee Hamilton (Democrat-Indiana), that the Federal Reserve Board should be made more accountable to the president.

Whatever the Fed's new philosophy, and whatever it did to accommodate other executive branch agencies, a major turf battle would erupt if it moved into a dominant position. Another development to add fuel to the fire would be the emerging influence of the Federal Deposit Insurance Corporation, which received significant new authority through FIRREA. Indeed, many experts are now questioning which agency—the

FDIC or the Federal Reserve Board—now occupies the dominant bank regulatory position in Washington. For their part, the FDIC and OCC are well aware that their powers may be reduced with the internationalization of regulation, as the history of U.S. representation on the Basle Committee strongly suggests.

At one time, the Federal Reserve fielded three representatives at Basle Committee meetings. The Comptroller of the Currency objected vigorously and was added, replacing one of the Federal Reserve Board representatives. But the FDIC was still excluded. Despite protests directed at Basle, no attention was paid to the FDIC, which finally resorted to the U.S. Congress. In 1983, as part of the International Lending Supervision Act, Congress specifically directed that the FDIC be represented on the Basle Committee.

In short, developments in the European Community may help bring to a peak a power struggle between the federal banking agencies that would have important implications for U.S. banks. As the European Community progresses toward monetary union and toward the establishment of a coordinating body for central banks (if not a single central bank), there may well be a resurgence of efforts to create a new super regulatory body for U.S. financial institutions, divorced from the central bank.

At the least, such a body would regulate all banks, probably all depository institutions, and possibly the SEC. Proposals of this kind have a long history in the United States. This very plan was advocated for many years by a governor of the Federal Reserve Board, J. L. Robertson, who was fond of pointing out that monetary policy responsibilities needed to be distinguished from bank regulation by saying that examiners should not be compelled to don "rose colored glasses or black glasses" depending on the monetary policy of the moment. This approach has been introduced on more than a few occasions in legislative form—for example, between 1975 and 1983, by former Senator William Proxmire (Democrat-Wisconsin), the chairman of the Senate Banking Committee, and in 1988 by Congressman Hamilton.

A single agency at the federal level in the United States, supervising and regulating all banking and securities institutions in the United States (or even just all depository institutions), would have broad implications for the conduct of financial business there. A great deal has been written on this subject, some of which expresses support for such a move because it promises to increase efficiency (for example, by eliminating overlapping jurisdictions), reduce regulatory costs for banks, and eliminate the so-called competition-in-laxity among the agencies. Opponents argue that the outcome would ensure stultifying federal regulation—and the demise of the dual banking system. All agree that the change to a single regulatory agency would be of first-order importance to the U.S. financial industry.

Some observers have already detected a slight shift in the balance between federal and state bank regulatory authority following the recent enactment of legislation to address the savings and loan crisis (FIRREA). State supervisory and regulatory officials fear that this may be a sign the United States is entering one of those periods when the federal government begins to flex its muscles and pull back from its traditional posture of delegating much of its bank supervisory responsibility to the states. If we are correct in assuming that Europe 1992 and monetary union will have a long-term effect on U.S. banking regulation, the uneasiness of state authorities is certainly warranted.

At least a hint that something may be in the wind can be found in the recent congressional testimony of David C. Mulford, Treasury under secretary for international affairs. Referring to the new reciprocity interpretation by the EC as a "club in the closet," Mr. Mulford noted that several states discriminate against EC banks, particularly when it comes to operating across state lines. Congress has long deferred to the states when it comes to rules affecting geographic expansion (that is, through multi-office banking), but in this case the under secretary commented: "It is true that a few individual U.S. states have practices which discriminate against foreign financial institutions. The Treasury Department has worked and will continue to work within the constraints of our federal system to change these practices."[35]

Several prominent state officials have expressed deep dissatisfaction at being excluded from the negotiations leading to risk-based capital regulations. "We were not even invited to the table," remarked one official. Since the state regulatory agencies supervise about two-thirds of all banks by number, holding perhaps 40 to 45 percent of all bank assets, why state authorities want to sit at future negotiating tables is obvious. It would not be surprising to find them going to the Congress for relief,

---

35. David C. Mulford, testimony before the Subcommittee on Financial Institutions Supervision, Regulation, and Insurance of the House Committee on Banking, Finance and Urban Affairs, September 28, 1989.

much as the FDIC did in 1983 when it was excluded from the Basle Committee.

Although the states have a great deal of political muscle when it comes to banking matters, at the moment their position is not strong. Rightly or wrongly, much of the blame for the S&L crisis has been placed on those state legislatures that gave great latitude to savings and loan associations. Whether the states will be able to convince others that it is not necessary for the central banks of the world to take responsibility for banking supervision is uncertain.

In the long run—the very long run in this instance—one could argue that the eventual demise of the dual banking system, which some see as inevitable (and others hope for), will be hastened by Europe 1992. Whether the U.S. banking system would be better or worse off as a result can be debated at considerable length and will not be addressed here. The purpose of this discussion is to draw attention to the fragmented supervisory structure of the financial system in the United States. Efforts in the past to achieve some rationalization and consolidation have foundered: first, because industry divisions have created a constituency within each agency that itself feels challenged; second, because agencies differ in their approach to regulation; and third, because many in the financial industry do not want to see the federal-state balance upset.

Sooner or later, Europe 1992 will compel the United States to speak with one voice on supervisory and regulatory issues that have bearing on international matters. This in turn will probably create pressure for changes in the U.S. regulatory structure. What those changes will be is not known; the most likely result would seem to be a more influential position for the Federal Reserve, but a small wager on the FDIC would not be imprudent.

### Competition among Financial Institutions

Two other pertinent questions about the future of U.S. financial institutions merit attention. How, if at all, will competition among banking organizations doing business in the United States be affected by Europe 1992? And what, if any, competitive opportunities will Europe 1992 make available for banking organizations headquartered in the United States?

In the short term, Europe 1992 will have little impact on competition among financial institutions within the United States. In the long term, the story will be different. On the simplest level, but in many ways the most important, the impact will be felt in the guise of changing customer demands on financial institutions. Although evidence of the increasing interest of U.S. firms in Europe 1992 is anecdotal, it is still impressive.

The largest U.S. financial organizations, most of them already doing a substantial business in Europe, are engrossed in devising ways to take advantage of the changes to come. The business press is filled with accounts of greenfield plants and acquisitions. The *Economist* (May 13, 1989) reports that in a survey by the Bank of Boston of 1,200 chief executive officers of manufacturing companies, 84 percent saw the prospect of expanded sales and 53 percent saw the need to alter their marketing and production strategies as a result of 1992.

One thing is clear: the business firms affected by Europe 1992 will not only be the customers of multinational financial institutions but also the customers of many other U.S. banks. One CEO of a major regional bank recently asked for an update on what is happening with respect to Europe 1992 "because my customers are beginning to ask us questions about it." Developments in the Community may be a large "yawn" for the overwhelming majority of U.S. banks today, but far fewer will be yawning tomorrow. They run a significant risk of losing important customers to the U.S. multinational banks, unless they learn to handle Europe 1992 themselves.

The competitive implications are particularly important for the regional banking organizations, notably the so-called superregionals. The consolidation movement among U.S. banking organizations is progressing rapidly, as more and more states grant bank holding company entry to out-of-state organizations, and is likely to accelerate as the United States approaches nationwide banking. Many states that are now members of regional state groups are planning to open their markets on a nationwide basis at specified dates, one of which (Indiana) happens to be the year 1992!

As a result, regional banking organizations are developing rapidly, sometimes seeming to appear out of nowhere. A number of banking organizations that were virtually unknown except in their own localities just five or ten years ago now equal or exceed the traditional money-center banks. For example, First Union, based in North Carolina, exceeds the Bank of New York and Chemical Bank in market capital; Barnett Banks, headquartered in Florida, has a greater market capital than First Interstate in Los Angeles, First Chicago, and Manufacturers Hanover.

Most, though not all, of the emerging regional banking organizations are focused on domestic business and are heavily retail-oriented. They have little or no presence in the European Community. But as they expand in size and develop, directly or through acquisitions, an important domestic customer base, some kind of presence in the European Community will become necessary. Those interests may coincide with the expansion plans of EC financial institutions seeking to gain retail markets in the United States. Community officials may see this as an opportune moment to flex their "reciprocity" muscle. A fascinating question is whether the U.S. regionals will ultimately be hobbled in their drive to unseat the traditional U.S. banking organizations by being "cut off at the pass" when the time comes for them to expand their wholesale activities into the European Community.

We noted earlier that Europe 1992 is a retail phenomenon; all that we have learned points to the development of large retail banking organizations (possessing securities powers) in the European Community following 1992. Furthermore, it looks as though EC-based institutions will quickly learn to match the abilities and aggressiveness of U.S. institutions engaged in the full range of investment banking activities. Meanwhile, the United States will probably adopt some form of universal banking in the not-so-distant future. If all this transpires, the U.S. financial market will look increasingly attractive to EC-based financial institutions, once the dust settles in the Community and attention turns to other markets.

Those EC-based institutions that are able to put together retail banking operations across the Community may well find the whole United States as tempting as Japanese banks have found California. The new group of EC-based institutions would certainly face barriers, not the least of which would be the reactions of the U.S. Congress. Nonetheless, Europe 1992 may bring large new competitors into the U.S. retail arena, operating in the United States but headquartered in Europe. These competitors would exert pressure on margin spreads and on the general profitability of retail banking throughout the United States.

If reciprocity issues are taken care of, what competitive opportunities will U.S.-headquartered financial institutions find in Europe after 1992? According to one banker, unless the United States thoroughly reorganizes its banking system and repeals the McFadden and Glass-Steagall acts, the more appropriate question is, "At what point does it become advantageous for a U.S.-based financial institution to consider changing its headquarters?" This question is of interest to only a few U.S. organizations. For virtually all other U.S.-based financial firms, the question remains, "What changes will Europe 1992 bring to this country?"

As stated earlier, in the short run the answer seems to be very few, except for the increased volume of business going to the multinational organizations. The prospects of doing a retail banking business in the Community nations with a single banking license would not seem attractive to many U.S. institutions. As best as we could learn from our conversations and interviews, the markets for retail business in the Community have already been divided up, either formally or informally. Only one U.S. organization was mentioned as a possible entrant— Citibank. Whether it intends to be a large retail player in the Community, and, if so, whether it will succeed, are questions on which we received a variety of answers.

Another question we asked is whether U.S.-based investment banking firms will be able to muster forces in the next several years to establish permanent lead positions in the wholesale banking markets of Europe. One official of a major U.S. investment banking firm suggested that this would not be possible unless U.S. firms obtained deposit-taking capabilities and then became full universal banks. Others disagreed with the importance of deposit taking. However, everyone agreed that U.S. companies doing an investment banking business in the Community currently enjoy decided advantages over their EC-based counterparts and probably will continue to do so over the near term.

One commercial banker suggested that there will be numerous opportunities in the Community for U.S. commercial banks, both on a wholesale and on a retail level, but that most of these opportunities will consist of discovering niches to be exploited, possibly in conjunction with EC-based institutions. The development of new retail products by U.S. commercial banking organizations may be a profitable way of gaining limited entry into these niches. In any case, those U.S. firms now doing a "wholesale" banking business in Europe will no doubt find a surging market for their services. Whether their current competitive strength will enable them to establish permanent positions in the Community nations is another matter.

The overwhelming majority of U.S. financial firms—particularly commercial banks—are heavily engaged in the retail banking business. Once

Europe 1992 is implemented, the EC is likely to witness the rise of large retail banking firms with considerable expertise and, eventually, expanded appetites for growth. The U.S. retail banking market is attractive. Hence U.S. banking organizations may find their already intensely competitive world becoming even more competitive.

APPENDIX 2–1. Adopted and Proposed EC Legislation on Banking, 1960–89

| Title | Year adopted and legal form | Aim | Comment |
|---|---|---|---|
| | | **Pre–1985 White Paper** | |
| Abolition of Restrictions | 1973; Directive 73/183/EEC | To abolish restrictions on freedom of establishment and freedom to provide services in respect of self-employed activities of banks and other financial institutions | The first directive to abolish restrictions on banking services; limited to certain services linked to capital movements. |
| First Banking Directive | 1977; Directive 77/780/EEC | To coordinate laws, regulations, etc., relating to the taking up and the pursuit of the business of credit institutions | Defined credit institutions, prescribed minimum capital requirements, and mandated supervisory cooperation between member nations. |
| Consolidated Supervision | 1983; Directive 83/350/EEC | To ensure that credit institutions are supervised on a consolidated basis | Specified that the accounts, exposure, and management of an institution must be reviewed annually on a consolidated basis. |
| | | **Post–1985 White Paper** | |
| Accounts of Banks | 1986; Directive 86/635/EEC | To harmonize the published accounts of banks and other financial institutions | Specified the format and contents of published accounts. |
| Large Exposures | 1987; Recommendation 87/62/EEC | To monitor and control large exposures of credit institutions | Recommended standards for controlling large exposures (15 percent or more of a credit institution's own funds); exposures to a single client not to exceed 40 percent of own funds; aggregate large exposures not to exceed 800 percent of own funds. |

| | | | |
|---|---|---|---|
| Deposit Guarantee | 1987; Recommendation 87/63/EEC | To list minimum requirements for deposit guarantee plans and to encourage such plans | Recommended compensation schemes to protect depositors from loss as a result of bank failure. |
| Electronic Payments | 1987; Recommendation 87/598/EEC; not a White Paper proposal | To establish a European Code of Conduct relating to electronic payments | Recommended proper relationships among financial institutions, business firms, and consumers. |
| Payment Systems | 1988; Recommendation 88/590/EEC; not a White Paper proposal | To establish the relationship between card issuers and cardholders | Recommended rules of conduct between card issuers and cardholders. |
| Second Banking Directive | 1989; Directive 89/646/EEC | To coordinate the laws and regulations relating to the taking up and pursuit of the business of credit institutions | Promoted a single banking market by building on the First Banking Directive of 1977: harmonization of essential supervisory rules; mutual recognition of other rules. A banking license from one supervisory authority will enable an institution to offer services throughout the EC. If permitted by its home country, the institution may engage in underwriting and securities activities throughout the EC. Establishment of an EC subsidiary by a non-EC institution will depend on the quality of reciprocity. |

APPENDIX 2–1 (*Continued*)

| Title | Year adopted and legal form | Aim | Comment |
|---|---|---|---|
| Bank Branch Accounts | 1989; Directive 89/117/EEC | To eliminate the need for publication of separate accounts by branches located outside their home state | Specified branches are to provide the consolidated accounts of their parents; branches with non-EC parents can be required to provide branch accounts. |
| Winding Up | Proposed directive, not yet adopted | To establish measures for the reorganization and winding up of institutions in trouble | Home country authorities would be responsible for reorganization and winding up. |
| Own Funds | 1989; Directive 89/299/EEC | To harmonize the definition of own funds (capital) | Proposed a standard minimum definition of bank capital compatible with the Basle Committee definition. |
| Mortgage Credit | Proposed directive, not yet adopted | To permit mortgage lenders to operate throughout the EC | Permitted EC-based mortgage lenders to raise funds and make loans in all EC countries; provided for close cooperation among supervisory authorities. |
| Solvency Ratios | 1989; Directive 89/647/EEC; not a White Paper proposal | To harmonize and strengthen solvency ratios among EC credit institutions | Proposed minimum capital ratio of 8 percent of risk-weighted assets for credit institutions. |

APPENDIX 2–2 (Continued)

| Title | Year adopted and legal form | Aim | Comment |
|---|---|---|---|
| | | **Pre–1985 White Paper** | |
| Admissions | 1979; Directive 79/279/EEC; amended by 82/148/EEC | To coordinate the conditions for the admission of securities to official stock exchange listing | Established minimum conditions for the admission of securities to official listing on stock exchanges in EC member nations. |
| Listing Particulars | 1980; Directive 80/390/EEC; amended by 82/148/EEC, 87/345/EEC | To harmonize listing particulars to be published for the admission of securities to official stock exchange listing | Coordinated the requirements for the drawing up, scrutiny, and distribution of the listing particulars to be published for the admission of securities to stock exchange listing. |
| Interim Reports | 1982; Directive 82/121/EEC | To require regular reports by companies whose securities have been admitted to official stock exchange listing | Required that investors must be supplied with adequate periodic information; complements Directives 79/279/EEC (Admissions) and 80/390/EEC (Listing Particulars); together these three directives establish the information that is to be provided for listed securities. |
| | | **Post–1985 White Paper** | |
| UCITs | 1985; Directive 85/611/EEC, amended by 88/220/EEC | To coordinate laws and regulations regarding UCITs (undertakings for collective investment in transferable securities) | Permitted UCITs, which include trusts similar to mutual funds, to be marketed throughout the EC on the basis of a single license. |

APPENDIX 2-2 *(Continued)*

| Title | Year adopted and legal form | Aim | Comment |
|---|---|---|---|
| Major Holdings | 1988; Directive 88/627/EEC | To coordinate policy regarding disclosure of changes in major share holdings | Required disclosure by persons who acquire or dispose of major share holdings in listed companies; threshold reporting levels are 10, 20, 33.3, 50, and 66.6 percent. |
| Prospectus | 1989; Directive 89/298/EEC; not a White Paper proposal | To ensure adequate disclosure of information concerning public offers of securities | Established requirements for the content of prospectuses for securities offered to the public; provided for mutual recognition of prospectuses. |
| Insider Trading | 1989; Directive 89/592/EEC; not a White Paper proposal | To harmonize rules on insider trading | Prohibited insiders from using inside information to buy and sell securities. |
| Securities Transaction Tax | Proposed directive, not yet adopted | To harmonize taxes on transactions in securities | Eliminated differences in securities transactions taxes. |
| Investment Services | Proposed directive, not yet adopted | To promote a single market in investment services | Allowed investment firms established in one EC member state to set up branches in other EC states (credit institutions providing investment services are not covered by this directive; they are covered by the Second Banking Directive); establishment of an EC subsidiary by a non-EC firm will depend on reciprocity. |

APPENDIX 2–3. Adopted and Proposed EC Legislation on Capital Movements, 1960–88

| Title | Year adopted and legal form | Aim | Comment |
|---|---|---|---|
| | | **Pre–1985 White Paper** | |
| First Directive | 1960; Directive of May 11, 1960; amended by 63/21/EEC, 85/583/ EEC, 86/566/EEC, 88/361/EEC | First directive for the implementation of Article 67 of the Treaty of Rome (Amendment 63/21/EEC of 1963 was especially noteworthy) | Liberalized capital movements, but extensive safeguard clauses enabled member nations to avoid implementation to a large extent. |
| Invisible Transactions | 1963; Directive 63/474/ EEC | To liberalize transfers in respect of invisible transactions not connected with the movement of goods, services, capital, or persons | Helped to liberalize such invisible transactions as banking charges, representation expenses, and overhead expenses between related companies. |
| International Capital Flows | 1972; Directive 72/156/ EEC, amended by 88/361/EEC | To regulate international capital flows and neutralize their undesirable effects on domestic liquidity | Recognized the right of national monetary authorities to discourage exceptionally large capital movements. |
| | | **Post–1985 White Paper** | |
| UCITs | 1985; Directive 85/583/ EEC | To liberalize capital movements for transactions in UCITs | Amended First Directive of 1960 on capital movements to include UCITs. |

APPENDIX 2–3 (*Continued*)

| Title | Year adopted and legal form | Aim | Comment |
|---|---|---|---|
| Certain Capital Transactions | 1986; Directive 85/566/ EEC | To liberalize certain capital transactions | Required member states to permit: long-term commercial credits; acquisitions of non-stock-exchange securities; and admission of securities to the capital markets. |
| Complete Liberalization | 1988; Directive 88/361/ EEC; effective July 1, 1990 | To remove all restrictions on capital movements | Obliged EC member states to abolish restrictions on the movement of capital between EC residents; capital transfers are to be made at the same exchange rates as those applying to current transactions; only temporary safeguards permitted in exceptional situations. |

## APPENDIX 2–4. Excerpt from Second Banking Directive: Definition of Banking Activities

These are businesses which are integral to banking and are to be included within the scope of mutual recognition:

1. Acceptance of deposits and other repayable funds from the public
2. Lending, including in particular: consumer credit; mortgage lending; factoring, with or without recourse; financing of commercial transactions (including forfeiting)
3. Financial leasing
4. Money transmission services
5. Issuing and administering means of payment (credit cards, travellers cheques and bankers drafts)
6. Guarantees and commitments
7. Trading for own account or for account of customers in:
   (a) money market instruments (cheques, bills, CDs, etc.)
   (b) foreign exchange
   (c) financial futures and options
   (d) exchange and interest rate instruments
   (e) securities
8. Participation in share issues and the provision of services related to such issues
9. Advice to undertakings on capital structure, industrial strategy and related questions and advice and services relating to mergers and the purchase of undertakings
10. Money broking
11. Portfolio management and advice
12. Safekeeping and administration of securities
13. Credit reference services
14. Safe custody services

## APPENDIX 2–5. Proposed Investment Services Directive: Definition of Investment Activities

### Section A: Activities

1. Brokerage, i.e., the acceptance of investors' orders relating to any or all of the instruments referred to in Section B below and/or the execution of such orders on an exchange or market on an agency basis against payment of commission.
2. Dealing as principal, i.e., the purchase and sale of any or all of the instruments referred to in Section B below for own account and at own risk with a view to profiting from the margin between bid and offer prices.
3. Market making, i.e., maintenance of a market in any or all of the instruments referred to in Section B below by dealing in such instruments.
4. Portfolio management, i.e., the management against payment of portfolios composed of any or all of the instruments referred to in Section B below undertaken for investors otherwise than on a collective basis.
5. Arranging or offering underwriting services in respect of issues of the instruments referred to in point 1 of Section B below and distribution of such issues to the public.
6. Professional investment advice given to investors on an individual basis or on the basis of private subscription in connection with any or all of the instruments referred to in Section B below.
7. Safekeeping and administration of any of the instruments referred to in Section B below otherwise than in connection with the management of a clearing system.

### Section B: Instruments

1. Transferable securities including units in undertakings for collective investment in transferable securities.
2. Money market instruments (including certificates of deposit and Eurocommercial paper).
3. Financial futures and options.
4. Exchange rate and interest rate instruments.

118

Chapter 3

# Automobiles

ALASDAIR SMITH & ANTHONY J. VENABLES

T HERE ARE three reasons for paying special attention to the
European car market in a general study of the effects of
Europe 1992. First, Europe's auto industry provides an important test
of the political viability of the Europe 1992 Program. Is the wide political
support for the general principles of the program strong enough to
overcome the considerable difficulties of actually creating a single market?
In the case of the European car market, harmonization of regulations
and standards, tax harmonization, and the control of state aid are all
proving contentious. External trade in automobiles faces even trickier
difficulties, although, oddly, the initial public discussion of the 1992
program almost totally neglected external trade implications.

Second, the car industry will test the underlying economic objective
of the 1992 program: to make the European Community more competitive
in the world economy. The health of the auto industry is not the sole
indicator of economic success, but the industry is important, and its
problems reflect more general problems in the European economy. The
fate of this industry in the post-1992 market may have wider implications
for the global competitiveness of the European Community.

Finally, the car industry provides a unique perspective on U.S.
interests in Europe 1992. Past U.S. involvement in the European auto
market has largely been in the form of foreign direct investment. Both
Ford and General Motors have long-established European operations
that apparently enjoy considerable independence from their U.S. parents
and that are now organized on a pan-European basis to a greater extent
than are Europe's own car producers. The impact of 1992 on Ford of

Alasdair Smith is professor of economics at the University of Sussex and co-director of
the International Trade Research Program at the Centre for Economic Policy Research.
Anthony J. Venables is Roll Professor of Economic Policy at the University of Southampton
and research fellow at the Centre for Economic Policy Research.

Europe and GM Europe is one of the principal issues addressed in this chapter. Because direct investment may become the dominant mode of U.S. involvement in many sectors in Europe, general lessons might be drawn from the particular case of the car industry.

But the interests of the United States in the European car market go beyond those of the European subsidiaries of the big two producers. Although U.S. car exports to Europe have been low, to the point of insignificance, they are now growing. Japanese "transplant" producers in the United States will probably seek to export to the European market, and the scale of their exports could dwarf existing export flows. This development in turn raises a set of key questions about the true nature of U.S. interests in the European car market. Since the interests of Honda are different from the interests of Ford, to which set of interests should the United States government give the higher priority? Specifically, should the United States allow an understanding between Brussels and Tokyo to regulate the flow of transplant exports from Ohio to Europe? To what extent is it sensible or useful to regard the interests of the European subsidiaries of U.S. multinationals, like Ford and GM, as U.S. interests? Are the interests of U.S. consumers in the substantial flow of car imports from Europe in danger of being ignored in discussions that focus on the interests of different groups of producers?

## The EC Automobile Market

The structure of the European car market is summarized in table 3-1, which shows the 1988 registration of passenger cars of producers in various European markets. The major producer groups are Volkswagen (West Germany), Fiat (Italy), Peugeot/Citroën and Renault (France), and Ford and General Motors (United States). The seventh row of the table groups together the registration figures of the smaller, more specialist, and mainly up-market producers: Volvo and Saab (Sweden), Mercedes and BMW (West Germany), and Jaguar and Rover (United Kingdom).[1] The last two rows give the registration data for Japanese producers and for all other producers, principally Korean and East European. The

1. These six producers make uneasy bedfellows. Rover is a former mass-market producer with ambitions to be an up-market specialist, but probably destined to be absorbed into Honda's European operations. In late 1989 Jaguar was taken over by Ford, and General Motors acquired a controlling stake in Saab, while in February 1990 Volvo and Renault agreed upon a partial merger.

FIGURE 3–1. European Car Market Shares, 1988

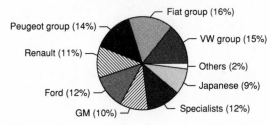

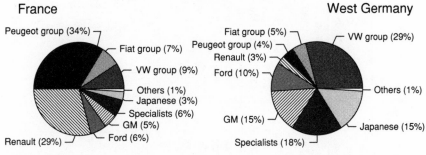

SOURCE: Same as table 3-1.

columns of the table refer to the different markets. The largest four European markets are separately identified, but to keep the table of manageable size, the other European markets are grouped as Iberia (Spain and Portugal), the rest of the European Community (Belgium, Denmark, Ireland, Greece, Luxembourg, and the Netherlands) and EFTA (European Free Trade Association countries: Austria, Finland, Norway, Sweden, and Switzerland).

The most striking feature of the data displayed in table 3-1 is that the sales pattern of different producers varies greatly across countries. Figure 3-1 contrasts the distribution of sales in the EC market as a whole with the distribution of sales in France and in West Germany. At the Community level the picture is one of six large groups, each with significant market shares but none dominant. For the French market alone, however, the picture changes dramatically, with the two French groups taking a commanding share of more than 60 percent of their home market. The West German market is a little less concentrated, with 53 percent of the market taken by Volkswagen, Ford, and General Motors (both U.S. multinationals produce in West Germany), and a further 16

TABLE 3–1. The European Car Market, 1988

| Producer | France | Germany | Italy | United Kingdom | Iberia[a] | Rest EC[b] | EC total | EFTA[c] | Western European total |
|---|---|---|---|---|---|---|---|---|---|
| | *Passenger car registrations (thousands)* | | | | | | | | |
| VW group | 189.7 | 825.2 | 255.6 | 130.2 | 223.1 | 149.5 | 1,773.3 | 164.1 | 1,937.4 |
| Fiat group | 160.5 | 132.0 | 1,308.5 | 82.8 | 123.6 | 61.1 | 1,868.5 | 60.7 | 1,929.3 |
| Peugeot group | 757.7 | 108.6 | 168.6 | 193.8 | 229.6 | 145.3 | 1,603.6 | 74.1 | 1,677.7 |
| Renault | 642.5 | 78.4 | 155.0 | 85.6 | 253.9 | 64.5 | 1,279.9 | 33.6 | 1,313.5 |
| Ford | 142.9 | 281.8 | 79.8 | 583.8 | 159.9 | 116.9 | 1,365.1 | 100.0 | 1,465.1 |
| GM | 106.6 | 430.1 | 71.5 | 303.6 | 182.9 | 141.8 | 1,236.4 | 122.3 | 1,358.6 |
| Specialists | 122.0 | 503.9 | 98.8 | 507.9 | 66.4 | 109.8 | 1,408.8 | 204.6 | 1,613.4 |
| Japanese | 66.0 | 425.8 | 19.9 | 252.7 | 26.9 | 305.8 | 1,097.0 | 369.6 | 1,466.6 |
| Others | 29.2 | 22.3 | 26.7 | 75.3 | 7.2 | 52.9 | 213.6 | 29.8 | 242.3 |
| TOTAL | 2,217.1 | 2,807.9 | 2,184.3 | 2,215.6 | 1,273.5 | 1,147.6 | 11,846.1 | 1,157.8 | 13,003.9 |
| | *Market shares (percent)* | | | | | | | | |
| VW group | 9 | 29 | 12 | 6 | 18 | 13 | 15 | 14 | 15 |
| Fiat group | 7 | 5 | 60 | 4 | 10 | 5 | 16 | 5 | 15 |
| Peugeot group | 34 | 4 | 8 | 9 | 18 | 13 | 14 | 6 | 13 |
| Renault | 29 | 3 | 7 | 4 | 20 | 6 | 11 | 3 | 10 |
| Ford | 6 | 10 | 4 | 26 | 13 | 10 | 12 | 9 | 11 |
| GM | 5 | 15 | 3 | 14 | 14 | 12 | 10 | 11 | 10 |
| Specialists | 6 | 18 | 5 | 23 | 5 | 10 | 12 | 18 | 12 |
| Japanese | 3 | 15 | 1 | 11 | 2 | 27 | 9 | 32 | 11 |
| Others | 1 | 1 | 1 | 3 | 1 | 5 | 2 | 2 | 2 |
| TOTAL | 100 | 100 | 100 | 100 | 100 | 100 | 100 | 100 | 100 |

|  | | | | | Producer shares (percent) | | | | |
|---|---|---|---|---|---|---|---|---|---|
| VW group | 10 | 43 | 13 | 7 | 12 | 8 | 92 | 8 | 100 |
| Fiat group | 8 | 7 | 68 | 4 | 6 | 3 | 97 | 3 | 100 |
| Peugeot group | 45 | 6 | 10 | 12 | 14 | 9 | 96 | 4 | 100 |
| Renault | 49 | 6 | 12 | 7 | 19 | 5 | 97 | 3 | 100 |
| Ford | 10 | 19 | 5 | 40 | 11 | 8 | 93 | 7 | 100 |
| GM | 8 | 32 | 5 | 22 | 13 | 10 | 91 | 9 | 100 |
| Specialists | 8 | 31 | 6 | 31 | 4 | 7 | 87 | 13 | 100 |
| Japanese | 4 | 29 | 1 | 17 | 2 | 21 | 75 | 25 | 100 |
| Others | 12 | 9 | 11 | 31 | 3 | 22 | 88 | 12 | 100 |
| TOTAL | 17 | 22 | 17 | 17 | 10 | 9 | 91 | 9 | 100 |

SOURCE: Automobile Industry Data Ltd., *1989 Car Yearbook*.
a. Spain and Portugal
b. Belgium, Denmark, Ireland, Greece, Luxembourg, and The Netherlands.
c. European Free Trade Association countries: Austria, Finland, Norway, Sweden, and Switzerland.

percent by Mercedes and BMW (who account for almost all of the specialist car sales in Germany). Despite their common border and the customs union to which both have belonged for more than thirty years, France and Germany have sales patterns with virtually nothing in common. Nor are these two countries special cases. Table 3-1 shows similarly idiosyncratic sales patterns in the Italian and U.K. markets.

As strong as the national bias in purchasing patterns is, it is less pronounced than it was in the past. In the mid-1950s the major European markets all had domestic producers' shares in excess of 90 percent.[2] National purchasing patterns could, of course, reflect genuine differences in national tastes rather than barriers to intra-European trade. Italian and German car buyers may have different needs, and Fiat's model range may reflect the needs of Italian consumers while the Mercedes range responds to German taste. However, the wide differences among the prices of identical cars in different EC member states show that there continue to be barriers to intra-EC trade in cars.[3] Although the past three decades have seen a considerable growth in international trade in cars within Western Europe as all tariff and some nontariff barriers have fallen, the market is still a long way from being a single market.

There is another way of looking at the European market asymmetries. Not only does the Fiat group command a large share of the Italian market, the Italian market absorbs a large share of Fiat's output: 68 percent of the Fiats sold in Western Europe are sold in Italy. Similarly, 45 percent of Peugeot's sales and 49 percent of Renault's sales in Western Europe are actually in France. These numbers imply that these three producers are vulnerable to changes affecting their home markets.

The pattern of national markets dominated by national champion producers is broken by the two U.S. multinational producers. Ford established a plant in England in 1911 and several plants elsewhere in Europe (including Germany) in the decade after 1919, while General Motors acquired the English manufacturer Vauxhall in 1925 and Adam Opel of Germany in 1929. Both producers also own substantial production facilities in other EC member states: Ford in Spain, Belgium, and France; GM in Spain and Austria. It was only in the 1970s and 1980s that Ford

---

2. Yves Bourdet, *International Integration, Market Structure and Prices* (London: Routledge, 1988), p. 61.

3. Bureau Européen des Unions de Consommateurs (BEUC), *Car Prices and Progress Towards 1992*, report for the EC Directorate-General for the Environment, Consumer Protection, and Nuclear Safety (Brussels, October 15, 1989).

and GM integrated their operations on a Europe-wide basis starting with the establishment of Ford of Europe in 1967.

The European producers too are becoming multinationals, although far less so than Ford and GM. Volkswagen has a controlling interest in SEAT of Spain; Peugeot and Renault have Spanish production; and Peugeot, having taken over Chrysler's European operations, produces in Britain.[4]

Alliances are an important feature of the world motor industry. Appendix 3-1 lists important mergers and acquisitions, joint ventures, and cooperative agreements affecting the major European producers. These alliances point to the possibility that increased competition in the post-1992 European car market need not force some producers out of business. An alternative is more cooperation and joint ventures (see chapter 6).

Another striking feature of table 3-1, the differing Japanese share of individual European markets, reflects distinct national policies on imports from Japan. The Community's common external tariff on cars is set at a rate of 10.3 percent (compared with 3 percent in the United States and zero in Japan). Quantitative restrictions imposed by various EC member states, however, imply that the Community is far from having a common external trade policy. Spain virtually prohibits imports of Japanese cars. Italy has a quota limit of 2,300, although 14,000 more cars are imported through other EC countries. Since 1977 an industry-to-industry voluntary export restraint agreement has limited Japanese producers to 11 percent of the U.K. market. A voluntary restraint agreement between the Japanese industry and the French government limits the Japanese to 3 percent of the French market. The EC markets aggregated in table 3-1 as the "Rest of the EC" have essentially no limits on Japanese imports, which took 26 percent of these markets in 1988. Similarly, the largely unrestricted EFTA market has a Japanese share of 32 percent.[5]

Japanese imports into the German market pose a minor puzzle. As the Japanese market share grew rapidly at the end of the 1970s, the German government put pressure on the Japanese to moderate the rate

4. The Peugeot and Renault plants in Spain, like Ford and GM's Spanish operations, may have been established to get access to the protected Spanish market.

5. One qualification to the statement that EFTA markets have no restrictions on Japanese imports is that the Swedish government has put pressure on the Japanese to limit their sales in Sweden. There is also anecdotal evidence of restraint of Japanese sales in Belgium.

of growth of their sales to Germany. Although the pressure was temporary, the Japanese share of the German market has been constant at almost 15 percent since 1986, a fact that gives rise to the suspicion that imports are unilaterally restrained by the Japanese producers. Another puzzle is the monitoring by the Ministry of International Trade and Industry (MITI), at the request of the Commission, of Japanese sales to the European Community as a whole.[6] Because Japanese sales to Britain, France, Italy, and Spain are subject to national trade restrictions, and because the Japanese share of the "Rest of the EC" market is large and shows little evidence of sales restraint by the Japanese, there is little scope for EC-wide monitoring to have a real effect, except through restraint in sales to Germany. Perhaps the two puzzles are related: do the Japanese moderate their German sales to comply with a perceived need to moderate sales to the European Community as a whole?

Japanese transplants have been slower to appear in the European market than in the United States, but they have now arrived. In 1986 Nissan established a plant in England that produced 56,000 cars in 1988. Expansion is planned to raise capacity to 200,000 cars a year by 1992 and to 400,000 by the end of the century. In 1989 Toyota announced plans for a plant, also in England, with an initial capacity of 100,000 cars a year by 1995, rising to 200,000 within two or three years. Honda plans an English facility with an output of 100,000 cars a year by 1994, in addition to a collaborative arrangement with Rover for the production of 40,000 Honda cars at a Rover plant. Both Toyota and Honda also have plans for new engine plants in England.[7] Comparing these numbers with the data in table 3-1 shows that the already announced Japanese transplant capacity in the United Kingdom amounts to 3 to 4 percent of the total EC market for cars.

Japanese firms have several possible motives for the establishment of transplants in Europe. First, the transplants provide a means of circumventing restrictions on imports from Japan. Second, they bring the Japanese producers closer to the markets and should help them to be more responsive to local tastes. Third, they provide producers with a

6. "Japan Automakers Agree to Restrain Exports to EC," *Wall Street Journal*, April 6, 1989.

7. Kevin Done and Ian Rodger, "Honda Chooses U.K. for First European Car Assembly Plant," *Financial Times*, July 14, 1989, p. 1; David E. Sanger, "Honda Raises Its Stake in Europe," *New York Times*, July 14, 1989, p. D1; and Kevin Done, "Japanese Springboard," *Financial Times*, September 13, 1989, p. vi.

FIGURE 3–2. The Changing Structure of World Car Production, 1960 and 1986

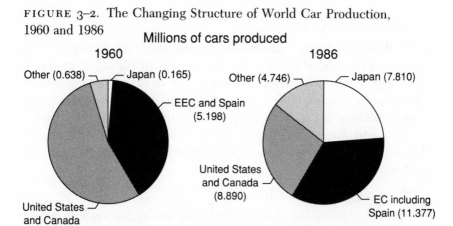

Millions of cars produced

SOURCES: Organization for Economic Cooperation and Development, *Long Term Outlook for the World Automobile Industry* (Paris, 1983), p. 26; and Society of Motor Manufacturers and Traders, *Motor Industry of Great Britain, 1987: World Automotive Statistics* (London, 1987), table 1.

measure of insurance against the risk of exchange rate swings, balancing revenues in European currencies with production costs in European currencies rather than in yen. It remains to be seen to what extent transplant production will substitute for direct imports. The U.S. experience has been that transplant production supplements rather than substitutes for imports.

Finally, it is important to see the European car market in the context of changes in the world trade pattern in cars. Figure 3-2 shows how the distribution of world production changed between 1960 and 1986.[8] The rise in the Japanese share of world production has been largely at the expense of American rather than European producers. West European sales to the rest of the world and to North America have declined somewhat as Japanese competition in these markets has grown. But European production has grown more or less in step with the growth of the European market. By contrast, in North America the growth of the market has been met almost entirely by increased imports. The key issue for the European industry over the next twenty-five years is whether its former pattern of growth can be maintained in the face of Japanese competition.

8. See the figure for production data sources. The information about the relationship among production, sales, and exports comes from Kevin Done, "The Complicated Global Square Dance," in Survey of the World Car Industry, *Financial Times*, September 13, 1989, p. xiv.

## 1992 and Beyond

Of the different interpretations of Europe 1992, the narrowest takes the text of the 1985 White Paper as the agenda. At the other extreme is an interpretation that embraces every aspect of the continuing process of European economic integration, whether or not linked to the White Paper. Without going so far as to endorse the latter view, we find it necessary to discuss, in addition to the White Paper agenda, several issues that are outside the strict letter of the White Paper agenda but within its spirit.

### The Strict 1992 Agenda

The single European market is to be created by the implementation of a broad range of deregulatory measures aimed at reducing the cost of cross-border transactions. For cars the aim of the 1992 program is to remove the barriers that create nationalistic sales patterns. Three items on the 1992 agenda are of particular relevance to the car industry: the harmonization of technical regulations, the harmonization of value-added and excise taxes, and the control of state aid to industry.

The first item on the 1992 agenda is the harmonization of technical regulations, standards, and testing. At present cars sold in the European Community have to satisfy national regulations that vary markedly from country to country. Harmonization of regulations should reduce costs by allowing greater standardization of production and by permitting access to all Community markets on the basis of a single battery of tests.[9]

9. An auto sector study, by Ludvigsen Associates, conducted as part of the Commission's research program on the cost of non-Europe, does not directly address the question of the costs of different regulatory standards. It identifies some potentially "substantial" cost savings from such changes as technical harmonization and simplification of type approval, but points out that there is already a tendency in the European industry to standardize features even where regulatory requirements are not standardized. Ludvigsen Associates, *The EC 92 Automobile Sector, Research on the "Cost of Non-Europe": Basic Findings*, vol. 11 (Luxembourg: EC Commission, 1988). The Commission's own study states that "the formal barriers to intra-Community trade in the car industry turn out to have a relatively marginal impact." Michael Emerson and others, "The Economics of 1992: An Assessment of the Potential Economic Effects of Completing the Internal Market of the European Community," *European Economy*, no. 35 (Luxembourg, March 1988), p. 74. By contrast the Commission's Cecchini report cites research undertaken for Ford of Europe as finding that the costs of differing national standards in Europe were very large. Paolo Cecchini and others, *The European Challenge 1992: The Benefits of a Single Market* (Aldershot, Eng.: Wildwood House for the Commission, March 1988), p. 27. It is, however, plain that the cost saving per car will be much more significant for products with low sales levels than for mass-market products.

The attempt, starting in 1970, to replace national regulations with Community-wide whole vehicle type approval (WVTA) required agreement on forty-four specific items. Agreement on forty-one was achieved, but the remaining three have been held up for twelve years. The three items are of no great significance or difficulty in themselves, being concerned with weights and dimensions, glass, and tires, and the delay appears to be a result of industry (particularly French industry) fears that EC WVTA would increase external competition. WVTA is, in essence, being held hostage to the settlement of external trade policy. This was confirmed by the statement in the November 1988 Commission progress report on the implementation of the White Paper that "the introduction of Community type approval, which is essential to free movement, depends on the formulation of a common commercial policy in this sector" (p. 16). The WVTA agenda is supposed to be wrapped up in 1990, but it may take longer if external trade policy remains unresolved.[10] An important question is whether national regulations and EC regulations will coexist, in effect allowing producers a choice between regulators; the Commission currently proposes to forbid the continued existence of national regulations.[11]

A further set of regulatory problems was raised by the attempt to harmonize exhaust regulations. Here the problem was the existence of perceived conflicts of interest between member states. EC member states without significant local production pushed for relatively demanding standards; others pressed for standards that potentially could be met with "lean-burn" engine technology, rather than with expensive catalytic converters; and a third group was particularly concerned at the disproportionate cost of catalytic converters in small cars. In the event, agreement was reached in 1989 that small cars should meet U.S. emissions standards, an agreement that will require the installation of catalytic converters. An earlier agreement on large and medium-sized cars was revised so that the same set of U.S. standards should apply to all market segments. Even though the European Community has adopted U.S. standards, European testing procedures will differ from those in the United States, and there is no expectation of agreement between the

10. Kevin Done and William Dawkins, "Giving the Green Light to Japan," *Financial Times*, July 3, 1989, p. 6; and Bruce Barnard, "EC Acts to Lift Japan Car Quotas," *Journal of Commerce*, December 7, 1989, pp. 1A, 5A.

11. William Dawkins, "End of Trade Curbs in Sight," *Financial Times*, September 13, 1989, p. x.

United States and the Community on the mutual recognition of test results.

The second item on the 1992 agenda is the harmonization of rates of value-added tax and excise taxes. As displayed in appendix 3-2, tax rates on car purchases differ significantly between EC member states. Excise taxes on gasoline also differ significantly. Fiscal harmonization is a more complex issue in the car market than in other markets because of the special sales or registration taxes applied to cars in many European markets. The Commission is testing the legality of some of these taxes by taking action against EC governments in the European Court. Nonetheless, elimination or harmonization of these taxes was not on the original White Paper agenda. Differences between the special taxes from state to state mean that if fiscal harmonization is confined to VAT and excise taxes, the major source of fiscal distortions would remain untouched. The Commission's current proposals for the European car market include case-by-case action to deal with such taxes.[12]

Tax differences, whether VAT, excise, or special taxes, give rise to two kinds of costs. In the first place, high taxes, whether on cars or on fuel, tend to make consumers buy cheaper cars, especially when taxes are disproportionately high on larger cars (which is not uncommon). In addition, different tax rates affect the product range that firms offer to the market, not only raising prices, but also distorting consumer choices. In the second place, tax differences lead to the administrative cost of border tax adjustments—rebating VAT already paid in the country of production and imposing VAT at the rate appropriate to the country of importation. The EC-1992 agenda calls for the abolition of all such border adjustments.

The difficulty with removing border tax adjustments is that EC member states with high tax rates will lose revenue as consumers make their purchases in member states with lower tax rates. The high-tax states would then come under pressure to reduce their tax rates. The Commission now proposes to avoid this problem in the car market by imposing a VAT, at the appropriate national rate, at the point of vehicle registration, just as the special car taxes are imposed. This proposal will help ease the direct pressure on government revenues, but cross-border shopping in other durable goods in the same tax category as cars will keep up the pressure to harmonize rates.

12. Done and Dawkins, "Giving the Green Light," p. 6.

Anything the Commission does to protect the revenue of high-tax states will, unfortunately, increase consumer price differences between member states, differences that can already be quite wide. When cross-border shopping is difficult, firms tend to set lower pre-tax prices in high-tax markets such as Denmark. If, however, it becomes possible for West German consumers to buy at the lower Danish pre-tax prices and then pay tax at the West German rate, firms will respond by narrowing the dispersion of pre-tax prices, and the intra-Community spread of post-tax prices will increase. In short, differences in national tax rates inevitably imply costly distortions. Although alternative rules can shift the incidence of the distortion, no set of rules about the tax treatment of goods that cross borders can eliminate all distortions if underlying tax rates differ.

The previous Commission sought to tackle the problem of fiscal harmonization by setting bands that would confine differences in EC member state tax rates. The new approach outlined above for cars takes a more laissez-faire view, relying on "fiscal competition" to harmonize rates, much the same way that mutual recognition of standards leads to harmonization of national standards through regulatory competition (see chapter 1). At the time of writing, it is not clear whether this new approach to a tricky set of issues will succeed. Since the high-tax countries will already be facing the loss of tax revenue for almost all goods other than cars, it is fair to predict that they will doubly resist the elimination or harmonization of the special car taxes. Moreover, most of the countries with high tax rates import all of their cars. For them, the sales taxes are effectively import taxes whose reduction could have painful balance of trade effects, yet another obstacle to the harmonization.

The third item on the 1992 agenda, state aid, is important because of the long history of European state involvement in the car industry. In recent years, debts have been written off at SEAT by the Spanish government, at the Rover Group by the British government, and, most recently, at Renault by the French government. Debt write-offs are only part of the story; producers also receive state aid in the form of regional development assistance. Both forms of aid can distort the market. As Jan Candries, director of European Affairs for Ford of Europe, argued in October 1987:

This massive selective state aid is promoting market distortions and thereby retarding progress toward the establishment of a true "Common Market" for cars in Europe. This arises because such aid, for example, enables some competitors to avoid the need to:

—price vehicles on a normal commercial basis

—generate adequate funds for future product and manufacturing investments

—close uneconomic manufacturing facilities, thus adding to Europe's overcapacity problem.

In a properly functioning free market in Europe, the European car industry would today look very different—for example, some competitors would probably have gone bankrupt, most would either be selling considerably less or considerably more products than they do now, their current product line-ups would most likely be different and more realistic prices would be charged in some continental markets.

The situation in France provides an excellent example of the disruptive effects of such aid.[13]

The Commission has restricted debt write-offs for Rover and Renault, and, since January 1989, has required Commission approval for all state aid for projects whose value exceeds ECU 12 million.

The case of Renault is the most difficult so far. In March 1988 the Commission and the French government agreed on conditions associated with government aid to Renault of Fr. 20 billion, of which 12 billion was a debt write-off. The conditions included a change in Renault's legal status from the "regie" status that protected it from bankruptcy and a cut in its production capacity. In November 1989 the Commission, alleging that the French government had failed to stick to the agreement, set a three-month deadline for compliance.[14] The eventual outcome of the dispute may provide a test of the effectiveness of the Commission's policy on state aid. The dispute between the Commission and the French government is not the only test faced by the Community on state aid: in West Germany EC control is seen as infringing on the constitutional rights of the state governments within the German federal system, while the Spanish government objects to limitations on its control over industrial policy.

13. Jan F. Candries, "Automotive Industry View of the Single European Act," presentation to the conference "Single European Act: Make or Brake," organized by the EC Committee of the American Chamber of Commerce in Belgium, Brussels, October 20, 1987.

14. Lucy Kellaway and William Dawkins, "EC Threatens France over State Aid," *Financial Times*, November 16, 1989, p. 32.

## Beyond the White Paper Agenda

Besides the harmonization of special car taxes, other important car-related issues that lie outside the strict 1992 agenda are the "block exemption" of exclusive dealerships in cars from the provisions of Article 85 of the Treaty of Rome (see chapter 6), currency integration, and the social dimension of integration. The treatment of quantitative import restrictions falls partly in the "strict 1992" category and partly in the "beyond 1992" category, but it is of such importance as to require separate discussion.

The Commission's study of the economics of 1992 pointed out that the costs of a segmented European market are not only the direct costs to producers and consumers of regulatory, fiscal, and other border barriers, and the distorting effects of state aid, but also the indirect effects that such barriers have on reducing competition.[15] In the case of the car market, much attention has been given to the price differences in the different national markets within the European Community.[16] Consumer interest groups, notably the Bureau Européen des Unions de Consommateurs (BEUC), argue that the price differences are the result of monopolistic behavior on the part of producers. Firms argue that the differences arise from tax differences, exchange rate variations, and demand differences. In fact, a price differential requires both an underlying economic cause and a market structure that permits it to be maintained. To go back to our earlier example, the coexistence of high car tax rates in Denmark and low tax rates in Germany gives producers an incentive to charge lower pre-tax prices in Denmark than in Germany, but producers can act on those incentives only if barriers restrict cross-border purchasing by consumers. In this context it is of some importance whether national regulations are permitted to coexist with EC regulations: if they are, then firms may have an incentive to produce differently specified vehicles to satisfy different national regulations in order to enable them to continue to segment their markets.

15. Emerson and others, *Economics of 1992*, chaps. 7, 9.
16. In Thomas Wieser, "Price Differentials in the European Economic Space (EES)," Occasional Paper 29, European Free Trade Association (Geneva, August 1989), it is shown that the dispersion of prices between national markets in the EC is much higher for motor vehicles than for almost all other traded goods. The only other categories of traded goods with comparable dispersions are pharmaceuticals, a tightly regulated market, and books, magazines and newspapers, where there are obvious linguistic and cultural barriers to cross-border trade.

If tax harmonization and other EC-1992 measures succeed to the point that it becomes almost as easy for consumers to buy cars in another Community member state as in their home state, then firms' pricing behavior would change. Instead of having a certain amount of freedom to set prices in individual country markets, they would see themselves as setting prices for the European market as a whole. The implications of this change should be seen against the background of the asymmetrical sales patterns for cars described earlier. When firms see the Italian market as separate from other European markets, they will set their prices in Italy knowing that the Fiat group has a dominant share of the Italian market: other firms will be wary of competing too aggressively against Fiat, and Fiat itself will, therefore, not have to compete aggressively. The same is true in the other national markets where there are clear market leaders. If, however, firms look at the European Community as a single market, they will see a structure in which there are several firms with market shares of less than 16 percent and no firm with a position in the single market comparable even to that of Ford in the United Kingdom or of Volkswagen in Germany, much less to that of Peugeot in France and Fiat in Italy.

With the far more even distribution of market power likely to encourage more competitive pricing strategies, price cutting and the consequent restructuring of production could have effects well beyond the direct effects of the removal of the border barriers.[17] Evidence supporting the proposition that integration can lead to changes in the pricing behavior of firms is provided by a study that showed that EC-wide concentration is becoming more important than national concentration in determining price-cost margins.[18]

The block exemption of exclusive car dealerships from the antitrust provisions of Article 85 of the Rome Treaty has the effect of segmenting the European car market. At present, car dealership areas do not cross national boundaries. The mere fact that they do not would not necessarily

---

17. In a similar manner, EC restrictions on state aid could have a pro-competitive indirect effect. State aid to national champions may deter other firms from competing aggressively if they feel the national champions can dip into the public purse to maintain their market position. Restrictions on state aid may therefore increase competition.

18. Leo Sleuwaegen and Hideki Yamawaki, "The Formation of the European Common Market and Changes in Market Structure and Performance," *European Economic Review*, vol. 32 (September 1988), pp. 1451–75. The phenomenon was found in geographically integrated markets, excluding such sectors as cement products where studies of United States markets had found evidence of geographic fragmentation.

permit market segmentation; but if consumers lack confidence that warranties will be honored on cars bought from foreign dealers, or face bureaucratic difficulties in registering cars bought across the border, then the exclusive dealership arrangements can help to maintain national price differentials.[19] It is possible that when the block exemption comes up for review in 1995, the Commission will seek to modify it to facilitate cross-border purchasing. However, the producers, who see exclusive dealerships as protecting the character of their products, will argue for their retention in some form.[20]

A still more obvious barrier to cross-border purchasing is the existence of different national currencies subject, in the case of the pound sterling, to unlimited daily exchange rate fluctuations against other EC currencies, or, in the case of the currencies within the exchange rate mechanism of the European Monetary System, to limited daily fluctuations and occasional realignments. Progress toward European monetary union would surely encourage consumers and producers to see the European market as a single market and permit the realization of the indirect gains from competition.

Another important issue beyond the strict 1992 agenda is the "social dimension" of the single market. Pressure to harmonize social provisions and workers' rights inevitably operates in the direction of upward harmonization. One of the advantages to producers of pan-European operation is the ability to shift production between locations as relative costs of production change. Harmonization of social legislation and pan-European trade unions will erode that advantage. Specifically, it could become somewhat less attractive to locate new plants in low-cost Spain and the United Kingdom, as against high-cost Germany.

## Europeanization of the Japanese Quotas

Restrictions on Japanese car imports into several European markets vary widely. Some are official quotas, some are unofficial "gray area"

19. Centre de Recherche et d'Information des Organisations de Consommateurs Belgique, *Les Prix des Automobiles dans Six Pays de la C.E.E.* (Brussels, January 1989), discusses in section 3 the difficulties that consumers can face when attempting to import cars across borders within the European Community. See also BEUC, *Car Prices and Progress Towards 1992,* sec. 3.

20. See the discussion of the issue of interbrand and intrabrand competition in chapter 6.

restrictions, some limit the level of imports, and some limit the market share of imports. For simplicity, we refer to all the limits as quotas.

The principal effects of quotas on Japanese car imports are straightforward. Car prices to consumers in restricted markets are higher, so consumers lose. European producers enjoy larger market shares, and the combined effect of higher prices and larger shares will benefit European producers. The prices of Japanese cars rise most, however, benefiting Japanese producers by offsetting their loss of market share.

Import restrictions also have subtler effects on the nature of competition in the car market. When Japanese firms face import restrictions, European firms know that an important group of their competitors faces limitations on their ability to compete. European firms can then set prices higher than they would if they had to worry about their Japanese competitors cutting prices to increase sales. Because the Japanese industry itself administers the restrictions, new Japanese firms are unlikely to enter the market. Thus a quantitative restriction on imports has an inherently anticompetitive nature. Import restraints on Japanese firms tend to push prices up, not just because of the direct effect of fewer cars on the market, but also because European firms have less incentive to be aggressive competitors.

## The End of National Quantitative Restrictions?

National trade policies are incompatible with the single market program. Since, for example, Belgium has no quota, France can maintain the effectiveness of its quota only by stopping the supply of Japanese cars to the French market through Belgian intermediaries. The obvious mechanism is a border inspection, though national quotas could be enforced at the point of registration rather than the point of import. The point is that any mechanism to support the quota must impede the free circulation of goods within the Community. This is not to say that national quotas must be abolished to prepare the way for a single European market for cars; rather, measures to establish a single market will eventually make national quotas ineffective and irrelevant.

The 1985 White Paper calls for the abolition of national quotas and the associated Article 115 border inspections. Technically speaking, this call has limited application to the car market, since the French and U.K. restrictions on Japanese imports are "gray area" measures not entitled to Article 115 support. It was reported early in 1989, however, that the Commission was setting aside such ambiguities and taking the straightforward view that the national restrictions on Japanese car imports are incompatible with the single market program:

> The Commission appears to have reached a surprising unanimity in the past couple of months that national import quotas can play no part in the single market post-1992, although officials privately accept that some form of transition period will have to be granted to countries such as Italy and France. . . . [Commissioner Bangemann] will discuss [with the countries that have quotas] a timetable for ending the quotas—the Commission's opening bid is the end of 1992—as well as the operation of a transitional monitoring system of Japanese imports.[21]

Removing national import quotas, however, does not pose a problem for *all* interest groups in such countries as France and Italy: there can be no doubt of the benefits to consumers in those markets from trade liberalization. Rather the difficulties are for the French and Italian producers whose sales are heavily concentrated in their home markets, markets that will be opened up to the Japanese. The question then arises whether there should be a Community-wide restriction on Japanese car imports to replace the defunct national restrictions, in order to protect European producers from the effects of open competition.

A related question is whether opening the Community market to Japanese imports should be made conditional on reciprocal liberalization of the Japanese market. The previous Commission took the line that the 1992 program should not be allowed to lead to unilateral trade liberalization. As Commissioner Willy De Clercq put it in a speech to the Europaeisches Forum on August 29, 1988, "Where international obligations do not exist . . . we see no reason why the benefits of our internal liberalization should be extended unilaterally to third countries. We shall be ready and willing to negotiate reciprocal concessions with third countries."[22]

Although De Clercq's statement was not directed specifically at the issue of national quotas, the logic of his argument implies that the national auto import restrictions should be replaced by EC-wide restrictions in the absence of negotiated reciprocal concessions from Japan. The reference to international obligations, however, is important, since it is not self-

21. Done and Dawkins, "Giving the Green Light," p. 6.

22. Michael Calingaert, *The 1992 Challenge from Europe: Development of the European Community's Internal Market* (Washington: National Planning Association, 1988), p. 120.

evident that the replacement of national "gray area" restrictions by equally "gray" EC-wide restrictions can be regarded as compatible with international obligations.

The European industry has pressed for strict reciprocity, with both the Coordinating Council of European Car Manufacturers and the Committee of Common Market Car Makers seeking a firm limit of 10 percent on the Japanese share of the EC market until 1997, or until the European share of the Japanese car market is substantially increased.[23] Jacques Calvet, president of Peugeot-Citroën, urged on December 6, 1989, that Japanese sales in the Community not be permitted to exceed twice the number of European cars sold in Japan.[24] While Commissioners Martin Bangemann, Leon Brittan, and Frans Andriessen are reported to be unsympathetic to this viewpoint, Commission President Jacques Delors has announced the deliciously ambiguous intention "to have discussions with Japan to reach a good agreement between better imports and exports."[25] According to a July 1989 *Financial Times* report, however, "The European car makers' calls for a freeze of Japanese imports and for reciprocity from Tokyo in terms of improved market access for European cars to the Japanese market have received short shrift in Brussels."[26]

On the question of an EC-wide quota, U.S. Trade Representative Carla Hills expressed the view of the United States before a congressional committee in May 1989:

EC 1992 should reduce the level of protectionism in the EC and not substitute Community-wide restrictions for existing national restrictions (in areas such as automobiles). . . . Our position is that the 1992 package cannot be the excuse for new external trade barriers, and we have repeatedly made known our intention to challenge any new barriers in the GATT should they be introduced by the Community.[27]

23. Hans Glatz, secretary general of the Coordinating Council of European Car Manufacturers (CLCA), was quoted in *Europe-1992*, vol. 1 (May 24, 1989), as lobbying for a 10 percent limit on Japanese imports up to 1997. François Perrin-Pelletier, secretary general of the Committee of Common Market Car Makers (CCMC), reportedly wants a firm quota on Japanese auto imports after 1992. See Done and Dawkins, "Giving the Green Light," p. 6.

24. Lucy Kellaway and William Dawkins, "Brussels Says Japan Must Curb Car Exports," *Financial Times*, December 7, 1989, p. 2.

25. Keith M. Rockwell, "EC's Delors to Press Japan to Restrain Auto Exports," *Journal of Commerce*, June 16, 1989, p. 3A.

26. Done and Dawkins, "Giving the Green Light," p. 6.

27. Carla Hills, statement before the Senate Finance Committee, May 10, 1989.

Like the EC pronouncements, this statement is not without its ambiguities. It is not entirely clear what kinds of substitution of Community trade policies for national trade policies would be regarded by Ambassador Hills as constituting new external trade barriers.

Whatever the views of Commissioner Bangemann and Ambassador Hills, it can be expected that car producers, working with the French and Italian governments, will continue to fight for a long transitional period, for firmer EC-wide restrictions on Japanese imports to replace the national restrictions, and for a more aggressive line on reciprocal concessions for European imports in the Japanese market.

The key problem for the Community is that abolishing national restrictions could increase the share of Japanese imports as high as 20 to 25 percent (not allowing for the inevitable flow of cars produced by Japanese transplants). Such a tide of imports would cause severe adjustment problems, at least for the French and Italian producers, and cushioning these adjustments is a legitimate aim of Community policy; hence the temptation to replace the national trade restrictions with an EC-wide quota.

Such a quota, however, may be less attractive than it appears at first sight. In the first place it will reduce Japanese sales in European markets that presently have no quota, and impose substantial costs on consumers in these markets. An EC-wide quota will also confer unambiguous benefits on the Japanese producers, who will reduce sales in presently unrestricted, therefore low-price, markets such as Belgium, and increase sales in presently restricted, high-price markets such as France.

Nor will an EC-wide quota fully shield European producers from increased competition. Even if the European Community were to restrict Japanese imports tightly—say, fixing imports at their current level of less than 10 percent of the overall EC market—there would be severe problems for the French and Italian producers—Fiat, Renault, Peugeot—who sell so much of their output in their domestic markets. The Japanese share of these markets would surely rise to well over 5 percent. Indeed, it is not clear that a Europe-wide quota will significantly reduce the adjustment problems of the French and Italian producers. Japanese sales will take time to react to the removal of the trade restrictions, as distribution networks are established only gradually, so the growth of Japanese sales following removal of national trade restrictions may be little faster without an EC-wide restriction than with one.

If trade liberalization does lead to adjustment in the European car industry, car producers will press for measures to ease the pain of adjustment. Claims on the Community's structural funds could be allocated in a way that would discriminate in favor of national champion producers. Producers would also demand retention of the block exemption in its present form. One tilt of the playing field could be replaced with others. Also relevant is the link between external trade policy and the implementation of the final stages of EC-wide whole vehicle type approval and other measures to eliminate barriers to intra-EC trade in cars. Pressures arising from the external market may hold up the implementation of a more competitive internal market.

## Japanese Transplants in Europe and Rules of Origin

Quite apart from imports, the role of the Japanese firms within the European market is rapidly changing as transplant operations are established. The capacity of transplants announced or already in operation will by 1995 amount to some 400,000 cars a year or more than 3.3 percent of the total EC market, and rise to 500,000 (more than 4 percent) by 1998. Restrictions on Japanese imports are one, though not the only, reason for the establishment of these transplants. If their products are treated as EC-produced cars, then Japanese transplant operations get around the import restrictions, and eventually render the import restrictions wholly ineffective. Indeed, when import restrictions attract transplants that would not otherwise have been established, the net result can be increased competition for European firms. Once established in the European market, Japanese producers can be expected to be even more responsive to consumer needs in that market, quite apart from their freedom from sales restraint.

To some extent, European-produced "Japanese" cars will substitute for Japanese-produced cars, but a total share for the Japanese firms of 30 percent of the EC market seems quite attainable. Such a share implies sharply increased price competition and product rationalization.

Of course, this scenario depends on transplant output being treated as European cars. There was a well-publicized dispute between the United Kingdom and France in 1989 on the specific issue of whether Nissan cars assembled in England should be treated as European or as Japanese cars. One result has been confusion between two related but distinct concepts: local content and rules of origin. The agreement between Nissan and the U.K. government on the establishment of the plant included an understanding that Nissan would over a period of years raise the local content of its U.K.-produced cars to 80 percent. The French government argued that the same local content criterion applied by the British government as an investment requirement should be applied as a rule of origin, so that the Nissan cars should be treated as Japanese cars subject to import restrictions unless they satisfy the 80 percent European content criterion. The fact that both the British and French governments were arguing on the basis of local content percentages gives the mistaken impression that the Community had already adopted some sort of local content rule as the criterion of origin.

From a legal point of view, the French position had no merit. Articles 9 and 10 of the Treaty of Rome require that goods in free circulation in one Community country freely circulate throughout the Community. An exception is that where there is a recognized national restriction on foreign trade, Article 115 permits the restriction to be maintained by border controls on intra-EC trade. The U.K.-assembled Nissan cars are regarded by the U.K. government as European products in free circulation in the United Kingdom and the French quota on Japanese cars is not a legally recognized trade restriction. From these two points it follows that the Treaty of Rome grants free circulation in France to the English Nissans. Rules of origin should play no part in intra-EC trade except where Article 115 restrictions are invoked.[28] A further point is that the rule of origin in general use by the European Community treats a product as of EC origin if the "last substantial transformation" occurred in the European Community. It is an activity test, not a local content test, and it is clearly met by Nissan U.K.

This legalistic view, however, ignores the reality that "gray area" measures, like the voluntary export restraints (VERs) limiting Japanese sales to the U.K. and French markets, are tolerated, connived at, or encouraged by *all* the EC member states involved. If the governments of EC member states other than France accept the existence of the French VER, then they have to accept that border restrictions that have the same effect as Article 115 restrictions must be implemented to maintain the VER. Further, the implementation of such restrictions requires rules to identify which goods are subject to restriction, and for "gray area" restrictions these rules can be "gray rules of origin" based on content.

The French withdrew their objections to the British Nissans (although not conceding the general point) on the reported grounds that Nissan

28. We are grateful to Peter Holmes for advice on this point.

would in the fairly near future meet the local content standard demanded so that there seemed little point in prolonging the dispute over an issue that would soon disappear. The French may also have feared that what was an undoubted attempt to extend the scope of the French VER might lead to scrutiny of its shaky legality.[29] We should perhaps see this dispute as an attempt by the French government to put pressure on the Commission to take a restrictive line on Japanese imports and Japanese transplant production in general rather than as a dispute about the British-made Nissans as such. This interpretation is consistent with past experience: France used import restrictions on Japanese videocassette recorders to pressure the Commission to negotiate an EC-wide VER, and France resisted EC-wide WVTA in the absence of an acceptable common commercial policy on cars.

From all this it is not surprising that many expect the European Community to adopt, for the purpose of administering any EC-wide import restriction on Japanese cars, a "gray rule of origin" based on a demanding level of European content. This view is probably mistaken. It is reported that Commissioner Bangemann opposes such a change.[30] It would be a radical departure from existing practice, even after the Commission's actions in the Ricoh case and in semiconductors (see chapter 4).[31] One argument that can be advanced by those, like Commissioner Bangemann, who do not want to have "gray rules of origin" is that if the objective is to keep Japanese car producers out of Europe, it is unlikely to succeed, as both Nissan and Toyota seem confident that their U.K. plants will soon have European content of 80 percent. It is difficult to predict what levels of local content would be reached in the absence of pressure. The history of Japanese transplants in the United

29. The Italian and Spanish governments took the same position as the French on this issue, but the Italians at least seem to have retreated along with the French.

30. William Dawkins, "Opening the Gates of Europe's Car Market," *Financial Times*, May 19, 1989, p. 2; and Done and Dawkins, "Giving the Green Light," p. 6.

31. The Commission has been active in its pursuit of antidumping actions in sensitive products and has tried to protect and strengthen the European electronics industry. In both cases there was a concern that the Japanese were circumventing EC restrictions by establishing "screwdriver" plants for final assembly of Japanese-made products. For semiconductors the rules of origin seemed to be rewritten to ensure a suitably protective outcome. William Dawkins, "Some Original Ideas on the Limits of Free Trade," *Financial Times*, February 10, 1989, p. 9. In the antidumping case involving Ricoh photocopiers, the Commission took the view that Ricoh could not avoid the consequences of earlier antidumping action by moving the final assembly from Japan to California. (See chapter 5 in this volume.)

States, where there seems to have been less overt pressure on local content, suggests that assembly plants naturally draw on local components to shorten their lines of supply.

## The Commission's Proposals

An official statement of the Commission's view, awaited for much of 1989, did not appear until December 6—yet more evidence of the difficulty in arriving at an agreement. The statement seems to represent a retreat from Commissioner Bangemann's earlier reported position as it includes a transitional "monitoring" of Japanese imports, which is to take account of the number of cars assembled by Japanese-owned transplants in Europe. Neither local content rules nor a "reciprocal" formula linking Japanese sales in the European Community to European sales in Japan is to be imposed. The statement calls for the rapid phasing out of national quotas but is quite vague on how long Japanese imports will be monitored.[32]

In light of our analysis of the likely effects of an EC-wide trade restriction, the detailed implementation of the monitoring is a key issue. If the proposed monitoring were equivalent to the imposition of an EC-wide quota and were to be maintained for the decade or so that it might take for transplant production to grow large enough to make a quota irrelevant, then it would entail all the disadvantages of an EC-wide quota. But if it were focused only on the markets with the most severe adjustment problems, it could be regarded largely as cushioning the effects of eliminating national quotas. There is a strong case to be made that monitoring focused on particular adjustment problems is both more efficient at meeting the legitimate need for adjustment assistance for the European producers and more likely to achieve the long-run goal of a truly open competitive market. The Commission's aim is evidently for monitoring not to reduce sales to currently free markets, but to reduce the adjustment pressures in the presently restricted markets.[33] The Commission may then have retreated somewhat from its initial liberal intentions, but seemed in early 1990 still to be trying to maintain a balance between its conflicting objectives.

Arriving at a consensus on policy toward the car market may have been hard for the Commission. Reconciling the views of the EC member

32. Kellaway and Dawkins, "Brussels Says Japan Must Curb Car Exports," p. 2.
33. Guy de Jonquières, "Brussels Faces Rough Ride in Drive for Consensus on Japanese Cars," *Financial Times*, February 5, 1990, p. 4.

states will be far harder. The French and Italian governments regard the Commission's position as dangerously liberal, and it is not clear when and whether agreement can be reached.[34] The mass-market European producers have since 1985 enjoyed high profitability.[35] A market downturn that adversely affected profitability would strengthen protectionist pressure. Because the Commission proposals involve "understandings" with the Japanese producers rather than formal quotas, the true shape of policy may emerge only gradually. Given the Commission's position, and the strong views of West Germany, the Netherlands, Denmark, and the United Kingdom, it may be reasonable to assume that the "Fortress Europe" option is foreclosed. Nevertheless, it is hard to predict how liberal the eventual trade policy of the Community in the car market will be.

## The Impact of the Program on the European Automobile Market

What then will be the effect of 1992 and 1992-related measures in the European car market? At this point, no definitive answer can be given because key details of the program are still unclear. Even in 1995, it will be difficult to give an answer, because of the difficulty of disentangling effects of the 1992 program from changes that might have taken place anyway. This problem is particularly acute with respect to the scale economies obtainable from the restructuring of production. The Ludvigsen contribution to the Commission's study on the economics of 1992 predicts considerable restructuring of the industry, generating economies of scale and driving costs and prices down some 6 percent. The report does not, however, separate whatever restructuring would have happened anyway from the effects of fiscal and regulatory harmonization, changes in the exchange rate regime, and changes in external trade policy. There are also grounds to be a little skeptical of Ludvigsen's estimates of economies of scale, in that they may not take sufficient account of the increased degree of flexibility that seems to characterize recent technological developments in the motor industry.[36]

34. Lucy Kellaway, "EC Still Split over Japan Cars," *Financial Times*, February 6, 1990, pp. 1, 26.

35. Kevin Done and Nick Garnett, "Being Special Is Not Enough," *Financial Times*, September 23, 1989, p. 6.

36. Ludvigsen Associates, *EC 92*. Ludvigsen's appeal to the small number of producers in the United States as indicating the scale economies achievable by post-1992 restructuring

Pan-European restructuring of production is already a central feature of the operations of Ford and GM, and it has more recently become apparent in developments at Peugeot and the Volkswagen group. Conceivably, the 1992 program will do no more than speed up the existing Europeanization of national car industries. But surely it will also help reduce unnecessary product variety and minimize uncertainty about component flows across borders. The question is how much. The direct effects of the reduction or removal of border barriers associated with the 1992 program may be small. But if the removal of border barriers, perhaps accompanied by progress on monetary union, erodes the national segmentation of markets and leads to a qualitative change in the nature of competition in the European car market, then the effects could be much more dramatic.

Another possible development that could lead to dramatic effects would be a leap in European productivity to Japanese and U.S. levels. If this occurs, Ludvigsen's estimates of the potential gains associated with 1992 will be too small. A study by John Krafcik of the Massachussetts Institute of Technology, described in appendix 3-3, reports remarkable differences in labor productivity between different car plants in different countries. Krafcik's figures suggest great scope for reducing European costs if European producers can attain foreign productivity levels. The potential production cost reductions implied by Krafcik's statistics are much greater than any estimate of the cost reductions associated with economies of scale. That such cost reductions are in principle attainable, at least in the medium run, is suggested by the productivity performance of the best European plants. This is confirmed by a reported statement of Raymond Lévy, chairman of Renault: "We also could build a modern plant that uses 3,000 employees to build 200,000 cars a year, but to do that we would have to close one of our plants that employs 10,000 people."[37]

Indirect evidence on the competitive lag of the European industry is provided by the decline of European exports to the United States. Of course, the Europeans export to the top end of the U.S. market, where they are now meeting serious Japanese competition for the first time. Exchange rate changes too have been unfavorable. Nevertheless, one

---

of production in Europe is not entirely convincing at a time when the number of producers in the United States has risen, with the arrival of Japanese transplants.

37. Steven Greenhouse, "Europe's Agonizing over Japan," *New York Times*, April 30, 1989, p. F1.

has to see declining exports as another symptom of the European productivity gap. The 1992 program will not restore European fortunes in the U.S. market unless it helps bring about a substantial improvement in European competitiveness—at best, a long and painful process.

It is surely increased Japanese competition rather than the 1992 program itself that is most likely to stimulate a dramatic productivity response from the European producers. The implications for EC policy toward Japanese imports are clear. In the long run, a restrictive policy will draw in more transplants and thus more competition that will drive less efficient European plants out of production. A less restrictive policy will increase competitive pressure in the short run, but could force a speedier and more successful response from the Europeans.

## U.S. Interests in the 1992 Program

Discussion of the effect of Europe 1992 on the interests of the United States requires, first, making a clear distinction between the interests of U.S. multinationals operating in the European Community and the interests of exporters operating from the United States. It also requires stepping back from the mundane details of short-term commercial interests and taking a long view of Europe 1992.

### U.S. Multinationals in the EC

Some observers worry that U.S. multinationals suffer from discrimination compared with European firms in the 1992 policymaking process. One concern is that standard-setting practice in the Commission does not include the open consultation with foreign firms that takes place in the United States and that lack of consultation with foreign firms could result in discrimination against their products. Ford of Europe and GM Europe are, in fact, excluded from membership in the Committee of Common Market Car Makers (CCMC), which is consulted about regulations and standards, but Ford and GM participate in national associations that come together in the Coordinating Council of European Car Manufacturers (CLCA). Moreover, just because of their exclusion from the CCMC, Ford and GM are sometimes consulted individually by regulators, when the CCMC members are consulted collectively. In the end, both multinationals feel that they have adequate access to regulatory discussions and are treated as European producers.

For the rest of the 1992 program, there seems little prospect of serious discrimination against the U.S. multinationals. Fiscal harmonization is unlikely to affect some manufacturers significantly more than others. If anything, effective control of state aid will be of particular benefit to the multinational producers, by limiting the preference given to the national champion European firms. On the face of it, the adoption of U.S. emissions standards in the EC market might seem to favor producers whose U.S. parents have accumulated experience in meeting these standards (but because all European exporters to the United States have had to meet these standards the advantage to Ford and GM may be rather small).[38] On the other hand, there are elements of Community preference in some Community actions. It is not clear, for example, to what extent U.S. multinationals will be permitted to participate in EC programs to foster technological development, but this is probably not a serious matter in the car industry.[39]

If, as we expect, the 1992 program and associated changes bring dramatically more competition to the European car market, the resulting restructuring need not imply the demise of existing producer groups entirely but will surely require the reshaping of some of them and the development of increased collaborative links. It is unwise to make predictions about who will benefit most from such a process, but Ford and GM are better placed than most European producers to cope with the effects of 1992. Their sales are more evenly spread across the Community than are those of any of the local producers; in particular, they show no undue concentration in those markets in which the competitive effects are likely to be fiercest. Their ability to move production between different countries might give them some edge in cutting costs. The perceived wisdom in the industry is that unit costs at Ford and GM might not be as low as those of Fiat or Nissan, but that they are on average at the lower end of the European spectrum. It should be emphasized, however, that the prediction that Ford and GM may do better than European firms in the 1990s is a prediction of relative performance in a market that will be difficult for all producers.

The restructuring of the European industry has already started, although so far it is confined to the top of the market. Ford took over Jaguar in November 1989, defeating GM's attempts to woo Jaguar into

38. Suzanne Perry, "U.S. Companies to Profit from New E.C. Emission Standards," *Europe-1992*, vol. 1 (August 30, 1989).

39. Insofar as U.S. multinationals are excluded from the EC's R&D programs, it is in response to the exclusion of European multinationals from U.S. programs such as Sematech.

a collaborative relationship.[40] Competition between Fiat and GM for control of Saab resulted in a victory for GM in December 1989.[41] An alliance has been formed between Renault and Volvo.[42] Several years of booming sales have been profitable for the volume car producers, and they are not under the immediate pressure to restructure that drove Jaguar and Saab into the arms of Ford and GM.[43] If a downturn in the European car market, however, should coincide with the increased capacity of Japanese transplants and with growing imports from Japan and the U.S.-based Japanese transplants, this picture could quickly change.

## U.S. Exports to Europe

Standard textbook analysis of economic integration suggests that when barriers to trade are reduced among a group of countries, one effect is trade diversion. Countries outside the group find their exports replaced by intra-group trade. Exports of cars from the United States to Europe, however, have risen over the past several years, and the public announcements of U.S. producers point to a continuing growth of exports.

General Motors and Ford both have announced the intention to expand their exports from the United States to Europe. These exports will be of specialized niche vehicles rather than mass-market cars, a trend that reflects little more than the slowly increasing globalization of the production of GM and Ford. GM Europe's sales of U.S.-sourced vehicles might rise from 12,000 units in 1988 to 30,000 by 1992; but it seems unlikely that Ford (under less pressure than GM in the U.S. market, and shipping fewer than 4,000 units in 1988) will export to Europe on this scale. Chrysler, however, has reentered the European market with sales of 31,000 vehicles in 1988, possibly rising to 100,000 in the 1990s.[44]

40. Kevin Done, "Ford Wins Jaguar Board's Acceptance of $1.66 Bn Bid," *Financial Times*, November 3, 1989, p. 1.
41. Robert Taylor and Kevin Done, "GM Agrees to Take 50 Percent of Saab in $600m Deal," *Financial Times*, December 16–17, 1989, p. 1.
42. Kevin Done and Paul Abrahams, "Renault and Volvo to Link," *Financial Times*, February 24, 1990, p. 1; and Kevin Done, "With This Committee I Thee Wed," *Financial Times*, February 26, 1990, p. 16.
43. Done and Garnett, "Being Special Is Not Enough," p. 6.
44. Interview with the president of GM Europe in the Economist Intelligence Unit, *European Motor Business*, no. 12 (May 1988); Perry, "U.S. Companies to Profit"; and Andrew Fisher, "Chrysler Close to Mini-Jeep Site Choice," *Financial Times*, September 14, 1989, p. 2.

This small- to medium-scale trade will undoubtedly be facilitated by the 1992 program as it lowers the cost of obtaining the necessary type approvals.

The most interesting questions about U.S. exports concern the possibility of sales in Europe of cars made by the Japanese transplants located in America. Honda, which already exports cars from Ohio to Japan, has announced its intention to export to Europe, and the other Japanese transplant producers can be expected to follow suit. With Japanese transplant capacity in the United States rising above 1.5 million cars, the flow of exports to Europe could conceivably reach 250,000 cars a year, worth more than $2 billion to the trade balance. There seems no realistic prospect of EC-1992 leading to such a burst of European competitiveness as to make such exports uneconomic for the transplant producers, though the growth of transplant capacity in Europe reduces the prospects for exports from American transplants.

Despite the controversy over the local content of the U.K.-produced Nissans, it is virtually inconceivable that the Community would seek to treat U.S.-produced Hondas as Japanese cars subject to an EC quota unless their U.S. content is 80 percent.[45] The application of a European local content criterion as a rule of origin has itself a very shaky basis. Quite apart from the virtual impossibility of so twisting rules of origin, the issue would arise only if the European Community were attempting to impose a GATT-illegal formal quota on Japanese car imports. In fact, what the Commission proposes is an "understanding" with Japanese producers and the monitoring of their sales in the European Community.

---

45. Whatever the likelihood is of the EC's attempting to implement such a measure, it should be noted that it can apply only to "Japanese" cars produced in the United States. A report of the House Subcommittee on International Economic Policy and Trade made the statement: "Honda . . . has announced plans to export 20,000 of its U.S.-assembled automobiles to the EC by 1991, and the other transplants have the capability to export to Europe. Chrysler does export automobiles to the EC and does not have a European plant. The export option for these U.S.-assembled automobiles, many of which have a majority U.S. content, must be preserved from an EC-92 automobile policy which provides for an unfair rule of origin. Otherwise, these companies may choose to abandon plans to increase the size of their existing American plants or to open additional plants." *European Community's 1992 Economic Integration Plan*, Subcommittee on International Economic Policy and Trade of the House Foreign Affairs Committee, 101 Cong. 1 sess. (Government Printing Office, May 19, 1989), pp. 37–38. The proposition that the EC's rules of origin could exclude U.S.-produced Chrysler cars ignores the crucial fact that the rule of origin under discussion is one applied in the enforcement on limits on imports of *Japanese* cars. The only U.S.-produced Chrysler cars that could conceivably be affected are those produced in the plant jointly operated by Chrysler and Mitsubishi.

The monitoring is to take account of forecasts of sales from European transplants, but the question of sales from U.S. transplants has not been addressed. One interpretation of this silence is that the Commission believes that the level of such imports will not be significant. Or it may simply be seeking to avoid problems with the U.S. government. The Commission may also be relying on the restraining effects of Japanese fears of the Community's reaction to increased sales from North America. If the Japanese firms believe that rapid growth of such sales will lead to tighter monitoring of imports from Japan, then that belief will itself lead to sales restraint without the need for any explicit statement by the Community. Such subtleties fall far short of a firm quota backed by a restrictive rule of origin, but could amount in essence to a Brussels-Tokyo agreement on exports from the United States.

U.S. components exports to the EC may also be affected by EC rule of origin requirements. In May of 1989 a representative of the Motor and Equipment Manufacturers Association warned a U.S. congressional committee of the possibility of "reduced long-term opportunities for U.S. exports of original equipment automotive parts if EC rule of origin requirements are set at an excessive level (a minimum of up to 80 percent is under discussion)."[46]

This possibility brings to the surface a further ambiguity from the already murky swamp of rules of origin and local content requirements: whether local content requirements imposed on Japanese transplant producers in Europe make it difficult for U.S components manufacturers to supply these producers. Since local content requirements are the subject of understandings between incoming producers and host governments, rather than the subject of statute law, it is difficult to discover whether there is in fact such discrimination.[47] Both Ford of Europe and GM Europe note with pride that virtually all their components are European produced. Before concluding that U.S. components manufacturers are thereby victimized by serious EC discrimination, one would

46. Christopher Bates, statement before the Senate Finance Committee, May 11, 1989.
47. The apparent objective of the EC's local content requirement is to keep the EC's trade policies from being circumvented by "screwdriver" plants. To meet that objective, the appropriate rule would be one that sets a maximum Japanese content rather than a minimum European content, in which case there would not be discrimination against U.S. components manufacturers. But an appeal to logic may be a poor guide to how rules are applied in reality! See the discussion of this issue in the context of the semiconductor industry in chapter 5.

want evidence that Ford and GM acted on the basis of pressure to be European rather than on commercial considerations.

Finally, in the light of the increasing importance of electronic components in motor vehicles, it is worth noting that U.S. components exports could be affected by EC nationalistic trade policies in electronics. The motor industry is no different in this respect from other users of electronics products (see chapter 7).

## What Is the Real U.S. Interest in 1992?

A formidable volume of paper has been generated over the past year conveying U.S. views of 1992. Much of it has a depressingly narrow focus on how U.S. commercial interests might be affected by this or that piece of legislation in Brussels. A full U.S. perspective on 1992 requires a broader view. Some uncertainty lingers about the extent to which the 1992 program will be inward-looking, mercantilist, and discriminatory in character, but the evidence so far offers strong grounds for optimism that fortress features will not predominate. Much more uncertainty remains about the extent to which the 1992 program will raise European economic efficiency and thereby affect Europe's position in the world economy. Here the optimism must be more modest. There is, of course, a link between the two questions: it is hard to see how an inward-looking program can increase competitiveness. The United States must consider *both* aspects of Europe 1992 in assessing its overall interests.

First, U.S. pressure can appropriately be applied on the European policy process to prevent discrimination against U.S. interests. Apart from the issue of external trade policy, there is a strong presumption that both U.S. exporters and the U.S. multinationals in Europe will gain from the 1992 program. The question remains whether the adoption of EC-wide restrictions of some kind on Japanese imports will have such unfair effects on U.S. interests as to justify action to carry out Ambassador Hills's promise to "challenge any new barriers in the GATT should they be introduced by the Community."

Ford of Europe and GM Europe will gain, at least in the short run, from restraints imposed on imports of Japanese cars into the Community. They have been less vocal than the Italian and French producers in advocating restraints, but Lindsey Halstead, chairman of Ford of Europe, is reported as arguing that abandoning import restrictions "should be conditional on the development of a fair degree of reciprocity from the Japanese."[48]

Import restraints in the European market, however, will increase the pressure of Japanese competition in the U.S. market. A more serious concern may be that the adoption of import restraints by the Community, even if replacing national restrictions of equivalent effect, represents an unacceptable further step toward making such restrictions a permanent feature of the world trading system. There is a case for low-key pressure to ensure that EC-wide restraints are short lived and genuinely focused on easing adjustment, and for making a serious attempt to deal with quantitative restrictions in multilateral negotiations. But the case for aggressive and unconditional challenge of any EC-wide restrictions is less obvious.

A nice problem arises for U.S. policymaking when U.S. interests are in conflict. The interests of the owners of Ford of Europe and GM Europe are different from the interests of the U.S. workers and suppliers of Honda and Toyota. The effectiveness, from the viewpoint of European producers, of restraints on Japanese producers will obviously be greater if they cover U.S.-produced as well as Japanese-produced cars.

The U.S. government, however, should not acquiesce in EC-imposed restraints on imports from transplants. First, the United States probably gains more from exports of Japanese-produced cars than from the earnings of the multinationals. Gains to Ford and GM stockholders from restraints on sales by U.S. transplants are almost surely less than the losses to U.S. interests involved in the Japanese transplants.[49] Second, while extending

48. Kevin Done, "Car-Makers Warn of Unbridled Japanese Competition," *Financial Times*, September 14, 1989, p. 2.

49. However, in the absence of supporting evidence, it is surely going too far to say, as does the report of the House Subcommittee on International Economic Policy and Trade on the EC's 1992 plan, that "Japanese car companies, furthermore, have already accepted the inevitability of locating new plants in Europe rather than expanding their production facilities in the U.S. Toyota recently selected a site in the United Kingdom for a European plant, and other Japanese manufacturers are sure to follow. The prospective EC policy on automobiles is already causing a distortion of international trade and investment, although the effect on the U.S. of this distortion may not be felt for a number of years." *European Community's 1992 Economic Integration Plan*, House report, pp. 38–39. No evidence is offered for the proposition that, in the absence of restrictive EC policies, Toyota would have supplied the European market from the United States rather than Japan. We should also not allow to slip by unnoticed the implicit judgment that foreign direct investment in the United States, which may be related to U.S import restrictions, is part of the natural order of the world, while foreign direct investment in the EC that may be induced by the EC's trade restrictions is an unacceptable "distortion of international trade and investment"!

import restraint agreements to third countries would not be an unprecedented step, if only because the U.S.-Japan semiconductor agreement has shown the way (see chapter 5), taking the world car market down this road would be a big step in the direction of globally managed trade. The real danger is not a new formal trade barrier on U.S.-produced Japanese cars. Rather, the danger is that the Community may be moving to an implicit market-sharing arrangement with the Japanese, covering car sales, of whatever origin, of all Japanese producers in the European Community. The United States has historically opposed the cartelization of world trade, and Ambassador Hills has vigorously reaffirmed the traditional U.S. position. For all the reasons that Europe bristled over the effects of the Washington-Tokyo semiconductor agreement on the European market, the United States should take umbrage, and action, over indirect limits on transplant exports, however deftly negotiated or subtly expressed. But the more subtle the understandings between Brussels and Tokyo, the harder it will be for Washington to react.

U.S. commercial diplomacy on this issue should take account of divided European interests. In the 1990s a very significant proportion of the U.K. motor industry will consist of Japanese-owned plants, and the question of how their output will be treated by the Community is not yet fully resolved. It seems unlikely, however, that the Community will treat U.K.-manufactured Hondas, Nissans, and Toyotas less favorably than it treats U.S.-manufactured products of the same firms. It follows that the U.K. government can be expected to oppose attempts to apply EC import restraints to U.S.-produced cars of Japanese firms.

U.S. interest in the second aspect of Europe 1992, whether it will raise European competitiveness, is less direct than its interest in minimizing fortress effects. In the long run, however, the competitiveness issue is the more interesting. No external trade policy can shield the European industry indefinitely from the need to face up to free competition from foreign producers with higher productivity levels. We have argued that opening up the European market to free competition sooner rather than later is more likely to induce an increase in European productivity. The fate of U.S. interests in the post-1992 European car market may then depend less on how aggressively or effectively the U.S. government pursues its commercial diplomacy than on how effectively U.S. producers pursue their commercial interests. In the short run, countries have an ambiguous interest in the competitiveness of foreigners. The more successful the 1992 program is in making the European motor industry competitive, the harder life will be for the U.S. producers, but the better for U.S. consumers and U.S. sellers of other goods to European consumers. In the long run, given time to adjust to changes in the pattern of international competitiveness, countries generally gain from the increased efficiency of their trading partners. The United States, in this as in other sectors, should look at the 1992 program in the spirit of the Marshall Plan rather than that of the 1988 Omnibus Trade Act.

APPENDIX 3-1. Alliances in the European Car Industry, 1970–90[a]

| Year | Acquiring firm[b] | Acquired firm[b] | Percent acquired[c] |
|---|---|---|---|
| 1972 | Volvo (S) | DAF (NL) | 33 (53) |
| 1974 | Peugeot (F) | Citroën (F) | 38 (53) |
| 1977 | Peugeot (F) | Chrysler Europe (U.S.) | 100 |
| 1977 | Chrysler (U.S.) | Peugeot (F) | 15 |
| 1979 | Renault (F) | American Motors (U.S.) | 5 (46) |
| 1979 | Renault (F) | Volvo (S) | 10(25+) |
| 1982 | Nissan (J) | Motor Iberica (E) | 89.5 |
| 1986 | General Motors (U.S.) | Lotus (GB) | 94 |
| 1986 | Volkswagen (D) | SEAT (E) | 75 |
| 1986 | Fiat (I) | Alfa Romeo (I) | 50+ |
| 1987 | Chrysler (U.S.) | Maserati (I) | 15.6 |
| 1987 | Chrysler (U.S.) | Lamborghini (I) | 100 |
| 1987 | Ford (U.S.) | Aston Martin (GB) | 75 |
| 1989 | Honda (J) | Rover (GB) | 20 |
| 1989 | Ford (U.S.) | Jaguar (GB) | 100 |
| 1989 | General Motors (U.S.) | Saab (S) | 50+ |
| 1990 | Volvo (S) | Renault (F) | 20+ |

SOURCES: Christian Marfels, *Recent Trends of Concentration in Selected Industries of the European Community, Japan and the United States* (EC Commission, 1988), p. 34; and *Financial Times* as cited in text notes 7, 40–42.

a. In addition, Marfels reports many joint-ventures and cooperative agreements, including assembly by Alfa Romeo of a Nissan-designed car; joint design and production of cars by British Leyland (now Rover) and Honda; joint design of an executive car by Saab, Alfa Romeo, and Lancia; and technical cooperation between Fiat and Peugeot. Marfels notes, however, that European joint ventures are almost exclusively intra-European, in contrast with the major links between General Motors and Toyota, Ford and Mazda, and Chrysler and Mitsubishi.

b. Letters in parentheses indicate the nationality of the firms involved (D = West Germany; E = Spain).

c. Numbers in parentheses indicate a subsequent change.

APPENDIX 3–2. Car Tax Differences in the European Community, 1988

| Country | Type of tax and rate[a] |
|---|---|
| **VAT on new car purchases** | |
| Belgium | 25 percent on sale price, 33 percent on larger-engined cars |
| Denmark | 22 percent on ex-customs value |
| Ireland | 23 percent on ex-customs value and excise tax combined |
| France | 28 percent on sale price |
| Greece | 6 percent on sale price |
| Italy | 18 percent, 38 percent on larger-engined cars |
| Luxembourg | 12 percent |
| Netherlands | 20 percent on sale price |
| Portugal | 16 percent on sale price |
| Spain | 33 percent on sale price |
| United Kingdom | 15 percent on sale price including car tax |
| West Germany | 14 percent on sale price |
| **Other taxes on new car purchases[a]** | |
| Belgium | 25 percent on difference between catalogue price and sale price 33 percent on larger-engined cars |
| Denmark | 105 percent on VAT inclusive price up to certain price; 180 percent on balance of price |
| Ireland | 21.7 percent or 24.7 percent of VAT inclusive price, depending on engine size |
| France | No tax |
| Greece | 80–400 percent depending on engine size, price |
| Italy | No tax |
| Luxembourg | No tax |
| Netherlands | 17.3 percent on tax-inclusive price up to a certain level; 25.9 percent on balance of price |
| Portugal | Import tax up to 110 percent depending on price and engine size |
| Spain | No tax |
| United Kingdom | 10 percent of ⅚ of the catalogue price |
| West Germany | No tax |

SOURCE: Krish N. Bhaskar and others, *A Single European Market? An Automotive Perspective* (University of East Anglia, Motor Industry Research Unit, 1988).

a. In the case of both kinds of taxes, it should be noted that not only are there substantial differences between countries in their tax rates, but also that some countries levy taxes at different rates depending on price and engine capacity. This last factor gives an incentive to firms to produce cars that are just below rather than just above such "fiscal break points." But then differences between fiscal break points encourage the production of different cars for different national markets.

This kind of costly diversity is also encouraged by further fiscal differences. There are different taxes on vehicle ownership, with break points in some countries; and there is a fair amount of variation in the taxation of motor fuel. In the United Kingdom there are income tax concessions on the provision of cars by employers, and these concessions too have break points.

APPENDIX 3–3. International Productivity Differences in the
Auto Industry: The Krafcik Results

A study by John F. Krafcik of the Massachusetts Institute of Technology reports remarkable differences in labor productivity between different car plants in different countries. The figure on page 158 reproduces the results reported in Krafcik's figure 2. It illustrates the range of hours of worker input per vehicle produced (standardized to allow for differences between car model requirements) in different categories of plant. Japanese-owned plants located in Japan have the best performance with an average score of 19.1, the best plant having a score of 16, and the worst scoring 24.2. Japanese producers in North America are a little less efficient on average but have less variance. U.S.-owned plants in North America have not succeeded in attaining Japanese levels of productivity, but the gap is not unreasonably wide. By contrast, productivity in Europe lags far behind on Krafcik's estimates, with an average of 30.9 for U.S.-owned or Japanese-owned European plants and of 35.9 for European-owned European plants. The best practice in Europe is within sight of the rest of the world, at 22.8 for U.S.-owned or Japanese-owned plants in Europe, 22.6 for European-owned plants, but the worst scores in the two European categories, 47.6 and 53, respectively, fall woefully behind.

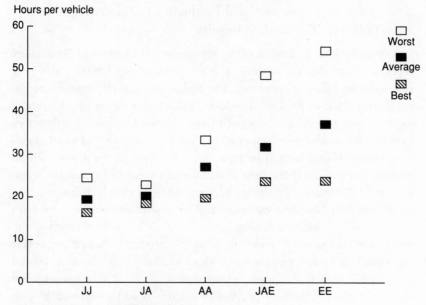

Hours per vehicle

JJ   Japanese-owned plants in Japan
JA   Japanese-owned plants in North America
AA   American-owned plants in North America
JAE  Japanese or American-owned plants in Europe
EE   European-owned plants in Europe

SOURCE: John F. Krafcik, "Triumph of the Lean Production System," *Sloan Management Review* (Fall 1988), pp. 41–52.

# Chapter 4

# Telecommunications

PETER F. COWHEY

ALTHOUGH the Europe 1992 process has significantly increased competition in the European telecommunications market, the European market today is less open than the U.S. market has been since the settlement in 1984 of the federal antitrust suit against American Telephone and Telegraph Company. Quasi-competition within Europe poses three sets of questions for the United States.

First, which markets will be open enough and lucrative enough for entry by U.S. firms? I contend that the U.S. policymakers should redefine their strategic conception of the European telecommunications market. A strategy for enhancing American competitiveness in information technology and services is vital. Particularly important is a new "growth triangle," the intersection of global information services, advanced radio communications services, and the supporting telecommunications transmission equipment and terminal equipment. This triangle could reshape the industry and play to American strengths in information markets. Moreover the triangle's high growth rates make entry by U.S. firms less politically contentious.

Second, what happens over the longer term? How will the EC blend of industrial policy and increased competition balance out in telecommunications? I argue that the combination of growing Japanese inroads in the European market together with EC industrial policies will ensure a continuing agenda of trade issues between Brussels and Washington.

Third, how do the U.S. negotiations with Europe about telecommunications fit into the broader agenda of managing the world trading system and ensuring American competitiveness? I call for a reconsideration of U.S. positions on issues ranging from government procurement through

Peter F. Cowhey is professor of Political Science and International Relations at the University of California at San Diego and co-author of *When Countries Talk: International Trade in Telecommunications Services.*

international voice services, an emphasis on the role of smaller U.S. firms in the European market, a reformulation of U.S. policy toward the regional Bell operating companies ("Baby Bells"), and U.S.-Community bilateral talks within the framework of GATT negotiations.

## Transformation of the World Telecommunications Market

Telecommunications was once a rather simple industry, though it spawned complex technologies. Worldwide, a phone call was a phone call, and a mixture of large network equipment, like the central office telephone switches (COS), and small terminal equipment (the telephone handset) made it all possible. In Europe, national governments granted authority over communications to a single monopolist, which also served as the government ministry and often ran the post office (hence the name post, telephone, and telegraph administrations, or PTTs).

In the United States, in many respects, the old AT&T system operated as a European PTT. It was universally accepted that a PTT (or AT&T) could best exploit the presumed natural monopoly created by telephone technology: economies of scale and scope arising from expanded central switching capability and denser networks, and positive externalities generated by larger numbers of interconnected users. In turn, the PTT monopoly permitted politically attractive cross-subsidies in favor of residential as against business users, in favor of local calls as against long-distance calls, and in favor of rural as against urban areas.

Traditional electromechanical equipment was highly standardized. Public policy encouraged PTTs to pick a few local producers (preferably nationally owned firms) as exclusive suppliers, thus breeding monopoly equipment manufacturers. In theory, this tight cartellized system of equipment supply enabled producers to reap economies of scale and scope for their wares, ensured network reliability, and boosted the local electronics industry. In practice, the system also yielded idiosyncratic national standards and pushed up labor and equipment costs.

Given the coalition of interests in favor of the status quo, it is not surprising that PTTs were exempt from the government procurement code negotiated in the Tokyo Round (1973–79) of GATT talks. But other events, in the form of new technology, came along to disrupt the comfortable world of PTTs and their suppliers. Digital and fiber-optic technologies accelerated the growing interdependence of computers and telecommunications. Troubling regulatory questions were raised as the telephone network became the medium for organizing global financial exchanges, airline reservation networks, and just-in-time delivery systems. Who should design and sell these services? The telephone company or the firms using the telephone company's facilities? Whose equipment should deliver the service? A bewildering array of data terminals, computers, and private automatic branch exchanges (PABXs) now allowed a customer to duplicate or surpass many network control functions once available only on the central telephone switch. (See appendix 4-1 for definitions of telecommunications equipment.)

The problems and choices posed by technological innovation first emerged in the United States, the home of the world's most advanced financial and service industries, the biggest and most diverse computer industry, and the largest number of multinational corporations. But the same coalition of users has since surfaced in other industrial countries to demand a new telecommunications policy. The few large corporations and government agencies who are oligopoly users of communications services have both motives and resources to influence regulation. Typically, 5 percent of all users generate more than 50 percent of long-distance traffic and more than 30 percent of local phone traffic. In the U.S. experience 20 percent of equipment customers make 80 percent of the purchases.[1] Many of the users hope to become suppliers of telecommunication-related services. Meanwhile the microchip revolution attracted important companies such as IBM to the telecommunications industry, companies that wanted to break up the cozy system of protected markets for telecommunications equipment.

### Impact of American Deregulation

In 1984 the United States decided that competition, rather than regulated monopoly, was the better way to organize the telecommunications market. The exception was local phone services, where the arguments for monopoly still prevailed. The 1984 consent decree resulting from the federal antitrust challenge led to the split of AT&T from the regional Bell operating companies (RBOCs).[2] The consent decree imposed

---

1. Czatadana Inan, "Big Business = Big Bucks in Telecommunications," *Telephony*, August 5, 1985, p. 38.

2. Peter F. Cowhey, "Bringing the Politician Back In: Political Choice and the Origins of American Foreign Economic Policy," Social Science Research Council Conference, Stanford University, May 1989.

severe restraints on lines of business open to the RBOCs in an attempt to prevent the unfair competitive advantage that would supposedly derive from their abuse of local monopoly power if allowed to compete in other segments of the telecommunications industry. The consent decree also curtailed the potential abuse of remaining monopoly powers inherent in the technical aspects of the major phone networks. It required AT&T, the RBOCs, and others to ensure equal access to all users of unbundled network features, such as network billing information or the network signaling channel, and to ensure full disclosure to all service providers of the network design through open network architecture (ONA).

Deregulation became the American policy template for the information era. It permitted users to choose their own equipment, it reinforced the extensive decentralization of distributed computing power, and it bolstered customized design. For example, many corporate networks will evolve in modular style, from local area networks (LANs) that connect terminals and computers in offices over many desktops, to enterprise-wide networks that link offices in many cities. The specialized equipment for channeling and integrating this traffic (such as bridgers and routers) not only opens new markets, but also reshapes competition in older ones (such as PABX markets). Semicustomized software programs tailor the ensemble for the individual user.[3]

The U.S. market combined the flexible choice of standards with a large base of customers that followed the IBM and AT&T protocols. Hence a reasonably coherent infrastructure of standards has emerged. While the United States worries whether it can sustain this mix of diversity and conformity, European countries face a more severe problem: they lack the integrated telecommunications starting point that is equivalent to AT&T, or the all-purpose computer firm that is equivalent to IBM (except IBM Europe). The European Commission has, therefore, identified interconnected open systems of information and communications (not dependent on IBM) as a key priority, and the Community has an active industrial policy to achieve this goal. The challenge facing the United States government is to accommodate this valid European goal, while preserving the flexibility, diversity, and competition in information network design characteristic of the open U.S. systems.

Once opened, the U.S. market soon attracted extensive entry by foreign companies. The U.S. trade balance in telecommunications equip-

---

3. John McQuillan, "Routers as Building Blocks for Robust Internetworks," *Data Communications*, September 21, 1989, pp. 28–33.

TABLE 4-1. U.S. Telecommunications Trade Balance, 1985 and 1988
Millions of dollars

| Imports and exports | 1985 | 1988 |
|---|---|---|
| *Imports* | | |
| Terminal equipment | | |
| Telephone sets | 501 | 927 |
| Terminals | 687 | 1,470 |
| Of which: fax | n.a. | (918) |
| Wireless equipment | 170 | 685 |
| Of which: Cordless phones | (169) | (403) |
| Of which: Cellular phones | n.a. | (282) |
| Answering machines | 200 | 379 |
| SUBTOTAL | 1,188 | 2,397 |
| Telephone apparatus | 275 | 556 |
| Telephone switches | 526 | 431 |
| TOTAL | 2,358 | 4,449 |
| *Exports* | | |
| Telephone switches | 363 | 546 |
| Telephone apparatus | 314 | 464 |
| TOTAL | 677 | 1,010 |

SOURCE: Communications Workers of America, *Information Industry Report* (Washington, August 1989), p. 13.
n.a. Not available.

ment swung from a $0.5 billion surplus in 1979 to a $3.4 billion deficit in 1988, largely because of massive imports of terminal equipment (see table 4-1 for 1988 data). At the same time, foreign markets were not nearly as open to U.S. exports. Moreover, competition stimulated American use of the international phone network for outgoing calls while high prices in other countries discouraged calling to the United States. Under the conventions governing the division of international telephone revenues, this imbalance created growing net U.S. payments to foreign telephone companies that reached $1.2 billion annually in 1986.[4]

Deregulation in the United States shook the foundations of regulation on a global scale and quickly spilled over into trade policy. Deregulation offered an alternative model for voice and data networks, and it turned AT&T's old business customers into rivals with telephone network facilities

4. Unless otherwise noted, all dollar figures in this paper have been converted at the rate of $1.20 to an ECU. Leland L. Johnson, "International Telecommunications Regulation," in Paula R. Newberg, ed., *New Directions in Telecommunications Policy*, vol. 1 (Duke University Press, 1989).

for many functions.[5] The United States soon mounted a vigorous campaign to export its new brand of deregulation and competition. Japan was the leading target, but Europe also attracted interest. The U.S. Congress decided that telecommunications warranted special attention in the 1988 Omnibus Trade and Competitiveness Act. The 1988 act required the U.S. Trade Representative (USTR) to open bilateral negotiations with countries posing a serious trade problem in telecommunications and to achieve fair market access by spring 1990.

The USTR targeted the EC for bilateral talks regarding both communications equipment and services (see appendixes 4-1 and 4-2 for a listing of equipment and services). The combined approach was dictated by technology: as the next section explains, the equipment and service markets are highly interdependent.

Brussels responded in two ways. First it insisted that bilateral negotiations would undermine the spirit of multilateral GATT talks. More fundamentally, Brussels argued that trade talks are unnecessary: in the natural course of the Europe 1992 process, the telecommunications market will be opened to foreign competition. While the U.S. government praised the EC agenda, it insisted on negotiations because the European approach may entail continued intervention in ways that U.S. industry does not find congenial.[6]

## Changing Composition of the Market

Telecommunications equipment and services are intimately tied to computing and other information markets. The European Commission foresees a dramatic increase in the share of European GDP represented by the combined markets—a rise, perhaps, from 2 percent in 1988 to 7 percent by the year 2000.[7]

---

5. For example, Digital Equipment Corporation computers can provide network control functions that make it unnecessary to upgrade the COS software system. Conversely, Centrex is a substitute for a PABX.

6. For example, the Commission might favor uniform terminal equipment standards to assure Community interoperability, whereas many U.S. designers view uniform standards as an impediment to creative design. Commission documents state that compulsory standards may have to go up to designs for application software programs and terminal equipment (layers 6 and 7 of the Open Systems Interconnection reference model adopted by the International Standards Organization), and other new standards may be required for network equipment. See W. von Pattay, "The Role of Compatibility and Service Quality in Teleprocessing," *Telecommunications Journal*, vol. 56 (1989), pp. 172–78.

7. James Capel, *Special Report on the Impact of 1992 on European Industrial and Financial Markets* (Brussels, September 1988), p. 18.

TABLE 4-2. EC Market in 1986 and 2000

Billions of dollars

| Market segment | World 1986 | EC-12 1986 | EC-12 2000 |
|---|---|---|---|
| Telecommunications services | 360 | 84[a] | 277 |
| Voice | n.a. | 74 | 190 |
| New services[b] | n.a. | 6 | 88 |
| Telecommunications equipment | 108 | 25[a] | 47 |
| Computing equipment[c] | 150 | 30 | 138 |
| TOTAL | 618 | 139 | 740 |

SOURCE: Author's calculations based on the data in appendix 4-3.
n.a. Not available.
a. 1987 figures, including telex and telegraph.
b. All enhanced and overlay services as defined in appendix 4-2.
c. Integrated office equipment and software (including typewriters, data terminals, computers).

The estimates in table 4-2 (derived from appendix 4-3) suggest that the market for telecommunications equipment will be rocked by dramatic changes in the larger markets for computing, office equipment, and new services. The total market for services will far surpass the market for equipment, but only new service markets will surely be contestable within the EC. Hard bargaining will be needed to open not only the equipment market but also many service markets. The result of effective bargaining will be the creation of a new "growth triangle," comprising enhanced services on a global basis, advanced radio communications services, and advanced transmission and terminal equipment.

The U.S. experience helped blur the line between the domains of hardware and service. Indeed, definitions beyond the tautological ("services are everything other than hardware") are virtually meaningless. Numerous firms are now searching out profitable synergies by crossing the border between these domains, although AT&T's and IBM's frustrations in storming the other's core markets show the difficulties of doing so. The next two sections of this chapter analyze the service and equipment markets, respectively, with an eye on their interaction.

## Telecommunications Services

The shape of the services market has changed rapidly, and the policy debate has shifted in response. A symbol of change is that the PTTs are coming to be known as telecommunications authorities (TAs)—a more modest claim to power.

## Evolution of the EC Market

Most European telecommunications authorities want to retain a monopoly on basic telephone services, which still generate about 90 percent of all revenues, in the name of social equity for smaller users.[8] Many European TAs also propose to expand universal service beyond simple phone service to enhanced services, which include an unspecified range of new information services. They insist that this requires a monopoly on certain fundamental value-added services, particularly packet switched networks (for definitions and the distinction between value-added and information services, see appendix 4-2). The TAs advocate that all users, including residential users, be connected soon by fiber-optic cables. Although critics argue that such a speedy recabling of public networks would pose economic risks of underutilized plant, the TAs counter that it could also speed a new era of information services for residential and corporate customers alike.

By the early 1980s, however, private analysts concluded that the TAs would not deliver an integrated services digital network (ISDN) on a continental basis and would not cut their high prices for large users. Alienated corporate customers intensified their efforts for control over their communications systems. They won case-by-case exemptions from reliance on TA networks, thus threatening Europe's public network with a dearth of sophisticated new continental services and a declining customer base.

The TAs initially responded to their critics by backing Community initiatives for an accelerated introduction of a Europe-wide ISDN based on common technical standards.[9] They also supported limited competition in segments less vital to their core monopoly, such as pure information services (those dealing solely in content) and parts of the terminal equipment market.

The TA strategy for services posed many problems for U.S. firms—even when served up in its most progressive form, the EC's 1987 Green

---

8. The TAs also argue that competition is unfair until they can rebalance their tariff structure, a problem hampered by prior welfare policies.

9. Council Recommendation 86/659/EEC, *Official Journal of the European Communities*, no. L382 (Luxembourg, December 31, 1986), p. 36 [hereafter *O.J. Eur. Comm.*]. Council Decision 88/28/EEC, *O.J. Eur. Comm.*, no. 16 (January 21, 1988), p. 44, established the RACE program to promote a succeeding generation of broadband services.

Paper on Telecommunications.[10] Appendix 4-4 outlines the problems as they stood at the start of 1989.

By 1989 European customer firms were echoing the complaints of U.S. firms. The EC Commission concluded that it would get caught in a political quagmire if it tried to limit competition in value-added services. Influenced by the U.K. decision in 1984 to legalize competition in basic phone service by introducing a second competitor, owned by Cable and Wireless, to British Telecom, the Commission hoped that the impact on households would be small if TAs rebalanced their rate structures and operated more like private firms.

The experience of British Telecom paralleled the experience of U.S. carriers after the breakup of AT&T: a combination of reduced costs and rebalanced rates can hold down prices for basic phone services (especially local calls), while stimulating demand for other services (notably long-distance calls) and boosting earnings. As a result, revenues from traditional phone services can continue to grow at a healthy rate. But profit margins on long-distance calls (especially international calls) will decline radically, and local calls will bear more of their true costs.[11] The British government had also concluded that residual restrictions on competition in data-related services, which offer vast growth and profit potential, are counterproductive. The potential loss to voice telephone service revenues due to the growth of private networks was not large enough to justify retarding the growth of new services.

In response to the U.K. experiment and the Commission's leanings, the European TAs argue that uniformity in standards and network tariffs—uniformity that only they can provide—is vital for the development of data-related services. Experience, however, suggests that demand is far too heterogeneous to be served by uniformly designed services, a notion hard for long-time monopolists to absorb. User-specific design of com-

---

10. EC Commission, *Towards a Dynamic European Economy—Green Paper on the Common Market for Telecommunications Services and Equipment* (Brussels, June 1987).

11. Although the U.K. network was especially decrepit at the onset of competition, any loss in economies of scale was offset by gains in other efficiencies. The growth rates for standard phone service in Europe may be even higher than the projected 5 to 6 percent annually because the demand for services may be stimulated by lower terminal prices. For example, most European households do not have a second phone, and international services are overpriced. In 1985 international services provided 10 to 12 percent of France Telecom's total income, even though they were only 1 to 2 percent of chargeable minutes. Interviews, with officials of France Telecom, summer 1985.

munications packages and application software is the byword.[12] Digital technology offers great flexibility in the location where value is added, since the distance and volume of transmission become smaller components of total cost in a value-added system. Indeed, the communications component of a value-added network (VAN)—which usually combines leased circuits and some private overlay facilities—often accounts for less than 15 percent of the value-added. Still, this cost component is critical to the competitive advantage of private services.[13] Within a VAN, communications costs are much lower than they are in TA networks; the service is far more reliable than that provided by public networks; and it is optimized for the particular needs of its client base.

VANs largely make their profits from the applications software designed for customers that use data networks, and from designing private corporate networks. Tymnet (a U.S.-based provider of value-added networks), for example, estimated that it was the source of design and software for 50 percent of the private U.S. networks created in 1984.[14] Perhaps the most conspicuous successes in the world of VANs are systems that require detailed knowledge of industry-specific operations. These include the airline reservation systems, such as American Airlines' Sabre, and the credit card validation networks, such as the financial network of American Express.

The most important externality of VANs is the cumulative learning effect they offer both producers and consumers: the greater the use, the lower the cost, both to producers and consumers.[15] An important part of this learning effect is the transformation of users into providers of enhanced

12. General Electric Information Services, for example, does not use the X.25 standard for data communications because the GE system is optimized for two-way data transactions, and X.25 works best at simple one-way transport. C. C. van Weizsaecker and others, "The Economics of Value Added Network Services" (University of Cologne, June 1987).

13. TAs often urge that entry in VANs should be limited to firms in which communications do not exceed 15 percent of total value-added. (This will block services that are nothing but pure resale of circuits with a little window dressing, argue the TAs.) The problem with the 15 percent rule is that even a network whose general operations may easily meet this criterion often has specific routes that do not.

14. Dwight B. Davis, "Making Sense of the Telecommunications Circus," *High Technology*, September 1985, pp. 20–30.

15. Van Weizsaecker persuasively argues that current consumption in these industries is a function of total previous consumption because of a variety of forces associated with learning effects, such as consumer knowledge and declining costs. Higher costs for the communications component of enhanced services have a significant cumulative effect over time. I expect the industry for mass information services to approximate Chamberlain-style competition with many entrants, highly differentiated products, and increasing returns.

services—an established trend in the United States, where Sears and Westinghouse resell and customize their own private networks for other firms, and an emerging trend in the newly deregulated Japanese market. In Europe this trend is stifled by restrictive TA leasing practices, high tariffs, and inflexible access to the public network. Some countries (notably West Germany) are reducing these barriers.[16]

Meanwhile, many European government and corporate officials doubt that communications traffic will soon move, as once thought, to a fiber-optic pipe that ties together an all-purpose integrated broadband communications system to European business and residential users in the late 1990s.[17] One reason for skepticism is the rapid emergence of cellular and radio technologies in the so-called overlay services (see appendix 4-2). The European cellular mobile market will soon exceed $1 billion annually, and its growth consistently outperforms the forecasts.[18] But this is only the beginning. Britain is creating a national personal communications network (PCN), a slightly less powerful radio system than cellular radio. By 1996 the number of British subscribers to the PCN could reach 8 million, as prices drop to the equivalent of a pay telephone call.[19] One telephone company is considering the use of radio

16. West Germany is investing in infrastructure to make flexible selection among ISDN and other service packages feasible, rather than insisting that all users convert to ISDN.

17. Advocates of the integrated broadband communications (IBC) system assume that a single fiber-optic "pipe" is more efficient than multiple systems. This implies that competition involving multiple specialized networks will yield smaller efficiencies than the economies of scope provided by a single broadband network. IBC enthusiasts also assume that the added costs of rapid replacement of existing systems (compared with gradual upgrading and replacement) are justified by massive benefits at an earlier date. Neither assumption is self-evidently correct. I thank Eli Noam for sharing unpublished work on these points with me. "Establishing Advanced Communications in Europe," *IBC Strategic Audit 1988* (EC Commission, February 1989), pp. 24–26.

18. This has occurred even though regulation has hindered the market except in the United Kingdom and Scandinavia. By May 1989 the U.K. subscriber total was about 600,000 and Scandinavia was approaching 700,000 (almost a doubling in ten months). Della Bradshaw, "Europe Places Call for Mobile Telephone Network by 1991," *Financial Times*, July 20, 1988; and "Telephones That Get Up and Go," *Economist*, September 16, 1989, pp. 71–72.

19. The U.K. government has not selected a definitive version of PCN, but it will operate in the 1.7 GHz to 2.3 GHz section of the spectrum. The system will thus be able to send and receive calls (whereas yet another U.K. system, Telepoint, permits only local outgoing cordless calls), but the equipment will be more costly. Racal-Vodafone believes that a special interface would be required as an option to be covered by both micro and macro cells, and that automatic handoff (as a user passes from cell to cell) may only work at lower mobile speeds than cellular. A PCN network will cost about $1.5 billion to create

to provide the final digital link to households.[20] While the ultimate limits on radio's bandwidth mean fiber optics will dominate eventually, the share of radio could be quite large in the next ten to twenty years. Radio could entrench support for competing network infrastructures.

Other innovative radio services are coming, and many are supplied by non-European firms. Mobile data and facsimile networks, especially for trucking, and Europe-wide paging and air telephone systems are in the works.[21] The rapid expansion of satellite transponder capacity provides a further boost to overlay services because price cutting and relaxed use restrictions are almost inevitable.[22] Indeed, overlay services could grow to $30 billion by the year 2000, and enhanced services could reach $60 billion. These estimates may prove conservative.

Meanwhile, the traditional market for international voice services is changing. Large corporations dominate usage, and they are operating both private voice and data networks. The corporations may lease circuits from TAs and do everything themselves, or they may hire TAs to serve as subcontractors for selected services. This development is forcing national TAs to work as a team, both to woo corporate customers and to customize their prices and services.

Progressive liberalization and more intensive competition are the likely order of the 1990s. But the United States should remain wary because EC thinking about advanced services assumes EC-wide guidance of the

and requires about 3.5 million subscribers for profitability. One major problem for PCN is how its technical standards will fit with the European digital cellular system that is expected to have 3 million to 4 million subscribers by 1995. Forecasts made in 1988 of 1 million EC cellular subscribers by 1994 were surpassed by May 1989, as surely will also occur to the predicted 9 million by 1999. "UK Government Says New Mobile Services Are Aimed at Cellular," *Fintech Telecom Markets* (London, Financial Times, June 29, 1989), pp. 1–2; "Racal-Vodafone and the Personal Communication Network Market," *Fintech Telecom Markets*, July 27, 1989, pp. 7–8; and "Telephones That Get Up and Go," pp. 71–72.

20. Interview with official of European telephone company, July 1989.

21. U.S. government estimates suggest that mobile satellite service revenues will grow globally at $150 million to $250 million in 1992 and $1 billion in 1995. Technologies differ depending on whether the entrant uses existing satellites or designs new satellites. Ron Schneiderman, "Tracking Trucks by Satellite," *High Technology Business*, May 1989, pp. 24–28. Yet another business is airphone and related services for airline passengers. Bell South controls AirCall in the United Kingdom, which in turn holds a share of Europage, another British entrant in the business. *Telecommunications Reports*, March 6, 1989, p. 31.

22. Some hope to divert the new satellite capacity to direct broadcasting services to protect the core service monopolies of the regional European satellite system, Eutelsat. The success of this gambit is uncertain. Raymond Snoddy, "Ambitions to Be the Best," and "Eutelsat—A Second Generation," *Financial Times*, July 28, 1988, pp. IV2–3, and IV4.

market. For example, the EC assumes that its Research and Development for Advanced Communications in Europe (RACE) will provide technical research, extensive policy coordination, and even financial incentives for trans-European transmission facilities to nourish videoconferencing, high-speed data, high-speed color facsimile, and videophony.[23] This underlying assumption practically ensures an ongoing transatlantic dialogue over subsidies, administrative guidance, and competition.

## U.S. Firms in the Service Market

The explosion of enhanced and overlay services is the first-generation outcome of the services era. The second generation will come as primarily national and continental markets become enmeshed in global competitive networks and intersect with traditional voice services. The mingling of voice with data and videoservices on enhanced and overlay networks will gradually erode the network monopoly on voice services.

By and large, phone companies around the world have done poorly in enhanced services while thriving in overlay services. This is partly due to learning curve gains, since governments typically set aside at least one overlay franchise for the local phone company. But hybrid ownership of overlay services—phone companies plus independent suppliers—is becoming more popular because second-generation global networks require combined skills in voice and data. These networks will be shaped by how their developers assemble operating licenses, much as airline development is shaped by route assembly. The networks will also feature the selective reintegration of service and equipment suppliers. This section explores the changes in competitive positioning, with an emphasis on the role of U.S. firms.

By contrast with European TAs, which have generally lagged in all-purpose VANs and whose networks generally lose money and perform poorly, U.S. firms are well positioned in the world market, despite the surprisingly weak start of America's foremost network, AT&T. U.S. strength grew backward from computers into the communications network. Two computer firms, General Electric's GEISCO network and

---

23. Without market stimulation the EC estimated that there would be a 2 percent penetration rate for videoconferencing and 7 percent for high-speed data. With an active market approach, the numbers rose to 16 and 17 percent, and color fax and videophony would hit 3 percent and 21 percent respectively. (The market was defined as businesses with more than fifty employees.) EC Commission, "Towards Advanced Telecommunications for Europe," COM 88/341 Final (Brussels, June 21, 1988), pp. 24–25.

Control Data, created first-class data networks as a by-product of their futile challenge to IBM. Later, IBM turned to building its own global VAN. Meanwhile, three other U.S. VANs, open for public business, became prominent: Tymnet, U.S. Sprint's Telenet, and Computer Science Corporation's Infonet.

The next generation of entrants moved closer to offering integrated computing and communications services. Electronic Data Services (EDS), now a General Motors subsidiary, set the pace by offering to operate all computing and related communications tasks for major multinational firms. GEISCO and IBM offered the same service for selective global tasks, such as the electronic data interchange needs of their multinational customers.[24] Although trailing the U.S. industry, European firms have also done well in specialized application networks. The lead example is Reuters, which, along with Telerate owned by Dow Jones, dominates the $3 billion market for electronic financial trading.[25]

With the conspicuous exception of Telenet, most U.S. phone companies have sputtered in their attempts to market traditional VANs in Europe. AT&T was reluctant to challenge its equipment customers, the European TAs. Repeated signs that British Telecom intended to bypass AT&T in the VAN market finally prompted AT&T's 1989 purchase of Instel, a large British VAN. Meanwhile, the RBOCs were banned by the consent decree both from establishing comprehensive VANs within the United States and from interconnecting any global VAN to their home territories. This relic of antitrust doctrine forced the RBOCs to enter, without a comprehensive global plan, various ventures to explore local VANs overseas. These ventures are sometimes described as showcases, awaiting the day when the consent decree is modified.[26]

24. GEISCO reports that its business in Europe is growing 25 percent annually. Peter Heywood and Lee Mantelman, "Untying Europe's Tangled Web of Communications," *Data Communications*, March 1989, pp. 171–82.

25. Another pair of European successes are SITA and Swift, specialized closed user groups that provide airline and banking VANs for their members. In 1982, the European Information Providers Association estimated that all of Europe produced $532 million of information services, compared with $2.6 billion in the United States. It concluded that Europe lacked economies of scale and scope. Its definition included the production of data bases, on-line services, videotext, electronic publishing, microfilm production, document delivery software, consulting and information brokerage, and training services. Reuters fit into this definition. "Survey of the European Information Industry—Its Electronic Developments," *Business International*, European Information Providers Association (Geneva, June 1984).

26. The most extreme example was Nynex's 1989 purchase of the telephone system of the Rock of Gibraltar in Spain to demonstrate what it could do technologically in Europe.

Quiescence on the part of AT&T and the RBOCs may hurt the United States in the global market for value-added services, especially when mixing voice and data becomes more vital. Meanwhile, European interests have acquired a significant stake in U.S. VANs. British Telecom (BT) has just purchased Tymnet, and in 1989 twelve TAs bought 70 percent of the Infonet global packet switching network.[27] The TAs hope to use Infonet as the packet switching backbone for a venture with other TAs to provide an integrated international data network available on demand. In addition, the TAs hope to preempt American service providers from entering the European market by using independent networks; instead, the TAs want the American entrants to rely on the European data transmission network.

While the Infonet deal went through, the ambitious managed data network system (MDNS) collapsed because of Community antitrust scrutiny, bickering among TAs, and the decision of British Telecom and Deutsche Telekom that they could do better on their own. While a more limited agreement on electronic data interchange was salvaged, some European TAs are negotiating partnerships with U.S. suppliers of VANs, especially EDS and GEISCO, to serve the market for large users.[28]

Oddly enough, U.S. authorities believe that Europe is doing much better than the United States in mixing traditional VANs with low-cost terminals and innovative information services for small businesses and the general public. This claim has a potent political appeal, but it hinges on the very interesting Minitel videotext system in France. Minitel is important because it has already spent over $1.3 billion to deliver information services to small businesses and households—for example,

27. The ownership split stops Computer Services Corporation from exercising a unilateral veto on key decisions, which would have required a one-third equity holding. (In 1990 CSC agreed to sell its stake to MCI, a U.S. phone company.) The shares are 5 percent each to Scandinavian Teleinvest, Belgium, and Spain. Fifteen percent each went to West Germany and France (Transpac). Another 10 percent went to other European nations and 15 percent was allocated to Nippon Telegraph and Telephone of Japan and the Overseas Telecommunication Service of Australia. It is estimated that only 20 percent of the European international data traffic stays within Europe; the remainder ultimately goes elsewhere. "PTT-Infonet Deal Offers Glimpse of Post-1992 VAN Reality in Europe," *Data Communications*, September 1988, pp. 60–66; and Jeanie M. Wexler, "EDI Firms Forge Global Alliance," *Computer World*, December 1, 1989, p. 16.

28. For example, STET, the Italian state telecommunications company, paid $20 million for a 40 percent share in GEISCO's local subsidiary. Spain's Telefonica has worked for a partnership whereby it provides the packet switching and EDS provides systems integration in Spain. *Fintech Telecom Markets*, June 29, 1989, p. 10; and *Telecommunications Reports*, September 21, 1987, p. 50.

electronic yellow pages for the mass public at low prices. Yet Minitel is a doubtful commercial success, and it has yet to draw imitators.[29] If there is a European success in boosting enhanced services, it is not yet Minitel. Instead, the European success may be government efforts at creating common standards for the format of such services as electronic funds transfer.

While the RBOCs complain that even the latest changes in the consent decree restrict them from providing the American equivalent of an improved Minitel, the RBOCs are proving more adept in new overlay services.[30] Pacific Telesis, U.S. West, and Motorola are partners in the three new personal communications network licenses in the United Kingdom; Pacific Telesis is a partner in the second cellular license in West Germany; and U.S. West is a partner in one of the two cellular licenses in France.[31] U.S. West also owns a 25 percent stake in three different South London cable television franchises that plan to provide data, fax, and some voice telephone services along routes paralleling those of Mercury, British Telecom's main competitor.

What does this RBOC activity add up to? Whether it is only a portfolio play or something more fundamental is difficult to tell. Three strategies are emerging. Because frequency spectrum is scarce, it is quite valuable. Therefore, one cautious strategy is to become the equivalent to a skilled

29. Among its 4.5 million subscribers about 40 percent of the business is looking up phone numbers at a cost of about 6 cents per minute. Another 30 percent is from subscriber services, such as business and banking information. About half of the remaining 30 percent of the business is dating and electronic sex services (Minitel "rose"). More important, the videotext's slow speed and (comparatively) primitive graphics have made it a commercial failure in most countries, although Minitel is hoping to succeed in Spain and Switzerland. The terminals were originally offered free of charge. France Telecom is introducing a more sophisticated terminal in a partnership with Telic-Alcatel to lure business users. Even in France the service is probably a money loser, although the TA reports that the revenue gains for the supporting packet switched network largely offset the losses. For details of the endless debate over Minitel's economics, see "France Telecom's New Minitel Terminal for Business Users," *Fintech Telecom Markets*, May 18, 1989, p. 5; "French Minitel Service Will 'Remain in Deficit until at Least 1995,' " *Fintech Telecom Markets*, July 13, 1989, p. 2; and "High Wired Society," *Economist*, August 19, 1989, p. 55.

30. The consent decree changes permit RBOCs to offer a "gateway" for overlay services. U.S. West is using Minitel technology in a test system.

31. In the United Kingdom, Motorola (20 percent share) will be a partner to Cable and Wireless (60 percent) and Telefonica of Spain (10 percent) in one PCN license. Pacific Telesis is partnered with British Aerospace and France's Matra. U.S. West has Thorne EMI, the West German phone company, and FTS as partners. For a comprehensive overview of RBOC activities in the Community, see "The Baby Bells Scramble for Europe," *New York Times*, December 10, 1989, sec. 3, pp. 1, 8.

real estate developer and design firm. Many telecommunications firms define their comparative advantage in a global market in terms of skills at assembling, financing, designing, and operating systems. Holding several licenses in the same foreign region creates specialized human capital and information with a knowledge of local markets. It allows Nynex, for example, to argue to New York firms that it can help manage their communications needs in Europe. Many firms employing this first strategy are also exploring a second strategy of melding equipment and service markets selectively. The third, and most preliminary strategy, is the "globalization" of overlay and enhanced services networks. This requires new partnerships to put together specialized service skills and the right package of licenses.

British Telecom has the potential to combine all three strategies in assembling a global network for overlay and enhanced services, especially in air calling, paging, cellular, and voice messaging systems. Its most dramatic move was a $1.5 billion purchase of 22 percent of McCaw Cellular, America's largest cellular network. British Telecom has also invested in U.S. paging and voice messaging service companies, and it has won air call franchises on the Atlantic and Pacific routes. All these offerings can be marketed in a package with global VAN offerings from its recently acquired Tymnet. A single universal telephone (or phone number) is not at hand. But the new British Telecom network may provide better integration of pricing and services (for example, a single set of rates for the United States and the United Kingdom) than the traditional system of painstakingly negotiated joint agreements for individual service elements between nationally owned phone companies.[32]

Other groups would like to follow British Telecom's lead. Their efforts at global networking are powerfully influenced by the regulatory system for overlay services. In most countries the number of licenses for each specialized overlay service (air calling, cellular, mobile data, and so forth) is restricted, and foreign equity is typically limited to around 20 to 25 percent of ownership. The resulting race for franchises that combine local and foreign players generates some interesting market features.

---

32. Differences among frequency allocations in the regions of the world currently make it impractical to build a low-cost portable terminal (for example, a cellular phone) that can be used everywhere. But a single company's leadership permits the reduction of the infighting that plagued the MDNS initiative. I should add that British Telecom's overseas subsidiaries are still only about 3 percent of total revenue. "European P77's MONS Plan Falls Foul of New Competition," *Fintech Telecom Markets*, November 2, 1989, p. 3.

Because licenses are necessarily limited in number, they command a premium when sold.[33] The value of an individual license to a potential purchaser depends not only upon the inherent characteristics of the license (type of service and territory covered) but also the characteristics of the potential purchaser's other licenses. It is those other licenses that open up new possibilities for networking. As a result, shrewd companies are trying to build synergies in their mix of domestic and international licenses.

If the sale of licenses were left to the free play of market forces, a relatively few giant network organizers (like British Telecom) might emerge. But many countries circumvent the markets by using licenses to distribute political benefits and to protect the dominant role of domestic companies. Consortia organized to seek licenses therefore often include large users (especially if they also have global network needs) and local equipment manufacturers. This pattern in turn is educating a large pool of potential new entrants, such as the automobile companies. General Motors is already a major player through Hughes and EDS, Toyota is exerting itself in Japan, and Mercedes is stirring in West Germany.

In the face of rapid proliferation of new players and changing technology, the boundaries distinguishing among different overlay services and separating overlay services from traditional public networks are getting blurred. Cellular services, for example, currently connect to the main public network to place routine phone calls. While limited bandwidth means that radio networks cannot wholly abandon terrestrial systems, specialized networks for mobile users or private corporate networks not requiring video could be purely radio. Likewise, Cable and Wireless is leading the private fiber-optic alternative to public international voice service by developing Atlantic and Pacific cables that specialize in private voice and enhanced services networks. In a way, Cable and Wireless is the voice counterpart to the British Telecom experiment with a global data services network.[34] Someday, a British firm could own cellular franchises in the United States, Canada, and Britain and interconnect

33. Spectrum is scarce, and it is not allocated efficiently. Therefore, a license represents control of an inherently scarce commodity. The following discussion is based on interviews with companies in 1988 and 1989.

34. Similarly, France Telecom owns a minority share in an international long-distance carrier in the United States and in Japan. Therefore, it can profit from both ends of a call from the United States to France. All these developments pose major questions for regulators.

them over a private oceanic cable to provide a united bypass network for corporate customers.

Service providers are also experimenting with selective manufacture of equipment that complements new services. British Telecom owns Mitel, a PABX firm, and also manufactures and markets a line of data communications modems and multiplexers.[35] Electronic Data Services has just taken a 20 percent partnership with Hitachi in buying the U.S. National Advanced Systems, which manufactures Hitachi mainframe computers in the United States.[36] Meanwhile, Reuters has joined Sony in developing specialized bilingual financial terminals for the Japanese market.[37] Several overlay consortia groups feature equipment suppliers, such as Motorola and Hughes, as important members.

## Telecommunications Equipment

Europe has a bilateral trade deficit with the United States and Japan on every single item of telecommunications equipment, and even the strongest nations, France and West Germany, are in deficit on all but switching equipment.[38] France and West Germany are the only countries not in an overall trade deficit on telecommunications (see table 4-3 and appendix 4-5). Community firms are trying to unify the European internal market in order to become more competitive. At the same time, the "growth triangle" is changing the importance of different market segments and the types of firms that can compete effectively.

Repeated U.S. charges of unfair trading practices in European telecommunications have created the impression that U.S. firms are hard pressed to succeed in Europe. There is some truth in this impression. Obstacles are surely plentiful. The TAs overwhelmingly favor national suppliers, a significant barrier inasmuch as the combined network and terminal equipment purchases of the TAs of France, West Germany, Italy, and the United Kingdom account for 52 percent of the sales of

35. *Telecommunications Reports*, February 29, 1988, p. 16; June 27, 1988, p. 25; August 1, 1988, p. 31; and August 8, 1988, p. 50.

36. The new venture, Hitachi Data Systems Corporation, has sales of about $900 million. Jean S. Bozman, "NAS Gives Hitachi a U.S. Label to Wear," *Computer World*, May 8, 1989, p. 14.

37. "In Brief," *Computer World*, May 29, 1989, p. 66.

38. Based on pp. 53–57 of R. A. Cawley with P. Verburgt, *Intra-EC and Extra-EC Trade Flows in Telecommunications Equipment in 1988* (EC Commission, June 1989), p. 6. My calculations converted the data into categories of switching, transmission, terminal, and radio equipment. See table 4-3 and appendix 4-5.

TABLE 4–3. EC Performance in Intra-EC and Rest of World Trade in Telecommunications Equipment, 1988[a]

Billions of dollars

| Item | EC-12 | Big two[b] | Middle three[c] | Other seven[d] |
|---|---|---|---|---|
| Intra-EC exports | 4.1 | 2.4 | 1.1 | 0.6 |
| Intra-EC imports | 4.1 | 1.9 | 1.7 | 0.4 |
| ROW exports | 4.6 | 2.8 | 1.2 | 0.6 |
| ROW imports | 4.4 | 1.6 | 2.3 | 0.6 |
| ROW balance | 0.2 | 1.2 | (1.1) | (0.0) |
| Of which: | | | | |
| United States | (0.6) | (0.0) | (0.4) | (0.1) |
| Japan | (1.4) | (0.5) | (0.7) | (0.2) |
| Other countries | 2.0 | 1.7 | (0.0) | 0.2 |

SOURCE: Author's calculations based on R. A. Cawley with P. Verburgt, *Intra-EC and Extra-EC Trade Flows in Telecommunications Equipment in 1988* (EC Commission, June 1989), pp. 15, 52.
a. Rounded to nearest ECU 0.1 billion. Figures may not add up as a result of rounding.
b. France and West Germany.
c. United Kingdom, Netherlands, and Italy.
d. Other members of EC.

European equipment manufacturers.[39] While the United States still runs a positive trade balance on equipment, the surplus has declined from its 1985 peak of about $960 million to a 1988 figure of $575 million.[40] The EC program to unify the internal market, coupled with competitive pressure from the Japanese, portends further inroads on the U.S. export position.[41]

More generally, the United States faces three problems. First, the U.S. domestic market is declining in its role as a "platform" to support American firms on the world market. Competitive pressure has meant smaller margins for equipment suppliers, narrowing their financial scope to price aggressively abroad. Meanwhile, because the U.S. market is becoming a smaller share of the world total and is fragmented among more suppliers, the ability of U.S. firms to spread their R&D costs over comparatively long production runs is eroded. Second, the central office switch market, the traditional focus of U.S. trade policy, is growing comparatively slowly but remains a very expensive venture. Third, the

39. EC Commission, *Panorama of EC Industry* (Paris and Luxembourg, 1989), table 2, p. 6.
40. Cawley with Verburgt, *Intra-EC and Extra-EC Trade Flows*, p. 6.
41. Moreover, many hoped that European ISDN data services would finally provide an integrated alternative to relying on IBM architecture for computer communications and give European manufacturers an edge in designing for the new telecommuting environment.

"growth triangle" holds more promise for U.S. suppliers, but the U.S. government has yet to sort out how the fate of U.S. firms in Europe relates to the treatment of Japanese firms.

## The Central Office Switch Market

The United States historically commanded the largest share of the world central office switch (COS) equipment market, both as a producer and a consumer. Although risky, the COS market remains the strategic prize for large suppliers, both because it is the biggest component of the overall telecommunications market and because COS shapes the total network design. Therefore, it was alarming when AT&T's share of the U.S. central office switch market shrank from near dominance in 1980 to 58 percent in 1988.[42]

Throughout most of the postwar era, the world COS market might have been America's for the asking—if vastly different antitrust policies had prevailed at home and if far more open trade policies had been pursued abroad. AT&T and International Telephone and Telegraph enjoyed economies of scale and learning curves that might have conferred a decisive advantage in the world arena. However, U.S. antitrust policy deliberately impeded AT&T's overseas sales until the 1984 consent decree. Meanwhile, Europe, Japan, and Canada largely closed their markets to external competition. The European preference for local suppliers prompted ITT—the largest U.S. competitor for network equipment overseas—to become a decentralized manufacturer with most of its key research facilities located in Europe, alongside its principal markets.[43] Once ITT and a few other firms had slipped into their role of quasi-local suppliers (usually as second sources in large markets), most European equipment markets were frozen.

The opening of the U.S. market, following the consent decree, was a

42. AT&T purchased GTE's share of the market to bolster its position. National Telecommunications and Information Administration, *NTIA Telecom-2000: Charting the Course for a New Century*, Special Publication 88-21 (Washington: U.S. Department of Commerce, October 1988), p. 314.

43. GTE also expanded, particularly into Canada and Italy. It lacked major scale economies and decided to abandon its major equipment lines by selling its overseas business and U.S. transmission business to Siemens. It sold the U.S. and Canadian COS business to AT&T. ITT abandoned the COS business units after its newest generation switch had major software troubles that disqualified it from the U.S. market during the time when Northern Telecom won much of its new business. ITT sold the majority share of its business to Alcatel, which had the resources to finance correction of the problem.

critical ice-breaking event: for the first time in the postwar period, telecommunications procurement became a central issue of trade policy. This happened because the U.S. market was thoroughly penetrated by foreign suppliers very quickly, and the RBOCs wanted to become less dependent on the equipment of AT&T, a rival in services.[44]

In addition, a Canadian firm, Northern Telecom (itself a 1956 offspring of Western Electric), exploited its knowledge of North American network standards to expand aggressively, with the result that over half of its sales and production is now located in the United States. The RBOCs are searching for a third major source of switching technology. Siemens of Germany has already qualified with three RBOCs; and NEC of Japan, GPT of Britain, and Ericsson of Sweden have all qualified with at least one RBOC.[45]

The battle over central office switches also points to a broader issue concerning the U.S. market. Even as AT&T has stumbled in its efforts to replace ITT and General Telephone and Electronics Corporation (GTE) as an American champion overseas, the RBOCs are prevented from entering the equipment manufacturing market (and most COS software) under the consent decree. They argue that this restriction has amplified their dependence on imports because they cannot create their own captive alternative to AT&T and Northern Telecom. But manufacturing is no cinch, and many doubt that the RBOCs could do well in this business without entering into partnerships with foreign producers.

At the same time, table 4-4 shows that the United States is becoming a smaller share of the world market, a development that could hinder U.S. competitiveness, not only because fixed cost and scale problems are especially prominent in COS, but also because, as table 4-5 shows, COS growth rates do not match other equipment segments.[46] Yet it has

44. The RBOCs were also enticed by attractive equipment prices quoted by foreign suppliers. They were also mindful of the fact that the network switch contains software vital to services, and they did not want AT&T's service operations to enjoy advantages based on prior knowledge of its Western Electric network architecture.

45. Intense competition will keep profit margins down, although all the competitors hope that ISDN and other advanced network services may induce operating companies to purchase switches with more "bells and whistles" and fatter margins. The National Telecommunications and Information Administration estimates the U.S. telecommunications sales of Alcatel at $533 million and Siemens at $810 million in 1986. NTIA, *NTIA Telecom-2000*, p. 333.

46. This shrinkage in the importance of COS may be even more rapid because the giant COS may continually lose market share to smaller scale, high-performance data switches, PABXs, and computing equipment, much as mainframes lost share to minicom-

TABLE 4–4.  Expenditure by Top Fifty National Markets
for Telecommunications Equipment, 1986, 1990, 1995, 2000

Billions of dollars unless otherwise specified

| Item | 1986 | 1990 | 1995 | 2000 |
|---|---|---|---|---|
| Total world market | 83 | 112 | 133 | 185 |
| Total top 50 market | 81 | 110 | 131 | 181 |
| U.S. market | 24 | 27 | 30 | 42 |
| Top 50 as share of world market (percent) | 97 | 98 | 98 | 98 |
| U.S. as share of world market (percent) | 29 | 24 | 22 | 23 |

SOURCE: Author's calculations based on Telecommunications Research Centre, *Telecommunications World Outlook and Forecast, 1986 to 2000* (West Sussex, U.K., 1989), pp. 6–9, 13.

already cost about $1 billion to develop the current generation of switches, and the next generation may cost $2 billion. The minimum share of the world market necessary for survival is at least 10 percent and may be as high as 15 percent.[47] These developments explain why the number of market participants will shrink to five or six major equipment suppliers.

A successful strategy for central office switches requires a combination of world-scale size and local production. Local production fills the political demand to nurture home industry, and answers the local telephone company's demand for responsive manufacturing and design capability. (European firms claim that RBOCs ask the same features of their suppliers.) The political demand for local production will, by itself, ensure that "offset" arrangements endure. In these arrangements, an Italian telephone company that purchases $700 million of COS components from, say, AT&T, will insist that AT&T offset that purchase by buying, say, $500 million of terminals from Italy.

Offset arrangements clearly distort trade patterns, but the extent of distortion will be diminished as offsets are increasingly tuned to global standards of design and pricing. Indeed, even before the current liberalization push in the Europe 1992 context, implicit specialization emerged in switching equipment through components trade at the

---

puters. (A good example of the breed of newcomers is Digital Switching Corporation's entry that provides the COS for one of the new Japanese phone networks, Dani-Denden.) Table 4-3B in appendix 4-3, using somewhat higher estimates of COS markets, still points to low growth rates in key markets.

47. Müller estimates that half of the value added of a switch is software, which has a cost independent of market size. Switches also require some specialized components, although some manufacturers (like Ericsson) do not make most chips internally. Jürgen Müller, *The Benefits of Completing the Internal Market for Telecommunication, Research on the "Cost of Non-Europe," Basic Finding*, vol. 10 (Brussels: EC Commission, 1988).

TABLE 4–5. Market Segments for Equipment in Top Fifty Markets, 1986, 1990, 2000

Billions of dollars unless otherwise specified

| | 1986 | | 1990 | | 2000 | |
|---|---|---|---|---|---|---|
| Equipment | Total | Percent | Total | Percent | Total | Percent |
| COS[a] | 22 | 27 | 29 | 26 | 39 | 22 |
| Data switch and communications[b] | 5 | 8 | 10 | 10 | 26 | 14 |
| PABX and key systems | 6 | 8 | 9 | 8 | 13 | 7 |
| Transmission[c] | 19 | 23 | 25 | 22 | 35 | 19 |
| Cable[d] | 7 | 9 | 10 | 9 | 15 | 8 |
| Satellites[e] | 3 | 3 | 3 | 3 | 5 | 3 |
| Terminal equipment[f] | 8 | 9 | 9 | 8 | 15 | 8 |
| Mobile communications[g] | 5 | 6 | 9 | 9 | 21 | 12 |
| Other equipment[h] | 6 | 7 | 5 | 5 | 12 | 6 |
| TOTAL | 81 | 100 | 110 | 100 | 181 | 100 |

SOURCE: Author's calculations based on Telecommunications Research Centre, *Telecommunications World Outlook and Forecast*, pp. 45, 46, 48. TRC estimates have been modified in light of author's interviews to increase shares for data switch and communications (includes both wide area networks and LANs) and mobile communications, and to reduce shares for COS and PABX and key systems in 2000.

a. Local, toll and trunk switches, plus telex switches.
b. Modems, statistical multiplexers, packet switches, pads.
c. All equipment, outside plant, multiplexers.
d. Network and subscriber cabling, both copper and fiber.
e. Includes earth stations.
f. Handsets, feature and cordless phones, telex, and fax machines.
g. Cellular and traditional mobile radio, pagers, switches, and mobile data equipment.
h. Includes components, pay phones, and so on.

intrafirm and interfirm level.[48] The move toward "efficient offsets" reflects tremendous pressure on profit margins.

Another type of procurement distortion will also be diminished because of pressure on profit margins. As service markets become more competitive, TAs are less willing to retain their previous levels of cross-subsidies and quasi-exclusive supply contracts with national champion European firms. The average cost of COS per switched line runs between $225 and $500 in the EC, compared with about $100 in the United States.[49]

48. In 1986 West Germany had a switching market of DM 4.5 billion and imports of DM 800 million, largely in components for systems made and sold by local German producers. Thomas Schnöring, "Changes in Telecommunications Equipment Trade—The Case of Germany," paper presented to the International Telecommunications Society, Wissenschaftliches Institut für Kommunikationsdienste der Deutschen Bundespost, October 25–26, 1987.

49. "Europe's Internal Market," *Economist*, July 9, 1988, p. 33. Müller uses the AT&T production plant of 7 million lines per year as the benchmark for estimating that European

Terminal equipment is also overpriced. Müller has estimated that full liberalization of the equipment market would have saved more than 25 percent of a $21 billion market.[50]

The current reorganization of the European market may produce so much tumult that it will mislead policymakers about the trade opportunities in COS. Even the proposed Community directive that would liberalize procurement of telecommunications equipment would still allow TAs to demand a 50 percent European content level.[51] Besides, the top COS markets are largely locked in for the next few years (see table 4-6).

Four major changes in the COS market relate directly to the role of U.S. firms in Europe. First, majority control of ITT's network business was assumed in 1986 by France's Alcatel. This immediately boosted Alcatel to the number two position in the world switch market; its 40 percent share of the European market generated 87 percent of its revenue.[52] Like the other COS takeovers of recent years, the advantage of new market share is partly diminished by having to manage more than one switching technology.

Second, Siemens and Northern Telecom took advantage of the U.K. and Italian consolidation of their switchmakers. A troubled British venture in building digital switches was rescued by forming GPT, which is now controlled by the General Electric Company of the United Kingdom and Siemens. In addition, Siemens absorbed GTE's shares of the Italian and Belgian markets. Altogether, Siemens has about 25 percent of the European switch market and 15 percent of the world market, about

---

scales are at least 20 to 30 percent less on plants of 1 million lines per year. Müller, *Benefits of Completing*, p. 10. Interviews suggest that this is probably an exaggeration.

50. The large R&D costs and significant scale economies of COS seemingly make it an ideal fit for the strategic trade policy prescription of temporary protection of a home market in order to bestow a sustainable competitive advantage in exporting. As many critics point out, even the ideal examples of the theory leave many doubts about its applicability. However, I believe that a bargaining solution to the strategic trade issue has already arrived: some local production plus increased opening of the world market among governments of principal suppliers on the basis of (unspoken and imperfect) conditional reciprocity. Subsidy estimates are from Müller, *Benefits of Completing*, pp. 39, 52.

51. A powerful testimonial to the political dimension is that European firms seeking the COS market in the United States assume that they will have to deliver substantial local content.

52. Assuming control of ITT's holdings meant that Alcatel acquired the political problem of balancing sensitivities of a major French electronics company controlling key firms in West Germany and Belgium.

TABLE 4–6.  EC COS Market Size in 1990, Supplier Shares in 1989, and Contestability in the 1990s

| Country | Market size in 1990 (millions of dollars) | Supplier shares in 1989 Firm | Share (percent) | Contest-ability in the 1990s (percent) |
|---|---|---|---|---|
| West Germany | 2,200 | Siemens | 50 | 10–15 |
| | | Alcatel | 25 | |
| | | DTW | 10 | |
| | | TN | 15[a] | |
| France | 1,400 | Alcatel | 80 | 0 |
| | | Ericsson-Matra | 20 | |
| Italy[b] | 1,800 | Face-Alcatel | 20 | 20–30 |
| | | Fatme-Ericsson | 20 | |
| | | AT&T-Italtel | 50 | |
| | | Siemens-GTE | 10 | |
| United Kingdom | 1,200 | GPT (GEC and Plessey)-Siemens | 60 | 15[c] |
| | | Northern Telecom–STL | 20 | |
| | | Ericsson-Thorn | 20 | |
| Netherlands | 220 | AT&T-Philips | 82 | 4 |
| | | Ericsson | 10 | |
| | | Siemens | 4 | |
| | | Alcatel | 4 | |
| Spain[b] | 800 | Alcatel | 60 | 20–25 |
| | | Ericsson | 40 | |

SOURCE: Market estimates supplied by one telecommunications firm; and table 4-3B in appendix 4-3.
a. DTW and TN license Siemens technology.
b. High-growth market.
c. Primarily in firms other than British Telecom.

double its 1985 position. In 1987 Northern Telecom took a 28.5 percent share in STC, the smallest supplier of COS in Britain. STC has secured contracts from Cable and Wireless and may score at British Telecom.[53]

Third, the shakeout provided AT&T with its European entree. Italy's Italtel has teamed with AT&T for its 51.1 percent of the Italian market; while Philips N.V. of the Netherlands has subordinated its COS business

53. Northern also built a PABX plant in France. It promised to build up the transmission export business of STC, which also made a joint venture with SAT in France (a subsidiary of Sagem)—STC and SAT each had about a 30 percent share in their home market. David Thomas, "Northern Telecom Gains a Name," *Financial Times*, October 8, 1987, p. 6. Fujitsu has a PABX factory in Spain, and NEC, Toshiba, and Matsushita have ventures in the United Kingdom. EC Commission, *Panorama of EC Industry*, p. 12-8.

to AT&T.[54] AT&T has sold a few switches to British Telecom for special applications, but its best prospects are in the new networks. All in all, the North American presence in the European COS market has largely been reduced to one firm, AT&T, with Northern Telecom playing a weak secondary role.

The fourth change is that Ericsson of Sweden has also scored, largely at AT&T's expense. France sold its weak second supplier (which has a 15 percent share of the French switch market) to a strong new consortium led by Matra and Ericsson, thus diffusing a fight between the United States and West Germany over the French market.[55] Meanwhile, Ericsson also bolstered its position by forming a joint venture for switching with Thorn to control 20 percent of the U.K. market.

As table 4-6 shows, between reorganization and strategic positioning, most of the COS action will come down to

—Spanish and Italian procurement (because both have large markets requiring catch-up modernization);

—The West German decision on whether to introduce a third switch supplier; and

—U.K. choices as new networks enter the market and British Telecom modernizes.

While European COS orders will not dramatically alter the U.S. trade balance, they will help U.S. firms by enabling specific components to be produced efficiently on a global scale, by contributing to sunk costs for research, and by enhancing their credibility outside the U.S. market.

### Other Equipment Markets

The overall mix of the European equipment market is shifting in favor of non-COS items, particularly equipment associated with the "growth

54. AT&T had majority control of its joint venture with Philips, AT&T Network International. This entity swapped 20 percent of its ownership and paid $130 million in cash for a similar share of Italtel to cement the market relationship. Italtel will retain its own switching architecture. Alan Friedman, "AT&T to Invest $130m in Telecom Pact with Italtel," *Financial Times*, June 6, 1989, p. 23.

55. The TA and Alcatel preferred AT&T because AT&T was to help establish French equipment for COS and transmission (especially cellular and microwave) in the United States. David March, "France Sends Friendly Signals across the Atlantic," *Financial Times*, July 5, 1985, p. 3. West Germany then objected to Alcatel controlling 40 percent of the German market while letting AT&T into France in preference to Siemens. While France rejected this thesis, it diplomatically elected to choose a French firm, Matra, which had chosen a 20 percent share for Ericsson as its joint venture partner (and technology source).

triangle."[56] The equipment markets in question range widely in terms of types of equipment, their scale economies, and fixed research and marketing costs. For example, standard transmission cable (which suffers from global overcapacity) is a basic technology with some economies of scale. By contrast, fiber optics—which will grow from $0.3 billion in 1985 to $1.5 billion in 1991—has significant scale economies and high research costs.[57] U.S. firms retain leading roles in both fiber optics and satellites.[58]

Japanese suppliers, who do not do well in central office switches, do well in fiber optics, much to the distress of European officials who see a closed Japanese market. The U.S. role in Europe is also under pressure from Japan. An issue for U.S. policy, therefore, is how hard (if at all) the United States should oppose European reciprocity demands leveled against Japan. A good guess is "not very hard," so long as EC reciprocity demands do not deliver a glancing blow against U.S. interests.

In terms of market characteristics, the most vital changes are, first, the growth of specialized network equipment designed for data switching and high-speed, high-volume transmission and, second, the growth of equipment designed for advanced combinations of voice, optical, and data, along with complementary terminal equipment. Radio, advanced transmission, and terminal equipment will lead the overall market (see table 4-5).[59] Markets for mobile and radio communications gear are exploding, with annual growth rates of 25 percent and the prospect of a

56. Dataquest estimates that public digital COS will be virtually constant at roughly $3 billion, as will private PABX switching at roughly $2.5 billion. Hugo Dixon, "Telecommunications Markets Boom in Europe Predicted," *Financial Times*, October 25, 1988, p. 5.

57. In comparison, the United States will go from $0.77 billion in 1986 to $2.9 billion in 1992. NTIA, *NTIA: Telecom-2000*, p. 266.

58. Thanks to their patent positions, AT&T and Corning dominate fiber production in the U.S. market, holding more than a 75 percent share. Corning further bolstered its European role through joint ventures with Siemens and BICC for fiber cables. Japanese firms, however, have made major inroads in the world market, especially by price cutting. The International Trade Commission estimates that the United States held about 35 percent of the Community market for optical fiber (worth $22 million in U.S. exports). ITC, *The Effects of Greater Economic Integration within the European Community on the United States*, USITC publication 2204 (Washington, July 1989). This treatment largely skips the special properties of the satellite communications market. Hughes, General Electric, and Ford remain strong in satellite systems despite repeated European assaults on the market. Satellites have been revived because high-powered systems linked to VSATs (very small aperture terminals) have made them a vehicle of great appeal for private networks with intermittent transmission needs.

59. Dixon, "Telecommunications Markets Boom."

$2 billion market in 1992. Many U.S. companies are using leased circuits to set up private high-speed data networks (called T1 networks), thereby creating a U.S. market for local area network connections, multiplexers (which mix and route digital data over transmission channels), modems, and related network control equipment.[60] This market was $5.2 billion in 1988. A similar market will soon emerge in Europe.

The growth of advanced transmission and associated terminal equipment has two implications. First, these segments are ripe for newcomers seeking niche markets. Telecommunications authorities are more willing to accept the new entrants because fixed costs and scale economies are not so high as to create the prospect of a severe shakeout, with the wholesale demise of new firms. U.S. leaders include older firms with specialized lines in telecommunications (for example, Rockwell-Collins in advanced transmission) and smaller firms, such as those for the T1 switch and multiplexer market (NET, Newbridge Networks, Timplex, and Digital Communications Associates and Proteon).[61]

Second, the growing sophistication of this equipment enables a newcomer to build its own relationship with a TA, comparable to what was once possible only between the COS supplier and the TA. For example, AT&T—a newcomer in this context—is concentrating on selling transmission equipment systems for high-speed fiber-optic systems, not only for immediate earnings, but also as a way to build long-term relationships suitable for later success in the COS market.[62] AT&T teamed with Spanish Telefonica's firm, Amper, to take over ITT's old Marconi holdings in Spain for transmission systems; and many AT&T dealings with Philips N.V. and Italtel focus on joint efforts in the new markets.

The natural complement to transmission is advanced terminal equip-

60. One estimate is that 37 percent of the $13.7 billion in U.S. private purchases in 1985 went for data communications equipment (excluding PABX) and value-added features such as voice mail and local area networks. Czatadana, "Big Business = Big Bucks in Telecommunications," pp. 32–48. U.S. growth rates are declining because the initial wave of new corporate private networks has just peaked in the United States, but it will soon take off in Europe where the number of wide area networks will double in the next three years. Nigel Tutt, "Delays in Standards, Doubts about Marketing," *Telecommagazine* (Netherlands), August 1988, pp. 26–36. Also Davis, "Making Sense of the Telecommunications Circus."

61. Britain's Racal recently bought part of the DCA line. Elisabeth Horwitt, "Newbridge Follows NET's Footsteps," *Computer World*, October 24, 1988, p. 61.

62. AT&T sold such a system to the French TA. AT&T is relying on smaller U.S. firms to supply many of the key items (for example, T1 networking multiplexers and packet switching) for its expansion. John T. Mulqueen, "AT&T: Clever OEM or 'Sugar Daddy' of the Industry?" *Data Communications*, March 1988, pp. 103–08.

ment. The European market posed special problems for new entrants until now. For example, several TAs retained their monopolies on the "first instrument attached to the network" and other additional items. National standards were often so idiosyncratic (and sometimes not fully disclosed) as to make the cost of entry into each market prohibitively high (thanks to reengineering outlays). In addition, U.S. firms faced costly, time-consuming government certification procedures. Not surprisingly, U.S. firms much prefer the use of recognized commercial laboratories to test systems and to certify compliance with applicable standards.

European obstacles are starting to disappear. Recent liberalization of the advanced terminal equipment market has already pressed European suppliers hard. The quickly growing terminal market is akin to consumer electronics and sophisticated personal computers. Producer strength at the lower end flows from labor and component cost advantages or from quick responses to market niches. Entry is easy, and both U.S. and European markets have largely fallen to Asian suppliers, which not only have lower production costs but also dumped certain items.[63]

European firms, however, take pride in nurturing a consumer electronics industry in spite of the Japanese challenge. Internal unification of the EC market is crucial for making the Europeans and Americans once again competitive in at least mid-level terminal equipment, like key telephone sets.[64] Many hope that high-definition television (HDTV) can leverage this industry into a lower-end terminal market for new network services (in addition to supporting advanced graphics technology

63. Although Japan ran its original trade surplus on lower-end technology like telephone keysets, now developing countries are displacing Japanese firms in these markets. Japanese companies are emphasizing terminal equipment that uses advances in microchips and imaging technology to add value to inputs provided by public networks—for example, the image processing available on its new television and fax equipment. *IBC Strategic Audit*, p. 27, estimates that fax systems were 40 percent and 70 percent of terminal equipment markets of ECU 4 billion and ECU 8.6 billion in 1987 and 1992, respectively. LANs will be half of an ECU 5.2 billion market for data communications equipment in 1992. See also Dixon, "Telecommunications Markets Boom." European manufacturers freely acknowledge that they cannot compete on the lower end under current market conditions. Residential terminal equipment (about 8 percent of the market at ECU 1.3 billion) is dominated by Asian producers. EC Community, *Panorama of EC Industry*, p. 12-7.

64. The problem is worse for U.S. companies. One American manufacturer estimates that it requires a minimum production of 500,000 key telephone set units of the same basic design to be cost effective. Yet a realistic market share in any individual European nation is about 50,000 to 70,000 units. Therefore, a firm has to design and sell to a single European market if it is to produce in Europe. Interview, May 1989.

and signal processing chips). However, as in the United States, European doubts about the precise payoffs of HDTV technology are growing.[65]

Entry is almost as easy at the upper end of the terminal market, but significant advantages flow from customization for specific users and expertise on emerging regional standards. U.S. firms excel at equipment in the range from desktop computer up through the private corporate network. By contrast, because of their close association with the TAs, European firms made considerable investment in new ISDN-compatible equipment and think that they are globally competitive on this front. For example, Siemens stressed these capabilities in its joint venture with IBM for Rolm PABXs. (Assisted by AT&T's failure in the European PABX game, Siemens now dominates the market.)[66] However, given the uncertainties about the timing and size of the ISDN market, the European emphasis is a bit of a gamble.[67]

The other major segment of the new market is radio and mobile. This technology alters the prospects of fiber optics and COS.[68] The major network equipment suppliers largely missed the initial cellular revolution, and only Ericsson has emerged as a co-leader with a specialized U.S. supplier, Motorola. So far, Motorola (13 percent of the European market) and assorted Japanese firms (about 43 percent of the market) also dominate mobile telephone sets.[69] U.S. firms (like Harris and Scientific Atlantic)

65. Unlike U.S. plans for fiber optics, direct satellite broadcasting may be the vital mechanism for delivering HDTV in Europe.

66. It takes a great deal of money, time, technical resources, and knowledge of local public networks' idiosyncracies to introduce a successful PABX. So this remains a market with significant entry barriers, and even in Japan significant market consolidation is under way. U.S. firms do not shine in this market overseas. The Rolm-Siemens deal will boost Siemens into first place in the world PABX market with sales of $2.3 billion in 1987 (including Rolm), while Northern Telecom has $1.7 billion and AT&T and NEC have $1 billion each. Both AT&T and Northern Telecom have about a 20 percent share of the U.S. PABX market, Japanese firms have a 24 percent share. Booz Allen and Hamilton, *Europe 1992: Threat or Opportunity?* Special Report (New York, 1989); and Shuichi Saito, "PBX Makers Find Joint Marketing Solves Problem of Development Costs," *Japan Economic Journal*, October 7, 1989, p. 20.

67. Customers claim that the equipment costs are far too high, so European firms are anxious to unify the market to gain scale economies. Moreover, high-speed local area networks may make ISDN far too slow for large users, and the ISDN market for smaller customers is still uncertain.

68. For example, U.S. cellular network equipment will grow from $0.5 billion in 1987 to $5 billion in 1990, while terminal equipment will increase from $0.5 billion to $1 billion. The pager equipment market will be $1 billion in 1990. NTIA, *NTIA: Telecom-2000*, pp. 286–87.

69. The International Trade Commission estimates that U.S. exports to the Community

also do extremely well in the VSAT and ROE satellite terminal markets (see appendix 4-1 for definitions), but European restrictions on their use may inhibit the market.[70]

European firms hope that the conversion to digital cellular services and other radio technologies, whose markets may reach $1.6 billion by 1991, will create a lucrative second chance.[71] For example, Racal Vodafone, a British firm, selected Orbitel of the United Kingdom and Ericsson of Sweden as its equipment suppliers for the next generation of services.[72]

Reflecting the changes discussed here, the global ranking of telecommunications manufacturers in 1987 came down to the results shown in tables 4-7 and 4-8. These figures largely reflect positioning in the COS market, and they understate U.S. competitiveness because leaders in many new markets are not on the list. In a similar way, sales of mainframe computers distorted industry rankings in the computer sector for many years. The figures do suggest that major switching firms have diversified their lines of telecommunications equipment; notable examples are

---

were $109 million for transmitters, receivers, transceivers, television cameras, cellular digital land systems, and papers. ITC, *Effects of Greater Economic Integration*, pp. 4–41. The European leaders for these terminals are Nokia (13.4 percent), Ericsson (3.9 percent), Siemens (3.1 percent), and Philips (3.6 percent). Bert Wiggers and Marc van der Heyden, "Digital Mobile Telephone Network Threatened from Space?" *Telecommagazine* (Netherlands), Autumn 1988, p. 45. Motorola just received a $100 million contract from Telefonica of Spain for its joint venture with Amper in Spain to provide a national analog cellular system and digital system for Seville. *Telecommunications Reports*, September 4, 1989, p. 33.

70. The U.S. market for VSATs that can both send and receive will quadruple from its current $200 million level by 1994. "When Big Birds Have Little Ears," *Data Communications*, vol. 18 (September 1989), pp. 67–70.

71. Although no U.S. firm has yet pressed the point, the linkage between the service and equipment goals of the Community in this area opens the possibilities of trade complaints in the future.

72. Orbitel is a joint venture of Racal with Plessey. Digital pocket phones will be an EC business market of ECU 2.5 billion by 1995, says the Commission. This covers home cordless phones at 1–1.5 billion and business phones at 1 billion and prices of ECU 200 to ECU 250 per set. Pocket phones used near telepoints will add another ECU 1–1.5 billion from business users and ECU 0.2 billion from residential users. Hugo Dixon, "EC Proposals for Freeing Telecom Services Criticised," *Financial Times*, March 17, 1989, p. 2. Ericsson, in turn, has teamed up with General Electric to form a new joint venture that will encompass patent firm assets in mobile radio, cellular telephones, and mobile data systems for North America and Europe. The joint venture, 60 percent owned by Ericsson, expects a $1 billion business by 1990. *Telecommunications Reports*, August 28, 1989, p. 13. In addition, a German (AEG), Finnish (Nokia), and French (Alcatel) consortium appears to be the likely supplier of choice for the German and French digital cellular systems.

TABLE 4–7. Leading Manufacturers of Public Network Equipment, 1987[a]

Billions of dollars unless otherwise specified

| Firm | Network equipment sales | Percent of top ten firms | Total equipment sales | Total equipment sales as percent of total firm revenues |
|---|---|---|---|---|
| AT&T[b] | 7.1 | 25 | 10.2 | 30 |
| Alcatel[c] | 5.2 | 19 | 7.8 | 61 |
| Siemens[d] | 3.7 | 13 | 6.2 | 22 |
| Northern Telecom | 3.0 | 11 | 4.8 | 98 |
| Ericsson[e] | 2.4 | 8 | 3.3 | 64 |
| NEC | 2.4 | 8 | 5.0 | 31 |
| GPT/Stromberg[f] | 1.4 | 5 | 2.0 | 100 |
| Fujitsu | 1.3 | 5 | 2.0 | 16 |
| Telettra/Italtel[g] | 1.1 | 4 | 1.1 | 95 |
| GTE[h] | 0.7 | 1 | 1.1 | 7 |
| Motorola | . . . | . . . | 3.5 | 57 |
| IBM[i] | . . . | . . . | 2.4 | 3 |

SOURCE: Author's calculations based on Telecommunications Research Centre, *Telecommunications World Outlook and Forecast*, p. 223; and Herbert Ungerer with Nicholas Costello, *Telecommunications in Europe* (Brussels: EC Commission, 1988), p. 128.

a. These firms account for 49 percent of the world sales of telecommunications equipment.
b. Includes joint venture with Philips. If half of Telettra/Italtel and two-thirds of GTE are included, the AT&T adjusted share of the top ten firms would be about 29 percent.
c. Includes all ITT holdings.
d. If all of GPT group and a third of GTE are included, the Siemens adjusted share would be 19 percent of the top ten firms.
e. Includes sales of CGCT in France.
f. Includes Stromberg Carlson sales in the United States; this group is becoming part of Siemens alliance structure.
g. Before AT&T partnership with Italtel.
h. Before splitting holdings between AT&T and Siemens.
i. Before partnership on PABX with Siemens.

Siemens, AT&T, and to some extent Ericsson. Other contenders are part of well-diversified firms (like NEC).

U.S. industry as a whole finds its best prospects in the equipment segment of the growth triangle. Overlay services are especially important for U.S. firms, because it is here that they shine, not in terminal equipment items, such as fax machines, that resemble consumer appliances.

U.S. reliance on the upper end of the market means that U.S. firms selling in Europe are highly vulnerable if the EC does not make the design of its future information network fully transparent, and if it does not pursue a philosophy of decentralized computing and network management. In any event, the upper-end market will feature a sharp battle

TABLE 4–8. Breakdown of Sales of Leading Telecommunications
Companies, 1988

Billions of dollars[a]

| Item | Siemens | AT&T | Ericsson | Alcatel |
|---|---|---|---|---|
| Network systems | 4.4 | 6.8[b] | 4.4 | 8.8 |
| Switching | 2.3 | n.a. | 2.1 | 3.3[c] |
| Transmission[d] | 1.5 | n.a. | 0.2 | 2.0 |
| Cables | 0.6 | n.a. | 0.5 | 3.5 |
| Communications/information | | | | |
| systems and terminals | 5.8[e] | 7.9[f] | 0.6 | 3.2[g] |
| Components | 1.6 | 0.5[h] | 0.1 | . . . |
| Special items | 1.5[i] | 20.0[j] | 1.7[k] | 2.0[l] |
| TOTAL SALES | 33.0 | 35.2 | 5.0 | 13.5 |

SOURCE: Author's calculations based on 1988 annual reports.
a. Converted at DM 1.8 to dollar, 6.3 kroner to dollar, and $1.22 to the ECU.
b. Breakdown of category not itemized in AT&T report.
c. Includes digital radio switches.
d. Items other than cabling, for example, microwave, multiplexers.
e. Roughly 50 percent is computer equipment, 30 percent is equipment for private communications networks, and 20 percent is communications terminals and other peripherals.
f. Includes PABX, all terminal equipment, and computers.
g. Includes PABX, facsimile, and cellular equipment.
h. Including sales to federal government.
i. Includes home security systems, radio systems, and so forth.
j. Largely network services.
k. Network services, engineering, defense work, radio systems.
l. Primarily specialized applications software.

for share among European, U.S., and Japanese firms. Because Europe views the Japanese market as closed, the Community will very likely impose reciprocity requirements on Japan. These requirements could be fashioned in ways that inadvertently or otherwise affect U.S. interests. So the U.S. government may well be drawn into EC-Japan negotiations.

## Broad Directions in EC Policy

The effort to retool the European economy to meet the Japanese challenge is a critical dimension of the 1992 process. Because Europeans believe that telecommunications and information industries are crucial, and because Europe is a recognized laggard, there is broad support for reorganizing this large market. The key issues are the balance between competition and administrative guidance, and the degree to which the market should be open to foreign suppliers. The substantive resolution of these issues will depend on the decisionmaking process.

The Community relies on a system of consensus building staffed by the Commission directorates. For telecommunications policy, the most concerned directorates are DG-13 (telecommunications), DG-4 (competition), and to a lesser extent DG-1 (external relations).[73] Usually, final approval of Commission proposals rests with the Council of Ministers of member states. For example, national communications ministers approve the proposals made by DG-13, while ministers of justice approve the proposals made by DG-4.

In practice, DG-4 can block (and DG-1 can influence) major telecommunications proposals, if they try hard. But this still leaves considerable discretion to DG-13, a directorate committed to blending more competition into the industrial policy mix. It is natural for U.S. firms to worry how that mix will work, especially because DG-13 relies heavily on the TA-dominated Senior Officials Group–Telecommunications and its Groupe d'Analyse et de Prevision. DG-13 has tried to manipulate the process to force the TAs to propose major reforms, but this ploy has also conferred great influence on the TAs.

The telecommunications program of the Common Market is largely carried out by binding directives that allow for limited member state differences when incorporated into national legislation.[74] There are two routes for issuing binding directives. The normal route is to obtain approval from the Council of Ministers. Although the 1987 Single European Act curtailed unilateral national vetos, a minority can still block action. A second route for issuing a directive involves Article 90(3) of the Treaty of Rome. Article 90(3) permits the Commission to issue a directive without Council approval, to deal with "cases where the dominant position of state monopolies is being abused, resulting in a violation of EC rules."[75] In theory a directive issued under Article 90(3) only specifies how the existing power of the EC applies to a particular

73. For a full description of the legislative process, see chapter 1. Commissioners are picked by national governments, but they are assigned to their posts by the Commission president. Sir Leon Brittan heads DG-4 (competition), and Filippon Maria Pandolfi of Italy heads DG-13 (telecommunications). Both directorates have strong bureaucracies, although DG-4 is traditionally one of the most powerful in the Commission. Brittan has blended ministerial experience in competition and industrial policy with credibility won from previous conflicts with Margaret Thatcher to bolster his strong commitment to market competition. Pandolfi, a finance expert, has proved a less vital political force. But this balance could shift with new commissioners, to be selected in 1993.

74. DG-13 has also used nonbinding recommendations to prepare the way for building a consensus on legally binding regulations and decisions.

75. Neil Gibbs, J. M. Didier, and associates, "Telecommunications in the Single European Market," 1992: The External Impact of European Unification, vol. 1, pt. 2 (April 7, 1989), p. 14. Also, Wayne Sandholtz and John Zysman, "1992: Recasting the European Bargain," World Politics, vol. 42 (1989), pp. 95–128.

problem posed by state monopolies. In practice this route was created because member states recognized that the special political influence of public utilities might someday block enforcement actions necessary for the efficient functioning of the internal market. Article 90(3) was crucial for adopting key elements of the 1987 Green Paper on Telecommunications, but its use for this purpose in itself became a point of controversy because many governments worried about the precedent being set for other issues.

A final wrinkle is the principle of "mutual recognition," which serves as the "default option" under the 1992 program. Simply put, if there is no explicit program for harmonizing technical regulations, the member states must accommodate the regulations of the home country of a Community firm. The Commission is pushing to apply the mutual recognition principle to the right to establish and provide services throughout the Community. In the case of telecommunications, the highly competitive U.K regulatory regime means that British-domiciled firms would have significant latitude throughout Europe, if no general EC rules on standards for equipment and services are adopted. Conservative TAs, therefore, have a powerful incentive to reach a consensus on standards.

The amount of competition in the reform mix is still precarious. Organized labor, still politically powerful, remains skeptical of competition. Closer ties with Eastern Europe will bolster supporters of a strong public sector as part of a single "mixed" economy for Europe. Finally, no political leadership in Europe will tolerate a major rate shock for small households as a result of competition. The Commission strategy of liberalizing the market in stages is partly a testing process, designed to establish that competition will not significantly penalize smaller users.

The strongest opposition to competition came from France, Italy, Belgium, and Spain. For many reasons France was the pivot of the opposition.[76] Mitterrand's motivation was primarily political and philosophical: public telecommunications services are in some sense the last refuge of the socialist pledge that the public sector can be more efficient

---

76. The political problems concerning regional politics in Belgium have greatly strengthened the power of its unions and reduced its credibility on this issue. Many suspect that Spain may change its position as Telefonica expands aggressively overseas, and most do not think that Italy can overcome internal political divisions sufficiently to be a firm advocate. Special Community redistribution programs for telecommunications are supposed to satisfy Greece and Portugal.

and innovative than the private market, especially in serving smaller users. Thus France advocated a monopoly, or strictly licensed competition, on such "basic" data services as packet networks. In theory this would have prevented "cream skimming" by newcomers that would erode the ability of TAs to create innovative services. In fact France may have feared that decisive use of Article 90(3) would prompt a massive rush of voice traffic to private networks. In December 1989 France settled for a compromise that permits licensed competition in basic data services, but makes licensing subject to Commission review to ensure transparency, nondiscrimination, and conformity to EC competition rules.[77]

The strongest support for competition came from the United Kingdom, the Netherlands, and West Germany. This coalition initially prevailed because the Commission, especially Jacques Delors, was reminded by the collective voice of European industry that a firm competition policy was essential to the EC's credibility. One hundred endorsements—from senior executives of European user firms—played a major role in EC decisions on telecommunications services, reflected in the December 1989 compromise. The business community also worked hard in the European Parliament to modify Commission proposals so as to give a greater role to users in setting policy. In addition, some TAs preferred reform on favorable terms because they believed that the mutual recognition approach would eventually enable users to bypass restrictive national networks. Finally, the TAs and some unions recognized that monopoly could no longer ensure manufacturing jobs in the equipment sector. In the new era of digital products, traditional levels of employment simply cannot be maintained.[78]

The December 1989 compromise leaves much discretion to the Commission. If West German competitive reforms are as extensive as they seem, that will make the Commission's task easier. The pro-competition camp depends on a group of like-minded political leaders within the member states to favor the largest telecommunications users, thereby boosting economic efficiency, while still protecting local house-

77. Hugh Dixon, "Untangling Europe's Telecommunications Networks," *Financial Times*, December 11, 1989, p. 5.

78. A. D. Little reported that the total number of employees in a 500,000 line plant for COS should drop from 1,250 for analog systems to 160 for digital. EC Commission, *European Telecommunications—Strategic Issues and Opportunities for the Decade Ahead*, annex A (Brussels, November 1983), p. 54.

holds. These leaders can blame the Commission for any disruption of the TAs, or their suppliers, or the labor unions. Finally, the EC rules will leave national leaders with some latitude for hidden but curtailed protectionism. This blend of credit taking, blame avoidance, and hidden protection provides an ideal backdrop for a political process that relies heavily on building a consensus over time.[79]

One factor that could disrupt the consensus would be a further major swing in the trade balance in favor of Japan. The Community would then have to decide whether to challenge the Japanese overtly on a bilateral basis or simply to step up hidden protectionism against all foreign products. A second danger is that the European Court of Justice could reject the use of Article 90(3) as the basis for directives on telecommunications, and force a replay of the decisionmaking process that would favor the coalition inclined to less competition.

## Equipment and Services in the EC Market

The Commission used Article 90(3) to issue a sweeping directive on terminal equipment that ends the monopoly privileges of TAs and liberalizes the market for the supply, sale, installation, and services for terminal equipment. Directive 88/301 even covers the "first instrument" attached to the network, from telephone through VSAT and ROE satellite terminals.[80] TAs must publish all technical standards for terminal equipment, including the network interface specifications, a move that ensures that no TA will have a competitive advantage in equipment sales or supply of enhanced services due to its exclusive knowledge of the interface.

U.S. firms are happy with the Commission directive, and rightly so. But two areas of concern remain. The first is the timeliness of its implementation. France, Italy, and Belgium affirmed support for the content of Directive 88/301 but protested the use of Article 90(3) for this purpose. They have accordingly challenged the directive in the European Court of Justice, and a ruling is expected in March 1990. If the challenge

79. Roland Vaubel, "A Public Choice Approach to International Organization," *Public Choice*, vol. 51, no. 1 (1986), pp. 39–57.

80. As a result, a third-party systems integrator (like Electronic Data Services) can purchase, configure, and maintain any set of equipment at the request of a client. This greatly facilitates the installation of private corporate networks, including the use of satellite receiving stations to move data to many locations.

prevails, there will be a delay until a new directive following conventional routes is adopted. Meanwhile, eight member states have failed to meet the implementation schedule, and the Commission is preparing enforcement actions against them.

The other concern pertains to the types of standards and the testing and certification for compliance. While Directive 88/301 abolished TA control of type approvals as of July 1989, ineffective implementation could open major loopholes for TAs to block competition. Draft Directive COM 89/289 (released in July 1989), dealing with types of standards and compliance issues, lays down more stringent approval procedures than the United States follows. U.S. rules require only that equipment may not hurt the network or pose safety dangers. Unlike the United States, the Community would allow the TA to require greater uniformity in design to facilitate interconnecting equipment.[81] The draft directive moves Europe closer to the United States on testing procedures, enabling certification for the entire EC market by any independent testing authority certified by member states.[82] Trade negotiators might extend this use of the mutual recognition principle, on a reciprocal basis, to the testing authorities of other nations.

## Public Procurement of Network Equipment

Network equipment was a particularly troubling problem for the Commission because, as government entities, most TAs were subject to the byzantine world of public procurement policies and were exempt from EC procurement rules. The Commission decided, in 1989, to extend new rules for open procurement to telecommunications, transport, electricity, and water utilities. But the Council has not yet approved this proposal. (See appendix 4-6 for details.)

The Commission had a tough political problem because, while most TA procurement is made by government entities, a few, notably British Telecom, are private firms. The Commission feared that private firms

81. DG-4 reached agreement with DG-13 that interoperability requirements would be kept to a minimum. Directive 86/361 in 1986 set out the requirement for mutual recognition of test results. The Article 90 directive to liberalize terminal equipment by December 31, 1990, was adopted in May 1988.

82. Oversight of the process and the issuance of additional necessary standards rests in the hands of the Approvals Committee for Telecommunications Equipment (ACTE), which has two members appointed by each government and votes according to the qualified majority procedures of the Community. It is worth noting that Draft Directive COM 89/289 (Luxembourg, July 27, 1989) is not an Article 90(3) decision.

with monopoly licenses (or operating in markets where the number of licenses was very limited) might make procurement decisions in the same discriminatory manner as any government entity. Accordingly, the Commission has fashioned a proposal (Directive 88/378) that effectively binds both public entities that offer telecommunications services to the public and private entities in telecommunications, if they have special or exclusive rights of operation (for example, a license to operate a basic telecommunications network).[83] The proposal governs procurement of network equipment, terminal equipment, software, and installation and service contracts. (It does not include terminal equipment resold to customers, a market where the telephone companies have no monopoly position.) TAs retain considerable discretion over the precise method of procuring equipment, and the TA can still require 50 percent European content. But all purchases are subject to greater transparency and tougher rules on nondiscrimination (see appendix 4-6).

U.S. firms have many worries about the procurement directive, but six stand out.

First, will the EC extend its coverage to other public entities? Many of the largest purchasers of telecommunications products are government ministries in finance, defense, and transportation. The current directive excludes them.

The second issue is a matter of broad principle. Europe sees the procurement directive as its negotiating tool to obtain access to the RBOC market in particular. So the Community has offered to drop its own European content requirements if the GATT code on government procurement is extended to cover telecommunications, including procurement by RBOCs. Failing this, the Community wants to negotiate a bilateral accord. But it wants any code or accord to match the scope of its own new rules on covered purchases. The United States adamantly argues that private firms should be exempt, including AT&T and the

---

83. The current proposal combines COM (88) 377 (Brussels, October 11, 1988) and (88) 378 (Brussels, October 11, 1988). The coverage is defined in Article 1 of the directive. It will include cellular phone licenses. There is a plausible political case that political pressure can be exerted on an exclusive franchisee to purchase locally. Even if the competitive pressure is too great for the franchisee to surrender to inefficient procurement, many European politicians would reject the notion that public TAs might be less efficient than private ones. (Oftel's recommendation that British Telecom buy no more than 20 percent of its switches from Thorn-Ericsson illustrates all of these issues.) "BT and Its Suppliers," *Financial Times*, July 24, 1985, p. 12.

RBOCs. This disagreement raises a fundamental issue about the surveillance of the procurement decisions of quasi-public firms.[84] On this issue, the EC has the better argument. Indeed, if the United States were negotiating with Japan, it would surely want private entities with licensing privileges to be covered.

Third, what constitutes 50 percent European content, so that the supplier can be treated as a European firm? Will eligibility be based on content for the particular project or on the firm's total degree of European value-added on all network products? Content probably will be judged on a project basis, and this test would pose difficulties for many U.S. firms. A large part of the value-added of telecommunications equipment resides in the research and software that, typically, are part of joint costs of a broader production and research effort.

The related fourth concern is over software and research and development. Most U.S. firms, including AT&T, will find it hard to meet European content rules—if the 50 percent standard prevails project-by-project—because software and R&D are such major cost elements. U.S. firms might have to shift more software and R&D to Europe, but the types and amount will depend on how European nations apportion credit for these outlays. Whatever the precise rules, the United States has no interest in losing its own software and R&D base as a by-product of Community content rules.

Fifth, will the 50 percent rule be supplemented by additional local content rules specifying, for example, a minimum level of technological sophistication? This type of rule has already surfaced in semiconductors and copying machines.

Network equipment may well become intermeshed with local content decisions concerning semiconductors, particularly if disputes with Japan escalate. Large orders in network equipment often include substantial orders to semiconductor groups. If local content rules on chips impinge on semiconductor operations (see chapter 5), a further problem will be created for exports.

Finally, how can this directive be effectively enforced? Much is left to national discretion because mixing and matching equipment for network design requires considerable judgment (see appendix 4-7). What remedies

---

84. One European firm has suggested that all equipment firms should be prohibited from joining membership in consortia for new service licenses. This would influence procurement but would fall outside conventional trade rules.

exist other than the bilateral trade confrontations that everyone would like to reduce?[85]

## Basic Public Services

The directive "On Competition in the Markets for Telecommunications Services," adopted in July 1989, retains simple public telephone services and the requisite network infrastructure as the only permissible monopolies. (By virtue of using Article 90 to adopt this directive, the Council did not have to number and publish it in the *Official Journal*.) DG-4 (competition) was skeptical about retaining any telephone monopolies, and it wanted to limit the infrastructure monopoly to a bare minimum. But it was not politically prepared to challenge the TAs on these fundamental points. The voice and infrastructure monopolies will again come up for review in 1992; meanwhile, the directive on competition in services could open a significant segment of voice services to competition over time.

The new directive enables private corporate networks to provide voice services. Third-party providers may also offer a shared private network for a group of companies. And, in all likelihood, a supplier of enhanced services may be able to offer voice as part of its total package of competitive services, although simple resale of voice services is not sanctioned. These measures will eventually liberalize competition in voice services for at least larger users.

The scope of private corporate network service is not set by a rigid technical boundary line; rather it will be determined as a matter of policy, subject to the discretion of regulators. This approach has the virtue of common sense, but it could allow restrictive interpretations if the political winds shift against competition.[86] In any event, private networks will not be allowed to challenge the fundamental TA monopoly over public telephone services.

Change is slower for international basic services. The Community has nothing directly to say about international basic telephone services (except that a monopoly is legal on the European end), but this will change

85. Bilateral disputes become Community disputes because the Community has binding jurisdiction over foreign trade policy.

86. Pure resale of voice services would probably not be allowed (see p. 18 of the Summary Report of the Green Paper, *Towards a Dynamic European Economy*) unless combined with some other value-added features or offered in the context of a closed user group. Specialized closed user groups have been permitted for some time. The new approach ends the demand for specialization (for example, all airline companies).

because high European prices annoy business. Europeans often justify their voice monopolies by noting that each EC member is no bigger than an RBOC that enjoys a monopoly on local services. But the Community-wide market for long-distance services across national boundaries is roughly equivalent to the interstate market of the United States. Someday it should be ripe for competition. Moreover, current rules poorly address the full implications of a TA that owns companies on both sides of the international connection. For example, the U.S. telephone company affiliates of European TAs can boost profits of the European TAs by routing traffic to Europe through that TA.[87] The U.S. company can also refer customers to its sister TA for enhanced services. This will put new competitive pressure on major U.S. carriers, especially AT&T, and European TAs without U.S. affiliates.

## Enhanced Services

The telecommunications services directive liberalizes enhanced services. The attempt by France and others to retain selective monopolies, particularly on packet network services and possibly on ISDN data transmission services, was rejected. However, as noted earlier, member states can inaugurate a licensing procedure subject to Community review. The directive permits a grace period for phasing in liberalization that effectively postpones competition until January 1, 1993 (and up to 1996 for the poorest countries). This will give TAs additional time to pay off investments made on the expectation of monopoly.

Importantly, the EC granted the right to lease and to resell leased circuits within the Common Market. These are the vital building blocks for VANs and private corporate networks. Just as important, Community competition rules imply that companies can run a network that resells circuits from the United States to the United Kingdom. In turn, the U.S. circuits are linked to Japan through special bilateral arrangements.[88]

87. The U.S. Federal Communications Commission has finally declared that the firm FTC Communications is a nondominant carrier for all international services except those to France. FTCC has a 14.9 percent indirect share holding by the U.S. holding company of France Cables et Radio, a subsidiary of France Telecom. Reliable sources indicate that France Cables et Radio is drumming up direct traffic back to France through FTCC. Interviews, July 1989; and *Telecommunications Reports*, July 17, 1989, pp. 24–25.

88. This is the judgment shared by several Commission officials and outside observers despite the statement in "Proposal by the 'Analysis and Forecasting Group' (GAP) on Open Network Provision (ONP) for Leased Lines in the Community" (Brussels, January 11, 1989), p. 7.

Therefore, in theory, companies can run such networks on an unimpeded basis all the way from Japan through Europe by way of the United States.

While the United States should applaud the directive, its practical meaning will depend on a second directive, on open network provision, that will follow normal ratification procedures (approval by the Council of Ministers). The open network provision directive, COM (89) 325, will set the terms at which services will be tariffed and will establish how enhanced service providers may access the basic network.

Many questions remain about this market. If member states establish strict licensing of data transport networks, that will retard competition. Even if the services directive survives legal challenge, U.S. firms fear that European TAs operating through their specialized regional organization, CEPT, may work against competition by adopting restrictive tariff policies. In addition, the Community may limit shared use and resale of ISDN services.[89] National governments may fail to establish a level playing field between the TA and its competitors: France, for example, imposes a 30 percent surcharge on VANs competing with its TA. In the end, effective competition will depend on DG-4 (competition) applying its antitrust surveillance standards not only to national regulations but also to collective talks among European TAs. Further, the Commission must give users and competitors a larger voice in shaping policy.

## Overlay Services and Facilities

The EC does not require competition for cellular telephone services, but the United Kingdom, France, and West Germany are allowing at least one competitor and at least partial foreign ownership. The Community has separately directed member states to reserve sufficient frequency spectra (enough to accommodate two networks), to coordinate

---

89. For example, in 1988 CEPT drew up a modified recommendation (PGT 10) that proposed to charge an access fee or set variable tariffs on leased lines, both of which could harm U.S. service providers according to documents supplied to the author on a confidential basis. The documents say that PGT 10 would "safeguard the financial viability of administrations" by levying an access fee of 30 percent on intracontinental leased circuits connected to public networks or carrying third-party traffic. It also recommended access charges or volume-sensitive tariffs for all international leased circuits interconnecting to the public network in the name of tariff harmonization. Shortly afterward, the consulting firm, Ovum, stated in a letter (dated September 13, 1989) concerning its consulting study for the EC: "[The EC may] impose certain conditions or restrictions on the ways in which ISDN can be used—for example, on the resale of capacity, on shared and third party use of ISDN connections, and on interconnection with public and private networks." Ovum was listing options, not making a prediction.

on technical standards, and to introduce pan-European digital cellular services by 1992. The status in EC policy of the next generation of radio voice services (such as the personal communications network in Britain) is not clear. But few observers expect a monopoly, and U.S. firms have good prospects.

The European approach still presents certain problems to American firms. Some countries shun competition. Others are using digital cellular service to pump up local manufacturers of cellular equipment (despite open procurement rules); or they impose penalties on service consortia that include hardware suppliers (in the German case). New (private) franchisees are under pressure to assure that they will not radically "rock the boat" on prices and services.[90] These restrictions may slow the growth of global service networks and hinder American hardware firms (such as Motorola) who often join service consortia in order to establish an equipment beachhead.

Satellites are a tougher problem because the TAs do not want to lose traffic to private satellite networks. A new directive is due in 1990. It will likely ensure a role for private suppliers of data transmission services only on send-and-receive VSATs that do not connect to the public network. The Community may retain the monopoly of the regional public satellite organization, Eutelsat, for European telephone traffic via satellite and for broadcasting within the European Broadcasting Union (with the exception of direct broadcasting services).[91]

Meanwhile, several European countries have established operating agreements with PanAmSat, a U.S. competitor to Intelsat, for private network and public data and video services.[92] PanAmSat charges that some countries, especially France, have purposefully delayed implementing actions that would make the operating agreements useful. All in all, restrictive EC policies on satellites inhibit any effort to build overlay networks that would completely bypass the public phone network.

90. This is based on interviews with two companies involved in franchise bids and an equipment supplier. One of the companies is not disturbed because it prefers nonprice competition in a booming market.

91. "EC Green Paper on Satellite Communications Is Delayed Again," *Fintech Telecom Markets*, September 21, 1989, pp. 1–2.

92. PanAmSat complained about informal restrictions in the case of France. Orion also won approval under restrictive conditions from Intelsat for its Ku-band services. British Aerospace owns 7 percent of Orion and is supplying it with two satellites. "Orion is Approved, but Is There a Market for It and PanAmSat?" *Fintech Telecom Markets*, June 29, 1989, pp. 2–3.

They could also lead to backup restrictions, as it becomes cheaper to transmit large amounts of data via satellite to the VAN customer.

## Open Network Provision and Technical Standards

Potential abuse of market power by the TAs is still possible because of their continued monopoly on most network facilities and because competitors may need selected service features from the dominant network to supplement an offering (such as "calling line identity" or "itemized billing").[93] Typical problems include unfair technical standards, failure to reveal standards, and inappropriate tariff principles. Similar issues surfaced in the United States, particularly in regard to the RBOCs that remain partial monopolists. The EC will address these issues through the forthcoming directive on open network provision (ONP), COM (89) 325.

That directive will provide much of the practical content of liberalization, and so will be a regulatory thicket (see appendix 4-7). Ultimately, policy officials have to make judgments about who gets the benefit of the doubt on technical questions. In the United States and the United Kingdom the initial answer was that challengers to the major established phone companies would get that benefit. Will the same be true in Europe? France, for example, succeeded in establishing the principle that ONP could be applied to competitive services of new entrants. But the Commission won agreement that rules on new entrants would be a low priority and very selective.

U.S. experience suggests that setting standards may be the toughest problem for ONP. The Community relies on established international standards whenever possible and requires full transparency of all standards. This approach still leaves many issues of uniformity and appropriateness.[94]

Users feared that if CEPT dominated the standards process, it would be too slow, too secretive, and too susceptible to control by the TAs. As

---

93. "ONP conditions will apply to efficient access to or use of public telecommunications networks and public telecommunications services for which the TAs are in law or in fact the sole or main providers. . . . ONP is not strictly limited to the area where special or exclusive rights do exist." The proposed directive lists required providers of ONP services, and they are largely the TAs and recognized private operating authorities. Specialized service providers will be exempt, much to the relief of U.S. VANs. Cor Berben, "Open Network Provision: Harmonized Access to Public Telecommunication Networks in Europe," Financial Times Conference on Telecommunications and the European Business Market (EC Commission, July 10, 1989), p. 6.

94. Ibid., p. 10.

a partial response, the European telecommunications ministers backed the European Telecommunications Standards Institute (ETSI) as an alternative to CEPT for coordinating the work of national standards bodies. The European Telecommunications Standards Institute has a permanent director and its membership is open to foreign companies with operations in Europe, although decisions are organized around national delegations. (IBM and Digital Equipment Corporation, for example, are active in ETSI.) U.S. companies report that all telecommunications equipment manufacturers are working together at ETSI to pressure TAs to adopt standards similar to those emerging in North America.

The ETSI standards are voluntary unless they are made compulsory by a special decision process elevating them into *norme européenne de télécommunications* (NETS) standards. This is done only for selected items. But will the Community impose mandatory standards for such items as data transmission in a way that would exclude the use of proprietary protocols on specialized networks?[95] Such a policy would clash with U.S. trade interests.

Moreover, though ETSI plays a coordinating role, there is still a large stage for CEPT. For example, CEPT's Groupe Speciale Mobile is the forum for shaping the pan-European cellular network.[96]

The United States has looked for a formula to protect its interests on network standards. With respect to representation, for example, the USTR advisory group on standards suggested that the United States ask the Community to rely on standards set by established global standards organizations to the maximum extent.[97] In addition, the United States

95. ETSI was created in April 1988. It is open to membership by TAs, suppliers, and users. It works closely with CEN/CENELEC. In December 1986, the Community issued a declaration requiring member states to use European standards and common technical interfaces for information technology. "ETSI Intends to Bring PTTs, Industry and Users Together," *Telecommagazine* (Netherlands), Autumn 1988, p. 42.

96. ETSI also depends on the work for terminal equipment standards done by CEN/CENELEC in which all European countries have a vote, but there are no non-European voting members. U.S. firms are often indirectly represented by their membership in national standards groups, and manufacturers generally are much stronger here than in CEPT.

97. ANSI has also requested an observer status at these Community organizations. The Community and the U.S. government are working out an arrangement to provide ETSI drafts to ANSI for comment. No doubt, all the U.S. organizations will have similar concerns about ACTE, which will supplement the work for terminal equipment. See the discussion by Greenwald in chapter 7. Accelerated progress toward a broadband network will, in the

has urged an expeditious and open process for demonstrating compliance with technical standards.

Beyond the ONP rules, the Community is coaxing European firms into a philosophy of open compatible systems by working together on future technologies through the Research and Development for Advanced Communications in Europe (RACE) research program. Participation in RACE projects can alert firms about technical architectures of the future. Access to RACE is vital to U.S. firms, but the terms of access are not yet settled.[98]

## Oversight of Telecommunications Policy

There is still no directive on what is, perhaps, the most important enforcement issue in the Green Paper's recommendation list: separation of operational and regulatory functions of the TAs. To get a sense of its importance, one merely has to examine the strongly competitive role played by Oftel, the specialized regulatory authority in the United Kingdom. To assure a successful launch for competition, Oftel's director, Sir Brian Carsberg, picked an early confrontation with British Telecom and threatened to recommend termination of its license if competition was not permitted. By contrast, many believe that the new French authority, the National Commission for Communications and Liberties, is much less pro-competitive.

At the EC level, two developments will influence enforcement of the substantive telecommunications directives. One is the industry advisory process. The claims of large users have prompted DG-13 (telecommunications) to rethink its entire advisory system, and some countries now include users in their delegation to Community meetings on telecommunications. But U.S. experience suggests that reform may also require a right to bring a legal challenge against the substance of policy if a thorough open review process is not followed for examining effects on

---

judgment of EC leaders, require intense collaboration with the United States and Japan, which are further advanced in devising standards. The United States has been championing a trilateral meeting in 1990 that will try to reconcile de facto standard setting by trilateral coordination with speedy action through the Consultative Committee in International Telegraphy and Telephony (CCITT). *IBC Strategic Audit*, p. 17; and interview with member of U.S. "T1" Committee, October 1989.

98. RACE is especially developing common functional specifications that would facilitate modular standardization of "service primitives" for layers 4 through 7 of the OSI reference model. RACE was adopted in December 1987. Its work follows from the 1986 Community recommendation for coordinated introduction of ISDN.

competition, consumer welfare, and international trade rules.[99] At a minimum, a process similar to the one used to initiate private antidumping complaints ought to be available concerning procurement decisions. Moreover, the U.S. government should continue to support aggressive use by DG-4 (competition) of antitrust policy by exploring reliance on action by DG-4 in lieu of trade complaints when feasible.

## Implications for the United States

Dramatic changes in the telecommunications market require new U.S. responses not only in international trade and regulation policies, but also in industrial promotion policies.

### Reinforcing GATT

The United States has cast itself in the role of a demandeur on telecommunications negotiations. This role speeds the pace of trade diplomacy but fragments the U.S. approach to a multistage negotiating problem. Even as the U.S. initiates fresh bilateral talks with Europe, it is seeking to close multilateral talks within the Uruguay Round of GATT negotiations.

The Omnibus Trade and Competitiveness Act of 1988 required the United States to retaliate by February 1990 if the European market had not been sufficiently opened. The deadline was yet another device for Congress to force the executive branch to accord greater weight to trade priorities, but a carefully crafted escape clause allowed the executive branch to delay retaliation up to two years. This permitted a constructive solution to the current U.S.-Community impasse over the propriety of bilateral talks.

In February 1990 the USTR announced satisfactory progress in the bilateral talks and delayed retaliation. Come December 1990 the USTR could announce the resolution of the talks in the context of a successful conclusion of the Uruguay Round. The United States and the Community could state that the GATT telecommunications agreements had resolved their primary disputes, and then jointly work out a detailed interpretation of how the GATT accords address the bilateral issues.

99. For example, the requirement of environmental impact statements in the United States has enfranchised environmental groups enforcing policy. J. Serge Taylor, *Making Bureaucracies Think: The Environmental Impact Statement Strategy of Administrative Reform* (Stanford University Press, 1984).

This approach would produce a striking payoff for the United States. It would resolve the substantive bilateral negotiating objectives while avoiding a nasty fight on the merits of bilateralism versus multilateralism. It would also give the Community a strong incentive to make significant concessions within the GATT context. In the case that the Article 90(3) basis of Community directives on telecommunications was overturned by the European Court of Justice, the United States could also count a GATT agreement as positive evidence of progress on the bilateral talks, and grant another extension to the Community. Just as important, it would provide the first important "case law" interpreting what is almost certain to be broad GATT language concerning the new trade regime for telecommunications services and equipment procurement. Having case law is useful because the chief danger of the GATT process is that conceptual breakthroughs will give way to muddled practical interpretations.

The Community would also benefit. It wants to reaffirm GATT preeminence to avert a series of bilateral disputes with the United States. This resolution would fudge the immediate issue of whether the United States is justified in demanding bilateral talks and assist supporters of multilateral talks in the United States. It would also help put a Community spin on interpreting global accords, a valuable tool when dealing with Japan.

## International Trade and Regulatory Policies

At the same time, the United States should change six features of its own trade and regulatory policy.

First, R&D programs play an important role in the execution of Community telecommunications policies. Research on a European basis assists EC firms to decide between more promising and less promising technologies; the research process also helps chart future standards and policy directions.[100] In general, the EC consortia have a greater mandate from governments to foster a particular set of policies than do their U.S. counterparts. Arguably they are subject to trade rules concerning transparency and representation in their decisionmaking processes. Some

---

100. "Major outputs from RACE are expected to influence standards directly and an executive team has been appointed to oversee the translation of RACE outputs into draft standards proposals. . . . RACE work is expected [to] contribute to the work of SG-XVIII in CCITT and NA5 in CEPT." EC Commission, *Working Towards Telecom 2000— Launching the Programme RACE*, COM (88) 240 Final (Brussels, May 31, 1988), p. 8.

U.S. firms already participate through their European subsidiaries, but both the United States and Europe have hazy policies on membership in their national research consortia.[101] The United States might urge more uniform U.S.-Community standards for antitrust oversight of these consortia, and it might reconsider the appropriate mission of these organizations (as it has in bilateral talks with Japan).

The United States should also push for broader discussions of how research and development expenditures fit into local content requirements. As noted earlier, the accounting formula is a critical part of any local content test. Agreement should be sought on what counts as R&D and how R&D in various locations is scored for purposes of meeting local content requirements. European firms like Siemens and Alcatel already have substantial R&D operations in the United States. The USTR should examine their operations closely to look for possible benchmarks.

Second, the United States should pursue a strategic compromise with the EC on procurement policy. It should put U.S. firms with significant market power and special or exclusive rights of operation under the review of procurement rules. Private or public ownership is not the issue; power in the marketplace and special legal rights are. Ideally, the strategy should cover RBOCs, but not AT&T; it should cover Nynex, not a small local phone company.[102] Opening this line of review should strengthen U.S. interests not only in Japan across a wide range of industries, but also in countries like Canada where Northern Telecom's parent, Bell Canada, is exempt from procurement rules.

Third, an equitable trade arrangement has to address the administrative process for setting regulatory policy. The United States has a relatively porous administrative structure; it does not exclude foreign firms from most administrative advisory structures. Moreover, the United States has a penchant for extending antitrust scrutiny to almost everything. U.S. firms do not have similar latitude in foreign telecommunications markets. Nor is antitrust scrutiny so vigorous.

101. See discussion by Kenneth Flamm on Esprit and JESSI in Chapter 5.

102. The EC itself makes the list of firms under its procurement rules a matter of administrative discretion, although it has clear guidelines. The small local phone company in the United States has few counterparts in Europe. It has special rights but no true market power as a buyer or competitor, so it should be exempt. AT&T has no special rights in long distance and is subject to substantial competition (its classification as a dominant carrier may be repealed). Both the RBOCs and the European TAs are subject to competition in sales of terminal equipment; therefore, they should be exempt from procurement rules in this part of their business. The EC already plans on this exemption.

The United States has to negotiate for adequate representation in the DG-13 (telecommunications) advisory process. At the same time, the United States should press the EC to monitor CEPT for possible antitrust violations and to insist on the clear separation of regulatory power and operating authority in each nation. It could also lobby the EC to rewrite its administrative law procedures to make it easier for private parties to challenge the process through the judicial system, much as has happened in the United States as a result of the Administrative Procedure Act, which was toughened in the 1970s. Such a move would allow firms to move a larger share of complaints about the regulatory arena from the channels of commercial diplomacy to the legal system.

Enforcement of procurement policy is a particularly rough problem. Realistically, the decisions on COS in the two or three swing Community markets will come down to a barely disguised exercise in bilateral diplomacy, even if the stated purpose is to keep politics out of the choice. Nonetheless, the United States cannot charge into every decision if EC sensibilities and the global trade order are to survive. One alternative is to create a specialized dispute settlement process between the EC and the United States. It might use a complaint procedure similar to the one permitting private firms to initiate antidumping cases under U.S. trade law. Another possibility is to rely on the separate EC directive that is being developed on the use of national courts to enforce EC procurement rules. This initiative has moved slowly, but the United States might work on its behalf.[103]

Fourth, the United States should oppose anything more than minimal licensing requirements for value-added services. It should also advocate freedom for overlay services to mix voice and data and to have no restrictions on transmitting large volumes of data.

Fifth, developments in the EC should prompt the United States to reconsider its regulatory policies for international voice services. While U.S. authorities favor more competition, they are reluctant to tamper with the joint framework for international voice services. This has produced two errors. First, the United States should begin to prod the EC about licensing Europe-wide long-distance carriers even if members retain monopolies on domestic voice services. This will strengthen the hand of DG-4 (competition) in future reviews of monopoly privileges. Competition in Europe-wide carriage will also boost competition in

103. Gibbs, "Telecommunications in the Single European Market," p. 15.

related equipment markets. The United States rigidly insists that U.S. carriers adhere to nondiscrimination in the selection of foreign service partners, and vice versa, for general telephone service. This insistence forbids discrimination in favor of AT&T by European TAs, but it undercuts the special partnerships designed to create new global networks (except that private networks of large companies are allowed). The United States should revisit these issues, particularly for overlay services.[104]

As an interim measure, the United States should insist that all telecommunications services potentially be subject to GATT trade rules for services because these rules could ultimately facilitate bargaining over reciprocal access for global networks.[105] But the United States should accept the right of countries to reserve specific services from initial coverage, with the proviso that future bargaining will address reserved services. (Under the standstill principle typically used in trade negotiations, no service could be switched from a competitive category to the reserved category.) This stance would allow review of international overlay and basic services over time among interested states, without a difficult advance commitment as to how far or how fast changes would go. The United States should also support a GATT mechanism that would allow parties to bilateral service agreements to "migrate" the agreement to GATT auspices, and to open it to other GATT signatories.

Finally, the United States should expect conflict between the EC and Japan over the trade balance on telecommunications equipment. There is already an effective informal boycott of Japanese COS in the Community. The problem may grow worse in advanced terminal equipment and new transmission equipment. Similar disputes concerning semiconductors have led to new antidumping rules in order for production to qualify as European.

Europeans carefully imply that any dispute with Japan will not ensnare the United States, but such distinctions may prove difficult as global alliances expand. The United States should urge the EC to emphasize market opening initiatives in Japan rather than new controls on sales and

104. Simultaneously, the Bush administration should keep pushing competition in international fiber-optic and satellite facilities in order to force European prices down, nurture competition in services, and stimulate traffic flows to the United States. This might pare the U.S. deficit on telephone service with Europe.

105. For example, national airlines like TWA run global networks. Countries bargain over reciprocal access for these carriers and the terms for access to domestic traffic. See Jonathan David Aronson and Peter F. Cowhey, *When Countries Talk—International Trade in Telecommunications Services* (Ballinger, 1988).

investment in Europe. If prior understandings can be reached, the United States might invite the Community and Japan to join in trilateral talks coordinated with the GATT negotiations. The explicit purpose should be to reconsider national practices so as to make future GATT accords more effective. The implicit purpose should be opening markets, while curbing the pattern of two-sided disputes that randomly wound the third party in a trilateral trade relationship.

## Industrial Promotion Policies

Industrial policy has rightly acquired a dubious reputation in American politics. But various measures to promote industry will not, and should not, disappear from the agenda. This study suggests the need to rethink three premises of U.S. policy.

To begin, the changes in the market suggest that traditional thinking about the benefits and costs of trade policy requires some careful consideration. The globalization of the telecommunications industry is profound. Economic and political forces are driving the industry toward local production and research, while merchandise imports and exports are declining in importance.

Economic forces represent a mix of high fixed costs, requiring a world market base, and localized needs, requiring customized products and services. Political forces generate the demand for local production content (or equity) for network equipment and overlay services, both for employment reasons and to secure membership in standard-setting groups.

Some illustrations can be given as to how these forces are working themselves out. International consortia are becoming more vital for VANs: a foreign telecommunications company provides specialized knowledge for the software design; a local telecommunications firm provides knowledge of the local customer base, technical standards, and regulatory system; and one or more large users help with customizing the services for their own use and those of suppliers and customers who connect with them. Similarly, makers of central office switches are becoming embedded in partnerships: the big switch supplier relies on its local partner for customization, local content, and knowledge of the ways of the local TA; the local partner also becomes a source of specialized network components for global customers of the COS company. This latter feature is more than a payoff for the local partner; no single firm can mobilize the money and bear the risk of developing each and every member in the full family of information products.[106]

In the midst of this wave of strategic alliances, globalization of the industry, and insistence on local participation, the United States should continue its call for open markets. It should not expect improved market access to boost exports dramatically (although like chicken soup, it won't hurt). Indeed, open European access may propel the export of telecommunications R&D from U.S. to European laboratories, because it will then be possible to create designs that not only cater to Europe, but also are priced at competitive global levels.

If export gains are limited, and if R&D losses are accelerated, why bother to open European markets? There are several reasons. Global competition will boost innovation, lower prices, and improve the range of supply options; in short, it will enhance consumer welfare, especially for businesses that intensively use telecommunications. At the same time, U.S. firms can retain their leadership in selective equipment and service markets by exploiting their own global mandates. Perhaps most important, competition will allow the United States to influence the overall design of the information and communications network of the future. It is less important that particular American firms win than that an open global telecommunications market will bring about the "American information standard."

At the same time, global competition raises serious questions about whether U.S. government rules and processes hinder the competitiveness of U.S. firms. The two most important classes of firms are the medium-sized firms interested in the European market and the RBOCs.

The newer equipment and services markets, where size is less vital, create many opportunities for specialized entrants. But complex standards and specialized regulations create formidable barriers. Effective participation in the formulation of regulations and standards, or in the design of U.S. policy toward services and equipment, remains a troubling problem for smaller firms. U.S. trade advisory groups seldom have representation from these firms, mainly because smaller firms do not allocate money for staffing such groups. (Small firms have some indirect representation through industry associations.) But smaller firms do

---

106. Gary P. Pisano, Michael V. Russo, and David J. Teece, "Joint Venture and Collaborative Arrangements in the Telecommunications Industry," in David C. Mowery, ed., *International Collaborative Ventures in U.S. Manufacturing* (Ballinger, 1988), pp. 23–70.

participate directly when similar issues are at stake in the procurement operations of the U.S. government. The financial consequences in that context are simply too large to ignore.

The U.S. government should more closely integrate its trade policy specialists with its procurement committees in two ways. First, it should begin to put representatives of the various U.S. agencies with large communications and information systems on trade advisory committees. These agencies are both large users and important agenda setters for the development of U.S. technology. Second, experts on trade policy need to be included in decisions on procurement policy in order to stimulate standardization of formats for information services in light of international competition. In short, procurement policy needs to be more responsive to foreign trade policy. This would provide an incentive for smaller firms to participate in trade issues, and it would respond to the reality that both the EC and Japan are pushing for more uniformity of standards than the United States. The National Telecommunications and Information Administration of the Department of Commerce is the logical vehicle for organizing these initiatives.

The RBOCs are also entering the European market vigorously, but they are hampered in two respects. First, once in the European market, they cannot interconnect to their home networks. Second, they cannot experiment with selective integration of services and equipment because all equipment ventures are banned in the United States.

The weakness of the RBOCs in the international arena is a significant problem for the United States because public policy makes the RBOCs the unique repositories of national experience at running sophisticated local exchanges. Thus much of the learning-by-doing in the U.S. domestic market is lost for international competitive purposes.

Is there a way to put the RBOCs more fully in play for the world market, while limiting the forms of market power that led to restrictions under the consent decree? This breaks into two questions, services and equipment. For services, the immediate priority is letting overseas network ventures of the RBOCs interconnect to their home market. The Japanese approach of encouraging joint ventures of service suppliers and customers for enhanced services suggests a model. The United States could require the RBOCs to run the international link to their home territory as a joint venture with a representative group of customers. The customers would help to monitor the performance of the venture.

The Federal Communications Commission could judge the appropriateness of consortium membership.

The United States should permit the RBOCs to enter the equipment market (including COS software) subject to continuing regulatory scrutiny. This review should follow a rule that the greater the market power of the RBOC as a buyer in an equipment sector, the more its movement into manufacturing should be subject to governmental review. Reliance on foreign suppliers for the new product would be a second trigger permitting entry into manufacturing, but this factor would not come into play unless the venture qualified in market power terms.[107]

More generally, the problem of the RBOCs illustrates many of the issues plaguing American competitiveness in Europe. Even if all trade and regulatory barriers suddenly disappear, U.S. industry will have to restructure significantly to meet competitive challenges. The days of the all-purpose equipment and service firm are over. The demand for firms that combine selective services and equipment on a global basis is on the rise. The United States has a regulatory system that works against global integration; at the same time, its trade policy system is too dependent on the strategic thinking of the largest firms. Until the United States catalyzes the most imaginative contributions of small and medium-sized firms—firms that will provide the largest share of American growth in overseas markets—U.S. participation in the growth triangle of global telecommunications will suffer.

107. The National Telecommunications and Information Administration has already suggested that the RBOCs should be free to enter the manufacturing business, but any joint ventures with foreign firms (particularly for network equipment) would be subject to special government scrutiny. The United States could also impose a rule, like the one used in Canada for the relationship between Bell Canada and Northern Telecom, that the RBOC could not pay a higher price for its affiliate's equipment than those prevailing on the open market. I have benefited from Leonard Waverman's thinking about the Northern Telecom experience.

## APPENDIX 4–1. Definitions of Telecommunications Equipment

**Network Equipment[1]**

1. Switching
   (a) Central office switching (COS)—the traditional heart of the public telephone network.
   (b) Private automatic branch exchange (PABX)—the focus of switching for private enterprises.
   (c) Specialized data switches—such items as packet switches for packet networks (described in appendix 4-2).

2. Transmission
   (a) Co-axial and fiber optic cables.
   (b) Traditional radio: microwave.
   (c) Overlay radio: cellular phone and mobile data transmission.
   (d) Advanced transmission systems: such items as high-speed T1 data lines and the multiplexers that allow multiple uses of the line.
   (e) Communications satellites.

**Terminal Equipment**

1. Conventional communications equipment: telephone handsets, key telephone sets, answering machines, telex machines.

2. New forms of radio technology: pagers, cellular and radio telephones, very small aperture terminals for satellites (VSATs), receive-only terminals for satellites (ROEs).

3. New optical and data technologies: fax machines, videotext, data terminals.

1. The growing power of terminal equipment is blurring the boundary between network equipment and terminal equipment. For example, some industry specialists count a PABX as network equipment, while others view it as terminal equipment.

APPENDIX 4–2. Definitions of Telecommunications Services

## Network Facilities

The equipment that permits the provision of services over networks open to all users.

## Basic Public Services

Basic public services involve no manipulation of the content or format of a message, and they are delivered over networks that are available to all customers. Many of these networks have "obligations to serve" (that is, to provide services to all citizens, even if it is not profitable to do so).

1. Telephone services: these divide largely into local and long-distance services; international services are a subset of long distance.
2. Simple document transmission: telegraph and telex services are the slowest growing segments of the market; some telecommunications authorities (TAs) also offer simple fax transmission.
3. Basic transport and service elements: the circuit service that simply leases transmission capacity. In the future, various switching and other network features will also be leased. Enhanced services often rely on the major public networks to provide these basic services.

## Enhanced (Value-added and Information) Services

These services may be offered by public or private networks and can include data, video, and voice. Enhanced services consist of either:

1. A value-added service that entails any substantial manipulation of the *format* of the message. For example, a packet switched network converts data into "packets" with addresses and error control codes, transmits the data, and then reassembles it.
2. Information services that provide *content* over the network (for example, access to a remote data base) or that *manipulate content* (for example, remote data processing on a supercomputer).

    Many services, such as electronic mail combined with electronic data interchange—as in networks that provide inventory and billing control, or communications between a large manufacturer and its suppliers—provide both content and format manipulation. Even ordinary voice services may graduate into the category of value-added services because of such technologies as voice mail systems.

## Overlay (Mobile and Radio) Facilities and Services

Many countries recognize that new mobile and radio technologies require selective new network facilities and services. Even though nations may try to retain a monopoly on basic public services, they will permit competition (often by offering two or more licenses) on overlay facilities and services. Overlay facilities may provide voice or enhanced services such as cellular telephones, mobile data and fax services, remote pager systems, airplane telephones, and navigation systems.

**ISDN and IBC**

An integrated services digital network is a way of providing any mix of voice, video, and data within the limits of its narrow bandwidth, speed, and technical design. Integrated broadband communications is the second generation and includes such items as switched video, which requires great bandwidth.

**Private Networks**

Regulatory authorities usually permit a single user (for example, Ford Motors) to establish a private internal network to provide all services within the firm. These networks are often global.

APPENDIX 4–3. EC Telecommunications in the Year 2000

Appendix table 4-3A starts with a snapshot of the 1987 market. It accepts the common estimate that conventional voice services will grow at 5 percent annually, while new services will achieve a 30 percent market share around the year 2000. The table then builds two scenarios. Both assume high growth for VANs and information services, a total European market of $5.9 billion in 1987 and (conservatively) about $58.2 billion in fifteen years. The first scenario projects a high growth rate for overlay services; the second assumes an explosion in overlay services. The more conservative scenario for overlay services assumes extensive mobile services but no effective penetration of the residential market. The second scenario allows for selective penetration of residential services. Depending on the overlay scenario, the EC telecommunications services market grows from $82.7 billion in 1989 to between $263 billion and $277 billion in 2002.

Appendix table 4-3B gives representative forecasts for telecommunications equipment. This market is growing less rapidly, and is considerably smaller, than the market for services.

Appendix table 4-3C completes the analysis by assuming that the total communications and information market will reach 7 percent of Community GDP in 2000. It optimistically assumes that Community GDP grows from $4.2 trillion in 1987 to $6.6 trillion in 2000. This implies a communications and information market of $463 billion in the year 2000.

APPENDIX TABLE 4–3A. Scenarios for EC Telecommunications Services, 1987, 1992, 1997, 2002[a]

Billions of dollars

| Year | Conventional voice services | Enhanced services | Overlay services Scenario I | Overlay services Scenario II | Total services Scenario I | Total services Scenario II |
|------|------|------|------|------|------|------|
| 1987 | 75.6 | 5.9 | 1.2 | 1.2 | 82.7 | 82.7 |
| 1992 | 102.8 | 17.6 | 2.4 | 4.8 | 122.9 | 125.3 |
| 1997 | 139.9 | 35.3 | 7.2 | 14.4 | 182.4 | 189.6 |
| 2002 | 180.0 | 58.2 | 14.4 | 28.8 | 262.6 | 277.0 |

a. These figures reflect the EC estimate of a 7 percent share of overall communications services for VANs in 1987. They also assume a total European communications services market of ECU 70 billion in 1987 and growth rates of 25 percent, 20 percent, and 15 percent in each subsequent five-year period for enhanced services. This follows the logic of the analysis of C. C. von Weizsaecker and others, "The Economics of Value Added Services" (University of Cologne, June 1917), p. 110. Estimates for the overlay market are based on interviews by the author in Europe in July 1989. All outcomes are rounded.

APPENDIX TABLE 4–3B. World Telecommunications Equipment
Markets, 1986, 1990, 2000
Billions of dollars

| Country or area | Total market | | | Public switching | | |
|---|---|---|---|---|---|---|
| | 1986 | 1990 | 2000 | 1986 | 1990 | 2000 |
| European Community | | | | | | |
| West Germany | 5.9 | 7.7 | 12.9 | 1.5 | 2.0 | 3.6 |
| France | 4.5 | 6.2 | 9.6 | 1.2 | 1.5 | 1.9 |
| Italy | 3.9 | 6.7 | 9.5 | 0.9 | 1.8 | 2.3 |
| United Kingdom | 3.1 | 4.7 | 6.5 | 0.9 | 1.2 | 1.4 |
| Spain | 1.4 | 3.0 | 5.2 | 0.3 | 0.8 | 1.2 |
| Netherlands | 0.5 | 0.8 | 1.3 | 0.1 | 0.2 | 0.3 |
| Belgium-Luxembourg | 0.5 | 0.5 | 1.1 | 0.1 | 0.1 | 0.2 |
| Denmark | 0.3 | 0.4 | 0.9 | 0.1 | 0.1 | 0.2 |
| Ireland | 0.1 | 0.1 | 0.1 | n.a. | n.a. | n.a. |
| Greece | 0.3 | 0.5 | 1.1 | 0.1 | 0.2 | 0.4 |
| Portugal | 0.1 | 0.2 | 0.7 | a | 0.1 | 0.1 |
| TOTAL | 20.6 | 30.8 | 48.9 | 5.2 | 8.0 | 11.6 |
| All Western Europe | 22.7 | 35.1 | 52.6 | n.a. | n.a. | n.a. |
| Japan | 7.1 | 8.5 | 13.3 | 1.7 | 2.1 | 3.3 |
| United States | 24.0 | 27.2 | 41.8 | 6.5 | 6.3 | 7.9 |
| World[b] | 83.4 | 112.8 | 184.5 | 21.9 | 29.4 | 43.0 |

SOURCE: Telecommunications Research Centre, *Telecommunications World Outlook and Forecast, 1986 to 2000* (West Sussex, U.K., 1988), p. 40.
n.a. Not available.
a. Less than $50 million.
b. Top fifty national markets.

APPENDIX TABLE 4–3C. Total EC Telecommunications Market
Projected in 2000[a]

| Market segment | Billions of dollars |
|---|---|
| Voice services | 190 |
| New services[b] | 88 |
| Telecommunications equipment | 47 |
| Integrated office equipment and software[c] | 138 |
| TOTAL | 463 |

a. These estimates are best read as broad magnitudes rather than precise forecasting. The underlying GDP forecast simply assumes a steady 3.5 percent annual growth and then adds a Europe 1992 "bonus" of 8 percent of GDP to the baseline forecast for 2000. The office equipment figure is derived as a residual between the other market segments and the grand total. This residual estimate was checked against other studies. A 1985 NTIA study estimated the computer industry globally at $195 billion in 1990. National Telecommunications and Information Administration, *NTIA Telecom-2000: Charting the Course for a New Century,* Special Publication 88-21 (Washington: U.S. Department of Commerce, October 1988). A modestly reduced growth rate for the 1990s would yield a rough doubling of the market to $480 billion by 2000, and the EC is likely to represent over 20 percent of the total. In addition, the EC Green Paper estimates for 1993 in the office market appeared consistent with the growth path suggested here. See Herbert Ungerer with Nicholas Costello, *Telecommunications in Europe* (Brussels: EC Commission, 1988), pp. 47–48.
b. Represents high estimate.
c. Includes full range of office equipment (including typewriters, data terminals, computers).

APPENDIX 4–4. U.S. Firms and the EC Services Market

Five major sets of complaints were voiced, prior to 1989, by U.S. sellers of enhanced services in the EC market and by U.S. companies that wished to run private corporate networks in the EC.

1. TAs would retain many enhanced services as a monopoly. For example, France wanted to reserve packet switched networks as a monopoly, and Italy wanted videoconferencing as a monopoly.

2. TAs might use their monopoly over basic telephone services and the physical infrastructure of the network to cross-subsidize their enhanced services, discriminate against competitors, or ineptly retard growth of the market. Items of special concern were:

   (a) availability and pricing of leased circuits (basic transport services);
   (b) rights to share or resell leased circuits;
   (c) rights to interconnect leased circuit networks to the public network;
   (d) technical standards for private networks.

   For example, U.S. firms wanted prompt leasing of circuits (it often took four to eight months to lease a cross-border circuit), flat monthly rates (paying by the message unit penalizes firms that use circuit capacity more efficiently); rates closely related to costs (lease rates for comparable circuits vary by several hundred percent across Europe);[1] freedom of choice of technical protocols (some countries refuse to permit innovative protocols even when there is no public standard); and the right to let users share a circuit or resell its use to third parties. Most countries have restrictions contradicting one or more of these requirements, or grant more favorable terms to their own TAs.

3. How would the EC treat American attempts to liberalize specialized overlay facilities and services? For example, would they reject the new American satellite competitors to Intelsat?

4. Would the EC grant U.S. firms entry to the many new Europe-wide research programs on telecommunications (for example, RACE) and related high-technology fields? Would U.S. firms participate in designing the networks of the future in Europe and have a voice on issues ranging from tariffs to technical standards?

5. Licensing rules for new services were arbitrary and capricious. Long delays, disclosure of sensitive commercial information, and an undue role for the TA in the process were among the complaints.

1. An analog leased circuit operating internationally at a distance of 2,000 kilometers at 9.6 kilobits should cost about $3,320 a year. The United Kingdom, with the lowest leasing rates, charges almost $15,000, while Spain charges $40,000 and Italy charges almost $50,000. *Ovum*, "Cost-Based Tariffs for Telecommunications: The Position in Europe," London, 1989. See also Peter Heywood and Lee Mantelman, "Untying Europe's Tangled Web of Communications," *Data Communications* (March 1989), pp. 171–82.

## APPENDIX 4-5. National Positions in the EC Equipment Market

The EC equipment market can be divided into three groups. All three groups ran deficits with the United States and Japan, yet the EC as a whole ran a modest surplus on its world telecommunications equipment trade because of exports to the rest of the world (see table 4-3). Europe has a bilateral trade deficit with the United States and Japan on every single item of telecommunications equipment. Even France and West Germany are in deficit on all but switching equipment. Transmission equipment and terminal equipment, which will take shares away from COS, are in particularly bad shape. The deficit with Japan is even more serious, because Japan imports very little and has swamped the terminal equipment market, especially in fax machines, which will account for $7 billion of a $42 billion European business equipment market by 1992.

The first group (the Big Two) comprises France and West Germany, both major exporters of telecommunications equipment. Alcatel and Siemens dominate these markets. They provide two-thirds of the exports, one-third of the imports, and most of the European surplus with the rest of the world (outside the United States and Japan).

France and Germany seek to open new markets for their champions while lowering their own costs as users of the technology. As the two largest equipment suppliers, they support unification of the EC equipment market. But they are also bargaining about reciprocal opening of their COS markets against reciprocal opening by other countries. France has attempted to resolve this issue by admitting Ericsson, while West Germany will face the issue soon.

The second group includes the Netherlands, Italy, and the United Kingdom. Members of this group are struggling to remain significant exporters. They provide about one-fourth of EC exports, absorb about half of EC imports, and run an equipment trade deficit with the rest of the world. These countries all have major indigenous suppliers—GPT in Britain, Philips N.V. in the Netherlands, Italtel and Telettra in Italy—struggling in world markets due to high costs, inadequate scale economies, or technological difficulties. They have all accepted roles as junior partners in new global partnerships. Italy's high growth rates and Britain's new networks are features of this group.

The third group of seven medium-sized and small European countries are largely purchasers of equipment, interested in getting the best deal while opening up prospects for selective exports to balance their trade figures. Belgium and Spain are prominent in this group. They constitute about 15 percent of EC imports and exports of telecommunications equipment, and almost exactly balance their accounts with the world. Spain, in particular, faces the question whether its traditional suppliers offer the best route for selective global expansion.

## APPENDIX 4–6. The Procurement Directive

Directive 88/378 covers purchases of ECU 200,000 and up (about $240,000) for supply contracts and ECU 5 million and up (about $6 million) for public works. Initially only 70 percent of procurement must be covered, but 100 percent coverage is required by 1992. Procurement can be open to all, restricted to a particular pool of companies (chosen on open and nondiscriminatory grounds), or closed. For example, procurement can be closed if prior network standards and equipment make it practical to buy only from a particular supplier.[1]

The EC has modeled its program for network equipment on the Buy America policy of the United States. A firm is judged to be European solely on the basis of the local European content of its products (50 percent of the goods and services embodied in the product) and its establishment as a firm in an EC member state, not the nationality of ownership. When considering bids, a non-European firm faces two potential penalties. First, it may simply be excluded from the purchase. Second, it may be allowed to compete, but it must compete against a 3 percent price preference given to European suppliers (assuming other aspects of the bids are comparable).

The directive lays out elaborate guidelines to ensure that the procurement process is transparent and nondiscriminatory. While the details are complicated, the major requirements include clear advance announcements of procurements, open and objective systems for choosing bidders (if bidding is not open to all), maximum compliance with European standards in project specifications, clear disclosure of the details of all awards, and assurances that all losers in the bidding process can find out why they lost or were disqualified from bidding. Ultimately the directive covers only a process, not results. There is still no EC enforcement mechanism as of yet. Although DG-13 is dedicated to writing tough rules, critics consider the process to be too complicated to be fully effective.

1. All national networks have embedded equipment with some distinct technical idiosyncracies. This fact opens the way to the following procurement game. A telephone company buys a new technology from a favored supplier on a noncompetitive basis for two years by making the amount less than ECU 200,000. It then develops national network standards especially geared to the idiosyncracies of the system. In the third year, it buys a large amount but declares an exemption from open procurement because of prior technical standards of the network. EC authorities hope to write regulations to make this type of game more difficult.

APPENDIX 4–7. Open Network Provisions and Leased Lines

As defined by COM (89) 325, ONP covers all public and private telecommunications organizations that have special or exclusive rights of operations, and it covers all services of those organizations (including those subject to competition).[1] ONP covers other service providers but only to the minimum extent necessary to assure interoperability of networks. ONP rules for such items as information services will be a lower priority. ONP requires service tariffs to be based on objective criteria (such as costs) that are transparent and published. It also grants equal nondiscriminatory access (including access to selective network features like call identification) to all users of the network. Practically speaking, this means setting specific rules for technical interfaces, usage conditions, and tariff principles for leased lines, public data networks, ISDN, and other services. It also means ensuring that special conditions for use of the network must fit some reasonable test of the public interest, such as data security and justifiable conditions for assuring interoperable services.

Consider how ONP may apply to leased lines. ONP will not set tariffs. It will try to harmonize pricing by stressing cost-based pricing, transparent published tariffs, and unbundling so that users pay only for what they specifically want. This may lead to additional rules on leased lines that will forbid volume-sensitive tariffs or any access charge not based on cost (for example, those based on social policy). However, deciding what determines a cost basis for access charges when current prices are so wildly out of kilter will be a major problem.[2] It will handle access issues by insisting on nondiscrimination (TAs must charge their own enhanced service subsidiaries the same published tariff that their competitors are charged; likewise, delivery terms, repair terms, and refunds must be the same). ONP will also assure rights to interconnect private networks to the public network.

1. This formulation came at the prompting of the European Parliament, which responded to the urgings of large users and VAN suppliers.

2. The GAP report on ONP encouragingly rejects the proposition that users can be charged for the cost of the infrastructure (as many TAs had in mind when setting initial connection charges). But the report opens the door to supplementary access charges related to cost. And it explicitly notes the costs imposed by the exit of firms from the public network and allows for a possible link between leased line rates and telephone rates (which remain on a monopoly basis). "Proposal by the 'Analysis and Forecasting Group' (GAP) on Open Network Provision (ONP) for Leased Lines in the Community" (Brussels, January 11, 1989), pp. 33–37.

Chapter 5

# Semiconductors

KENNETH FLAMM

A S 1992 and a more integrated European economy draw near, the semiconductor industry has emerged as one major source of friction between the European Community and its trading partners. On the face of it, there is very little in the EC's 1992 market completion program explicitly affecting the chip industry that would seem to warrant a substantial expenditure of political capital. Indeed, the issue that has been the lightning rod for foreign semiconductor companies worried about their future in the European market is a seemingly arcane and technical detail: a change in the EC rule of origin that determines whether a semiconductor is an "EC" chip or a "foreign" chip.

Minor points become major issues when they serve as surrogates for more serious matters. In this case, a much larger complex of interests is at stake. The rules of origin have become a litmus test for the attitude Europe will be adopting toward the trade regime in semiconductors.

In the 1980s the global semiconductor industry was the scene of a bitter struggle between U.S. and Japanese high-technology companies. The role of government and national policy was a central issue in the battle, as activist trade and technology policies were mustered to support the interests of national firms on both sides of the Pacific. A watershed of sorts was reached in September of 1986, when the United States and Japan formally approved the Semiconductor Trade Arrangement (STA). The STA, set to expire in 1991, represented a radical departure from the liberal trading system put into place after the Second World War: it set up a system for monitoring chip prices that in principle could be applied to virtually all semiconductors, and in a quasi-secret side letter the STA

Kenneth Flamm is a senior fellow at the Brookings Institution. Without implicating them in his errors, he would like to thank Peter F. Cowhey, Gary Hufbauer, Robert Z. Lawrence, Michael Maibach, Douglas E. Rosenthal, Charles L. Schultze, and Ulric Weill for their helpful comments. Yuko Iida Frost provided extremely useful research assistance.

specified a 20 percent quantitative market share target for foreign company sales in the Japanese market.

The idea of managed trade had suddenly become an operational reality. Perhaps more important, the arguments—intellectual and emotional—that had so altered the landscape of the semiconductor industry were applicable to a broad range of high-technology industries. The future of the trading system in high-technology products appeared to be up for grabs.

Seen in this context, the European Community's 1992-related measures affecting semiconductor trade must be aggregated with other recent EC policy initiatives not wearing the magical "1992" label and analyzed as a reaction to events and policies transforming the nature of international competition in high-technology industries. To what extent is Europe merely reacting reflexively to external events, and to what extent is it consciously attempting to define the directions in which the global trading system for high-technology goods evolves? How will its actions affect its own industries and their foreign competitors?

This chapter analyzes how structural changes have transformed global competition in semiconductors, raising new strategic issues for companies and countries. The chapter then tries to fit the European chip industry into an increasingly complicated global mosaic. European Community policies toward the European semiconductor industry are best understood as a response to the changing international environment, which has been critically shaped by American and Japanese policies.

One defensible line of analysis is that the EC is proceeding to build a protective barrier around its high-technology markets in general and semiconductors in particular, and that EC steps down this path represent a further push toward global protectionism in high-technology products. A more optimistic analysis, however, is that the EC has put into place within its boundaries the basic ingredients needed to maintain an open trading system in high-technology goods—the free flow of products, uniform antitrust standards to guard against anticompetitive exploitation of monopoly power, the gradual regionalization of national R&D subsidies, and vigorous advocacy of the reciprocity principle in access to R&D programs—in order to neutralize investment in technology as a tool of rent-seeking nationalistic industrial policy. If the EC experiment with these principles is opened up to wider international participation, creating a new sort of high-technology trading regime, Europe may be blazing a path that offers a way out of the rapidly increasing trade friction troubling global flows of technology-intensive products.

## Historical Overview

Semiconductors, the ubiquitous silicon chips at the electronic heart of all manner of high-technology goods, were developed during and after the Second World War. The first such solid-state components were diodes and rectifiers, used where certain types of vacuum tubes had previously been employed in electronic equipment. In 1947 the transistor was invented at the Bell Telephone Laboratories, and with it came the seed of a technological revolution. The transistor had the properties of both an amplifier and a switch and made it possible to replace the hot, bulky, and power-hungry vacuum tubes used for such purposes with fast, cool, and small semiconductor components. Right from the start it was realized that these devices could revolutionize the newly emerging technology of the computer. The U.S. military invested heavily in both technologies, and the link between computers and semiconductors continues to be central to the question of why governments pay so much attention to the semiconductor industry.

Transistors and diodes are discrete devices, however, with just one circuit element per semiconductor device. The microelectronics revolution began in earnest in 1959, with the invention of the integrated circuit (IC)—a semiconductor component with many devices, entire electronic circuits, constructed on a single silicon chip. Rapid improvements in processing technology made it possible to pack greater and greater numbers of miniaturized circuit elements on a single chip.

### Vertical Integration

More and more such elements were diffused onto the surface of a single sliver of silicon carved from a larger, circular silicon wafer on which many individual chips were actually fabricated. It became feasible to jam virtually the entire electronic guts of a complex computer system, industrial controller, or radio onto a single integrated circuit. With the ever-higher levels of integration onto a single chip came a realization that having access to the latest generation of semiconductor technology was increasingly critical to successful competition in all aspects of the electronics systems business. Higher levels of integration meant smaller numbers of chips, fewer interconnections, and lower manufacturing costs.

This continuing technological drive toward greater integration in turn led to an important change in the relationship between systems producers and chip manufacturers. In the beginning, small groups of electronic functions were combined into standard, "commodity" chips used as building blocks for more complex systems designs. At that time, relatively small numbers of circuit elements could fit within a single IC, so chip manufacturers developed standard parts that performed general generic functions that could be designed into more complex—and proprietary—systems. Today, however, when an entire system can be integrated onto a single chip, it is no longer economical to take standard building block chips and wire them together into a more complex system, since the cost of wiring together the standard components and testing the system is prohibitively expensive.[1]

This has meant that a systems designer building a complex electronic system has increasingly had to furnish proprietary design information to the component manufacturer producing the ICs used in the system. The need to transfer proprietary information from designer to component maker has made vertical integration an increasingly attractive option for systems houses. It has also made it risky for systems designers to purchase needed ICs from vertically integrated chip producers, since those firms might compete with them in downstream markets.

In the electronics marketplace, three sorts of changes pushed by the trend toward increasing integration between chip and systems producers have been evident. First, electronic systems companies with existing in-house chip-making capacity have strengthened and increased these activities. Second, "merchant" chip producers have integrated downstream into systems production. Companies like Intel and Texas Instruments have increased their involvement in computer systems production, while National Semiconductor recently acquired computer board manufacturer Quadram.[2] Third, chip makers and systems houses have been increasingly involved in strategic alliances, relationships where propri-

1. This is true except for systems built in small numbers, where the fixed costs involved in designing and fabricating custom ICs may be significant. Lower-density parts are more expensive per circuit element than higher-density parts, and making and testing connections between circuit elements mounted on a circuit board is much more expensive than making such connections within the internal microcircuitry of a single IC.

2. U.S. "merchant" producer Motorola has long been involved in systems production; indeed, chip sales account for only a third of its revenues.

etary design information is combined with chip manufacturing in exclusive product-based relationships. This may be regarded as a form of "virtual" vertical integration, in which a systems house combines its closely held design know-how with a chip producer's closely held manufacturing expertise.[3] Neither is threatened by potential competition from the other in the specific upstream or downstream markets involved.

But as entire proprietary designs for electronic systems are transferred onto a single chip, retaining control over that design becomes increasingly intertwined with finding chip suppliers who will not appropriate key elements and use them to manufacture a competitive product of their own. Access to a state-of-the-art chip supply, which combines leading-edge manufacturing technology with reasonable security for key elements of proprietary systems designs, has become a strategic issue throughout the global electronics industry.

### Industrial Concentration

Another technical change with implications for industrial organization has been the growing capital intensity of fabrication lines. Packing the maximum amount of circuitry onto a state-of-the-art chip has required increasingly expensive manufacturing equipment and facilities. The capital costs of a fabrication line for leading-edge chips rose from about 15 percent of the total fabrication cost in the mid-1970s to about half the cost by the mid-1980s, and were projected to pass 60 percent of total cost by the early 1990s. Total costs for a fabrication facility rose during the same periods from $30 million to $100 million, and were projected to reach $300 million.[4] Much of this equipment was highly specialized— it had little or no scrap value outside the semiconductor business—and, due to the rapid pace of technological change, it had a short economic life. Investments in semiconductor manufacturing facilities, therefore,

3. The term *virtual* is borrowed from the computer industry: virtual memory is memory space available to a program that may not actually be physically available to the computer system, but whose existence is mimicked by the system so that it operates as if such memory was actually available to the program. "Virtual" vertical integration therefore means a mode of operation where the firms behave as if vertically integrated, even though they are not actually linked by common ownership.

4. R. M. Reynolds and D. R. Strom, "CEM: Process Latitude in a Bottle," *Semiconductor International,* October 1989, p. 123. These refer to a state-of-the-art facility for manufacturing a high-volume, mass-produced commodity product. Facilities investments relative to other costs would be substantially lower for a smaller facility used in producing lower-volume, more specialized products. Manufacturing cost would also be a smaller share of product price for such more specialized, noncommodity products.

were often difficult to liquidate for more than a fraction of their acquisition cost. These investments took on the character of a sunk cost. The rising share of such sunk costs in total manufacturing cost made entry and exit from the industry more expensive and difficult. Moreover, because it typically took a year or more to get a new project up and running, another element of risk was added to a notoriously cyclical market.[5]

The rising capital intensity of a high-volume, state-of-the-art wafer fabrication facility is one factor behind increasing concentration within the IC industry, particularly in key mass-market products in which competitive success is tightly linked to manufacturing cost. A trend toward increased industrial concentration is clearly evident in mass-market products like commodity memory chips, particularly dynamic random access memories (DRAMS), the product segment with the single largest value in the semiconductor industry. The top eleven suppliers of DRAMs made nearly two-thirds of open market sales in 1981 and essentially all sales by 1988.[6]

All these factors—increasing capital intensity, greater risk, and the requirement for greater proprietary information transfer between chip producer and systems designer—played some role in the rapid ascent of the Japanese chip industry in the early 1980s. Japanese chip production has been dominated by large, vertically integrated systems houses, and both size and integration may have been increasingly advantageous in the changing environment for the semiconductor industry.

## Development of National Semiconductor Industries

International trade in semiconductors is complicated by regional differences in the development of the semiconductor industry. The organization and structure of the semiconductor industry evolved quite differently in Europe than they did in the United States. In the United States, established electronic component producers—mostly producers of vacuum tubes affiliated with electrical equipment manufacturers—

5. The world record for bringing up a new chip plant appears to be held by NMB Semiconductor, which claims that it took only nine months to go from initial groundbreaking on a new fabrication facility to initial production of 256K dynamic random access memories (DRAMs) in 1985. See Larry Waller, "DRAM Users and Makers: Shotgun Marriages Kick In," *Electronics*, November 1988, pp. 29–30.

6. Data collected by Nomura Research show the top three and top eleven DRAM merchants accounted for 37.6 and 62.6 percent of the global market, respectively, in 1981. In 1988 these shares were 50 and 97.5 percent. I am grateful to Makoto Sumita of Nomura Research for sharing these estimates with me.

became victims of technological change and fell by the wayside as entrepreneurial start-up companies were formed to push the development of new products.[7] As a consequence, by the mid-1960s the American semiconductor industry was dominated by so-called merchant producers, young companies that had specialized in the production of chips and then sold these chips at arm's length to an entirely different set of firms, electronic equipment producers.

The development of this distinctive semiconductor industry structure in the United States was linked to a number of factors. On the demand side, much was owed to the willingness of the military, the largest consumer of leading-edge components, to buy very expensive products from brand-new firms that offered the ultimate in performance in lieu of an established track record, and the rise of a highly competitive commercial computer industry that was also willing to buy the most advanced component technology from any source.[8] Other factors at work included the high degree of mobility within American industry, which encouraged engineers to leave established firms and start new firms if an existing company was slow to commercialize new developments; the ready availability of venture capital to fund such new spin-off companies; huge federal investments in R&D in the underlying technology base that spawned commercial products; and a first-class educational and scientific university infrastructure that fed research and personnel to the electronics industry (again, built with large doses of federal support and disposed to cooperate with industry as a consequence of the conditions tied to that federal funding).

The development of the semiconductor industry was quite different in Europe.[9] A more traditional, even hidebound, industrial structure prevailed—limited employee mobility among firms, little availability of venture capital to fuel start-ups, little government disposition (until much later) to plow huge amounts through public procurement or R&D subsidies

7. The standard source for this history is John E. Tilton, *International Diffusion of Technology: The Case of Semiconductors* (Brookings, 1971).

8. See Kenneth Flamm, *Targeting the Computer: Government Support and International Competition* (Brookings, 1987), chap. 4; and Flamm, *Creating the Computer: Government Industry and High Technology* (Brookings, 1988), pp. 13–19. In the 1950s and early 1960s, military purchases also accounted for the bulk of sales of the most technologically advanced computers.

9. An extensive discussion of the comparative development of the European semiconductor industry is found in Franco Malerba, *The Semiconductor Business: The Economics of Rapid Growth and Decline* (University of Wisconsin Press, 1985).

into leading-edge electronics or computers, and an academic sector with few links to, or interest in, industrial matters. Established electrical equipment manufacturers were the primary force driving investment in semiconductor electronics, as they sought to produce cheaper components for use in their product lines. For the most part, semiconductors were developed and produced within existing electrical equipment companies, and production took place within vertically integrated electronics producers. (The most conspicuous and important exception was the Italian producer SGS, a predecessor of what is today the only significant European producer that resembles a merchant vendor.)[10] Roughly the same (if vastly more successful) pattern of internalization of semiconductor production within larger systems producers took place in Japan.

Driven largely by demand for use in consumer and industrial products, European production of discrete semiconductors (transistors and diodes) grew nicely in the 1950s. However, the semiconductor market was revolutionized in the 1960s by the development of the integrated circuit, which was first used in significant quantities in computers, particularly by the military. The late 1950s and early 1960s witnessed an explosion in commercial demand for computers, and, because the European computer industry lagged well behind its U.S. competitors at that point, European electrical equipment producers largely missed the shift in the market. As the hot new boxes produced by the U.S. computer industry took over the European market in the early 1960s, local electronics manufacturers began to realize that much of the U.S. success was based on advanced semiconductors. When most European countries embarked on crash programs to develop national computer industries in the mid- to late 1960s, they often contained some support for ICs as an element of these programs.

But these national development programs for both computers and semiconductors were generally failures. Why they failed is an interesting and complex question that cannot be explored here.[11] In brief, the basic European computer strategy was to protect national markets with high tariff walls, then select "national champion" firms that were given favored

10. Although SGS was originally formed as part of a joint venture between office equipment producer Olivetti and telecommunications producer Telettra, their purchases accounted for little of SGS's sales over the years. See ibid., p. 91. SGS-Ates and the semiconductor division of France's Thomson electronics house merged to form SGS-Thomson Microelectronics (STM) in 1986.

11. See, for example, Flamm, *Targeting the Computer*, chap. 5; and Flamm, *Creating the Computer*, chap. 5.

treatment within the protected national market (generally receiving both direct subsidies and preferences in government procurement).[12] Some of the reasons for failure included: being sheltered from competition often meant lessened pressure to stay technologically abreast in a rapidly changing marketplace; being pushed by national policy to go head-to-head against IBM in existing markets and applications (rather than attempting to identify and enter new markets) has generally been a singularly unsuccessful strategy in the computer industry; and alliances to gain access to new technology were generally forged with U.S. producers following the same "clash of the titans" strategy of going directly against IBM in existing markets. When these American companies (such as RCA, General Electric, Xerox, and Honeywell) failed, their European partner "national champions" were generally left stranded with an installed base of orphaned technology.

The take-off in commercial computer demand in the early 1960s, and a soaring demand for high-performance semiconductors for use in these machines, marked the beginning of a steep decline in the competitive fortunes of European chip producers. The weakness of the European computer industry meant there was a relatively small demand there for the high-performance, state-of-the-art computer chips that were driving technology development in the United States. European chip production focused on discrete semiconductors and integrated circuits oriented toward the telecommunications and industrial markets, where European systems producers remained strong (see figure 5-1). Even today, European-manufactured chips are largely sold in Europe, with minimal sales in the United States, Japan, or other foreign markets. The emphasis placed on servicing the needs of local equipment manufacturers, rather than competing with foreign producers in the more rapidly developing global markets tied to the computer industry, is also evident in a relative focus on specialized proprietary chips and away from standardized commodity products where manufacturing cost and state-of-the-art processing skills are likely to be the keys to competitive success. One of the consequences of the avoidance of aggressive competition based on

12. One rather more complex case was that of International Computers Limited (ICL), the British national champion computer firm. Because ICL was formed through merger and acquisition from existing British electronics and computer companies, and because at least one of those companies remained a major player in the military electronics business, ICL was reportedly barred from selling in the military computer market in Britain, though it could bid into the smaller civil government market. Interview with ICL staff, August 1989.

FIGURE 5–1. Regional Semiconductor Sales, by Application, 1988

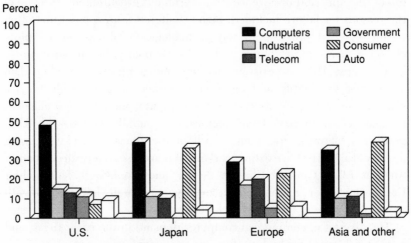

Percent

SOURCE: World Semiconductor Trade Statistics (WSTS) program, as cited in Electronics Industry Association of Japan, *The Reality of the Electronics Industry in Europe . . .* (in Japanese) (Tokyo, 1989), p. 123.

advanced manufacturing technology is that even today semiconductor production in Europe is much more tilted toward discrete devices than is the case in the United States or Japan (see figure 5-2).[13]

Attempts to protect the European semiconductor and computer industries from imports created a vicious circle of sorts. High tariffs and high costs for imported semiconductors meant higher prices—and diminished sales—for European computer systems makers in both national and global markets. Diminished computer sales meant a smaller demand for locally produced semiconductors to be used in those computer systems. A weaker national semiconductor industry meant greater political pressure for protection, and so on. This apparent contradiction between protecting a chip industry and fostering a competitive, chip-using computer industry downstream is not unique to Europe, of course; it became a major source of division within the U.S. electronics industry in the late 1980s after the Semiconductor Trade Arrangement was signed.

Since European chip manufacturers are largely vertically integrated

13. Although Japanese semiconductor makers started out producing relatively simpler discrete devices and ICs geared toward the consumer market, they (with government support) soon invested heavily in developing IC technology for the computer market. The share of Japanese semiconductor demand going into consumer electronics has steadily declined and today is surpassed by demand for chips going into office automation and computer systems.

FIGURE 5–2. Semiconductor Production, by Component Type and Producer's Base Region, 1987

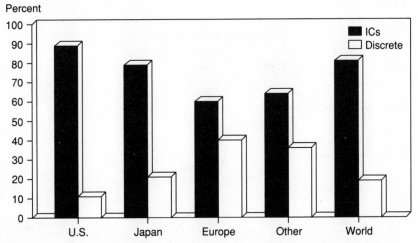

SOURCE: Integrated Circuit Engineering, *Mid-Term 1988* (Scottsdale, Ariz., 1988), p. 1-11. U.S. includes both captive and merchant.

divisions within electronics systems companies, this inherent policy conflict was internalized within European electronics firms. The solution chosen was to protect the domestic chip market but to permit free investment within Europe by foreign producers. In that way, access to leading-edge semiconductor technology developed abroad could be maintained; some degree of protection could be granted to the domestic industry; yet enough competition could be maintained over the long run in the domestic market to ensure that prices eventually approached costs. Only a mildly negative effect on the computer industry would be felt, to the extent that foreign producers of the latest, most proprietary technology might be able to practice price discrimination in the European market behind the shelter of tariff and other barriers impeding chip imports. But for mature products, with multiple sources of supply, competition within the European market would eventually drive prices down.

## Long-Term Decline of the European Semiconductor Industry

Figure 5-3 plots a number of different dimensions of how the European fit into the global semiconductor industry has changed over time. Historical data going back to the early 1970s can be pieced together for

FIGURE 5–3. Europe's Share in the World Semiconductor Market, 1970–88

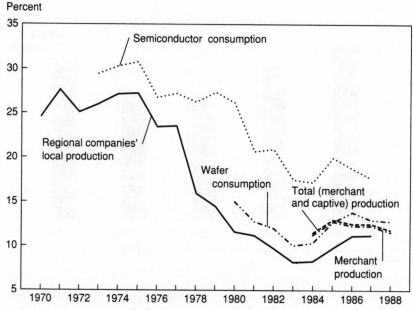

SOURCES: Author's calculations. Regional companies' global production based on WSTS and ICE data as reported in Thomas R. Howell and others, *The Microelectronics Race* (Boulder, Colo.: Westview, 1988), table A.1, and SIA presentations; data for 1973–75 semiconductors from William F. Finan and Chris B. Amundsen, "An Analysis of the Effects of Targeting on the Competitiveness of the U.S. Semiconductor Industry," Washington, Quick, Finan and Associates, n.d.; all other data are from Dataquest reports.

two of those measures, the market share of European-based producers and European consumption, in worldwide merchant sales of semiconductors. Both calculations show a halving of Europe's share in global merchant markets over the decade from 1975 to 1985. Other measures available for more recent years follow similar trends, for example, the global market share of European-produced semiconductors (with or without captive production), and physical silicon wafer volume (in millions of square inches) processed within Europe (merchant and captive). Since 1985, however, Europe's share has held fairly constant at 10–12 percent of the value of global chip sales produced within the region or by European companies. About that same share of the physical volume of silicon processed worldwide is used in European fabrication lines. Europe's recent share of global open market sales of semiconductors has stabilized at a higher level, about 17–20 percent of the world market.

The decline in Europe's electronic fortunes over the decade from 1975

FIGURE 5-4. America's Share in the World Semiconductor Market, 1970–88

Percent

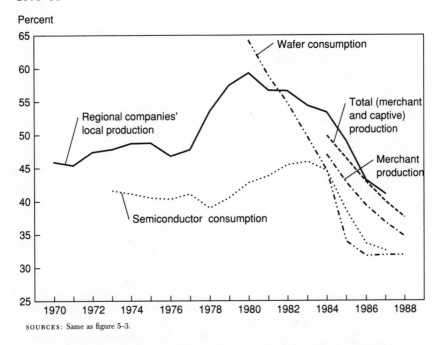

SOURCES: Same as figure 5-3.

to 1985 is usefully divided into two periods. From 1975 to 1980 Europe's share of world semiconductor consumption held relatively stable, while its production share declined sharply. The bulk of the lost European market share was picked up by U.S. firms, whose global market share rose to an all time-high (see figure 5-4). However, none of this lost European market share was squeezed out of the European market (see figure 5-5). U.S. companies gained global market share because of their rapidly increasing sales in the fast-growing U.S. and Asian chip markets. The global market share of Japanese companies basically stayed constant during this period (figure 5-6).

From 1980 to 1984, however, Japanese-based producers made significant inroads into global markets, at the expense of gradual erosion in both European and American firms' market shares. After the semiconductor industry slumped in 1985, there was a particularly large decline in the U.S. industry's share of world markets, with the vast bulk claimed by Japanese firms; in addition, a little lost ground was retaken by European companies.

FIGURE 5–5. Merchant Semiconductor Sales within Western Europe, by Country of Company Base, Selected Years, 1977–88

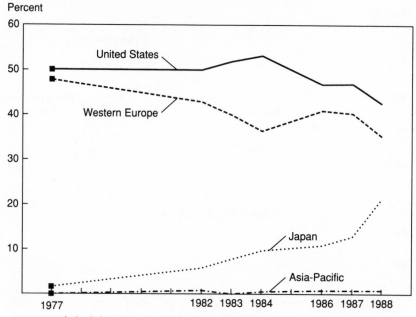

SOURCES: Author's calculations. Data for 1977 from Franco Malerba, *The Semiconductor Business: The Economics of Rapid Growth and Decline* (University of Wisconsin Press, 1985); for 1982–84, 1986, Marketing Research, Motorola Europe, October 1982–86; for 1987–88, Semiconductor Industry Association.

The fact that the regional shares of processed-wafer volume changed much more dramatically than market shares of the value of semiconductor production illustrates that it is in the commodity end of the market, where value per square inch of silicon processed is lowest, that American producers ceded the most ground to their Japanese competitors.

In short, the atmosphere of deepening crisis that surrounds semiconductor trade issues today differs markedly from the atmosphere of slow decline that informed European policy in the late 1970s. It is helpful to trace the precise changes in the semiconductor trade regime that set the stage for today's emotional debate.

### The European Chip Market in the Late 1970s

The barriers to trade that had been placed around the European semiconductor market in the 1960s were formidable. The European Community put a steep tariff on semiconductors in the 1960s—a rate of 17 percent—and this was not changed in either the Kennedy or Tokyo

FIGURE 5-6. Japan's Share in the World Semiconductor Market, 1970–88

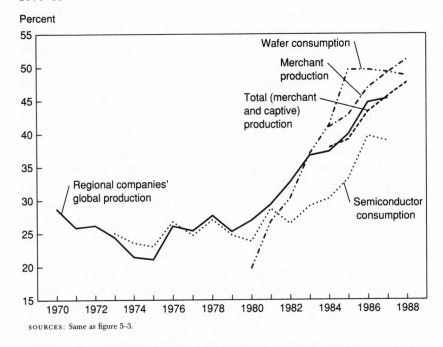

SOURCES: Same as figure 5–3.

rounds of global tariff reductions.[14] Rules of origin limiting duty-free preferential trade between the EC and the European Free Trade Association (EFTA) to electronic products with an import content of less than 5 percent of total value also effectively blocked the use of imported semiconductors in European electronics manufactures crossing the EC-EFTA boundary.[15]

The tariff on electronic boards and equipment has always been much lower than that on the semiconductors stuffed into those boards.[16] This has created some incentive to move equipment production offshore in

14. Britain had an even stiffer rate—20 percent—which came down to the EC level when it joined the Community. See Electronics Industry Association, submissions made in *Foreign Trade and Tariff Proposals,* Hearings before the House Committee on Ways and Means, 90 Cong. 2 sess. (Government Printing Office, 1968), pp. 3546, 3564.

15. See U.S. International Trade Commission, *Competitive Factors Influencing World Trade in Integrated Circuits,* USITC Publication 1013 (Washington, November 1979), p. 55.

16. In recent years, the tariff rate on computer boards was 4.9 percent, compared with a 14 percent tariff on semiconductors.

order to save on duties otherwise collected on the imported semiconductor content of the equipment.[17]

There is some evidence, largely anecdotal, that chip prices for leading-edge ICs tended to be somewhat higher in Europe than in the United States through the 1970s.[18] Unit costs for a variety of advanced ICs (like microprocessors and some advanced chips) tended to be significantly higher in Europe in the mid-1970s, while more mature products tended to be priced closer to (generally 10–15 percent over) U.S. levels (see table 5-1).

Nontariff barriers also encouraged U.S. firms to set up European production affiliates in the 1960s and 1970s. France and Britain—particularly France—were reported to have had a system of informal administrative quotas on semiconductor imports; both Britain and France pressured U.S. firms to set up local facilities to serve military markets on national security grounds; and much of the procurement of EC governments, particularly the purchases of national telecommunications monopolies, overtly favored domestic suppliers.[19]

U.S. companies set up two sorts of European affiliates in the 1960s and 1970s. The most common was that of a "point-of-sale" assembly

17. Moreover, if other computer parts are procured from abroad, the tariff structure creates an incentive to assemble offshore even if the semiconductors are fabricated in Europe. This is a consequence of the rules applied to offshore assembly (known as outward processing) using domestically made parts. Because duties on the assembled equipment (calculated at, say, 4.9 percent) are reduced by an amount reflecting the higher rate (say, 14 percent) that the exported semiconductor would be taxed at if reimported untransformed, the credit for the European semiconductor more than pays for its own share of the equipment's duty and even writes off some of the duty due on value added abroad.

18. This qualitative historical characterization of price differentials for leading-edge chips was supported in interviews with Europeans involved in the industry. William F. Finan cites a paper by Freund to the effect that prices for new, technically advanced transistors were 30–40 percent higher in Europe than in the United States in the 1960s, in support of his observation that similar price discrimination was an important feature of U.S. subsidiary sales in Europe in the early 1970s. Finan, *International Transfer of Semiconductor Technology through U.S.-Based Firms,* NBER Working Paper 118 (New York: National Bureau of Economic Research, 1975), p. 77. Edmond Sciberras, on the basis of his detailed case studies of pricing behavior by foreign affiliates in Europe, argues that centralized control of subsidiary pricing decisions by TI, Motorola, and Fairchild "is designed to guarantee against inter-subsidiary rivalry for markets, and against multinational customers exploiting inter-regional price differences by serving worldwide contracts from a low-price national subsidiary." Sciberras, *Multinational Electronic Companies and National Economic Policies* (Greenwich, Conn.: JAI Press, 1977), p. 246.

19. See Finan, *International Transfer of Semiconductor Technology,* pp. 71–75; U.S. Department of Commerce, *A Report on the U.S. Semiconductor Industry* (Washington, September 1979), pp. 95–98; and ITC, *Competitive Factors,* pp. 54–67.

TABLE 5-1. Prices of Integrated Circuits, by Region, 1976

Dollars per chip, average factory prices

| Product | Western Europe | United States | Japan |
|---|---|---|---|
| Calculator LSI | 2.75 | 2.45 | 1.86 |
| MOS | 3.20 | 3.00 | 3.20 |
| Bipolar digital | 0.85 | 0.75 | 1.36 |
| Bipolar linear | 1.10 | 1.00 | 0.70 |
| Microprocessor (including memory and support circuits) | 150 | 95 | 150 |
| Calculator and watch displays (4mm) | | | |
| LED | 1.80 | 1.70 | 1.50 |
| LCD | 5.00 | 4.50 | 4.50 |
| Clock displays (15mm) | | | |
| LED | 5.50 | 5.00 | 5.25 |
| LCD | 8.50 | 8.00 | 8.00 |

SOURCE: Mackintosh Consultants, *Market Survey of Semiconductors*, vol. 4: *Applications and Markets*, study prepared for the Ministry of Research and Technology of the Federal Republic of Germany (December 1976), tables IV-15 to IV-17. Note that quoted average costs reflect differences in product specifications and volume requirements.

operation (the local "back-end" assembly and testing of devices made from imported processed silicon wafers).[20] The attraction of this type of investment was that it reduced the dutiable value on which the tariff was levied (by the amount of value added by assembly and test in Europe) and often conferred local-origin status on the assembled product. Also, because the tariff rate on processed silicon wafers that had not yet been scribed and separated into individual chips was lower (9 percent rather than 17 percent), additional tariff savings could be realized by breaking the wafer into chips within the EC and then assembling and testing the product.

There was also a considerable amount of "front-end" wafer processing (diffusion of electronic devices onto the surface of the silicon wafer) in chip factories set up by U.S. companies in Europe. Initially, this was often linked to political pressure from national governments to set up local processing facilities.[21] In recent years, however, with the growing importance of fabricating customized chips on a rapid turnaround basis, the location of production facilities close to customers has become much more critical. This has increasingly furnished an economic rationale for location decisions that may have initially been political.

20. The point-of-sale terminology is that of Finan, *International Transfer of Semiconductor Technology*.

21. See ibid., pp. 80–85.

One respect in which the European subsidiaries of U.S. semiconductor companies differed markedly from their American brethren was the limited extent to which they carried out their assembly and test operations in low-wage offshore countries. In the late 1970s some 80–90 percent of semiconductors shipped in the United States were assembled and tested overseas. In Europe, in the mid-1970s, less than 20 percent of local production was assembled in offshore affiliates.[22] One of the reasons this was the case was the much higher tariff rate in Europe; another was the emphasis in Europe on producing discrete devices. (Since the value added in assembly was much greater relative to the value of the chip for discretes, the relative burden of the duty levied on any value added through offshore assembly was correspondingly higher.)

In the mid-1970s the market for advanced chips was dominated by specialized U.S. merchant IC producers selling to electronic equipment producers with whom they were not in direct competition. European chip producers concentrated on catching up through technical ties with U.S. chip companies (including significant acquisitions), in-house production of ICs for internal use to hone production skills, and reliance on U.S. suppliers for leading-edge products. While there was certainly awareness within Europe of the increased dependence on foreign-based chip suppliers and a shift in government policies toward more explicit support for national semiconductor industries,[23] large-scale investments within the European Community by U.S. suppliers seem to have blunted possible concerns. There were few visible signs of alarm in the European electronics sector and little palpable climate of crisis. This was to change in the 1980s.

## The European Market in the 1980s

Certainly, no urgent sense of crisis seemed to mark European trade policy as the 1980s opened. Indeed, formal barriers to semiconductor imports initially relaxed a bit. Starting in the late 1970s, European equipment producers (including some that also made semiconductors) began asking national authorities to seek tariff suspensions, to be approved by the European Commission, on selected semiconductor imports. The authority to suspend or reduce tariffs on selected products not produced

22. See Kenneth Flamm, "Internationalization in Semiconductors," in Joseph Grunwald and Kenneth Flamm, *The Global Factory: Foreign Assembly in International Trade* (Brookings, 1985), pp. 82–84, 85–86.

23. See Malerba, *Semiconductor Business*, chap. 6.

FIGURE 5–7.  New Tariff Suspensions Reviewed by the European
Community in the Microelectronics Sector, 1979–86

Number of cases

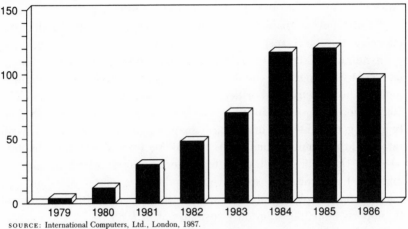

SOURCE: International Computers, Ltd., London, 1987.

within the EC or unavailable in sufficient quantity or quality there had
long been applied to (and was apparently inspired by) certain chemical
imports.[24] By the late 1970s creative minds in European systems houses
realized that this provision might also be applicable to chips. From 1979
on, there was a sharp increase in the use of full or partial tariff suspensions
in the semiconductor area (see figure 5-7). While one can count the
numbers of suspensions approved, the European Community has not
collected statistics on the value of imports entering under these provisions,
or the value of duty collections forgone. Nonetheless, there is a widespread
feeling that use of these suspensions has been a significant factor in
lowering prices in the European market.

As a consequence, it is easy to find Europeans involved in the industry
who assert that the use of tariff suspensions became so widespread as to
effectively open the European market, reducing the average collected
duty to 5–6 percent of import value.[25] To be fair, it is possible that other

24. Interviews with European industrial and official sources, summer 1989.

25. There is vast confusion on this point. During the summer of 1989, I spoke with
one EC official (directorate A) who cited a "vague" recollection of an estimate that one-
half to two-thirds of imports came in under some form of tariff suspension, another EC
official (directorate B) who spoke of an actual average duty rate of 5 percent on
semiconductors, an industry strategist (company C) who spoke of an average duty of 5.5
percent, yet another official from the same company who "guessed" that under 10 percent

ways of reducing duties on imported semiconductors—in addition to tariff suspensions—were factored into these calculations. Offshore assembly reduces the duties on reimported chips, as does the importation of finished wafers before they have been broken into chips.

But the best available—albeit rough—calculation suggests that the effect of the tariff suspension program was significant, though not overwhelming. Estimates that half or more of imports were affected seem far too large or perhaps count the effect of other tariff-sparing arrangements. The EC tariff authorities have estimated that an additional ECU 500 million in customs duties would have been collected in 1988 if all types of goods entering under tariff suspensions had paid the full tariff rate.[26] Of this amount, some ECU 100 million were allocated to chapters 84–99 in the tariff classification (machinery imports), of which approximately 80 percent were spared semiconductor imports. Based on this information, simple calculations suggest that perhaps 20–30 percent of IC imports benefited from duty suspensions in 1988.[27]

Despite the increased openness of the European market, resistance

---

of chip imports came in under tariff suspension, another producer's (company D) strategic planner who opined that the "real" duty on semiconductors was 7–8 percent and 40–50 percent of imports were covered by tariff suspensions, and another industry executive (company E, a large chip producer) who estimated that 25–30 percent of imports came in with some degree of duty suspension. Since the duty rate on ICs was 14 percent, and 9 percent on processed but undivided wafers in recent years, those who claimed a very large liberalizing effect on the tariff barriers to semiconductor imports were a clear majority in my not particularly random sample. However, as argued in the text, company E's well-informed minority opinion seems to carry the day based on the available evidence.

26. Interview with Mr. Casella, Directorate-General 21 (Customs Union and Indirect Tax), EC Commission, July 19, 1989.

27. In 1988, ECU 149.9 million of uncut processed chips on wafers (at 9 percent tariff) and ECU 3.47 billion of individual chip imports (at 14 percent tariff) would have generated tariff collections of ECU 499 million (official Eurostat statistics). EC customs authorities estimate suspended semiconductor duties to have been approximately ECU 80 million. If one (reasonably) assumes that the bulk of the value of tariff suspensions involved ICs and tallies up nominal tariff revenues due on IC imports, one concludes that all lost collections of suspended duties on ICs amounted to about 16 percent of the total due at the full tariff rates. If, on average, 100 percent of the tariff was suspended, this would imply that 16 percent of IC imports entered with tariffs suspended. If, on average, only 50 percent of the tariff was suspended, this would imply that 32 percent of ICs were imported with suspended duties. Casual perusal of lists of duty suspensions suggests that items benefiting from duty suspension very frequently have half or more of their duty suspended and most often all. On the basis of this admittedly crude judgment, 50 percent would be a loose upper bound. Therefore the available data seem to suggest that 20–30 percent of IC imports enter with duties suspended. The analogous calculation for all semiconductor imports would necessarily be lower.

to dismantling tariff barriers lingered on. In 1985, as Japan and the United States dropped all tariffs on semiconductors, Europe decided to lower the tariff on semiconductors by only 3 percent, to 14 percent (effective in 1986).[28] These apparent contradictions probably reflected political compromises, rather than a purposeful strategy. A certain amount of de facto liberalization was taking place as European equipment producers, struggling to stay competitive with mounting Asian imports, successfully lobbied for tariff suspensions on components where domestic production was nonexistent or technologically backward.

Use of offshore assembly also appears to have jumped. Imports from offshore countries (Asia-Pacific, except Japan and Australia) rose sharply, from 16 percent of IC imports in 1977 to 29 percent in 1988.[29] By 1988 it was estimated that only 40 percent of European company chip sales within the EC, and just a little over 20 percent of U.S.-based sales, were actually tested and assembled within the Community. The cost savings with foreign assembly of ICs must have outweighed the duties incurred when reentering the Community.

Despite the increasingly fluid flow of semiconductors into and out of the EC, however, European governments continued to commit resources to the technological development of the local electronics industry. After 1982 European national governments launched a major new set of programs of investment in technology.[30] Particularly significant was the Dutch and German governments' 1983 agreement to pay for a third of a billion-dollar joint investment by Philips and Siemens in the development of advanced semiconductor technology. This so-called Megaproject, which has just ended, played a catalytic role in the creation of the Joint European Submicron Silicon Initiative (JESSI) launched in 1989. Much earlier, in 1984, the first major Community-wide high-technology program, the European Strategic Program for Research and Development in Information Technology (Esprit), was formally begun by the EC. European analysts judge that the Esprit framework, in particular, has already greatly

28. Why this modest cut ultimately was implemented is variously described as the outcome of prolonged pressure by the British government or as a compensatory measure to offset the effect of increased protection for video cassette recorders within the European Community.

29. See Flamm, "Internationalization," p. 86; and unpublished Eurostat import statistics for 1988.

30. See Malerba, *Semiconductor Business*, pp. 188–200; and Mike Hobday, "The European Semiconductor Industry: Resurgence and Rationalization," University of Sussex, July 1989, pp. 6–11.

increased technical and strategic cooperation among European firms.[31] The recent move toward pan-European tie-ups greatly accelerated shortly afterward.

Chip demand began to deteriorate in late 1984, however, and a sharp downturn in the industry began shortly thereafter. But over the next two years, as the rest of the industry suffered through a major downturn in semiconductor demand, European manufacturers actually saw their market share rise within their home market. Although their pain may have been less acute, the European producers were also affected by the vicious price cutting that soon developed. Clamor for government action increased as the losses mounted. By the summer of 1986, it was clear that a negotiated peace—a deal between the Japanese and American governments—was in the works, to end the escalating tensions surrounding a succession of dumping cases being instituted against Japanese memory chip imports into the United States. In September of 1986 the Semiconductor Trade Arrangement between the United States and Japan was formally concluded, and the international electronics industry turned a historic corner. It is probably fair to describe the European Community as simply aghast at this development.

## The European Semiconductor Industry Today

While trade friction in semiconductors dates back to at least the 1960s, until recently it remained largely a conflict among the semiconductor producers of the countries involved and did not draw intense scrutiny from other industries (aside from sporadic concern over the potential cost-raising effects that protectionist trade remedies might bring about). This was because the semiconductor marketplace generally remained highly competitive.

Throughout the 1970s European systems companies grew increasingly reliant on chips produced by U.S. semiconductor companies. This posed no threat to their systems business, however, because these merchant chip companies were not in direct competition with their systems products in the downstream marketplace. Indeed, the intense technological competition among U.S. merchant semiconductor manufacturers meant a continuous stream of new leading-edge products was forthcoming, with prices dropping rapidly. While European systems companies may not

31. See Hobday, "European Semiconductor Industry," pp. 9–10.

have been happy about the poor showing of European-based chip producers (often components divisions within the same companies), cheaper components may even have decreased costs and prices and increased the overall size of systems markets.

In the early 1980s competition entered a new phase as Japanese companies reached the technological frontier in semiconductors and attacked international markets in force. Initially, this led to even more intense competition in the semiconductor market and put further downward pressure on chip prices, to the apparent benefit of systems producers. During this period, however, as the chip divisions of some vertically integrated Japanese companies became the industry's technological leaders in certain areas, the first inklings of a new concern became evident among some European and U.S. systems producers. Because Japanese chip producers were part of larger systems houses, foreign competitors began to suspect that systems divisions of the same Japanese companies were getting access to leading-edge products before their foreign competitors. This may have been perfectly natural, insofar as systems divisions and chip-making divisions collaborated in the design of new products, but it put foreign systems houses at a competitive disadvantage in getting timely access to the new parts. The resurgence of European support for semiconductors in the mid-1980s, in frameworks like the Megaproject and the Esprit program, in some measure reflected these mounting concerns. Similar worries also began to take root in the United States.

After 1985, and the exit of many U.S. merchant chip producers from the commodity DRAM market, trade friction in semiconductors entered a new phase. For the first time, the important commodity memory market—a cost-sensitive input important to a large number of downstream systems products—was dominated by a handful of integrated Japanese companies. At first, worries seemed highly academic. The Japanese companies producing these products competed ruthlessly against one another, and prices for DRAMs continued to plummet throughout 1985.

The signing of the Semiconductor Trade Arrangement in the fall of 1986 was followed by price stabilization and then by sharp increases— unprecedented in the forty-year history of the industry—in memory chip prices in 1987 and 1988. At that point, the troubles of semiconductor users made it clear that a whole new set of concerns had been created for corporate and public policy. Strategic issues, felt well beyond the boundaries of European chip factories, had come to the fore in semiconductors.

## Europe and the STA

Europe's extremely negative reaction to the STA had many roots. The perceived injury to European interests was procedural, economic, and psychological. The procedural damage involved the secret bilateral negotiation of a framework intended to affect international market conditions for semiconductors, without consultation with the EC and other affected parties. The economic damage included the implementation of export price "monitoring" mechanisms by Japan's Ministry of International Trade and Industry (MITI) designed to raise the price of semiconductors in third-country markets to levels prevailing on exports to the United States,[32] and the implementation of measures designed to increase U.S. firms' sales in Japanese semiconductor markets. (This latter fear, strictly speaking, was incorrect: the infamous 20 percent market share was to be supplied by "foreign-based" firms, not necessarily American companies.)[33] The psychological damage was the implicit message that Europe had ceased to be an important player in the international semiconductor industry and could safely be ignored. All three irritations moved Europe to complain to the GATT in September of 1986, and when consultations with the United States and Japan proved unsatisfactory, formally to request review of its grievances by a GATT panel in February 1987.

Why was Europe not consulted by the United States in order to head off these complaints and perhaps to form a stronger coalition to bring pressure to bear on Japan? Europeans certainly realized that the game was afoot in the first part of 1986 and shot off messages to the Americans and Japanese asking that strictly bilateral talks affecting third-country markets be broken off.[34] The EC and the United States were at the time embroiled in disputes over agricultural trade issues, and that may have

32. Actually, the MITI price-monitoring mechanism at first set lower standards for prices in third-country markets than for sales to the United States. MITI argued that the STA required it to end below-cost pricing in third-country markets, but only required the use of the Department of Commerce's cost accounting procedures on export sales to the U.S. market. For third countries, MITI argued, it would use its own costing guidelines, which would recognize lower marketing and distribution costs in non-U.S. markets. After further U.S. pressure, however, MITI capitulated and agreed to unify the two cost-monitoring systems for exports after November 1986. See *Asahi Shimbun*, November 23, 1986, p. 9.

33. Of course, since the so-called secret side letter was nominally secret, the Europeans had no way of knowing this.

34. Interviews with EC officials, summer 1989.

made cooperation on other issues more difficult. Since European producers accounted for only 10–12 percent of global chip production, they may have simply been viewed as a marginal player, an unnecessary complication in what were already difficult bilateral talks.

An irony in all this was that a movement was already under way in Europe to lobby for an STA-like outcome for the European market. By May 1986 European chip producers, in envy of the extraordinary political success of the American Semiconductor Industry Association (SIA), had followed its example by forming the European Electronic Component Manufacturers Association (EECA) in order to bring dumping cases against Japanese chip imports.[35] In December 1986 EECA filed a dumping complaint with the EC, and by April 1987 the EC had widened the investigation to include both DRAMs and erasable programmable read-only memories (EPROMs).[36] EECA argued that supplies diverted from the U.S. market by the STA were being shifted to the European market, further depressing prices.

American complaints about "below fair market value" chip sales by Japanese firms to third-country markets continued, however, and by early 1987 MITI had embarked on a more extensive program of restrictive measures to raise chip prices in foreign markets. ("Fair market value," or FMV, is legal jargon for the threshold price below which antidumping duties are levied. FMVs were used as minimum price floors, set by the Commerce Department.) In February 1987 MITI began issuing "requests" for production cutbacks to Japanese firms, and by March 1987, after some initial resistance, all Japanese producers (including U.S. producer Texas Instruments' subsidiary in Japan) were complying with these requests. MITI also tightened up its use of the export control machinery, which covered all semiconductor exports, to ensure that export prices were above the norms it had established.

Below-FMV sales continued, however. After a "sting" operation in Hong Kong in March 1987, in which Japanese producer Oki Electric's sales agents were lured into documenting sales at less than FMV prices, the United States announced a decision to impose trade sanctions (in the form of retaliatory tariffs) on selected Japanese imports. A memorandum

35. "Europe—Working Party to Investigate Japanese Chip Dumping," *Financial Times*, May 1, 1986, p. 6.

36. "EEC Receives Complaint from SC Manufacturers," *International Herald Tribune*, December 6, 1986, p. 13; and "EC to Investigate Claims of Japanese Dumping of EPROMs," *Financial Times*, April 10, 1987, p. 5.

circulated in Washington in April of 1987 in which MITI defended its attempts to raise prices in third-country markets. The memorandum specifically mentioned the MITI program of production guidelines to Japanese producers, and this was later to prove a crucial piece of evidence in the GATT decision that third-country pricing provisions of the STA were illegal.[37]

By May 1987 MITI's more stringent measures were taking effect, and the Europeans, no longer worried about excessive supplies to their market, were now asking Japan to increase supplies of chips to the European market. At that time, both prices and quantities for export to Europe were apparently under strict MITI guidelines.[38] At mid-year, computer industry sales—and chip demand—began to recover, and it was soon clear that a worldwide chip shortage was developing. Industry circles in Japan argued that the biggest factor in the developing chip shortage was MITI's continuing "guidance," and the fact that "MITI, which is concerned about the possibility of a flaring up of the Japan-US semiconductor friction again, maintains rigid supervision over the facilities investments of the major companies. As a result, these companies have drawn up moderate investment plans" despite the emerging shortage.[39]

The increasing signs of shortage satisfied the United States that MITI had acted forcefully to increase chip prices in worldwide markets. Indeed, by the fall of 1987 the agonized screams of chip users were being heard loud and clear, and the U.S. government had switched its public posture to one of encouraging MITI not to restrict chip production. On November 3, 1987, in a delicate ballet of communiqués, the U.S. government partially removed the spring sanctions and announced that it was satisfied that third-country dumping had ended. MITI announced that it was "imposing no quantitative or other restrictions on the production, shipment, or supply of semiconductors, except MITI continues to exercise export controls from the view point of COCOM."[40] This last qualification, it turned out, was crucial, since an extremely rigorous export control system was put into place during 1988 that effectively made it impossible

37. See General Agreement on Tariffs and Trade, *Japan—Trade in Semiconductors: Report of the Panel* (Geneva, March 24, 1988).

38. *Yomiuri Shimbun*, May 29, 1987, p. 6.

39. *Nihon Keizai Shimbun*, October 2, 1987, p. 20; and *Nihon Keizai Shimbun*, October 10, 1987, p. 10.

40. MITI, "Statement of Ministry of International Trade and Industry Concerning Trade in Semiconductors," November 3, 1987.

for foreign buyers to purchase Japanese chips at prices not directly controlled and administered by the chip manufacturers.

Behind the scenes, the U.S. government was less than enthusiastic about the concept of Japanese firms increasing chip capacity to meet the looming shortage.[41] Despite MITI protestations that it was acting to remove limits on chip production, U.S. trade negotiators continued to press MITI to limit investments by Japanese firms in new capacity well into 1988.[42] In January 1988 MITI reportedly switched its twice-yearly survey of Japanese industrial investment to a much more detailed and rigorous questionnaire in order to better monitor investments in trade-sensitive sectors, particularly semiconductors, and to ask business to scale back production plans that it judged to be excessive.[43]

Coupled with a recovery in the computer industry and an increasing

41. This attitude was aided and abetted by the widespread dissemination of a study carried out by the consulting firm of Quick and Finan, which forecast: "The tight supply conditions seen in late-1987 [are] only temporary. Several firms have just begun full-scale production and others will soon follow in the first half of 1988. Thus, throughout most of 1988, potential supply capacity will ramp faster than demand under any plausible market scenario." Quoted in Semiconductor Industry Association, *One and One-Half Years of Experience under the U.S.-Japan Semiconductor Agreement* (Cupertino, Calif., March 1, 1988), p. 26. This view conflicted sharply with the consensus view in Japan at that moment, where semiconductor manufacturers predicted a shortage lasting at least until the spring of 1989. See Mitsuhiro Takahashi, "Producers Slow to React to Chip Shortage," *Japan Economic Journal*, May 7, 1988, p. 1. Needless to say, the Japanese view—coming from the locale where more than 90 percent of merchant DRAMs were produced—was the correct one.

Despite their later stance of opposition to production cuts, important voices in U.S. government and industry actually welcomed the restrictions by MITI. A "U.S. official involved in the continuing chip talks with Japan" told a reporter from the *Wall Street Journal* (February 19, 1987, p. 6) that "MITI's production guidelines 'could potentially be helpful' in driving up Japanese prices around the world." And Joseph Parkinson, chairman of U.S. memory chip producer Micron Technology (which brought the original 64K DRAM dumping case against Japan), was quoted in a prominently featured interview in *Nihon Keizai Shimbun* (March 22, 1987, p. 3) as saying that "he appreciated MITI's guidance to industrial circles for the reduction of production as 'a correct approach,' and said, 'The problem is how quickly the Japanese side will achieve results by carrying out the Japan-U.S. Semiconductor Agreement, which includes the reduction of production by Japan.' "

42. Interviews with former U.S. government officials, 1989. MITI appears to have obliged and maintained its "guidance" to the Japanese industry well after the November 3 announcement. On December 23, 1987, a *Nihon Keizai Shimbun* article noted that "manufacturers maintain a cautious attitude toward the expansion of production under MITI's guidance" (p. 18).

43. See "Contents of Facilities Investments Also Will Be 'Supervised'; MITI Will Change Survey Method for Prevention of Friction; Reduction of Excessive Investments Will Be Urged," *Asahi Shimbun*, January 12, 1988, p. 11.

FIGURE 5–8. Sample One: 256K DRAM Price Comparisons, United States, Europe, Japan, 1986–89[a]

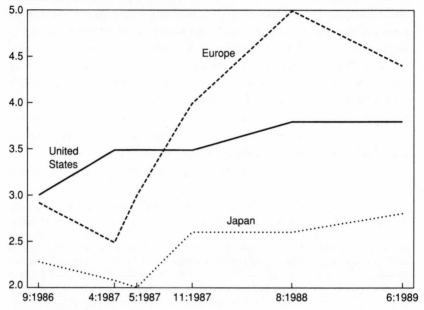

SOURCE: Company data.
a. These prices probably represent some mix of spot and long-term contract prices.

demand for memory chips, the restrictions had an extraordinarily dramatic impact. In early 1988 spot prices for DRAMs in the United States soared to historically unprecedented levels—the price of the best-selling 256K DRAM tripled over a four-month period—and the U.S. computer industry was plunged into crisis; producers scrambled for supplies of critical memory chips. Despite the developing crisis, however, production and investment increases within the Japanese industry were very modest. Within the Japanese trade press and financial circles, a belief persisted that MITI continued to offer informal guidance to producers on capacity expansion plans.[44]

European electronics systems producers found themselves in similarly dire straits. Figure 5-8 shows how the European subsidiary of one U.S.-based computer company with global procurement saw market prices for

44. For more on this point, see Kenneth Flamm, "Policy and Politics in the International Semiconductor Industry," keynote address, Semiconductor Equipment and Materials Institute, Newport Beach, Calif., January 1989.

the popular 256K DRAM change in the European market, compared with price levels in other major markets. After the STA was signed in September of 1986, prices continued to drop in the European market (as well as in Japan) through the spring of 1987. After U.S. sanctions were imposed and more restrictive production guidelines were imposed by MITI in the second quarter of 1987, prices quickly rose. In the fall of 1987 Japanese vendors were informing their European customers that an allocation system had been installed, and by late 1987 prices in the European market had risen substantially above U.S. levels. Through 1988 and into 1989 Japanese vendors continued to tell European customers that MITI restrictions limited their European shipments.[45]

Other data confirm the general outlines of this story. Figure 5-9 shows the average prices on long-term volume contracts for the purchase of standard 256K DRAMs by a sample of U.S. and European firms. Although these prices reflect only volume long-term contracts, and therefore are lower than those shown in figure 5-8, the same general pattern emerges: in the fall and winter of 1986 prices fell below American levels, then caught up by the fall of 1987 (as European purchasers heard about allocations), and rose above U.S. levels by mid-1988.

A similar tale is told by regional price statistics collected by the market research firm Dataquest (figure 5-10). Although these statistics are probably less reliable guides to price movements over time,[46] they too show European prices dropping (though just barely) below U.S. prices in the late spring of 1987, then shooting far above U.S. levels in mid-

---

45. One cannot, of course, neglect the possibility that this may have been a convenient excuse. However, according to a number of knowledgeable Japanese involved in that country's electronics industry (who spoke to me in late 1989), MITI continued administrative guidance on investment through the spring of 1988, continued to guide the regional allocation of DRAM shipments until mid-1989, and continued to offer opinions on companies' investment plans through the remainder of 1989.

46. Dataquest's pricing data—although they are virtually the only semipublic comparative data on international semiconductor pricing—appear to be significantly less reliable than some of Dataquest's other information products. Dataquest market researchers ask a small, nonrandom, continuously changing panel of vendors (not purchasers) what prices they received (or were asking, or would have been asking if no actual transactions at a specified volume took place) in "representative" transactions. These data appear to undergo significant retrospective revision. The most dramatic such example involved the U.S. government's use of Dataquest price data in its submission to the GATT panel investigation of the STA, in order to challenge price data furnished by European companies. The European data, however, were apparently also supplied by Dataquest. The data submitted by the U.S. government, in turn, differed from data furnished to me by Dataquest in February 1989.

FIGURE 5–9. Sample Two: 256K DRAM Price Comparisons, United States and Europe, 1985–88[a]

Average dollars per chip, long-term volume contracts

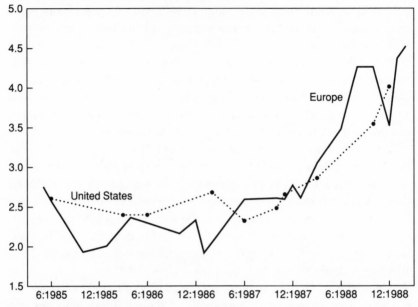

SOURCE: Data provided by industry sources.
a. The data track prices for the most widely used DRAM type over this period, the 256K chip with access times of 120 and 150 nanoseconds. (As manufacturers shrank their chip sizes in order to yield more usable product per wafer processed, device speeds increased, so that the average access time for the standard part fell from 150 to 120 nanoseconds.) A "volume" contract was taken to include a contract covering the purchase of 20,000 or more chips; average contract prices when the contract was negotiated were tabulated. The price reported is plotted against the date it was negotiated.

1988. Figure 5-11 shows that the overall price trend is quite consistent with trends in Japanese shipments of 256K DRAMs to the European market. Exports declined in the second quarter of 1987 and in the second half of 1988.

As a consequence, the STA provoked the extreme ire of both European chip producers and consumers. Producers first protested as European chip prices dropped below U.S. levels. Then, after American pressure resulted in reduced Japanese shipments to Europe and Asia and chip prices in Europe rose well above U.S. levels in 1988, European consumers began to shout and scream as they saw themselves disadvantaged in highly competitive global electronic systems industries. It is not evident that there was a deeper strategy behind the roller coaster path of U.S.-European memory chip price differentials: regional price differentials would inevitably arise under any regional supply rationing scheme.

FIGURE 5–10. Sample Three: 256K DRAM Price Comparisons, United States, Europe, Japan, 1986–88[a]

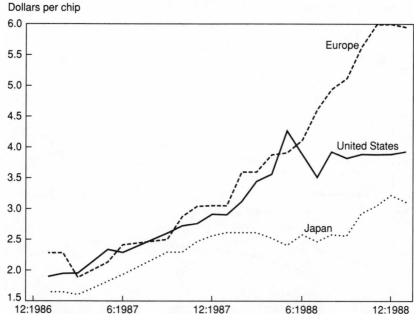

Dollars per chip

SOURCE: Dataquest "First Monday" data.

a. Volume contract pricing. Reference is to simple monthly averages of biweekly price quotations; chips are 150 nanosecond access times through August, 1988, 120 nanoseconds afterward.

Strategy or not, Europe was angry. The legal vessel in which the European outrage was deposited was the EC complaint before GATT. In March of 1988 a GATT panel ruled that the third-country pricing provisions of the STA were illegal, and the EC stood vindicated.

The GATT ruling posed a thorny dilemma for the Japanese. On the one hand, the United States was adamant that it would regard lower prices in third-country markets than in the American market as a subversion of the letter and intent of the STA. On the other hand, the GATT ruling clearly required the Japanese government to cease taking actions—by setting export prices or volumes or by fixing production— that had the effect of setting prices in third-country markets. How could Japan escape this quandary?

The dilemma was solved by the fact that chip prices had by this time risen far above FMV levels. Even with no guidance whatsoever offered, prices in Europe would certainly not fall under FMV levels any time soon. Thus for Japan to end official monitoring of European pricing and

FIGURE 5–11. Quarterly Shipments of 256K DRAMs from Japanese
Plants, by Destination, 1987–88

Millions of units to destination

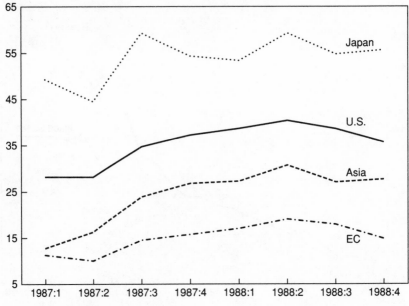

SOURCE: Unpublished Japanese government statistics.

exports would probably not lead to clashes with the United States in the
immediate future.

Ironically, the EC was shortly to ask MITI to implement an EC set
of standards for the monitoring of prices. The whole issue of price
monitoring remained moot so long as market prices hovered well above
FMVs. A formal resolution of the GATT complaint was not to be concluded
until over a full year later, in June 1989. At that point, Japan agreed to
retrospective monitoring of exports to non-U.S. markets, abolishing the
Forecast Committee (an industry-based committee that had formally
ratified MITI-developed "forecasts," which, at least in 1987, reflected
MITI guidance on production), and agreed to "refrain from interfering
with the level of production."[47] By that time, however, all but the final
details had been ironed out of a settlement of the DRAM dumping case
brought by the EC against Japanese firms. The settlement established
the EC's very own system of price monitoring.

47. EC Commission, "Japan to Implement GATT Recommendations on Trade in
Semiconductors," press release, Brussels, June 22, 1989.

A settlement of the DRAM dumping case was agreed on in principle by Japan and the EC in August 1989. The settlement proposed that a quarterly reference price on DRAMs be calculated on the basis of past historical cost data plus a generous 9.5 percent profit margin. Japanese manufacturers signing the undertaking would be required not to sell below this reference price. By early October 1989 the undertaking had been signed by eleven Japanese manufacturers and was scheduled to be passed on to the Council of Ministers for final approval. At Britain's insistence, it was also agreed that the five-year agreement be reviewed in 1991, when the STA is scheduled to expire.[48]

## Rising Significance of Strategic Concerns

Europe's experience since the STA was signed has almost certainly affected its attitude toward semiconductor industry issues. First, the manner in which Europe was excluded from basic political decisions affecting a vital industrial input drove home the message that the power to shape trade policy grows out of the barrel of a wafer stepper. Or to put it differently, the trade policy apparatus, national and international, largely deals with the interests of producers, not consumers, even when the consumer is itself an important industry. This lesson was also learned the hard way by the U.S. computer industry. Second, the vulnerability of European electronics systems companies to strategic action by foreign suppliers was demonstrated. For the first time, strategic concerns of user industries became part of the trade friction environment, and they remain a significant issue today. The user industries see two strategic threats.

The first strategic threat troubling chip users is that a small group of suppliers may use their market power to coordinate production or pricing in order to maximize profits collected on sales to outside customers, rather than compete as aggressively against one another as they have in the past. That this is more than a theoretical possibility was proven when MITI's 1987 production guidelines successfully reduced DRAM production on a scale large enough to boost DRAM prices significantly. To be sure, MITI guidelines were a response to external foreign pressure. But they succeeded in greatly improving the profitability of Japanese DRAM producers and showed that coordinated action by Japanese producers was feasible and profitable.

---

48. Lucy Kellaway, "Japan-EC Microchip Agreement Hits Snag," *Financial Times*, October 5, 1989, p. 2.

Although the subsequent rise in DRAM prices to levels far above FMV levels was undoubtedly due to other factors as well, particularly a recovery in semiconductor demand, restraint in expanding supply and production capacity by Japanese producers also was notable through mid-1988. By 1989 the concept of "bubble money"—supernormal profits due to abnormal scarcities of product—was widely used in Japanese industry circles to describe the profits being made on DRAMs. Estimates of bubble money being collected for DRAMs by early 1989 hovered around $3 billion to $4 billion a year.[49] This was quite a significant sum in an industry whose global sales in 1988 were about $45 billion. Some evidence of the extreme profitability of DRAM sales was apparent in the balance sheets of Toshiba, the largest producer of one-megabit DRAMs (with about one-third of the global market in fiscal 1988). Semiconductors generated only 21 percent of the company's fiscal 1988 sales revenues, yet semiconductor components were estimated to have earned 57 percent of that year's operating profit.[50]

More troubling were indications that Japanese companies were determined to put a permanent end to the "excessive competition" that had triggered rapid price declines in periods of slack semiconductor demand in the past. Beginning in the second quarter of 1989, despite price levels that by all accounts remained far higher than average costs of production (and vastly higher than marginal costs), firms began to reduce shipments in order to stabilize prices, rather than cut prices in order to continue to sell more chips, as would occur in a competitive industry. By late 1989 continued production cutbacks by leading Japanese firms appeared to have slowed down price declines in a seriously depressed chip market; rampant price cutting did not break out even though prices remained well above the average cost of production for leading Japanese producers.

To be fair, an outbreak of vigorous price competition might well have pushed prices down to the politically determined floor levels and provoked another round of recriminations from U.S. chip manufacturers. Japanese price competition and restraints on production could easily be defended as unavoidable consequences of continuing trade friction. The STA put

49. This value is roughly consistent with a report circulating in Japanese industry circles in the spring of 1989 that MITI had calculated that "bubble money" was running around ¥45 billion a month at that time. Other crude calculations that suggest a pure profit of about this magnitude are reviewed in Flamm, "Policy and Politics."

50. See Makoto Sumita, Yoshio Ando, and Kiyohisa Ohta, *Nomura Analyst Report: Electronics Review* (Tokyo: NRI, April 1989), exhibits 30, 31, 39.

the Japanese government in an unenviable position. If MITI kept chip prices up, U.S. users complained. If chip prices fell sharply, the U.S. chip producers complained even more loudly and could be counted on for a sharp political counterattack. Perhaps understandably, the choice to maintain relatively high chip prices appeared more attractive.

In any event, with or without MITI's assistance, Japanese DRAM manufacturers now seem determined to avoid the unbridled price competition of the past. There is widespread industry speculation that memory pricing in the future will follow the "bai-rule" rather than the "pi-rule." The "pi-rule" refers to the fact that historically DRAM prices for each generation of chip had tended to decline asymptotically toward the $3 level (pi = 3.14) as mass production of that generation peaked. Since a new generation of chip was introduced on average about every three years, and since each new generation of chip quadrupled the number of bits on a chip, this amounted to a 75 percent reduction in the cost of a bit of memory every three years, or an annual rate of decline of about 36 percent.[51] The "bai-rule" (bai is the kanji character meaning "doubling") suggests that in the future every new generation of chip will approximately double in price as mass production peaks. Following the previous logic, this means a 50 percent decline in bit cost every three years, for an annual rate of decline of about 20 percent, or about 50 percent less than under the pi-rule.

If this scenario comes to pass, it has serious implications indeed for the downstream computer industry. Technological progress, reflected in the declining cost of semiconductor memory, has contributed in a major way to the extraordinary decline in the cost of computing capacity. Computer demand, in turn, is quite sensitive to computer price. Some rough but conservative calculations suggest that the growth in the computer market due solely to declining semiconductor cost might change from perhaps 5.5 percent a year under the pi-rule to only 3.1 percent a year under the bai-rule.[52]

51. Remarkably, this is roughly the estimate of annual decline in memory bit cost produced by analyses of actual historical data.

52. These estimates are produced by noting that the elasticity of computer demand with respect to semiconductor price is approximately equal to the product of the elasticity of computer demand with respect to computer price, times the cost share of semiconductors in computer cost. I have also assumed in this approximation that there are constant returns to scale in computer manufacturing and that computer price is roughly proportional to computer manufacturing cost. Various studies suggest a price elasticity of computer demand of about −1.5, and I have used a very conservative figure of 0.1 as the share of semiconductor

Diminished industry growth is not the worst possible scenario for downstream users, however. What should trouble them more is the possibility that differential access to chips could leave them disadvantaged relative to their vertically integrated competitors—the second strategic threat facing chip users. Even though upstream chip suppliers can exercise monopoly power to collect rents from chip users, charging chip users a premium price will not maximize rent collection. In the case of an intermediate input like ICs, rent collection by a producer with monopoly power is maximized by integrating forward into the downstream industry, such as computers, and collecting the rent in the downstream industry.[53]

In short, if chip suppliers have the technological capability, they can maximize their return by integrating forward into systems industries and competing against unintegrated foreign competitors. Indeed, the U.S. market share of Japanese computer companies has risen sharply since 1986, at least in part due to differentials in memory chip cost. Three Japanese companies—NEC, Toshiba, and Epson—offered personal computer systems to the U.S. market that were very competitively priced compared with domestic manufacturers' products. Not surprisingly, U.S. PC market shares for all three companies have risen significantly.

## Implications for European Policy

The main point of this analysis is that trade friction in semiconductors has entered a new stage. Before the mid-1980s competition within the industry meant that strategic behavior by vertically integrated chip suppliers did not overly frighten systems companies that lacked their own leading-edge chip-making capability. Trade friction in semiconductors was largely a series of disputes among chip makers based in different regions.

Since 1985, however, increasing industrial concentration in the production of key products and the need to transfer increasing flows of proprietary information between chip producers and users have been coupled with the growing domination of merchant semiconductor markets

---

cost in computer systems' value. Under these assumptions, the pi-rule results in an annual increase in computer demand, all else being equal, of about 5.5 percent, while the bai-rule yields an annual increase of 3.1 percent.

53. Otherwise, the downstream user would normally substitute other inputs for the monopolized input as price is raised and dissipate some of the rent in inefficient production. See John M. Vernon and Daniel A. Graham, "Profitability of Monopolization by Vertical Integration," *Journal of Political Economy*, vol. 79 (July–August 1971), pp. 924–25.

FIGURE 5–12. The Theoretical Case for Domestic Production
of Semiconductors

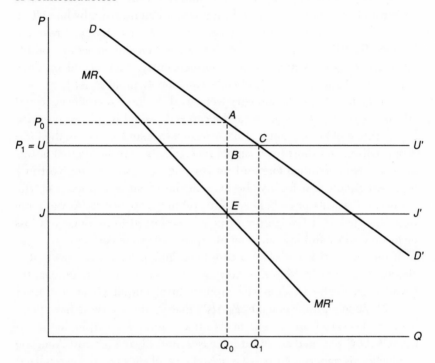

by vertically integrated Japanese chip suppliers. This has created strategic
concerns for other systems companies. These concerns will, in my view,
play a new and increasingly prominent role in semiconductor trade issues.

Regardless of whether monopoly power in chip supply is currently
being exercised and whether the hypothetical exercise of monopoly power
is undertaken by private firms on their own or under the guidance of
government in order to avoid trade friction, the potential exercise of
monopoly power creates an economic argument for coordinated defensive
action by user industries. Inefficient, high-cost domestic production may
be less costly to local users than efficiently produced foreign chips, if, in
the absence of competition, a foreign supplier acts as a monopolist and
marks up his price to extract a significant monopoly rent.

The essentials of this argument are spelled out in figure 5-12. For
simplicity, I have assumed constant returns to scale in chip production,
and I have assumed that technological investments and past learning
have created a cost advantage for Japanese chip producers, so that their

constant cost of production is $J$ dollars per unit (and their marginal and average cost schedule represented by line $JJ'$). Foreign companies have higher unit costs of $U$ dollars (and their cost schedule given by line $UU'$). Foreign demand is given by demand curve $DD'$, and marginal revenue by line $MR\text{-}MR'$. If Japanese producers were then able to act as a profit-maximizing cartel, without fear of foreign entry, they would produce output $Q_0$, charge price $P_0$, and collect monopoly profit $P_0\,AEJ$.

If entry and exit in the industry were costless, foreign producers could effectively contest the market, and a cap at $U$ would be placed on price by the threat of foreign entry. I have argued that sunk costs—in the form of specialized and short-lived capital investments—are substantial in this industry. No individual foreign firm is going to be willing to invest in a high-cost production facility, because in the event of a price war, the cartel can lower its price below $U$ and still fully cover costs. At the same time, the high-cost foreign producer will be forced to produce at a loss or to shut down and lose an amount equal to its sunk costs.

If the alternative is to face a cartel charging price $P_0$, however, it is clearly advantageous from the viewpoint of users in the foreign country to subsidize high-cost domestic production of output $Q_1$ at cost level $UU'$. Monopoly profits equal to $P_0\,ABP_1$ that would otherwise have been paid to the cartel are saved; in addition, consumer surplus equal to triangle $ABC$ is gained as output increases. Subsidy of high-cost domestic production is superior to passive acceptance of uncontested, cartelized imports. (I abstract from the issue of how domestic production is to be made available to users at cost—a production co-op organized by users would be one possibility.)

This analysis has some relevance for European semiconductor policy. The 1988 DRAM drought drove home a point that had already become visible in the earlier years of the decade. Back in the late 1970s, reliance by European systems houses on U.S. semiconductor companies for supplies of advanced chips, though far from welcome, did not pose a strategic problem for European industry. The U.S. merchant chip manufacturers were not, for the most part, vertically integrated into downstream systems. All competitors enjoyed roughly equal access to state-of-the-art components.

As the Japanese companies entered the European market in force in the early 1980s, this changed. At first, the changes were relatively advantageous for European users. Competition intensified and prices came down. The first inklings of a possible strategic issue came, by some accounts, when European equipment producers had some difficulties in obtaining the very latest high-performance chips from their Japanese suppliers, disadvantaging them in competition with the same suppliers in downstream equipment markets. When U.S. merchant suppliers dropped out of the most competitive commodity chip markets after the 1985 semiconductor recession, production of certain high-volume products was concentrated in just a handful of Japanese suppliers.

The STA was the catalyst for that handful of suppliers to act in a coordinated way.[54] The potential for the extraction of substantial monopoly profits by a well-disciplined group of foreign suppliers became evident. Henceforth policymakers could not ignore the potential for a concentrated group of producers of a key input to use that monopoly power to extract monopoly rents from users or, worse, to integrate forward into the user industry at the expense of existing firms in order to collect even greater returns. The counterremedy for such monopoly power is entry, or a credible threat of entry, by outsiders.

For two reasons—as the ante in a bid to play a role in shaping high-technology trade policy worldwide, and as a defense against the exercise of strategic control over a vital input to important user industries—this meant strengthening the European base in semiconductor technology.[55]

## The Emerging Rules of the Game

Strengthening the European semiconductor base is not an impossibly daunting task. Although European companies manufacture only a little over 12 percent of the world's semiconductor output, recent mergers have concentrated that production in just three firms, each of which ranks among the world's twenty top vendors of semiconductors (see table 5-2). In addition, some European companies are strong international

54. Voices within the U.S. semiconductor industry defend the STA by noting that in EPROMs, where production was much less concentrated, prices did not rise sharply. Therefore, they argue, the STA should not be blamed for the price gouging in DRAMs. Actually this reinforces the opposite point: the STA served as the organizing framework to coordinate producers in a market (DRAMs) that was already highly concentrated and transformed potential monopoly power into its actual realization.

55. It is sometimes asserted that technological spillovers from semiconductor production into other high-technology activities provide another strategic argument for support for a national semiconductor industry. However, it is not at all obvious that semiconductor manufacturing yields critical technologies needed in other industries (this author, at least, is hard-pressed to think of many significant examples). The strategic issues discussed earlier—the security of proprietary design information and the pricing and availability of leading-edge components—relate to the protection of intellectual property and the exercise of monopoly power in the market for an input, not technological spillovers.

TABLE 5–2. Top Twenty Semiconductor Vendors Worldwide, 1989

| Company | 1987 sales (millions of dollars) | 1989 sales (millions of dollars) | 1989 rank |
|---|---|---|---|
| NEC | 3,368 | 4,964 | 1 |
| Toshiba | 3,029 | 4,889 | 2 |
| Hitachi | 2,618 | 3,930 | 3 |
| Motorola | 2,431 | 3,322 | 4 |
| Fujitsu | 1,801 | 2,941 | 5 |
| TI | 2,127 | 2,787 | 6 |
| Mitsubishi | 1,492 | 2,629 | 7 |
| Intel | 1,491 | 2,440 | 8 |
| Matsushita | 1,457 | 1,871 | 9 |
| Philips[a] | 1,602 | 1,690 | 10 |
| National | 1,506 | 1,618 | 11 |
| SGS-Thomson[a] | 859 | 1,301 | 12 |
| Samsung | 327 | 1,284 | 13 |
| Sharp | 590 | 1,230 | 14 |
| Siemens[a] | 657 | 1,194 | 15 |
| Sanyo | 851 | 1,132 | 16 |
| Oki | 651 | 1,125 | 17 |
| AMD | 986 | 1,082 | 18 |
| Sony | 574 | 1,077 | 19 |
| AT&T | 802 | 873 | 20 |

SOURCE: Dataquest, as cited in *Electronic Buyers' News*, January 8, 1990, p. 3; and STM viewgraphs.
a. European companies.

competitors in the semiconductor equipment and materials industry. Two German companies, Wacker and Huels, sell about one-third of the world's unprocessed silicon wafers (the remaining two-thirds is shipped by a handful of Japanese companies). Wacker is also the world's largest producer and vendor of high-purity polycrystalline silicon, the not-so-raw material from which the wafers are made. A Dutch company, ASM International, is the world's largest manufacturer of chemical vapor deposition equipment for use in wafer fabrication.[56] Moreover, foreign-based companies have substantially increased their European production activities in recent years.

### The Players

The largest European-based semiconductor company is Philips N.V., headquartered in the Netherlands. Philips is the only European company

56. With 20 percent of the world market in 1988. See *Electronic News*, May 22, 1989, p. II-10.

to break into the ranks of the world's top ten semiconductor makers. In 1975 Philips acquired American IC manufacturer Signetics in a move that brought it both new technology and a large U.S. marketing base. In 1987 the American subsidiary was the sixth-largest merchant IC vendor in the U.S. market and produced almost as many ICs as the remainder of Philips's chip plants combined (Signetics was recently absorbed into the main Philips IC business unit).[57] Philips also owns 35 percent of Matsushita Electronics, which among other things manufactures DRAMs.[58] The extent of the technical and procurement relationship between Philips and Matsushita is not public, but does not appear particularly significant in the semiconductor area.

Philips was involved in the so-called Megaproject with Siemens over the period from 1983 to 1989. With one-third of the roughly $1 billion cost paid for by the governments of the Netherlands and West Germany, the two companies collaborated in the development of state-of-the-art semiconductor manufacturing technology. Philips focused on the design and production of a one-megabit static RAM chip, Siemens on the manufacture of a four-megabit dynamic RAM (since a static RAM requires roughly four times as many components as a dynamic RAM of the same size, they were technological equivalents). Although Siemens is today beginning to produce those four-megabit DRAMs commercially, Philips has not chosen to mass-produce its static RAM commercially.

The second-largest European producer is SGS-Thomson Microelectronics (STM), formed in 1987 from the merger of the semiconductor division of French electronics producer Thomson-CSF with Italian semiconductor producer SGS-Ates. Each of those companies has complex roots. A thumbnail sketch of the most important branches on the family tree would note that Thomson was the ultimate merger vehicle for a host of smaller and largely unsuccessful semiconductor start-ups subsidized by the French government over the years. In 1986 Thomson acquired a significant U.S. memory producer, Mostek, just as it was dropping out of the commercial DRAM business (although it continues to manufacture and sell DRAMs to the U.S. military). SGS-Ates has roots that include a joint venture with Fairchild in the 1960s, which ended in divorce. STM's two predecessor companies had historical ties to the Italian and

57. See Integrated Circuit Engineering, *Mid-Term 1988* (Scottsdale, Ariz., 1988), pp. 2-2, 2-20.

58. Philips apparently granted Matsushita the right to use key electrical equipment patents in exchange for a significant equity stake in Matsushita's electronics operations.

French governments. In 1986 SGS and Thomson had begun a joint development project (Megaproject 2) that apparently proved to be a catalyst for their merger.[59] In 1989 STM acquired British IC manufacturer Inmos, an innovative producer of microprocessors and fast memories (started with support from the British government). STM today is the largest seller of certain memory chips in the European market, number one worldwide in power control semiconductors, and a major vendor of EPROMs.

The third member of the European big three is Siemens, A.G. Until recently, Siemens was Europe's only producer of DRAMs (a position it held only briefly, since NEC and Motorola now fabricate DRAMs in Great Britain, and TI is building a large DRAM fabrication line in Italy). Like Philips, Siemens responded in the 1970s to its technological lag in IC technology by acquiring American semiconductor operations: in 1977, 20 percent of AMD and 100 percent of Litronix; in 1979, 100 percent of Microwave Semiconductor.

A respectable share of Siemens's chip production is consumed internally: in the mid-1980s Siemens was estimated to use 22 percent of its output within the company, roughly double the Philips figure of 10 percent.[60] Siemens clearly defines its involvement in semiconductors as a strategic issue, aimed at preserving its competitiveness in downstream equipment markets against vertically integrated Japanese competitors. In 1983, perceiving that it lagged three to four years behind the Japanese in semiconductor technology, it kicked off a catch-up drive aimed at reaching the Japanese by 1990. As part of this campaign, it launched the Megaproject with Philips in that same year. In 1985, in order to buy time in the face of an acceleration of the transition to next-generation DRAMs by its Japanese competitors, Siemens struck a deal in which Toshiba transferred its design and production know-how for one-megabit DRAMs to Siemens, which then set up production facilities in Europe. By 1988 Siemens was shipping one-megabit chips in volume.[61] Siemens today claims to have eliminated the technology lag vis-à-vis its Japanese

59. Hobday, "European Semiconductor Industry," pp. 10–11.

60. See Mackintosh International, *An Analysis of the Microelectronics Industry for Medium and Long Term Strategic Purposes*, report prepared for the EC Commission (Luton, U.K., June 1986); and Rob van Tulder and Eric van Empel, "European Multinationals in the Semiconductor Industry—Their Position in Microprocessors," University of Amsterdam, October 1984.

61. Interviews with Siemens company officials, summer 1989.

TABLE 5–3. Top Ten Semiconductor Vendors, by European Sales, 1988

Millions of dollars

| Company and nationality | Sales |
|---|---|
| Philips (Netherlands) | 1,002 |
| SGS-Thomson (France/Italy) | 650 |
| Texas Instruments (U.S.) | 636 |
| Motorola (U.S.) | 616 |
| Siemens (West Germany) | 571 |
| Intel (U.S.) | 485 |
| National Semiconductor (U.S.) | 390 |
| NEC (Japan) | 370 |
| Toshiba (Japan) | 349 |
| AMD (U.S.) | 279 |

SOURCE: Dataquest, as cited in *Economist*, February 18, 1989, p. 74.

competitors and views itself as the strongest semiconductor company in Europe from a strictly technological standpoint.

By the mid-1980s the European big three had largely moved offshore for the bulk of their semiconductor assembly and testing operations. According to EECA estimates, in 1988 more than 60 percent of ICs sold within the EC were tested and assembled outside the EC (see table 5-5). American producer sales within Europe were even more internationalized, with a little under 80 percent of U.S. sales tested and assembled outside the EC. Japanese producers, however, scored about the same as the European producers, drawing on the strength of their European test and assembly facilities.

Philips and STM do a substantial amount of chip fabrication in the United States in plants first established by their Signetics and Mostek acquisitions. Until recently, Siemens also did some specialized fabrication in New Jersey but has apparently phased that out. Philips and STM also fabricate chips in Southeast Asia: STM with fabrication lines in Singapore, and Philips through its Taiwan Semiconductor joint venture with the Taiwanese government, now the largest producer in Taiwan.[62]

In terms of sales within the European market, Philips has clearly been—and remains—the largest vendor (see table 5-3). Until quite

62. The scope of Philips's overseas fabrication activities recently increased with an announced expansion of its investment in Taiwan Semiconductor Manufacturing Corporation to a 51 percent majority interest. Philips is also building a fabrication line in Shanghai, China. See David Roman, "Philips to Up Stake," *Electronic Buyers' News*, November 6, 1989, p. 1.

recently U.S.-based producers Texas Instruments and Motorola occupied the second and third slots, followed by Siemens. The formation of STM from SGS and Thomson, however, catapulted that company into the number two slot. Other major U.S. vendors in the top ten include Intel, National Semiconductor, and AMD. (Of the American companies, all do some assembly and test within Europe, and all except Intel and AMD have European wafer fabrication lines, a point to which I shall return.) Until recently NEC was the only Japanese firm in the ranks of the European top ten, but it was recently joined by Toshiba, largely on the strength of Toshiba's dominant role worldwide in the supply of one-megabit DRAMs. Of the Japanese firms, only NEC had established a European fabrication facility until very recently, although the others had set up point-of-sale test and assembly operations in Europe (see table 5-4).[63]

Thus the major shifts in the European semiconductor supply base over the last decade have entailed consolidation and restructuring of European companies and the entry of the Japanese producers.[64] Changes over the next decade will undoubtedly hinge on how these same producers cope with the changing policy environment in Europe.

## The Rules

The DRAM crisis of 1987–88 stirred up considerable debate over Europe's semiconductor policy, and the high-profile movement toward European integration in 1992 has created an opportunity for that debate to foster significant changes in the rules of the semiconductor game. To see where Europe is going, one must review a collection of initiatives, rather than any single measure specifically tailored to 1992. Thus far three measures related to the 1992 program have held special significance for the semiconductor industry. The directives relate to protection of

63. In 1989 Fujitsu announced plans to set up a fabrication line in the United Kingdom and Mitsubishi announced a fabrication line in West Germany.

64. I have ignored in this brief discussion at least one potentially significant development, the emergence of a generation of new, relatively small-scale, specialized European producers of so-called application-specific ICs (ASICs). ASICs are circuits customized and tailored to the specific, often proprietary, design needs of a particular application. The most well known of these new start-ups is European Silicon Structures, a pan-European joint venture that has also benefited from government support. Other firms in this group include Mietec in Belgium, Advanced Silicon Corporation in the Netherlands, and Lassaray in Switzerland. Some analysts are relatively optimistic about the long-term prospects for these companies. See Hobday, "European Semiconductor Industry," pp. 14–17.

TABLE 5–4. Foreign Semiconductor Facilities in Europe, December 1989

| Company and location | Fabrication facility | Assembly only |
|---|---|---|
| United Kingdom, Scotland | | |
| Hughes | X | |
| DEC | X | |
| Seagate | X | |
| NEC | X | |
| National Semiconductor | | X |
| Motorola | | X |
| United Kingdom, England | | |
| Texas Instruments | X | |
| LSI Logic | X | |
| Fujitsu | X[a] | |
| AMD | | X |
| Harris | | X |
| Ireland | | |
| Analog Devices | X | |
| AMD | | X |
| Fujitsu | | X |
| NEC | | X |
| West Germany, northern region | | |
| IBM | X | |
| Toshiba | | X |
| LSI Logic | | X |
| West Germany, southern region | | |
| Texas Instruments | X | |
| ITT | X | |
| Mitsubishi | X[a] | |
| National Semiconductor | | X |
| Motorola | | X |
| ITT | | X |
| Hitachi | | X |
| Italy | | |
| Texas Instruments | X[a] | X |
| ITT | | X |
| France | | |
| IBM | X | |
| Motorola | X | |
| ITT | | X |
| Texas Instruments | | X |
| Spain | | |
| AT&T | X | |
| Portugal | | |
| Texas Instruments | | X |

SOURCE: Electronics Industry Association of Japan, *The Reality of the Electronics Industry in Europe* . . . (in Japanese) (Tokyo, 1989), p. 143; and trade press.
a. Planned.

intellectual property rights in semiconductor design, the use of national preferences in government procurement, and the rules of origin for semiconductors.

First, and least controversial of these measures, a directive ordering member states to enact laws protecting the masks used to produce semiconductors is part of the establishment of Community-wide standards on intellectual property rights. This protection is similar to one given to semiconductor masks in the United States and Japan and has been welcomed by foreign-based producers.

A second set of directives is aimed at establishing uniform rules and formal procedures governing the award of government contracts within the EC. In general, the proposed rules make the entire government procurement process much more transparent. They have been welcomed by U.S. companies. But four specific sectors where state-controlled corporations play major roles—water, energy, transport, and telecommunications—have been excluded from the new standards, and a different set of directives has been applied to them. Foreign-based companies are worried about national preferences extended to EC producers in public contracts in the excluded sectors. In particular, contracting organizations are permitted to throw out bids in which less than half the value of the contract is of EC origin, and they may also extend a 3 percent price preference to goods and services produced within the Community.

Because public sector purchases of telecommunications equipment may account for as much as 90 percent of U.S. companies' sales in Europe and as much as one-third of computer firm sales, the rules under which national origin is determined can potentially have a major effect on U.S. sales of these products.[65] However, the new rules are unlikely to represent a setback when compared with the far less transparent procedures frequently used in EC public procurement today. More important, telecommunications and computer equipment firms are large users of semiconductors, and the excluded-sector directives have a potentially significant effect on the use of U.S.-made semiconductors in the manufacture of equipment destined to be sold to the public sector in Europe, regardless of the national identity of the producer.

The new procurement directives have thus served to focus attention

65. See U.S. International Trade Commission, *The Effects of Greater Economic Integration within the European Community on the United States*, USITC Publication 2204 (Washington, July 1989), pp. 4–7.

TABLE 5–5. Share of European Company Sales Produced
Locally, 1988
Percent

| Headquarters of company | Definition of production | | |
|---|---|---|---|
| | Diffusion, all semi-conductors | Diffusion, ICs only | Test and assembly, ICs only |
| U.S. companies | 50 | 43 | 24 |
| Japanese companies | 12 | 5 | 39 |
| European companies | 98 | 94 | 37 |
| Rest-of-world companies | 0 | 0 | 0 |
| All companies | 58 | 52 | 31 |

SOURCES: Author's calculations based on data from Semiconductor Industry Association (first column) and European Electronic Components Manufacturers Association (second and third columns).

on what is probably, from the point of view of the U.S. semiconductor industry, the most controversial of the new measures, a change in the rules of origin for semiconductors. In February 1989 the European Commission approved a regulation that drastically altered the rules of origin for chips "made" in the EC.[66] Before then, the origin of a chip was assigned to the country "in which the last substantial process or operation that is economically justified was performed," as interpreted by national customs authorities.[67] In practice, assembly and test was generally accepted as a "substantial process," so that location of assembly and test was the de facto standard for origin. Under the new rule, origin is determined by the place of fabrication, or diffusion, the process by which electronic circuit elements are etched on the wafer.

This small change had very large consequences for the origin assigned to chips produced and consumed in Europe. Table 5-5 gives estimates, based on EECA data, of what share of IC production by U.S., Japanese, and European companies sold in Europe in 1988 would have been national based on both the new diffusion standard and the old test and assembly standard. The table also shows estimates, based on SIA data, of how much of European semiconductor output (including production of discrete devices) would have qualified for national origin under the diffusion standard. The SIA and EECA figures produce very similar overall portraits of the shares of companies' output that is diffused in Europe.

66. EEC Regulation 288/89, *Official Journal of the European Communities*, no. L33 (Luxembourg: EC Commission, February 4, 1989), p. 23 [hereafter *O.J. Eur. Comm.*].

67. Article 5, EEC Regulation 802/68, *O.J. Eur. Comm.*, L148 (June 28, 1968), p. 2.

The major loser was clearly Japan. About 40 percent of Japanese companies' sales in Europe qualified for national origin based on the old rules, though few underwent any processing beyond assembly and test. About the same proportion of European firm sales qualified for national origin despite the fact that almost all the chips were diffused within the Community. (It is useful to remember that the use of offshore assembly by European producers increased quite sharply over the last decade.) European companies are quite explicit that this situation—formal parity under the old rules despite quite different degrees of economic activity—was considered intolerable and thus was at the root of the rules change.

Interestingly, however, it was U.S. chip producers, and their lobbying arm, the SIA—not the Japanese—who reacted most negatively and publicly to the change. Curiously, the data in table 5-5 seem to show American producers as a group gaining by the change, with the share of their European IC sales qualifying for national origin roughly doubled. Why, then, was the reaction so negative?

Part of the answer is that the gains were very unevenly distributed. Certain U.S. chip companies—those with existing fabrication lines in Europe—were in private less than totally committed to the official SIA consensus that the rules change was contrary to U.S. interests. Indeed, officials at the EC happily point out that some European subsidiaries of U.S. companies—those with European fabrication lines—actually lobbied *for* the change in regulations. The big losers among the top ten vendors in Europe were Intel (with no European manufacturing) and AMD (which did test and assembly in Europe but had not invested in costly fabrication lines), and their smaller U.S. semiconductor brethren, like Siliconix, Hughes, Cherry, Cypress, PMI, and Harris, whose European test and assembly operations no longer qualified them for national origin. It was probably no coincidence that an employee of Intel, rather than an officer or full-time employee of the SIA, presented the SIA case against the new rules to Congress and the media.

Another part of the answer is that this seemed an open assault on the prevailing mainstream consensus concerning the determination of origin in the chip industry, since the test and assembly standard was virtually the international rule. In the rest of the world—outside Europe—where U.S. companies for the most part did not have existing fabrication lines, the consequences for national-origin status were clearly negative. A general, and perhaps costly, rethinking of origin concepts might be provoked by this EC precedent.

It turns out, however, that the use of diffusion as an explicit definition of national origin was not unprecedented. The 1989 Free Trade Agreement between the United States and Canada implies a diffusion test for the origin of semiconductors flowing between those two countries.[68] This was contained in a special provision designed to prevent the evasion of countervailing or antidumping duties through the use of test or assembly operations located in one of those two countries, not a change in the rule generally used for imports, as was the case with the European measure. But this fact did undermine the U.S. position and apparently was not discovered until after objections were voiced.

By that time it had become obvious that the rules of origin for semiconductors were not the real issue. After all, the change in the rules of origin made absolutely no difference in the cost of the chip within Europe. A chip fabricated in Europe but tested and assembled abroad paid the same duty upon entry into the Community as before. The same tariff as before was also paid for a chip fabricated abroad, and tested and assembled in Europe or entirely manufactured abroad. Clearly, the use of an imported chip *after* it has crossed the customs frontier must be the issue.

And that, as it turned out, was the heart of a murky debate. When the SIA presented its complaint to Congress, the example given of the losses being suffered was the case of a Japanese printer company that had opted not to use U.S. chips on its printed circuit boards because of the new rules of origin. Japanese printer companies had been found guilty of dumping in the EC.[69] With "antiscrewdriver" regulations (designed to prevent circumvention of a dumping penalty through the minimal performance of local assembly of imported parts), the EC had required that producers of dumped products use non-national components (that is, from countries other than the country where the dumped imports originated) amounting to more than 40 percent of the value of the product in order to escape penalties. In effect, a 40 percent minimum level of

68. This appears to have been the accidental consequence of a requirement that goods must change tariff chapters in order for a manufacturing operation to qualify goods for national origin.

69. "Dumping" no longer exclusively signifies its original meaning, namely, that a manufacturer is selling an identical commodity abroad for less than in his home market. Dumping today also has come to mean "less than my calculation of what your full average cost ought to be." Nevertheless, the word "dumping" retains the old pejorative connotation—profitable but predatory exercise of monopoly power—that rightly accompanied its original usage.

"non-dumped" content is required to avoid dumping penalties, even if the manufacturer then moves production inside the European Community.[70] The GATT legality of the antiscrewdriver regulations has been questioned, based on possible violation of both the "equal national treatment" provision of GATT itself and the antidumping code signed under GATT auspices.[71] In response to a complaint from Japan, a GATT panel is currently considering the national-treatment issue; however, the EC blocked consideration of the antidumping code issue by the GATT Antidumping Committee.[72]

Regardless of the GATT legality of the antiscrewdriver regulations, one might still be puzzled by the continuing U.S. concern. Japanese producers are faced with a requirement to use non-Japanese components, not European components, and do not seem to have any special reason to avoid U.S. components. The minutiae of European customs practice must be examined to make sense of the objection.

The problem is that assembled printed circuit boards for electronic products, on which components like semiconductors have been mounted, are treated as a single part. How is one to decide the nationality of a board in which many parts from many different countries have been assembled? One might argue that the principle embodied in the antiscrewdriver regulations would require 40 percent or more of the value of the board to originate in countries other than that of the offender.

This has apparently not been the case, however. Instead, it is alleged that the frequent practice of European customs officials has been to assign origin to the country with the largest single share of components in number or value.[73] In other cases, EC officials are alleged to classify

70. Note that the antiscrewdriver regulation applies only to products whose manufacture in the EC is carried out by a company found dumping and whose manufacture begins or substantially increases *after* a dumping investigation has started.

71. See Patrick J. McDermott, "Extending the Reach of Their Antidumping Laws: The European Community's 'Screwdriver Assembly' Regulation," *Law and Policy in International Business*, vol. 20, no. 2 (1989); De Bandt, van Hecke & Lagae, "1992 and Community Preference," New York and Brussels, 1989, pp. 29–37; and Dewey, Ballantine, Bushby, Palmer & Wood, "The EC's Application of Screwdriver Assembly Regulation in Products with Printed Circuit Boards Violates the GATT," New York and Washington, September 21, 1989.

72. See McDermott, "Extending the Reach of Their Antidumping Laws," p. 323.

73. These examples of alleged customs practice appear to be based on the reports of Japanese customers to U.S. semiconductor companies. See, for example, Dewey, Ballantine, "EC's Application of Screwdriver Assembly Regulation," p. 3.

boards as EC-made if 45 percent or more of the content comes from within the Community. The legal basis for this latter practice seems to rest on rules of origin for radio and TV receivers and VCRs set out in EC regulations dating back to the early 1970s.[74] Other informal customs procedures exposed by this episode are apparently not the result of formal regulations, and the EC is said to be in the process of formulating new regulations to define more precisely the national origin of assembled printed circuit boards.

The administrative practices of EC officials are also alleged to have created de facto preferences for European content in goods involved in dumping proceedings in another context. Screwdriver investigations in which the dumper is found to exceed the 60 percent ceiling are frequently settled with "undertakings," in which a manufacturer enters into a confidential commitment to alter the sourcing of components used in its European operations. The Commission has apparently suggested to manufacturers that they include a greater European content in order to produce an acceptable offer.[75]

In short, it may reasonably be suspected that government officials in the EC—like their counterparts in the United States or Japan—put their perceptions of national interests ahead of their obligations under GATT. One may occasionally detect these attitudes even in conversations with outsiders.[76]

74. Commission Regulations 2632/70 and 861/71 have apparently been used to determine whether radios, TVs, and tape recorders made by Japanese manufacturers are to be considered EC-produced. As applied, EC origin is granted if 45 percent of the value added in the price of the finished product takes place within the Community. See Kazuo Moritani, "Impact of the EC Unification on Japan's Automobile and Electronics Industries," JDB Research Report 16 (Tokyo: Japan Development Bank, August 1989), p. 34.

75. See De Bandt, van Hecke & Lagae, "1992 and Community Preference," pp. 33–34; and Gerwin van Gerven, "New Anti-Circumvention Rules in EEC Anti-Dumping Law," International Lawyer, vol. 22 (Fall 1988), p. 817. One recent concrete example seems to be February 10, 1989, draft regulations covering copying machines, which specify that EC product status would be granted Japanese producers who locally source certain specified components, including the printed circuit boards, lens systems, high-tension dynamos, and motors. Other less important components would not be considered significant. See Moritani, "Impact of the EC Unification," p. 34.

76. One memorable experience of this sort occurred in July 1989, while I was interviewing an EC official involved in EC dumping cases. I asked what the EC's attitude would be if Japanese firms responded to price floors for DRAMs and EPROMs by setting up integrated European production facilities that then proceeded to sell at prices below the floors set in the price undertakings. His response was that an undertaking can always be withdrawn, and that if Japanese producers sold chips produced in the EC at less than the undertaking price, it would have to be considered as possible circumvention! For this

This contradiction between the official legalities and the behind-the-door realities is not confined to the Brussels bureaucracy. European-based electronics companies have been sending out some very mixed messages to their customers and competitors. On the one hand, visitors from abroad are reminded that nothing in the regulations discriminates against U.S. content and that the worries about national content requirements reflect ignorant hysteria whipped up by the emotionalism of a false "Fortress Europe" image. On the other hand, some American chip companies complain that their European competitors are beating them out of new European business by telling customers that broader national content requirements are on the way. If they want to avoid looming problems, these customers are told, use European-made components. Occasionally some of this usually private talk even gets picked up in the trade press.[77]

It may be, of course, that all this is merely hard-sell marketing. If the inexperienced customer is foolish enough to believe these threats, one might argue, you cannot blame the zealous European vendor for a little creative salesmanship. And it may be that these signals are a form of "jawboning," a high-pressure but not binding indicator from European government and industry that they would be very pleased to see inputs sourced out of European factories. But given the clear existence of these

---

official, at least, the issue of a "safety net" for European producers took precedence over the legal basis for fixing the price of a domestically produced good.

77. Probably the most open recent such instance involved U.S. computer manufacturer Sun Microsystems' announcement that it was licensing its SPARC microprocessor design to Philips for manufacture and sale in Europe. A reporter noted that "Philips gives Sun the European supply of chips its plant in Scotland will need in 1992 when the European-content requirements become effective. Manufacturers will be required to buy many of their electronic components from companies that produce them on European soil." See Stephen Kreider Yoder, "Sun Microsystems to License Division of N.V. Philips to Design, Sell Its Chips," *Wall Street Journal*, August 9, 1989, p. B3. Unfortunately, the source of this seemingly incorrect report was Philips, not Fortress Europe–crazed U.S. trade lawyers. A subsequent account gave some further details: "Both companies [Sun and Philips] said that the chips will be used to help satisfy the 'European content requirement' of systems sold in Europe after 1992, but neither [Sun president Scott] McNealy nor [Philips Business Unit for Integrated Circuits director Peter] Draheim could say exactly what those European requirements will be. Draheim later told *Infoworld*: 'I expect that the place where the diffusion [chip fabrication] is done will determine the national origin of the chip. When we view a system's content, we will include European modules, assembly, and value added to determine if it is more than 50 percent European.'" An analyst, who asked not to be named, said, 'Philips and Siemens wield so much influence in Europe that the rules will be interpreted as they choose.'" See Martin Marshall, "Philips to Manufacture Sparc Chips," *Infoworld*, August 14, 1989, p. 33.

signals, it is disingenuous to dismiss all the Fortress Europe talk as uninformed paranoia.

Even if one concentrates on the current situation—not hints at the shape of the future—it is clear that the antiscrewdriver regulations will soon become vastly more important. In recent years "voluntary export restraints" (VERs), dumping actions, and associated undertakings have become increasingly popular weapons in a rather effective EC effort to impede the flow of Asian consumer electronics manufactures into the European market. Over the period from 1983 to 1987, the EC initiated 189 new antidumping investigations. In 1988 alone, the Commission began another 40 investigations.[78] Between September 1987 and May 1988 the number of VERs affecting electronic products imported into the EC doubled, from eight (out of eleven such agreements worldwide) to sixteen (out of a global total of nineteen).[79]

The EC dumping actions have largely targeted Japanese and Korean electronics exports. A large number of Japanese electronics exports have already been the subject of some sort of antidumping action or export restraint (see figure 5-13). In addition to the actions shown in figure 5-13, since 1983 at least eleven antidumping investigations have been aimed at Japanese products ranging from typewriters to car telephones. Four of these investigations have culminated in the imposition of tariffs, two have resulted in provisional tariffs, one has led to a price undertaking, and four are still under investigation.[80] Japanese producers, in attempting to glean clues from the historical record as to how the EC might apply the dumping laws to their electronics exports, have settled on three apparent criteria: the local market share for imports exceeds 50 percent; domestic companies manufacture the same product but are less competitive than foreign makers; and the products are high-technology.[81]

78. EC Commission, *Sixth Annual Report on the Community's Anti-Dumping and Anti-Subsidy Activities* (Brussels, March 21, 1989).

79. Most of the increase has come from new national VER arrangements negotiated by France, Italy, and the United Kingdom. Of the eight in force in September 1987, five were Community-wide, while three were national in scope. Of the sixteen counted in May 1988, eight were national. See Margaret Kelly and others, "Issues and Developments in International Trade Policy," Occasional Paper 63 (Washington: International Monetary Fund, December 1988), tables 12, 13.

80. See Electronic Industries Association of Japan, *The Reality of the Electronics Industry in Europe and the Way to Cope with the Integration of the EC Market: Issues of Developing Strategies for Internationalizing Japanese Corporations* (in Japanese) (Tokyo: EIAJ, November 1989), p. 47; updated by author.

81. Ibid., p. 133.

FIGURE 5-13. Trade Actions against Japanese Products, 1980–89

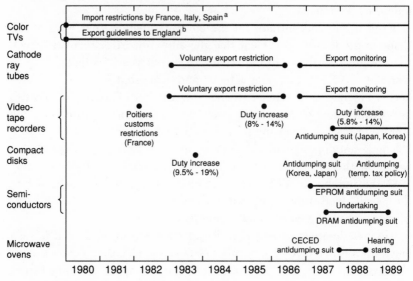

SOURCE: Same as table 5-5.
a. Began in 1968; Spanish restrictions expected to end in late 1989.
b. Began in 1972.

All EC member states' national quotas and VERs will have to be abolished by 1992 or replaced with EC-legal mechanisms. It seems safe to predict that there will be a sharp increase in Community-wide antidumping cases as national quotas and restrictions are phased out.[82] Arcane issues of administrative and customs practice will become central to the ultimate effect of this transition on the use of foreign components in electronics sold in Europe.

Finally, it seems possible that explicit national content requirements may be part of the transitional adjustment process for the European automobile industry. Given the increasing volume of electronics used in the auto industry, this would be a potentially significant mechanism in the current drift toward national content requirements for electronics.

In short, the rules of origin issue for semiconductors turned out to really be about the origin of printed circuit boards. And that, in turn, appeared to be most important as a disguised creep toward national content requirements and, beyond that, toward an explicitly protected regional market for selected electronics products.

82. This prediction was also offered by a top official involved with the EC's antidumping enforcement responsibilities in an interview during July 1989.

## Other Forms of Protection

At least two other sets of recent changes promise to create higher walls around the European semiconductor market after 1992. The first is a recent change in the rules for the tariff suspension program. The second is the price undertaking that settled the DRAM dumping case, which will most likely be the model for a forthcoming price undertaking to settle the EPROM dumping case.

Tariff suspensions came to play a significant role in IC imports in the 1980s, growing to account for perhaps 20–30 percent of imports by 1988. In early 1989 a draft European Commission regulation was sent to the Council of Ministers. It will significantly tighten the rules for tariff suspensions and is aimed at reducing their use. The most significant changes will limit tariff suspensions to items on which suspended duties will amount to at least ECU 20,000 and forbid suspensions where exclusivity agreements are in force. There is considerable uncertainty about precisely what the latter change means, but it does seem to signal a decrease in duty suspensions.

The DRAM dumping investigation instituted in early 1987 was suspended as a consequence of a price undertaking agreed to with Japanese producers in August 1989. (If nothing else, the delay bears out the complaints of European firms that the pace of EC dumping procedures is considerably slower—and hence less effective—than proceedings in the United States.) The intention of the price floors is to provide a "safety net" for European producers, to encourage them to increase their investments in an environment free of fear that prices will fall below production costs as a consequence of cutthroat Japanese competition. A target of 20 percent of the European market for European-based firms is sometimes mentioned as the desired outcome of the safety net.

Although the European price floors—as implemented in the EC DRAM price undertakings—seem superficially to resemble the American FMV system, they differ in some important respects. Rather than being producer-specific, a single general reference price for all imports from firms signing the undertaking is calculated and communicated to the Japanese producers on a quarterly basis. The quarterly reference prices are to be based on calculations using historical cost data from two quarters earlier.[83] Perhaps because of pressure from European chip consumers,

---

83. Each quarter's new reference price is to be calculated from cost projections for the

the undertaking includes procedures intended to set prices at relatively low levels: the cheapest device at a given density is used for reference price purposes for all chips of that density, and by taking a weighted average of costs across manufacturers, the more efficient, higher-volume producers will be given more weight. On the other hand, other features of the reference pricing scheme, including a profit margin of 9.5 percent added on to full cost (compared with a statutory 8 percent minimum profit margin used in U.S.-constructed cost calculations), might tend to produce higher cost calculations than the American FMV system.

Some European company officials rationalize the EC procedures in terms of drawing a distinction between "hard" dumping (selling at prices below even the most efficient producer's full average cost of production) and "soft" dumping (selling at prices below one's own cost, but not necessarily below the cost of more efficient producers). In this view, the American FMV system is more stringent in that it attempts to eliminate soft dumping, while the European system is more liberal in that it bans only hard dumping. A defender of the American system, on the other hand, might reply that it is more liberal, in that company-specific price floors permit efficient producers to expand at the expense of less efficient producers (whether U.S. or foreign). By contrast, the European weighted-average scheme hinders even the most efficient exporting firm by setting a price above its cost.

In many respects, this entire discussion is moot. More important is that an era is beginning in which different regions of the world are setting floor prices for key semiconductors using inconsistent and incompatible pricing formulas. Until recently this was not a problem, because market prices for DRAMs, in particular, were far above any of the various formulas used in Europe and the United States. This was one reason why European user resistance was ultimately overcome, enabling price undertakings with Japanese exporters to be completed in August of 1989.

No sooner had the undertakings been fixed, however, than DRAM prices dropped sharply in world markets. In August of 1989, for the first time since the introduction of the component into the marketplace and just after the DRAM price undertaking was announced, the spot price for one-megabit DRAMs dropped below the long-term contract price, marking a sharp decline in memory chip prices. The assumption factored

previous quarter, which in turn are based on actual data for the prior quarter (that is, two quarters earlier).

into the widespread acceptance within Europe of the DRAM price undertakings—that they were unlikely to act as constraints—was almost immediately overthrown.[84]

## Research Subsidies and Technological Integration

A final policy that has become increasingly central to the European strategy for competing in semiconductors is the growing flow of public subsidies into joint R&D activities in information technology and electronics in general and semiconductors in particular. The 1983 Megaproject, involving Siemens, Philips, and the German and Dutch governments, has already been mentioned; it was later pulled into the framework of the pan-European Eureka R&D initiative (proposed by François Mitterrand as a response to the U.S. Strategic Defense Initiative) established in 1985. Eureka projects are organized around collaborative, cross-national R&D involving European companies. Unlike EC technology programs, which are generally characterized as "pre-competitive," Eureka projects are aimed at development of technology with more immediate relevance to the commercial marketplace.

At roughly the same time as the initiation of Eureka, the European Community approved the first phase of its first truly large-scale R&D initiative, Esprit. The five-year program announced in 1984 (which ran through 1988) poured about ECU 1.5 billion (half provided by the EC budget and half by participating organizations) into research on advanced microelectronics, software technology, advanced information processing, office systems standards, and computer integrated manufacturing. Microelectronics accounted for about 25 percent of the Community's budgeted support for Esprit.[85] A key feature of Esprit was the requirement that collaboration among industrial firms and with the academic community be a feature of funding requests.[86]

---

84. Indeed, some observers (including the author) remarked at the time that the seemingly innocuous price floors would become a problem if there were a recession in the chip industry, or if Japanese producers decided on an aggressive pricing strategy with their next-generation four-megabit parts. Both predictions have to some extent materialized. See Peter Montagnon, "Brussels Chip Pricing Plan Floors Computer Makers," *Financial Times*, July 27, 1989, p. 3.

85. See EC Commission, *Esprit: The First Phase—Progress and Results*, Publication EUR 10940 EN (Luxembourg, 1987), p. 89.

86. The Alvey program, a national effort initiated by the British government in 1983, was the first European research program that made collaboration on joint projects a condition for participation.

One of Esprit's objectives was better technological integration within the Community. In 1985 this goal was made explicit by the European Commission with its proposal to EC heads of state and governments for a European Technological Community.[87] In addition to spurring investment in, and recouping greater returns on, research relevant to industrial technologies, an explicit part of the Esprit program was the encouragement of alliances and collaborations among European companies. Esprit is widely regarded as a success, particularly in encouraging pan-European industrial research alliances. In 1987 a five-year successor program, Esprit II, was approved with more than double the original Esprit budget (ECU 3.2 billion).

Since Esprit is nominally open to participation by Community companies, universities, and research institutes, the issue of who was a "Community company" was faced early on, and relatively transparent criteria were established. EC subsidiaries of American companies with European research facilities have been eligible to participate under the criteria adopted, and some do. American organizations with European research operations that participated in Esprit I include Analog Devices, AT&T (through its European telecommunications joint venture with Philips), the Battelle Institute, DEC, IBM, and Foxboro. Until very recently, major Japanese firms in Europe operated no significant research facilities, so Japanese participation was not an issue.

Most recently, in at least partial response to the U.S. Sematech initiative and large-scale R&D outlays by Japanese semiconductor companies, a major new pan-European R&D program in semiconductor technology was created. The Joint European Submicron Silicon Initiative (JESSI) was begun in 1989 with a planned budget of about ECU 4 billion over an eight-year period (ending in 1996). Originally conceived as a successor to the Philips-Siemens Megaproject, it too is organized as a Eureka program. Unlike the EC programs, there are few formalized procedures to determine eligibility for Eureka participation and no fixed rules for ownership and transfer of technology.[88]

---

87. EC Commission, Directorate-General 23 (Small and Medium-Sized Enterprises), *Esprit 1987 Annual Report* (Luxembourg, 1988), p. iii.

88. One of the hallmarks of the Eureka program is its emphasis on flexible procedures. "Eureka's organization and flexible procedures are designed to facilitate the process, by helping to overcome some of the traditional barriers to transnational cooperation, but it is up to individual organizations to initiate and pursue contacts with partners in other Eureka member countries *as they see fit.* . . . Once a partnership has been formed and the partners

JESSI is clearly quite a large semiconductor R&D program. By contrast, the U.S. Sematech program involves a budget of about $1 billion over five years. However, Sematech is much more narrowly focused on semiconductor manufacturing technology, while JESSI is to cover a larger territory, including equipment and materials and semiconductor applications and design tools. Public funding for JESSI will come from the national governments of Britain, France, Germany, and Italy, and from the EC itself. Although the EC is partially funding the program, it is not (at least now) an EC project and remains outside the scope of regulations governing EC projects.

Because of its size and scope, some U.S. companies—particularly IBM—have been eager to participate in JESSI through its European subsidiaries. Inquiries about participation in Sematech by U.S. affiliates of European companies, in particular the affiliates of Philips and ASM International, were rebuffed. Until recently, these same European companies were unwilling to permit IBM to join JESSI.

By virtue of its size, JESSI is an attractive bargaining chip, and Philips, in particular, had insisted that access to Sematech be made a condition for participation by U.S.-based companies.[89] IBM defused this conflict by inviting European companies to participate in its privately funded research program in X-ray lithography, to be used in the production of advanced semiconductors, and by agreeing to undertake joint R&D with Siemens on sixty-four-megabit DRAMs.[90] As a consequence, it was announced in January 1990 that IBM would be allowed to participate in JESSI. This idea of reciprocity in access to national and regional research programs looms as a major issue to be addressed in the semiconductor and other high-technology industries.

have elaborated contractual relations between them, the Governments of the firms and institutes involved will check that the project meets the Eureka criteria. . . . After such notification Eureka projects remain open to other parties, *should project partners so desire.*" See Eureka Secretariat, *Eureka* (Brussels, November 1987), pp. 2, 5 (emphasis added). Note that the absence of established procedures has led to some squabbling over how much of the Megaproject technology developed by Philips and Siemens must be transferred to JESSI partners who did not participate in Megaproject but who will be working with them on JESSI. The issue is complicated by the fact that the EC is funding a portion of JESSI, and there has yet been no clear decision made on whether the EC's policies on the ownership and transfer of technology will be applied to JESSI as a consequence of its financial participation.

89. Since Siemens does not have a significant semiconductor research facility in the United States, it has not attempted to join Sematech.

90. IBM recently announced that Motorola would be collaborating in the X-ray lithography research effort.

The focus within the European semiconductor industry seems to be increasingly the regionalization of R&D subsidies and the active encouragement of pan-European collaboration—in short, the regional integration of both public and private R&D activity. This shift away from competition among rival national champions is aided by the small numbers of significant European players in the semiconductor game and their pattern of relative specialization. In JESSI, for example, manufacturing process development can focus on memory chips as the vehicle for R&D without worrying about divisive competition among European producers because of the de facto specialization that has emerged. Siemens will apply the technology to its chosen market, dynamic RAMs; STM will use the same technology in its niche, EPROMs; and Philips will apply the same processes to static RAMs. The joint R&D effort would undoubtedly be much more difficult if each of these companies had a stake in the markets of other players.

Meanwhile, the EC seems embarked on a path toward technological integration of the Community. This means declining use of national R&D programs to favor national companies, increasing technical collaboration with non-national European partners, and a vastly larger role for the EC bureaucracy in organizing and administering national R&D initiatives. In many respects the semiconductor story fits in naturally with what has begun to emerge as the European model for the trade and investment regime in a strategic high-technology industry.

## The European Model

From the narrowest point of view, the path toward a regionally integrated European economic and technological community may well prove highly profitable for U.S. business. Because U.S. companies can draw on their extensive history of investment and manufacturing within the EC, they are far better positioned than their Japanese competitors quickly to increase sales of high-technology goods produced within the Community. Indeed, many protectionist EC measures seem specifically targeted at Japanese and other Asian producers, not U.S. companies. If reactions are quick and judgments sharp, U.S. investors could well gain from the barriers that might be erected around the European high-technology market.

To return to the broader issues I raised at the beginning, European Community policy regarding semiconductors seems to mix reflexive and contradictory short-term responses with a rather clear and coherent long-term view. A pessimist would interpret the long-term vision as highly protectionist, while an optimist might just catch sight of even grander and better regimes to come in a high-technology sector that desperately needs a way out of the current climate of political conflict and trade friction.

### Short-Term Dilemmas

The immediate future in the global trade regime for chips promises to be dominated by maneuvers to work out the contradictory pricing rules that are now superimposed on international trade in DRAMs. Conceivably, these contradictions can be resolved. When prices far exceeded both the European and U.S. price floors, there was of course nothing to be resolved. But as prices soften, a predictable problem will develop. The European reference price calculations are designed to yield chip prices that fall below the American FMVs. If that end is realized (after adding in the appropriate duty), prices in Europe will fall below those prevailing in the United States, and a central tenet of the U.S.- Japan STA—pricing in third-country markets at or above U.S. levels— will be broken. The United States undoubtedly will be extremely displeased and will attempt to change the situation.

The obvious solution for Japanese producers is to price at or above the U.S. FMV level when shipping exports to Europe. The Japanese government, however, in settling its semiconductor GATT case with the EC, agreed not to monitor the prices of exports to the EC and other third-country markets. The impasse might be solved if Japanese producers were privately able to collectively discipline their export pricing in a manner that satisfied the U.S. FMV standards yet did not overtly require Japanese government coordination. There is some evidence that this solution has already occurred to Japanese industrialists. Japanese semiconductor pioneer and Hitachi vice-president Hiroshi Asano, in an extensive interview, wondered out loud whether the industry could informally reconcile the STA with GATT on its own:

It is a problem for the Government as to how to maintain coordination between the Agreement and GATT. However, considering a time when demand and supply ease again, monitoring in accordance with the Agreement will probably be necessary as the "second best policy." In regard to the maintaining of order in industry circles, it is talked about, but as shown in the examples of textiles and iron and steel, I wonder if they can become so mature as to be able to really maintain order without Government intervention.[91]

There is some reason to believe that the required degree of maturity is now present in the Japanese semiconductor industry. After the semiconductor market began to weaken late in the spring of 1989, Japanese producers openly implemented and discussed cutbacks in DRAM production undertaken to bolster weak prices. Reports in the Japanese trade press over the last two years suggest that Japanese DRAM producers have acted in a coordinated fashion to stabilize prices. Japanese government policy over the same period has greatly strengthened manufacturers' control over distribution channels. Government gathering and dissemination of price and output information, coupled with a self-enforced industry discipline, may very well establish the coordination necessary to maintain two divergent price floors in two different markets.

Although MITI publicly denies any role in guiding producer behavior, sources within Japanese industry continue to report that MITI provides "opinions" to Japanese chip producers regarding their investment plans.[92] Reports from Japanese industrial circles continue to fuel a persistent belief that MITI maintains some elements of informal guidance to Japanese chip makers.

Private or public coordination of Japanese semiconductor producers is not an obviously rational policy, from the perspective of either Europe or the United States. Indeed, such action aggravates a potentially serious issue for consumers of high-technology products in both places: how to discourage collusion by foreign oligopoly suppliers extracting rents in their downstream industries or, in the worst case, integrating forward into these very industries. Apart from the cartelization problems facing users, the system of price floors for key semiconductors has been a bad

91. *Mainichi Shimbun*, March 26, 1988, p. 9.

92. When pressed on this point in an interview, one Japanese government official insisted to me that the only advice being supplied to producers concerned their foreign investment plans where political factors associated with the location of investments in Europe had become an issue. Approximately two weeks after this concession was made to my persistent skepticism, however, even this latter point was publicly denied: "MITI, Japan's Ministry of International Trade and Industry, has vigorously denied guiding Japanese companies to spread their investments around European Community countries rather than concentrating them in the UK. 'We have never given any guidance on this issue. It is a matter that is entirely up to companies themselves to decide,' Miti said yesterday." Ian Rodger, "Tokyo Denies Issuing Anti-UK Guidance," *Financial Times*, December 21, 1988, p. 3.

deal even for domestic semiconductor manufacturers. Neither U.S. nor European producers have gained more than a minimal share of the rents created by the chip shortage: instead, those rents have largely been gathered by Japanese firms and plowed back into Japanese R&D, which will create even greater pressure on non-Japanese vendors over the next cycle of competition.

Although some within the semiconductor industry continue to call for international pricing standards to reduce friction over dumping charges, it is hard to see how such a regime could be acceptable to chip users. All such proposals call for some calculation of long-run average cost to be used as a floor for export prices for selected semiconductors. Quite apart from the complex issue of how such an average cost is to be calculated—particularly in an industry where substantial R&D overhead expenditure is spread across a variety of products and where learning economies are a crucial feature of the cost structure—any price rule would seem to imply that regional price differentials for semiconductors must inevitably arise. Whatever price rule might be chosen, it would apply only to exports. In times of weak demand, economic pressures would drive chip makers (as has historically been the case) to drop prices in the domestic market to maintain sales and keep production lines up and running, so long as marginal costs were covered. But export prices would be kept above the calculated long-run average cost floor. In times of scarcity, however, all prices would exceed long-run average cost.

Users of imported chips would seem to be placed in a situation where, on average, they would be paying higher prices for chips, since they would not get the benefit of low prices in times of weak demand. These users would then be placed at a competitive disadvantage in downstream export markets relative to systems manufacturers who did not rely on imported chips. Furthermore, pricing rules would be entirely irrelevant to vertically integrated producers of both chips and equipment and would serve only to disadvantage unintegrated competitors.

A reasonable case can be made that both the United States and Europe—net users of chips—would have been better off with some temporary dumping duties on chips,[93] or, better yet, direct subsidies to domestic producers justified as an entry-inducing policy to reduce the monopoly power of Japanese suppliers. Rather than copy bad U.S. policy

---

93. The dumping duties would have to be levied on chips incorporated into equipment sold in the local market as well, in order not to disadvantage domestic manufacturers using imported chips vis-à-vis their foreign competitors.

and imitate the STA, Europe might have devised creative answers for its own short-term difficulties.

## Long-Term Prospects

Over the long term, however, a fairly clear and rational picture of European policy has begun to emerge. It is far from official, and no one in either the EC or member state governments would yet dare an explicit articulation. But the signs seem to point to a "technological bloc" under construction within the Community.

European electronics executives are less bashful about spelling out the vision. C. W. M. Koot, managing director of the IC business within Philips, recently said:

> ICs are the enabling technology for the continued advancement of industrial societies. As such, each region needs a viable IC industry to further its culture. Each region, therefore, needs to be substantially self-supporting.
>
> Being self-supporting means that all the elements of the so-called "industrial foodchain" must be available domestically: everything from manufacturing equipment, and chip design and fabrication, to making the end product for the consumer.[94]

At least part of this prescription may be rationalized with a vision of a world in which increasingly high fixed R&D costs and huge capital investment outlays in electronics create a significant degree of oligopoly power. Perhaps the most lasting effect of the STA will be its vivid demonstration of how potential market power can be transformed into concrete coordinated behavior. In the future, how can the EC prevent latent monopoly power from being similarly activated to collect rents from European consumer industries?

One approach—the road, I would argue, that Europe is currently edging down—is to require producers of high-technology inputs, like semiconductors, to manufacture the product within regional borders. That serves two purposes. First, it makes it more difficult for foreign-based companies to coordinate their actions, since it is much easier to observe what is going on inside those factories—for example, whether they are operating at capacity—and much easier to apply domestic

---

94. Cees W. M. Koot, "What Does 1992 Mean for the European IC Market?" speech delivered at the Dataquest Semiconductor Industry Conference, Tokyo, Japan, April 1989.

antitrust standards. Second, national security concerns are eased. If, as some have suggested, one nation might simply withhold vital chips to exert leverage on another region's foreign policy, the militia can be called in to occupy the local factory.

To be consistent with this vision, of course, suppliers for inputs to the oligopolistic industries, which are themselves organized oligopolistically, must also be forced to locate within the regional bloc. Otherwise, if semiconductor equipment or materials markets are highly concentrated, they could be used as effective leverage against the high-technology factories located within the bloc.

What are the potential costs of this approach? To the extent that economies of scale are important, fragmentation of the market into autonomous regional blocs means higher costs. It means that small niche markets may not be served with the best products. It means that regions enjoying a comparative advantage in one set of products or stage of production will not be able to specialize fully in that area. It means that, worldwide, efficiency gains from freer trade will be forfeited. And it means that the overall global pace of technical innovation will slow, as resources are absorbed and returns lowered by higher-cost production.

There are alternatives to this vision. International standards for competitive behavior, if enforced by a GATT-like body—perhaps the International Trade Organization originally proposed as an organizational sister to the GATT back in the 1940s—might alleviate some of the fears of anticompetitive behavior in concentrated high-technology sectors. The further development of a single Community competition policy would seem a promising model of how such standards might be ironed out, even within a group of nations with very different historical attitudes and institutions regulating market behavior.

Indeed, the European move toward regional technological integration might even become the first step toward a more functional trade regime for high-technology goods, a regime with two distinguishing character-istics. First, it would attempt to encourage investment in new technology by creating the widest possible market for high-technology goods (in-creasing the returns on fixed costs of R&D projects). The single EC market provides an obvious model here. Second, it would encourage the greatest possible social return on the collective international investment in technology (within the group of nations pledged to the new regime). Presumably this would mean not investing resources in national or regional production of every high-technology good, but instead specializing in particular market segments (because of the economies of scale created by high fixed R&D costs). Again, the Community-wide research consortia are instructive.

Technological specialization would be endangered if many would-be specialist firms feared that other members of the global community would manipulate this deliberate dependence on others in order to increase the collection of rents at their expense. Minimal safeguards would be needed against anticompetitive behavior by groups of firms within the boundaries of the regime. In this respect, emulation of the Community-wide competition policy would again seem to be the right idea.

Another danger would be the use of public subsidy to boost national firms selectively in world markets. Subsidies to production are already illegal, but subsidies to R&D are permitted by GATT. In high-technology industry, with large R&D costs, research subsidies are an easy and GATT-legal way to help the local team. Ending subsidies to R&D would be much more complicated than stopping subsidies to production.

Subsidies to high-technology industries have been advocated for two quite different reasons. One argument applies even in an economy cut off from international trade; it might be labeled the "domestic social" case for policy intervention. With the emergence of modern high-technology industry during and after the Second World War came an economic literature that argued that government support for research was desirable—if it corrected for market failures that caused private return to investment in technology to fall short of the full benefit to society. The principal cause for market failure was thought to be the difficulty investors encountered in trying to capture the full fruits of their R&D investment for their exclusive financial benefit. Both case studies and statistical analysis have confirmed the widespread empirical relevance of this argument. Furthermore, it is in more basic research—rather than pure development—that the gap between private and social return is largest and the case for government support is therefore easiest.

Indeed, international flows of goods and technology greatly complicate matters. Foreign producers may capture some of the total return on R&D that otherwise might have been reflected in greater profits for domestic producers or lower prices for domestic consumers, thus reducing the domestic social return. On the other hand, if foreign markets are open to domestic high-technology producers, additional technology-based rents that are collected overseas will increase domestic income and increase the social return. In principle, it is entirely possible for an investment in R&D to be socially worthwhile from the standpoint of the home country, even if none of the production embodying the technology is undertaken by domestic producers.

The possibility of collecting technological rents from foreign consumers (or avoiding payment of such a rent) raises a second ground for government intervention. If national policy can create a situation in which technology-based rents can be secured for national producers, then national income and the standard of living are increased. This may be called the "strategic trade" rationale for intervention in high-technology industries. The strategic trade argument for intervention does not rely solely on the existence of technology rents. A rent based on monopoly power protected by economies of scale, large sunk costs of any sort, or learning economies is also fair game and furnishes grounds for inspiring government intervention that might help capture part of this rent (or prevent it from being collected by foreign firms).

Thus, for several reasons, it seems inevitable that governments will be highly involved in national investment in technology and technology-intensive industries. The multiplicity of motives means that such involvement cannot be internationally regulated—in any operational way—by rules that strike at "forbidden" motives and tolerate "acceptable" motives.

The challenge, then, is to propose some way of neutralizing subsidies to R&D as a tool of rent-collecting strategic trade policy, yet preserve the ability of governments to engage in socially beneficial public investment in R&D. The concept of reciprocity in R&D—permitting firms from other countries to join domestic subsidized research programs in exchange for reciprocal access by home firms in the foreign country's R&D projects—would seem an important step in that direction. Exploration of how such bilateral or multilateral reciprocity in industrial R&D subsidies might be negotiated would seem an important subject for those interested in preserving an open international trading system. Here again, the EC would seem to offer one lead, with its deemphasis of national technical programs in favor of Community-wide technical links and its championing of the idea of reciprocity in access to research programs in its talks with the United States.

To conclude, the EC model of technological integration seems to be moving toward further development of Community-wide standards for competition, coupled with a regionalization of access to R&D funded out of the public purse. One way of looking at this is as Fortress Europe, building walls against the outside. Many Europeans seem to view it this way. But another way to look at it is as a model for the sort of arrangement that might work in high-technology industries on an even grander international scale. The same two EC principles could serve as ground rules for a technological community that included the United States, Japan, and any other country that wished to join. The wider the net, of course, the more difficult rulemaking becomes, as economies with very different institutions are included. Some method of apportioning the costs of public R&D investments would clearly have to be worked out. As public expenditure on technology becomes a truly international public good, equitably sharing the burden among nations and firms becomes that much more important.

The EC-1992 phenomenon demonstrates that the notion of an open international trading community is not hopelessly utopian. Reasonable nations can make reasonable compromises in their collective common interest. Nowhere is the common interest in an open trading system more threatened than in high-technology industries, particularly in semiconductors, where the world seems to be sliding rapidly toward a collection of balkanized regional markets. Can others seek refuge within the same common walls that the EC is building if an acceptable set of rules can be worked out? Will the EC cooperate in such an effort? For the electronics industry, this is the larger question raised by 1992.

# Chapter 6

# Competition Policy

DOUGLAS E. ROSENTHAL

TWO KEY GOALS of the Europe 1992 Program are to increase the competitiveness of EC enterprises and to promote consumer welfare. These goals are to be achieved by reducing governmental restraints that protect favored enterprises against open competition. But what if these two 1992 competition goals conflict? What if opening up and integrating internal European markets benefits major American and Japanese firms more than European enterprises? What if encouraging firms to be competitive globally, especially in high-technology fields, reduces competition within the EC market? Will governmental restraints be removed by January 1, 1993, and how unified will European markets be by that date? This chapter attempts to address such questions and, in doing so, to characterize the Community's competition policy, to contrast the Community's policy with U.S. policy, and to explore the transatlantic interplay of competition policies.

The conclusions are generally positive. European policy today favors open internal markets at least as strongly and consistently as does U.S. policy. The "ship" of opportunity for U.S. firms is not "leaving the dock," and "Fortress Europe" is no greater a threat than "Fortress America." The legal framework of EC competition policy, either in place or in view, should eventually promote significant European access for American firms on a generally nondiscriminatory basis. The antitrust enforcement bureaucrats of DG-4—the directorate-general most committed to maintaining competition—play an important role in the decisionmaking

Douglas E. Rosenthal is a partner in the Washington office of the international law firm Coudert Brothers. During the Carter administration, he served as chief of the Foreign Commerce Section of the Antitrust Division of the Justice Department. He received valuable research assistance from Cathy Issa in preparing this chapter. Peter Alexiadis, Jean Patrice de la Laurencie, Auke Haagsma, Georges Le Tallec, Jürgen Müller, and John Temple-Lang provided many useful criticisms of an early draft.

process. They speak with a strong voice on a broad range of EC competition policy decisions.

But the conclusions are not unconditional. There are risks. One, of course, is that a sustained recession could undermine public commitment to the 1992 program.[1] Even if the global economy continues to perform well, even if the dramatic changes in Eastern Europe do not brake the program, so much reform is proposed, so much that is established is to give way, that the ambitious time schedule for accomplishing competition reform is not likely to be met. Another danger is that the EC Commission will not be given enough resources to police newly deregulated markets adequately, a deficiency that private enforcement in national courts will be slow to redress, so that private barriers to market access could come to replace official barriers. A third risk is that competition in the Community and in some member states will be limited in the name of environmental, social, or health values, where a significant but disguised purpose or effect is anticompetitive. A fourth risk is that restrictions will be maintained in certain key sectors, especially the three discussed in this book—autos, telecommunications, and semiconductors—in the service of noncompetitive trade and industrial policy goals (especially limiting Japanese market access). A fifth related risk is that U.S. policymakers will be unable to assure the same degree of openness to U.S. markets for European enterprises that the Community may provide to American firms as both address the "Japanese problem." European competition policy might then be affected by pressures for reciprocity and retaliation.

## What Is Competition Policy?

The meaning of the term *competition policy* is unsettled. There are two polar notions. One is that competition policy is coincident with the antitrust laws and their enforcement. The other is that competition policy embraces any law or regulation that promotes or inhibits the free operation of the market mechanism.

The first definition is too narrow. While antitrust is at the core of competition policy, it does not cover the field. Antitrust laws are riddled with exceptions and exemptions: state immunity in the United States, industrial policy subsidies in the Community, agricultural exemptions

---

1. The economic unification of Europe noticeably slowed in the aftermath of the 1973 oil shock.

and voluntary restraint agreements in both jurisdictions.[2] In the United States, for example, the Antitrust Division of the Department of Justice plays no significant role when the government decides to enter into a semiconductor voluntary restraint arrangement limiting trade with Japan, even though that agreement vitally affects competitiveness in both the U.S. semiconductor and computer markets (see chapter 5). The antitrust laws deal primarily with that core of competition policy that sets and enforces standards for (1) legal business combinations—by acquisition or strategic alliance; (2) anticompetitive market-dominating behavior (monopolization); and (3) collusion between firms that is not directed by lawful governmental authority and that adversely affects competition in the market.[3]

The second concept of competition policy is too broad. Every governmental program, even those unrelated to an ambitious scheme of deregulation, has some effect, direct or indirect, planned or unintended, on competition in some market. The total hodgepodge of governmental rules and actions does not, however, add up to a "competition policy."

A definition of competition policy between these two extremes is used here. Competition policy is what a government says it wants and what it intentionally does (or refuses to do) to open (or close) its markets to competition and to protect (or fail to protect) competitors in the market against public or private trade restraints that impede the most able and promote the less efficient. It also includes the explicit balance between competition and other values in public decisions significantly affecting markets.

### Key Elements of EC Policy

Five aspects of European competition policy will have the most impact. First is the timing for and extent of removal of government barriers that

2. In the United States we speak of "antitrust" laws. In the EC and most other places, these are usually called "competition" laws. Since competition *policy* as used here is broader than the field of antitrust law, I shall refer to EC competition laws as "antitrust" laws.

3. U.S. antitrust law has three statutes that, together with interpretation and enforcement standards, frame this aspect of competition policy. They are section 7 of the Clayton Act and sections 1 and 2 of the Sherman Act. The parallel provisions of EC law are, in order, the merger regulation (see appendix 6-1; not yet in force), and articles 85 and 86 of the European Community Treaty. Until the merger regulation is in force, DG-4 of the European Commission (the EC antitrust enforcement agency) is relying upon imputed merger control authority in articles 85 and 86, which has not been fully tested before the European Court of Justice.

impede the "four freedoms"—the free flow of goods, persons, services, and capital within the Community. The removal of member state barriers obviously will have greater significance if those barriers are not replaced by restrictive, Community-wide "harmonizing" restraints. Second is how much market access is permitted, especially by merger or strategic alliance, based on the principles of national treatment and nondiscrimination. Free access requires that governments do not restrict market entry, or the opportunity to expand to realize efficiencies, or otherwise compete, once entry has been made, based on nationality or preferential criteria. Third is the extent to which outside firms, including U.S. firms, are targeted for private restraints perpetuated by European firms. Fourth is how much EC member states or Community institutions distort competition by providing subsidies to favored firms or consortia to make them "more competitive" or to give them "short-term relief" from market setbacks. Fifth is whether foreign firms can obtain equal access by exporting to European markets. A restrictive policy puts U.S. exporters, for example, at a disadvantage in comparison with U.S. firms that produce within the frontier.

To assess the likely impact of EC competition on U.S. industry and U.S. policy, this study accordingly examines five features of the 1992 program: deregulation, market restructuring, antitrust enforcement, industrial policy, and external trade policy.[4]

## Competition Policy and Noncompetition Values

The balance struck between competition and other values in public issue choices makes up a nation's competition policy. Not even the mainstream Chicago School argues that competition should be the ruling value in all transactions involving wealth creation or exchange. Competition is not an absolute good. Article 36 of the EEC Treaty identifies several values that may justify restrictions on competition in internal trade in goods between member states, so long as they shall not "constitute a means of arbitrary discrimination or a disguised" trade restriction. These values include "public morality, public security, the protection of health and life of humans, animals or plants, the protection of national

4. I am biased, but the best introduction to the legal structure of 1992 I have seen is the report prepared by Coudert Brothers. See Jacques Buhart and Dennis Burton, *Legal Aspects of the Single European Market: A Working Guide to 1992*, Euromoney Special Report (Tonbridge, Eng., 1989).

treasures possessing artistic, historical or archeological value, or the protection of industrial and commercial property."

The competitiveness of the Community and its accessibility to U.S. enterprises will be heavily influenced by how far the competition values of free markets give way to continuing member state or Community-wide restrictions justified on the grounds of national security, worker rights embodied in a social charter, health and safety, environmental protection, defense of intellectual property rights, cultural or historical patrimony, or public morality.

Implementation of the 1992 program, and the decision in the *Cassis de Dijon* case, laying the basis for mutual recognition of standards, should largely erode the force of most member state regulations restricting competition on Article 36 grounds—if member states comply fully and reasonably promptly with that program. *Cassis de Dijon* does, however, articulate four values that could theoretically justify anticompetitive restrictions: (1) effectiveness of fiscal supervision, (2) protection of public health, (3) fairness in commercial transactions, and (4) defense of the consumer.[5] Precedent suggests, however, that the first two claims are likely to be viewed skeptically in a competition context; the latter two should rarely if ever be antithetical to competition values.

To be sure, all the pending EC-1992 regulations and directives can be adopted, but if they are modified and implemented in ways that permit Article 36 justifications for several less competitive alternatives at points of difficult policy choice, the outcome will be significantly less competition than EC-1992 now promises.

The following issues with a competition dimension will be publicly debated in the coming years:

—Should a defense industry or domestic airline merger, arguably not justified on competition grounds, be approved on national security grounds?

—Should a firm be permitted to close its plants in West Germany with large worker layoffs in order to lower its labor and other costs by moving to a new facility in Spain or Portugal and, if so, at what price in closing costs?

—What food additive and nutritional labeling requirements will member states require, and will these promote market segmentation?

—Will arguably low-cost French nuclear power companies be per-

5. See *Rewe-Zentral AG* v. *Bundesmonopolverwaltung für Branntwein* (case 120/78), February 20, 1979, *Common Mkt. Rep.* (CCH), para. 8543 (1979).

mitted to compete freely with companies generating more expensive but "safer" power supplies?

—How far should patent and copyright laws be extended into frontier technology fields like computer software? What should be the trade-offs among stimulating innovation, promoting the dissemination and improvement of innovation, and restricting the opportunities for "free riders" to appropriate the intellectual property of others? Will expanded intellectual property laws retard competition and innovation?

—Should a Korean company be permitted to acquire, say, Chateau Chambord, or the La Scala Opera House, if those properties were put on the market?

It is too early to tell what balances will be struck in these areas of conflicting values. The same can be said, of course, for U.S. competition policy. While a few observations on these questions will be made in passing, the focus here is on factors other than these that will influence the shape and direction of EC competition policy.

## Who Makes EC Competition Policy?

While the Council of Ministers controls the timing and final form of directives and almost all regulations, including the merger regulation discussed in appendix 6-1, the treaty system has ceded primary responsibility for competition policy to the Commission. Of the 23 directorates-general of the Commission, perhaps the most significant in this policy area are:

*DG-4*, responsible for antitrust enforcement and for limiting the anticompetitive effects of state aids;

*DG-1*, responsible for external relations and trade negotiations;

*DG-3*, responsible for the formation of the internal market and industrial affairs policy;

*DG-15*, responsible for financial services, company law, and tax policy; and

*DG-12*, responsible for research and development policy.

The Commission decides policy by majority vote in secret. However, the views of the directorate primarily responsible for a particular policy area, and of the commissioner who leads it, if he chooses to be assertive, are given great weight during the consideration of policy initiatives, legislation, and enforcement actions. Where two or more policy areas are affected by a single policy option, cooperation between two or more directorates frequently occurs. For example, DG-1, which negotiated the semiconductor (DRAM) price undertaking with Japan, is reported to have consulted DG-4 to ensure that the Commission would not engage in price fixing. Conflict may, however, develop. In the Commission that served from 1984 to 1988, differences arose between then Competition Commissioner Peter Sutherland and Transport Commissioner Stanley Clinton Davis as to the degree and timing of proposed intra-Community aviation deregulation.

There are roughly 220 professionals in DG-4, but about 90–100 of these deal with state subsidies, not antitrust issues. There is talk of adding up to 30 more now that the merger regulation is adopted.[6] Still, this is absurdly inadequate staffing for an important policy area. DG-4, backed by its commissioner, has the potential to be more independent of the president of the Commission than the Antitrust Division is of the president of the United States. A strong president, like Jacques Delors, is quite influential. A member of his cabinet has, as one of two main responsibilities, the task of keeping an eye on competition issues. But even a Delors can only monitor so much. He does not have a staff equivalent to that of the White House with their broad control over U.S. competition initiatives. DG-4's independence does not mean it is insulated from lobbying on an industrywide basis. However, DG-4 is more independent of other government branches than the U.S. Federal Trade Commission is of the House and Senate Commerce Committees. Its personnel are also better paid, frequently more sophisticated, and accorded greater public respect than the personnel (especially the nonsupervisory personnel) of U.S. antitrust agencies. DG-4 can be constrained by a passive commissioner for competition or by a timid director-general, but, conversely, strong leadership in those positions strengthens its hand. Sutherland was regarded as a forceful commissioner. His successor, Sir Leon Brittan, is acknowledged to be very bright and politically skilled; his pro-competitive assertiveness as to difficult policy choices, however, is still largely untested.

DG-4 draws its greatest strength from the central role that the norm of competition plays within the Treaty of Rome. The Sherman Act may,

6. It is now accepted that the director-general of DG-4 should usually be a German national. This norm pays homage to the expertise and commitment to competition that Germany has demonstrated since the war. DG-4 has five subdirectorates; in addition, the staff of the Legal Services Department, assigned to provide legal advice to DG-4, also plays an important policy role.

as Justice Thurgood Marshall opined, have a quasi-constitutional status in U.S. jurisprudence,[7] but there is nothing "quasi" about Article 3(f) or Articles 85 and 86 of the EEC constitution. Armed with these articles, economics ministers in EC countries can, for example, stand up to PTT (post, telegraph, and telephone) ministers who are resisting more open telecommunications markets. U.S. antitrusters can take analogous action only with White House approval. The Rome treaty expresses a *norm* that markets must be open, that anticompetitive regulations must be narrow, that they ought to be phased out over time, and that they should be subject to constant monitoring. So far, other government officials and the informed public have accepted that a paramount competition norm will generally produce the best long-term public welfare results—notwithstanding possible short-term unemployment and elimination of certain services. Because the specific exemptions from U.S. antitrust enforcement are more clearly established in the U.S. system, U.S. competition officials have less authority than their EC counterparts to question elements of state intervention—especially in the realm of industrial policy.

DG-4 also draws power from its responsibility, delegated by the Commission, to conduct investigations, bring prosecutions, find liability, and impose fines of up to 10 percent of a company's annual worldwide revenue, as well as to obtain injunctions and divestiture orders. To date the remedy of divestiture, while available in theory, has never been ordered by the Commission. DG-4 exercises its considerable powers subject only to nonbinding advice from member state competition authorities via the Advisory Committee on Restrictive Practices and Monopolies, judicial review by the new Court of First Instance and potentially the European Court, and the views of the commissioner for competition (which tend to be binding, if he so chooses) and his fellow commissioners. One commentator has suggested that the exercise of these extraordinary powers, delegated de facto by the Commission to a

---

7. What he said is that the "[a]ntitrust laws in general, and the Sherman Act in particular, are the Magna Carta of free enterprise. They are as important to the preservation of economic freedom and our free-enterprise system as the Bill of Rights is to the protection of our fundamental personal freedoms. And the freedom guaranteed each and every business, no matter how small, is the freedom to compete—to assert with vigor, imagination, devotion, and ingenuity whatever economic muscle it can muster." *United States* v. *Topco Associates, Inc.*, 405 U.S. 596, 610, 92 S. Ct. 1126 (1972).

single directorate-general, would not happen again if the member states knew in 1962 what they know today.[8]

The European Parliament is playing a larger role in influencing the content of directives and regulations affecting competition policy. Members' prerogatives are not inconsiderable: they have the opportunity to amend draft proposals, and generally to do so at each of two separate legislative readings, as well as a committee system in which the role of lobbyists is likely to grow, coupled with a question period, when commissioners must personally appear to defend Commission policies. Other factors bear on parliament's increasing role. Many Commission "Eurocrats" are mindful both of the suspicion with which they are viewed (especially given the relatively low visibility of their decisionmaking) and of the fact that, unlike members of the European Parliament, they are not democratically elected. U.S. firms and trade associations, among others, are adding the European Parliament to their lobbying agenda.[9] For the more sophisticated, this agenda has for many years included the relevant commissioners and their staffs, as well as the relevant directorate-general officials. Even though the parliament is constrained by the Treaty of Rome to a much weaker role than that of the U.S. Congress, it could easily become a source of pressure to curb market "excesses" by seeking to protect jobs and worker rights. So far, the parliament has been generally supportive of the competition program of the Commission.

The trade and foreign ministries of member states are building their staffs to deal with the Commission and Council bureaucracies, both at home and in the Committee of Permanent Representatives (COREPER), which represents member states at the Council of Ministers. One reason the merger regulation has been delayed, however, is the recognition by member state trade and competition officials that, now it is approved, they and the Council of Ministers will exert relatively little influence over Commission merger policy. Regulation 17 obliges DG-4 to consult with the competition officials of member states before nonmerger enforcement actions are begun, and the merger regulation requires analogous consultation. The consultation process is a meaningful one. Never-

8. In 1962 the member states, acting through the Council of Ministers, approved Regulation 17, the implementing legislation for antitrust enforcement. See D. G. Goyder, *EEC Competition Law* (Oxford University Press, 1988), p. 36.

9. See, for example, Michael Bartholomew, "Lobbying Brussels in Anticipation of 1992," *Wall Street Journal*, March 6, 1989, p. A12.

theless, DG-4 is free to disregard the expert advice of member states. This fact is a matter of concern, particularly to some in the Bundeskartellamt (Federal Cartel Office) in Germany, which is justly proud of its commitment to competition, its professionalism, and its long record of enforcement success.

The thirteen judges of the European Court of Justice are responsible for deciding disputes between the Community and its member states, between institutions of the Community, and between individuals and Community institutions. Until now they have decided annually some twenty-five to thirty cases of importance to EC competition policy. The court has put muscle behind the competition provisions of the Treaty of Rome, often in cases initiated in and referred by the national courts of member states for definitive treaty interpretation. It has also generally supported Commission decisions, such as issuing enforcement orders against member states to retrieve illegal state subsidies from private firms.

The Court of Justice has been criticized for failing to give sufficiently close review to complex factual submissions in competition law cases. Responding to this criticism, the Single European Act authorized the Council to create a Court of First Instance, attached to the Court of Justice, to hear certain classes of legal actions. In October 1988 the Council created the new court, giving it jurisdiction over two categories of disputes: competition cases and cases involving job-related claims by Community civil service employees. An effort was made to extend jurisdiction to cases involving the application of import trade laws but, for the present, those will still be heard by the Court of Justice. In September 1989 the Court of First Instance began its work. Its decisions will be subject to review on legal (but not factual) questions by the Court of Justice.

A final set of governmental institutions of potential importance in the competition policy process are the national courts of member states. In the United States, 90 percent of the antitrust claims brought to the courts are private actions. To date in the Community, most antitrust enforcement actions have been brought by the Commission. This balance could shift; private claims could grow; and the role of national courts could expand. In fact, it is a matter of Commission policy to encourage the expansion of the role to be played by national courts. The national courts have the authority under the Treaty of Rome to apply Articles 85 and 86 in private suits brought by individuals or enterprises against other individuals, enterprises, or even governmental agencies.[10]

It is unimaginable that Americans would grant such political power as the Commission staff enjoys to a career bureaucracy. Not surprisingly, the people of Europe increasingly expect democratic accountability by Community political and bureaucratic leaders. If the Commission is to continue to grow in effectiveness in advancing a pro-competitive policy, it will need to continue to progress in two respects: become more transparent in its decisionmaking, and become even more vocal and persuasive in publicizing the benefits of competition.[11] Faced with these demands, the EC competition policy process could look quite different by the turn of the century.

## EC Competition Policy: Central Features

Deregulation will not, by itself, ensure that large, efficient Community-wide firms will emerge to compete effectively with U.S. and Japanese rivals in the world market. European firms must also be restructured. Both objectives have received near-total endorsement from member state governments and their main interest groups.

### Deregulation

The 1992 program is the most sweeping commitment to promoting competition by deregulation that any single nation, let alone any compact of nations, has made in history. While the United States has developed an integrated market over the course of 200 years, aided by a federal constitution that restricts the rights of states to burden unduly interstate commerce, significant regulatory barriers still impede a single open U.S. market. For example, there are wide variations in state tax rates; no national restrictions on selective state subsidies; discriminatory state

10. See generally, John Temple-Lang, "EEC Competition Actions in Members States' Courts—Claims for Damages, Declarations and Injunctions for Breach of Community Antitrust Law," in Barry E. Hawk, ed., *Antitrust and Trade Policies of the European Economic Community* (New York: Fordham Corporate Law Institute, 1983), pp. 219–304.

11. DG-4 has been doing the latter each summer for the past eighteen years through the publication of an annual *Competition Report* explaining what has been accomplished in the preceding year and indicating its enforcement priorities for the future. Commissioners Sutherland and Brittan have pursued an energetic program of education through speeches and interviews. There will need to be even more of these activities in the future.

government procurement and service qualification laws; significant variations in laws regulating the responsibilities of corporations in general, and in certain industries, such as insurance and liquor distribution, in particular; and federal and state laws restricting interstate and intrastate competition in financial services.

It is simply astonishing that the governments of all twelve EC member states—whether socialist, liberal, or conservative—have agreed in principle to remove longstanding national regulatory restrictions, both by modifying or overriding hundreds of national laws and by delegating to the European Commission, the European Parliament, the Council, and the Court of Justice more control over their economies than the fifty American states have ceded to the U.S. federal government.

The role of laws in establishing and preserving initiatives is easily undervalued. The commitment to the 1992 program may be weakened, but it will not be easily abandoned, even if the coming years bring recession and trade friction. That is because the treaty establishing the European Economic Community in 1957 *required* member states to create a single internal market by January 1, 1970 (Article 8), free of distortions to competition (Article 3(f)). In 1985 the deadline was extended to the end of 1992 (Article 8A).[12] The goal, if not its timing, was foreordained as a matter of law almost two generations in advance. Member states signed on to this when they acceded to the Treaty of Rome. They renewed that commitment when they approved, unanimously, the Single European Act treaty amendment in 1987, three decades later.

The scope and pace of market reform is now facing a critical test in the legal response to "default situations"—instances where directives have been adopted by the Council of Ministers but have not been implemented at all, or not enacted by member states in proper form, by

12. Article 8A of the Rome treaty states:

"The Community shall adopt measures with the aim of progressively establishing the internal market over a period expiring on December 31, 1992. . . .

"The internal market shall comprise an area without internal frontiers in which the free movement of goods, persons, services and capital is ensured in accordance with the provisions of this Treaty."

Article 3(f) states:

"For the purposes set out in Article 2, the activities of the Community shall include, as provided in this Treaty and in accordance with the timetable set out therein:

". . . (f) the institution of a system ensuring that competition in the common market is not distorted; . . ."

national legislative bodies.[13] The Court of Justice has indicated that directives adopted by the Council, but not fully or properly implemented, give rights to individuals and enterprises against the nonimplementing state. Whether Community directives can be enforced between individuals is currently being considered by the European Court.[14] Furthermore, the Commission may take a member state to the European Court to obtain an order directing it to implement directives if consultation and negotiation between the Commission and relevant state officials have failed to accomplish a satisfactory resolution (Article 169 of the Treaty of Rome). Important litigation concerning the "default" issue, now pending before the Court of Justice, involves the Product Liability Directive. This directive imposes stricter standards of liability on corporations whose products cause injury. As of fall 1989, only Greece had satisfied the Commission with its national law implementing this directive; consequently, an infringement action has been commenced against the remaining eleven states. The firmness and dispatch with which the Commission and the court enforce this and other directives in default could significantly affect the speed of market reform. In mid-September 1989, Commissioner Bangemann sounded an alarm bell that member states were not respecting European Court decisions.[15] He cited forty-six outstanding cases of noncompliance. Bangemann has threatened, somewhat rhetorically, that if member states do not mend their ways, the Commission may propose centralized regulations more frequently, in lieu of directives. The Commission is trying to hold to the January 1, 1993, deadline. Although they probably will not meet it, delay will not lead to abandonment.

Regulations establish Community law, which supersedes member state law. Unlike directives, their effect is instantaneous, without the inter-

13. The deadline for implementation by member states has passed for sixty-eight directives adopted by the Council of Ministers, but only seven of these have entered into force in all member states in a form acceptable to the Commission. Edward Cody, "Unified European Market Seen as Threatened by Delay," *Washington Post*, September 16, 1989, p. A15.

14. For enforcement of directives by individuals against the state, see *Van Duyn* v. *Home Office* (case 41/74), December 4, 1974, *Common Mkt. Rep.* (CCH) para. 8283 (1975). The pending case considering the rights of individuals to sue other individuals pursuant to improperly or inadequately enforced directives is *D.H. Barber* v. *Guardian Royal Exchange Assurance Group* (case 262/88) (reference for a preliminary ruling from the Court of Appeal, London).

15. See generally David Buchan, "The Good, the Bad, the Indifferent," *Financial Times*, September 25, 1989, p. 18.

mediation of national legislation. Two important and well-established antitrust laws (in addition to the merger regulation) are regulations: Regulation 17 of 1962, which established the procedural framework for antitrust law enforcement, and Regulation 19 of 1965, which gives the Commission the power to grant antitrust exemptions in the form of regulations on a block or group basis, without case-by-case review, so long as certain criteria are met (such as firm size and market share). Important block exemptions exist for research and development joint ventures and specialization agreements.

The principle of mutual recognition of goods produced in one member state in the markets of the other member states, even if produced according to differing national regulatory standards, is a central pillar of deregulation and market integration. It is a principle promulgated by the European Court in the 1979 *Cassis de Dijon* case.[16] It has provided the basic support for the change in EC policy away from efforts at detailed harmonization of disparate national product and service standards, to minimal harmonization and maximum mutual recognition of diversity. Commitment to this principle lessens the imperative for an extensive program of Community-wide regulation.

Interestingly, the 1992 program proposes no change in EC antitrust law. Competition law is already sophisticated and well established. True, the merger regulation is new, but merger control was not part of the 1992 program. (A merger regulation was first proposed in 1973.) The merger regulation is mainly important as a means to supersede partial and inconsistent merger regulation at the state level (some states, most notably Italy, having no merger control law on competition grounds at all), especially of large-scale mergers. A secondary purpose is to deregulate national merger controls that, it is feared, could be applied restrictively on noncompetition grounds. The conflicts between various member states on the one hand, and the Commission on the other, relating to the merger regulation are about who should be the gatekeeper in determining market access by acquisition in a unified market.

### Restructuring: An Overview

Even if internal trade barriers were suddenly lifted, a majority of European industries would still fail to participate in a single EC market. A significant price increase—say 5 to 10 percent for basic goods and

16. *Rewe-Zentral AG* v. *Bundesmonopolverwaltung für Branntweim* (case 120/78).

services, or 15 to 25 percent for luxury items—in one member state would not, in these sectors, attract a flood of competing products from other member states at lower prices—a rough test for defining geographic markets. In this sense, there probably now exists a single European market for high-technology machinery, bulk chemicals, steel and other raw and semifinished materials; for some but not all agricultural goods; and for many but not all processed foods, cigarettes, detergents, and consumer luxury goods. Increasing the number of industries and service sectors where such sales from afar will occur is a test of, and goal for, the realization of a single European market.

To approach that goal in a wider range of industries, analysts agree there will need to be larger enterprises, better able to compete around the world and better able to realize economies of scale and scope. European firms, even in capital-intensive and highly concentrated industries, are somewhat smaller than their non-European competitors. The only outstanding exceptions are in the chemical industry, where four of the world's five top firms are European, and in aerospace (figure 6-4). Figure 6-1, produced by the EC Commission, compares the market shares of the largest U.S., Japanese, and EC manufacturing firms in their respective national markets for 1986. Among the top five and ten firms in manufacturing, the U.S. level of concentration is twice that in the Community. To reinforce the broad picture, figures 6-2 and 6-3 show that, in several basic industries, Europe exhibits significantly less or about the same industrial concentration as the United States.

Some European firms have been able to survive in concentrated, capital-intensive industries primarily because of protective government regulations and procurement policies. Many of these firms will not be able to compete profitably in a single European (let alone global) market for locomotives, turbine generators, or telephone exchanges, to cite some obvious examples.

Preoccupation with a single market implies that local, country, and regional submarkets will largely disappear. In many cases, however, these submarkets will persist for many years. In a few cases they will persist indefinitely. For example, the costs of transporting ready-mix concrete beyond 75 kilometers are so high that local markets are effectively insulated from one another. While some consumer tastes may be acquiring a pan-European character, important national preferences still exist for beverages, medications, cultural products, and beauty aids—and such market defining preferences are unlikely to disappear.

FIGURE 6–1. Market Share of the Largest Manufacturing Firms in the EC-12, Japan, and the United States, 1986

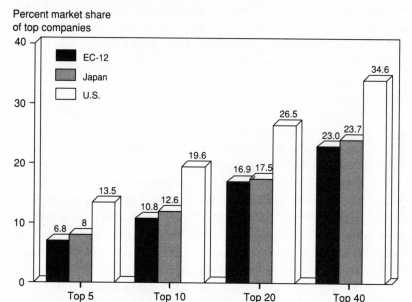

SOURCE: Alexis Jacquemin, Pierre Buigues, and Fabienne Ilzkovitz, "Horizontal Mergers and Competition Policy," *European Economy*, no. 40 (May 1989), p. 40.

FIGURE 6–2. Industries with European Concentration Lower than Japan or the United States, 1986

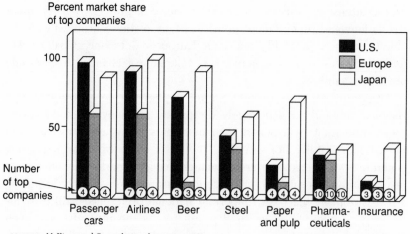

SOURCE: McKinsey and Co. analysis and estimates, 1986.

FIGURE 6–3. Industries with European Concentration Intermediate between Japan and the United States, 1986

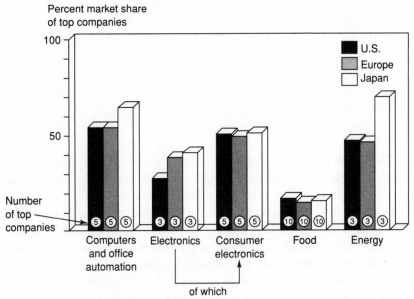

SOURCE: McKinsey and Co. analysis and estimates, 1986.

FIGURE 6–4. Industries with European Concentration Higher than Japan or the United States, 1986

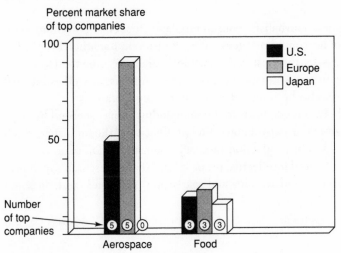

SOURCE: McKinsey and Co. analysis and estimates, 1986.

The continuing importance of submarkets lacking a "Community dimension" requires effective national competition policies that *complement* Community policy. At present, national competition law enforcement in many member states, especially the southern states and Belgium, is relatively weak. Parenthetically, submarkets are becoming a bigger problem in the United States too, as governments in the fifty U.S. states become more active in enforcing state antitrust laws (not always congruent with federal law) in an attempt to fill the vacuum left by diminished federal antitrust enforcement.

## Mergers

The competition policy of most member states and EC officials calls for greater European industrial and service concentration within the single European market. Pressure for an EC merger control law comes not so much from a desire to stop unwanted mergers that are economically beneficial as from an attempt to ensure that mergers are not impeded by either nonefficiency concerns of individual member states or a barrier of multiple and potentially inconsistent governmental merger reviews. In fact, West Germany and Britain were most concerned that the consideration of nonefficiency merger justifications should not rest with the Commission, thus giving it the power in effect to carry out industrial policy. There is also a counterpoint purpose of monitoring what goes on, served by a requirement of pre-merger notification for transactions with a Community dimension above the agreed threshold. The EC will be only the fifth sovereign with a broad antitrust pre-merger notification law. [17]

Most business journalists, consultants, and, it seems, corporate managers think of horizontal mergers—the acquisition of another firm in the same industry—as the best way to achieve dramatic growth. However, vertical mergers and strategic alliances between firms, as well as internal expansion, can also be quite attractive in certain situations.

Mergers between two firms in the same industry may succeed because new management usually knows the product and the industry. Such mergers may permit production rationalization, reduction of administrative expenses, shared intellectual property and shared research capability, the chance to consolidate sales and marketing personnel, and, in some

17. Germany was the first, in 1973, then the United States and Australia (1975), and Canada (1986).

instances, a rationalization of distributor networks. A toehold horizontal acquisition is usually a safer way to enter a new geographic market than *de novo* entry, especially if there are cultural and language barriers.

Vertical mergers entail the acquisition of upstream suppliers of raw materials, basic services, or components; or they involve the acquisition of downstream distributors or intermediate customers in the production process. They too may yield economies of scale and provide opportunities to ensure reliable supply (for example, items with exacting quality specifications) or effective distribution (for example, an eye-catching warranty program for machine tools). Vertical mergers are generally encouraged as a means of creating a unified market with larger and more efficient competitors. For the past twenty-five years U.S. antitrust authorities have rarely sought to block vertical mergers. It is not clear what the Commission's response will be. If it is committed to integrated markets, the Commission generally will be receptive to vertical mergers—except where they facilitate market dominance.

One consequence of European merger activity could be a restructuring of retailing within Europe, especially for processed food and beverage products, clothes, and other consumer goods. More than in the United States, local and national retailing in Europe is concentrated and not highly price competitive. In France, Le Clerc, Intermarche, and Carrefour heavily influence the national food distribution market. In England, there are J. Sainsbury, Tesco, and Argyll (Safeway); in the Netherlands, the Royal Ahold and Vendex Groups; and in Belgium, GB-INNO-BM and Delhaize.[18]

Excessive concentration and lack of competition in European retailing are difficult problems to solve. Land for new stores of efficient size in population centers is scarce, and local land use regulations limit new entry. Parking problems and traffic congestion limit the range of viable shopping alternatives. Some European consumers have reservations about shopping at supermarkets and seem to acquiesce in chronically high prices and poor service. Suppliers, who would like to increase sales where demand is elastic, find that retailers take supplier discounts for their own benefit. Supermarket discounting is much less frequent in Europe than in the United States.

The big national retailers are beginning to propose forming multifirm, multinational cooperatives. In May 1989 it was announced that Casino

18. See, for example, H. W. de Jong, ed., *The Structure of European Industry*, 2d rev. ed. (Neth.: Kluwer, 1988), p. 135.

of France had agreed to form a joint arrangement with Argyll and Royal Ahold. The precise nature of their proposed cooperation is unclear. At the very least it will apparently involve joint buying, and perhaps joint marketing and joint development, of new types of retail stores.[19]

There is some suggestion that the Commission may, reluctantly, approve such alliances in the hope that existing national oligopolists will be tempted to compete in other national markets. That would be a mistake. Such buyer cartels would increase the already sizable purchasing power of retailers who dominate their national submarkets. Their enhanced power would come at the expense of suppliers who are more highly motivated to expand consumer demand and promote price competition.

If retail competition does not emerge, sophisticated manufacturers invariably will seek to increase their bargaining power with established retailers by acquiring greater control over distribution. Meanwhile, maverick retailers likely will spring up, patterned after Walmart and Price Club. This combination could beneficially alter the face of retailing within European submarkets. DG-4 should pay more attention to limitations on retail competition than it has in the past, as the concept of a unified market invites the view that retailing has a Community-wide dimension.

A small number of American firms will capitalize on these trends. Coca-Cola, for example, will reportedly use much of the proceeds from its sale of Columbia Pictures to expand its investment in overseas bottlers, especially in Europe.[20] Coke has just completed a state-of-the-art canning plant in England (in a joint venture with Cadbury-Schweppes) and is building a second such plant on its own in Dunkirk, France.[21] Coke is apparently gambling that it will, within a few years, be permitted by EC competition law to serve a significantly larger volume of customers in virtually all member states from just a few highly efficient manufacturing facilities, through a network of noncompeting Coke distributors (see the section on intrabrand and interbrand competition below).

Conglomerate mergers, like ITT in the 1960s or BAT until recently,

19. "Three Retailers to Cooperate in Europe," *International Herald Tribune*, May 19, 1989, p. 15.

20. Steven Greenhouse, "U.S. Corporations Expand in Europe for '92 Prospects," *New York Times*, March 13, 1989, p. A1.

21. Betsy Morris, "Coke's Windfall from Expected Sales Is Likely to Go to Overseas Operations," *Wall Street Journal*, September 26, 1989, p. A18.

are no longer fashionable. Such firms attract corporate raiders who see the liquidation potential of underperforming divisions. Like ITT and Beatrice, many 1960s conglomerates have been pared down drastically. The one form of "conglomerate" that is thriving is the consumer goods manufacturer, such as Unilever and Procter & Gamble. These firms find synergies in the development of strong brands, and they bring persuasive merchandizing and effective distribution to a wide range of products. To the extent conglomerates are still put together by acquisition, the Commission is unlikely to challenge them.

With the announcement of the 1992 program, one would expect a significant increase in EC merger activity. This has, in fact, been the case. Table 6-1 shows a steady increase over the past four years—both for mergers between European firms in separate member states and for acquisitions of EC firms by foreign enterprises. There was a one-third increase in mergers between member states ("Community" mergers), and a threefold increase in foreign acquisitions of EC firms ("international" mergers). Community and international mergers were particularly evident in the food, chemical, metal, and transport industries. While Commission data show the number of purely national mergers between 1986–87 and 1987–88 to be essentially constant (table 6-1), this is probably a distortion of the data-gathering method employed. The Commission draws its universe from published news reports it spots. Data assembled by the French competition agency, the Directorate-General for Competition, Consumerism and the Repression of Fraud (DGCCRF), for example, indicate that French national mergers increased between 1986 and 1987 by almost 20 percent, and by 25 percent between 1987 and 1988.[22] It may be that similar increases in international mergers have occurred in other principal EC member states.

Ample opportunity still exists for further European consolidation within existing merger law standards, even in such highly concentrated industries as chemicals and electronics. Figure 6-5 shows differences in concentration levels in eleven major industries based on the market share held by the five largest firms. In none of these is further merger activity absolutely precluded by existing or proposed EC merger standards.

Market restructuring in Europe will be nowhere near "complete" by

22. Personal communication to author. See also (albeit with somewhat different figures) Edmond Abbou, "L'Evolution Récente du Mouvement de Concentration en France: Bilan, Situation Actuelle et Perspectives," *Revue de la Concurrence et de la Consommation*, no. 44 (juillet-août 1988).

TABLE 6-1. Merger Activity by EC Industrial Corporations, 1984–88

Number of mergers

| Sector | National | | | | Community | | | | International[a] | | | | Total | | | |
|---|---|---|---|---|---|---|---|---|---|---|---|---|---|---|---|---|
| | 1984–1985 | 1985–1986 | 1986–1987 | 1987–1988 | 1984–1985 | 1985–1986 | 1986–1987 | 1987–1988 | 1984–1985 | 1985–1986 | 1986–1987 | 1987–1988 | 1984–1985 | 1985–1986 | 1986–1987 | 1987–1988 |
| Food and drink | 20 | 25 | 39 | 25 | 1 | 7 | 11 | 18 | 1 | 2 | 2 | 8 | 22 | 34 | 52 | 51 |
| Chemicals, fibres, glass, ceramic wares, rubber | 25 | 23 | 38 | 32 | 23 | 28 | 27 | 38 | 5 | 6 | 6 | 15 | 53 | 57 | 71 | 85 |
| Electrical and electronic engineering, office machinery | 13 | 10 | 33 | 25 | 5 | 0 | 6 | 4 | 4 | 3 | 2 | 7 | 22 | 13 | 41 | 36 |
| Mechanical and instrument engineering, machine tools | 24 | 19 | 21 | 24 | 4 | 3 | 8 | 5 | 3 | 7 | 2 | 9 | 31 | 29 | 31 | 38 |
| Computers and data-processing equipment[b] | 2 | 1 | 2 | 2 | 0 | 0 | 0 | 1 | 1 | 0 | 0 | 0 | 3 | 1 | 2 | 3 |
| Production and preliminary processing of metals, metal goods | 13 | 14 | 15 | 28 | 3 | 1 | 4 | 9 | 1 | 2 | 0 | 3 | 17 | 17 | 19 | 40 |
| Vehicles and transport equipment | 8 | 6 | 15 | 3 | 2 | 0 | 6 | 9 | 0 | 4 | 0 | 3 | 10 | 10 | 21 | 15 |
| Wood, furniture, and paper | 10 | 18 | 17 | 24 | 5 | 4 | 7 | 6 | 3 | 5 | 1 | 4 | 18 | 27 | 25 | 34 |
| Extractive industries | 7 | 7 | 8 | 9 | 0 | 3 | 1 | 2 | 0 | 0 | 0 | 1 | 7 | 10 | 9 | 12 |
| Textiles, clothing, leather, footwear | 7 | 7 | 4 | 11 | 0 | 1 | 2 | 2 | 0 | 1 | 0 | 1 | 7 | 9 | 6 | 14 |
| Construction | 14 | 12 | 13 | 21 | 1 | 2 | 3 | 12 | 0 | 0 | 3 | 0 | 15 | 14 | 19 | 33 |
| Other manufacturing industry | 3 | 3 | 6 | 10 | 0 | 3 | 0 | 5 | 0 | 0 | 1 | 7 | 3 | 6 | 7 | 22 |
| TOTAL | 146 | 145 | 211 | 214 | 44 | 52 | 75 | 111 | 18 | 30 | 17 | 58 | 208 | 227 | 303 | 383 |

SOURCE: EC Commission, *Eighteenth Report on Competition Policy* (Luxembourg, 1989), p. 236.
a. Foreign acquisitions of EC firms.
b. In 1983–84 included under mechanical engineering.

FIGURE 6–5. EC Market Share of Five Largest Firms in Selected
Industries, 1986

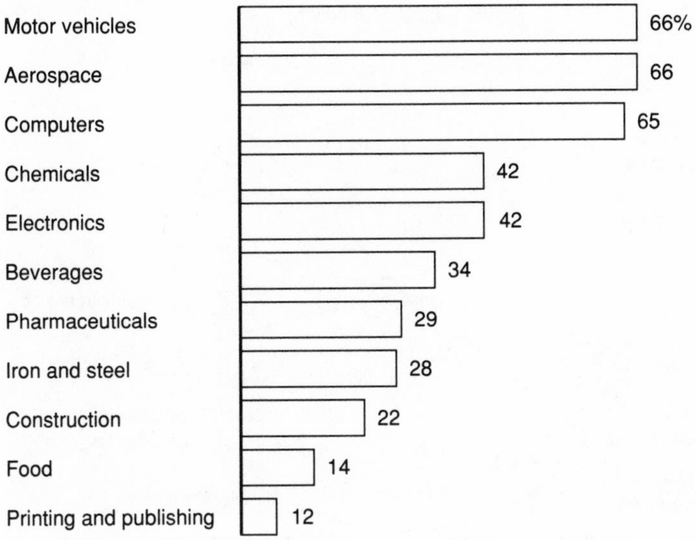

| Industry | Market Share |
|---|---|
| Motor vehicles | 66% |
| Aerospace | 66 |
| Computers | 65 |
| Chemicals | 42 |
| Electronics | 42 |
| Beverages | 34 |
| Pharmaceuticals | 29 |
| Iron and steel | 28 |
| Construction | 22 |
| Food | 14 |
| Printing and publishing | 12 |

SOURCE: Jacquemin and others, "Horizontal Mergers and Competition Policy," p. 41.

January 1993, and many merger opportunities in the Community should continue to exist for at least a decade thereafter. The Commission's positive encouragement of mergers for the purpose of promoting competition is evidenced by an EC pie chart that identifies several industries in which untapped economies of scale are thought to exist (figure 6-6). Even acquisitions by big companies are generally welcomed as a means to achieve world-class EC firms.

It is also interesting that European firms are making many more acquisitions in the United States than U.S. firms are making in Europe (see figure 6-7). In 1989 the total purchase price for U.S. acquisitions by EC firms monitored in the press ($34 billion) was six and a half times greater than the total purchase price of EC acquisitions by U.S. firms ($5.2 billion) in monitored transactions.[23] There are many possible explanations for this disparity (including the softness of the data). One is American caution about 1992. Many small and mid-sized American firms have not yet focused on market opportunities in Europe and do not have

23. *Mergers and Acquisitions Magazine*, M&A database, MLR Publishing (available on-line through Automatic Data Processing), February 12, 1990.

FIGURE 6–6. Potential Welfare Gains from Exploiting Economies of Scale

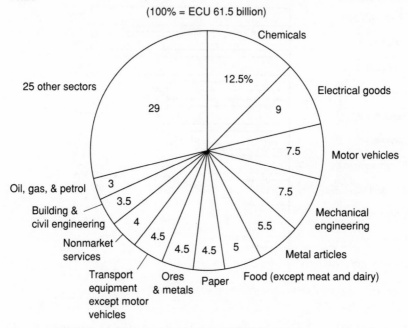

(100% = ECU 61.5 billion)

SOURCE: Michael Emerson and others, "The Economics of 1992," *European Economy*, no. 35 (Luxembourg: European Communities Directorate-General for Economic and Financial Affairs, March 1988), p. 185.
a. Total estimated gains approximately ECU 61.5 billion.

medium- or long-term 1992 business strategies.[24] My analysis suggests that they still have plenty of time to form alliances through the merger route. The big U.S. firms, of course, are already in Europe.

In broad terms the merger regulation seeks paramount EC surveillance over major mergers with a "Community dimension." It provides a safe harbor for mergers between firms with a combined market share not exceeding 25 percent of a product market in the total Common Market

24. In a survey conducted early in 1989 of senior U.S. and European executives, Booz-Allen & Hamilton reported that fewer than a third of U.S. firms have formal strategic plans for Europe 1992, and fewer than half of the U.S. executives were familiar with the Commission's 1985 White Paper on completing the internal market. On the other hand, about half of the U.S. firms surveyed already had an EC headquarters and another 11 percent were studying the possibility of establishing one. European executives, not surprisingly, were further along in planning for 1992. Paul A. Branstad and Martin M. Waldenstrom, *Europe 1992: Threat or Opportunity*, Booz-Allen & Hamilton Special Report (1989).

FIGURE 6–7. Merger Activity by EC and U.S. Firms, 1986–89

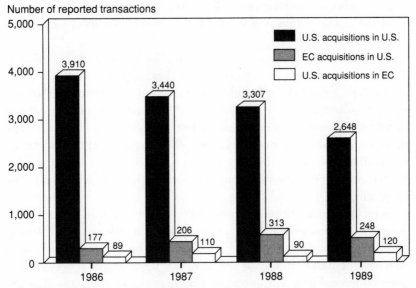

Number of reported transactions

SOURCE: *Mergers and Acquisitions Magazine*, M&A database, MLR Publishing (on-line through Automatic Data Processing), February 12, 1990.

or a substantial part of it (paragraph 15 of the preamble). Implicitly, the Commission might well deny an outright merger between two competing firms with a combined market share in excess of 30 percent, in a highly concentrated market, characterized by significant entry barriers, in which price leadership is exercised by a few powerful firms.

The merger regulation required unanimous approval of the Council of Ministers to be enacted.[25] The major battle had been over the proper scope of member state exceptions to Commission determinations based on nonefficiency grounds such as national defense, control of the media by nationals, and discouragement of corporate raiders who may, in the eyes of the national government, lack "suitable" qualifications. Differences of view could be partly compromised by providing concerned national competition authorities with an explicit role in the investigation and review of the facts of particular mergers. But the larger problem is that

25. Unanimity for the enactment of directives and regulations was generally required by Article 235 of the Treaty of Rome. As a general matter, the unanimity rule was replaced by qualified majority voting in the Single European Act; however, the merger regulation is an exception and still requires a unanimous Council vote.

some member states would give prominence to nonefficiency factors in deciding whether to disapprove some sensitive mergers, and others would limit the consideration of nonefficiency factors to the most exceptional circumstances.

Would the West German government, for example, be entitled to have the Commission, as a matter of EC law, approve a future merger of the type reflected in Daimler-Benz's recent acquisition of Messer-schmitt-Bolkow-Blohm, if Germany invoked a national security interest in having a strong German defense industry? Would it make a difference if, as was the case, the Federal Cartel Office disapproved the merger on competition grounds under German antitrust law, only to be overruled by the economics minister who had pushed the transaction from the beginning?

Some pro-competition officials in West Germany and the United Kingdom are concerned about retaining antitrust enforcement authority over national markets—even where there may be a Community dimension—in the belief, rightly or wrongly, that they may do a better job of competition enforcement down the road than the Commission. The turf battle over merger regulation thresholds is, therefore, not just between the Community as champion of competition and member states as promoters of industrial policy. Appendix 6-1 at the end of this chapter contains a summary of the new merger regulation just adopted at the beginning of 1990.

Commissioner Peter Sutherland was particularly frustrated by delays in obtaining Community merger legislation. In response, he championed the Commission's contention that a 1987 decision of theirs advances the proposition that Article 85 supports a broad program of merger enforcement against friendly merger agreements between competitors, even if neither of them holds a dominant market position. However, there seems to be little basis for applying Article 85 to review hostile takeovers that do not result in consensual takeover agreements.[26] (In transactions involving large companies, these are to be covered under the merger regulation.) The European Court has held that Article 86 (prohibiting

26. The decision held that Article 85 of the Treaty of Rome (outlawing concerted practices that distort competition) applies when one firm acquires a minority position in a competitor in a highly concentrated industry for the purpose of restricting competition between them. This finding is far short of a broad merger control mandate. *British American Tobacco and R.J. Reynolds* v. *EC Commission* (joined cases 42 and 156/84), November 17, 1987, *Common Mkt. Rep.* (CCH) para. 14,405 (1987).

the abuse of a dominant position) authorizes EC merger control where a dominant firm acquires a competitor.[27]

Until the merger regulation is in force in September, the Commission has used these positions drawn from Articles 85 and 86 to screen announced large mergers. For example, it negotiated further concessions from British Airways (BA) even after the U.K. Monopolies and Mergers Commission had approved BA's acquisition of British Caledonian Airways. It ordered BA to expand opportunities for new competing carriers to receive operating licenses and Heathrow slots for former Caledonian routes in Europe as a limitation on its otherwise likely market dominance.[28] This transaction illustrates what can be at stake in deciding who has the final say over mergers with both a Community and a national dimension.

Finally, it is worth noting that the merger regulation does not suggest that it may sometimes be appropriate to approve mergers that would tend to suppress competition in a unified EC market as a means of promoting a European "champion" big enough to compete with giant U.S. and Japanese enterprises. Indeed, Commissioner Brittan has made several speeches in which he has insisted, sharply, that

> such an approach would be profoundly misguided. Not because of any reluctance on my part to see powerful European companies facing world competition. Quite the reverse. It is misguided because companies that are allowed to operate in a monopolistic way in their own home markets, whether those are national or European, are in fact unlikely to become world beaters. Without the spur of competition in their own market they will inevitably be tempted to rely on and reinforce their dominance of that market and will not have the cutting edge needed to secure success on the world stage. Size will never be sufficient to ensure this success. And size brought about by the destruction of effective competition is likely to be a trap, rather than a spur.[29]

While the same position has been taken by U.S. courts and law enforcers in the twenty-seven years since the Supreme Court decided

27. *Europemballage Corporation* v. *EC Commission* (case 6/72), February 21, 1973, *Common Mkt. Rep.* (CCH) para. 8171 (1973).

28. EC Commission, *Eighteenth Report on Competition Policy* (Luxembourg, 1989), p. 86.

29. Sir Leon Brittan, "1992: Priorities in Competition Policy," *European Access*, April 2, 1989, p. 20.

*United States* v. *Philadelphia National Bank* in 1963,[30] the attitudes of some nonantitrust U.S. officials in the executive branch and Congress suggest that this policy may be more open to anticompetitive modification on this side of the Atlantic than in the Community.

## Strategic Alliances

The investment banking community promotes mergers and divestitures as the preferred means for restructuring firms and markets (the fees are better), even when permissible mergers are not always desirable. Mergers involve a total commitment to total integration. They frequently do not work out over time.[31]

Strategic alliances, such as technology-licensing arrangements, formal joint ventures between competitors to develop a new market where there is a high risk of failure, or more informal collaborations resulting from one company's taking an active minority shareholding in another, are alternatives to mergers that may accomplish the goals sought more directly, privately, cheaply, and with greater flexibility than a merger.

Strategic alliances have their problems too. Co-venturers often have different expectations, and conflicts are frequently exacerbated by changed circumstances. Questions of policy and day-to-day control may be hard to resolve. But, if things don't work out, separations are easier.

Strategic alliances that create a new joint venture entity not leading to the coordination of competitive behavior between the parent companies, or between them and the new entity, fall within the framework of merger notification and review under the merger regulation (Article 3.2). Other, less formal alliances will continue to be analyzed under Articles 85 and 86, subject to "block exemptions" (exemption from scrutiny of an entire category of cases).

Efficiency-enhancing joint venture arrangements are particularly important in the four industries examined in this book. Figure 6-8 shows the network of strategic alliances that General Motors Corporation has established with Japanese and European automakers (among others) in an effort to increase GM competitiveness in an increasingly globalized automobile market. U.S. antitrust authorities permitted GM to embark

---

30. *U.S.* v. *Philadelphia National Bank*, 374 U.S. 321, 83 S. Ct. 1715 (1963). See also *U.S. v. Ivaco, Inc.*, 704 F. Supp. 1409 (W.D. Mich. 1989).

31. David J. Ravenscraft and F. M. Scherer, *Mergers, Sell-offs and Economic Efficiency* (Brookings, 1987).

FIGURE 6–8. The Strategic Alliances of General Motors, 1989

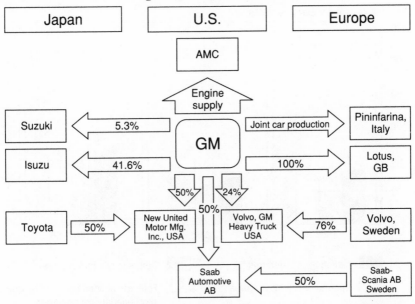

SOURCE: McKinsey and Co. research; and Bradley A. Sterz and Stephen D. Moore, "GM to Purchase 50 Percent Saab Stake for $500 Million," *Wall Street Journal*, December 18, 1989, p. 3.

on a production joint venture with Toyota (number three automaker in the world) for the production of less-expensive, high-quality cars in a California plant. On balance, the joint venture was viewed as having pro-competitive effects, even though it is hard to imagine any antitrust authority allowing an outright merger between GM and Toyota.

By the same token, strategic alliances may prove to be of even greater importance than mergers, both in promoting EC market access for U.S. firms and in upgrading EC firms to world-class status. Alliances are already important not only in the auto, semiconductor, financial services, and telecommunications industries, but also in the electronics, civil aviation, aerospace, defense, communications, computer, chemical, and pharmaceutical industries as well. Like mergers, EC joint ventures are increasing during the run-up to 1992 (see figure 6-9).

An important fact, little-known beyond a small fraternity of antitrust experts, is that there is no agreed set of standards for determining the likely competitive effect of strategic alliances between large firms that are actual or potential competitors in concentrated markets. A number of cases under both EC and U.S. law appraise the legality of joint

FIGURE 6–9. Joint Ventures in the European Community, 1985–88[a]

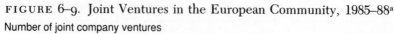

Number of joint company ventures

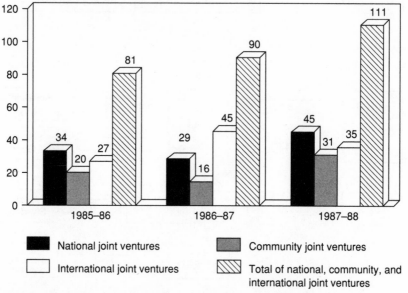

National joint ventures        Community joint ventures

International joint ventures    Total of national, community, and
                               international joint ventures

SOURCE: EC Commission, *Eighteenth Report on Competition Policy* (Luxembourg, 1989), p. 240.
a. Rate of change in total number of joint ventures between 1986 and 1987, 11.1 percent; rate of change in total number of joint ventures between 1987 and 1988, 23.3 percent.

ventures. However, each is quite limited to its individual set of facts and, taken as a whole, they do not exhibit doctrinal coherence.[32]

With current levels of concern about the need for greater productivity and innovation in the West, especially vis-à-vis Japan, it is likely that any proposed joint venture giving promise of adding something new to the marketplace, without transparently restraining trade in an existing market, will be sympathetically viewed either in Europe or in the United States. But transatlantic differences in the permissiveness of enforcement policies toward strategic alliances may generate frictions. It is too early to tell, but EC officials may be *more* critical of the claims for pro-competitive benefits of proposed alliances than U.S. federal authorities. It could happen, for example, that EC authorities would block an alliance between British Telecom and American Telephone and Telegraph Company on antitrust grounds; and U.S. authorities would view the denial

32. See, for example, Conference Board, "Antitrust Issues for a New Administration," Research Bulletin 223 (New York, 1989), p. 12. See also Joseph F. Brodley, "Joint Ventures and Antitrust Policy," *Harvard Law Review*, vol. 95 (1982), pp. 1521–90.

as a disguised means of curtailing AT&T prospects in the single European market.

There is a basic conceptual difference between Community and U.S. antitrust law. Article 85 (the analogue of Section 1 of the Sherman Act) prohibits all agreements that restrict competition in intra-Community trade (Article 85-(1)), unless a specific exemption is granted (under Article 85-(3)) because the restriction is reasonable and outweighed by beneficial effects. As a result, in most cases where two firms agree to forgo competition to the extent necessary to collaborate in a strategic alliance within an EC jurisdiction, they must obtain specific approval of the transaction or risk an antitrust violation. Under U.S. law, only unreasonable restraints of trade are illegal. No specific governmental clearance is required for strategic alliances between competitors. If the antitrust authorities disapprove of the strategic alliance, they must seek court disapproval.

The EC approach is more regulatory than the American. It puts a greater burden upon the staff of DG-4 to review hundreds of joint ventures each year, many of great complexity. One consequence is that there can be long delays before formal approval or disapproval is given—sometimes two or more years. If the parties are willing to accept less legal certainty than that afforded by an exemption, they can request a "comfort" letter from the Commission. While not binding on national courts or arbitrators, the comfort letter generally states that the Commission is "closing the file" without acting against the alliance.[33] This EC approach requires substantial DG-4 staffing if competition regulation is not to become a market barrier in its own right. In the past the Commission has pointed to the creation of categories of block exemptions that do not require case-by-case clearance in justification of its regulatory approach.

---

33. The joint venturers can seek either a formal comfort letter, issued after publication, in the *Official Journal*, of the essential terms of the agreements or an informal comfort letter issued without any such publication. The formal comfort letter generally carries more weight with courts and arbitrators but has the disadvantage of publicly disclosing the material terms of the scrutinized agreements. The informal comfort letter, on the other hand, provides security against an intervention by the Commission and has the additional advantage of being granted more rapidly than the formal comfort letter. However, in *Procureur* v. *Bruno Giry and Guerlain S.A.*, 1980 ECR 2327 (Court of Justice, cases 253/78 and 1 to 37/79), July 10, 1980, *Common Mkt. Rep.* (CCH) para. 8712, the European Court upheld the rejection of the authority of a comfort letter by a French national court that found that a joint arrangement acceptable to the Commission was nonetheless a violation of Article 85.

However, strategic alliances are too varied and fact-specific and involve firms of too great a size to make a block exemption useful.

## Anticartel Enforcement

Even if politicians and the public are generally enthusiastic about the potential benefits of greater competition, some business executives are privately ambivalent. Outright cartels, and the collusive exchange of price information, have been a comfortable way of life for many European industries throughout this century. The Commission has enjoyed only modest success in breaking up cartels and other collusive arrangements. In fact, only in this decade has the Commission shifted its enforcement priority from attacking vertical restraints upon intrabrand competition to attacking horizontal collusion. The Commission now seems eager to attack European members of European cartels, and a recent Court of Justice decision increases the Commission's enforcement powers in this regard.[34] But lack of resources undermines the Commission's will.

In the last year there were only two enforcement actions against Community-wide cartels. They involved an aggregate of twenty-three large firms in one important industry—thermoplastic products. The combined level of fines imposed was roughly ECU 60 million.[35] While the fines are large by Community or U.S. governmental standards ($1 million per firm per violation), they are not large by comparison with awards and settlements in comparable large private U.S. antitrust treble-damage lawsuits. In one recent U.S. case, damages were assessed against four plywood manufacturers in the amount of $367 million.[36] Even for these EC plastic cartels, one may ask whether the level of fines was sufficient to deter future cartel activity. In the United States an even more potent deterrent to cartel activity by large firms than treble damages is the risk that senior executives will go to jail if caught participating in price-fixing conspiracies. No such criminal deterrence exists under Community law.

A sensitive subject is whether the Commission is equally committed

34. The decision in the *Hoechst* case, arising out of plastics cartel investigations, increases the power of DG-4 officials to conduct effective "dawn raids" on the files of target companies under investigation. Tim Dickson, "Court Backs Investigative Powers for Commission," *Financial Times*, September 22, 1989, p. 1.

35. See William Darkins, "Victory for the Cartel Busters," *Financial Times*, April 12, 1989, p. 10.

36. *In Re Plywood Antitrust Litigation*, 76 F.R.D. 570 (E.D. La. 1976), *aff'd*, 655 F.2d 627 (5th Cir. 1981), *cert. dismissed*, 103 S. Ct. 3100 (1983).

to enforcing EC antitrust law against Community as against foreign enterprises. For many years an arguably disproportionate number of antitrust prosecutions were filed against EC firms with U.S. parents. Was prosecutorial discretion "tilted" against strong U.S. firms in Europe? Perhaps not. In the late 1970s, when U.S. antitrust enforcement against foreign firms located outside U.S. boundaries increased, several European governments made similar accusations against American enforcers. In that episode, U.S. firms were in fact sued more frequently than foreign members of international cartels. For reasons of scanty evidence and jurisdictional conflicts, U.S. prosecutive discretion was probably tilted in favor of foreign firms. Similar considerations have likely influenced the Commission. The roster of firms prosecuted in the plastics cartel cases was distinctly European. Only two of the twenty-three firms prosecuted were American, for the reasons cited, and also because U.S. firms are highly sensitive to the legal dangers of cartel conspiracies.

In September 1988 the European Court, in the *Wood Pulp* cases,[37] issued its most important decision to date on the extraterritorial application of EC competition (and other) law to reach conduct by foreign persons outside the territory of the Community. It holds squarely that anticompetitive agreements by, for example, U.S. firms operating in the United States to restrict direct sales into and within the Community will be subject to EC jurisdiction. Indirect involvement, even perhaps agreeing outside the EC to exclude goods from sale into the EC, are not, under this decision, necessarily subject to such jurisdiction. At present, therefore, EC law has an extraterritorial scope, but it is not yet as extensive as that under U.S. law. Nonetheless, potential jurisdictional conflicts with U.S. legal jurisdiction and with U.S. political interests are likely to increase as EC law is further clarified and applied. U.S. companies exporting to Europe, especially if acting jointly with U.S. competitors in export trading associations, need to consider carefully the application of EC antitrust law to their U.S. export activities.

The enforcement problem increases in an environment of deregulation. Regulated markets legitimate collusion among the regulated. When regulatory restrictions are lifted, it is tempting to engage in business as usual. At present there is no indication that the Commission plans a large increase in DG-4 staffing to police cartel practices in a unified

37. A. Ahlström Osakeyhtiö v. EC Commission (Wood Pulp cases) (joined cases 89, 104, 114, 116, 117, 125–29/85), September 27, 1988, Common Mkt. Rep. (CCH) para. 14,491 (1988).

market. Without such an increase, private cartelization and collusion is likely to continue and may even grow as a problem for competition policy. This situation poses a particular threat to American firms. Those already well established in Europe will still tend to be inhibited from participating in EC cartels by their U.S. experience and values. New American entrants may be further handicapped by the lack of network relationships that would avert discriminatory behavior by their suppliers and customers—for example, a quasi-boycott inspired by the cartel against new entrants.

The formulation of new national health and safety standards, pursuant to the 1992 program, provides fresh opportunities for collusive arrangements at the expense of vigorous (especially foreign) competitors. Foreign firms may be particularly disadvantaged by standard-setting collusion because often they do not participate on an equal footing in the relevant standard-setting bodies. This issue is illustrated by a deregulated standard-setting practice that occurred in Belgium in 1980. The Belgian government conferred statutory responsibilities on local members of a washing machine and dishwasher trade association, in conjunction with a water supply trade association, to certify appliances that could be legally connected to Belgian public water supplies. The European Court found that certificates were provided on a discriminatory basis to exclude low-cost imports.[38]

Collusion in standard-setting has been a long-standing problem in the United States as well.[39] In recent years it has not received much public enforcement attention here or in Europe. It should receive more. The best antidote to collusion can probably be found in the mutual recognition of appropriate national standards, both within the Community and between the Community and its trading partners. As the EC-1992 program emphasizes, the mutual recognition approach should be followed to the maximum possible extent.

The Commission will usually investigate any complaint about cartel (or other anticompetitive) behavior brought to its attention by a private person. At the beginning of 1989, there were 3,451 cases pending, of which 2,909 were applications or notifications (376 made in 1988), 357

38. *IAZ International Belgium SA* v. *EC Commission* (cases 96-102, 104, 105, 108, 110/82) November 8, 1983, *Common Mkt. Rep.* (CCH) para. 14,023 (1983). See also D. G. Goyder, *EEC Competition Law* (1988), pp. 340–41.

39. See, for example, *Allied Tube & Conduit Corp.* v. *Indian Head, Inc.*, 108 S. Ct. 1931 (1988), a suit challenging an alleged conspiracy by manufacturers of electrical conduit made of steel, to deny National Electric Code certification to makers of plastic conduit, not dismissed on state action grounds.

were complaints from firms (83 made in 1988), and 185 were proceedings initiated by the Commission on its own (44 begun in 1988). The pending caseload remains the same as compared with the beginning of 1988.[40] When one considers that key Commission documents relating to a proposed or announced case must be translated and published in nine languages, significant nonenforcement and noncompliance is likely. The interim remedy for U.S. firms may be self-help, taking the initiative to enforce Community antitrust law in national courts, or to provide for antitrust enforcement in contractual relations by arbitration. The potential exists. So far, few European firms have availed themselves of the opportunity except, to some extent, in disputes between suppliers and distributors.

### Intrabrand and Interbrand Competition

Over the past thirty years, the main difference between U.S. and EC competition policy has been significantly greater Community concern with vertical restrictions imposed by manufacturers on their distributors, and especially restrictions on parallel imports of the same branded product into one member state from a supplier in another member state of the Community. This set of issues relates to what is known as intrabrand competition. During the years when the single market initiative stagnated, the Commission sought to force the free flow of goods into and out of national markets by declaring absolutely illegal agreements that defined exclusive national sales territories and prohibited the transshipment of the same brands from neighboring states.[41]

By contrast, in 1977 the U.S. Supreme Court said that territorial restrictions on intrabrand competition in U.S. markets were not categorically prohibited. Instead, they could be justified if, on balance, they tended to help smaller firms compete more effectively against larger horizontal competitors—that is to say, if the benefits of resulting interbrand competition outweighed the diminution of intrabrand competition.[42] Over the past twelve years, U.S. judge-made law has moved even further away from concern with promoting intrabrand competition. The currently prevailing U.S. view—though not a matter of consensus—is

40. EC Commission, *Eighteenth Report on Competition Policy*, p. 62.
41. The leading case establishing this principle is *Establissements Consten SA* v. *EC Commission* (cases 56 and 58/64), July 13, 1966, *Common Mkt. Rep.* (CCH) para. 8046 (1966).
42. *Continental T.V. Inc.* v. *G.T.E. Sylvania Inc.*, 433 U.S. 36 (1977).

that exclusive territories that prevent intrabrand competition can generally be justified because they strengthen firms and make them better able to compete against other brands. In this view, discounters who transship from another territory are seen as unreliable "free riders" who undermine the incentives for authorized distributors to put effort and money into effective brand marketing and after-sale service. Camera discounters in Manhattan who import branded Japanese cameras from clandestine transshippers in Asia or the Caribbean, in violation of supplier policy, have fared well in U.S. courts, enabling Americans to buy such cameras at a 20 percent discount.[43] Because *import* transshipping does not promote a single internal market, this kind of transshipping from outside the EC into it can, in contrast, be more easily prevented, even though it promotes intrabrand competition.[44]

The Commission is familiar with changing U.S. attitudes toward intrabrand competition. In Europe intrabrand competition is still almost universally regarded as desirable. The emerging debate is over how much of it and what particulars can be sacrificed to the promotion of interbrand competition. There is increasing awareness that, as a single market becomes a reality, transshipments are not so necessary as a stimulus to integration. Moreover, the goal of facilitating the creation of large, efficient European firms—better able to compete in world markets and better able to cut costs to consumers by realizing economies of scale in the European market—may conflict with the traditional EC enforcement policy against vertical restrictions.

A watershed development was the Court of Justice decision in the *Pronuptia* case in 1986.[45] There, the court upheld a franchise agreement providing an exclusive right to sell trademarked wedding dresses within three local German markets, notwithstanding that the agreement restricted both the franchisor and the franchisee in making sales to third parties. The court recognized that such franchise agreements (1) benefit

43. *K Mart Corp.* v. *Cartier, Inc.*, 108 S. Ct. 1811 (1988).

44. See *EMI Records Ltd.* v. *CBS Grammofon A/S* (case 86/75), June 15, 1976, *Common Mkt. Rep.* (CCH) para. 8351 (1976); *EMI Records Ltd.* v. *CBS Schallplatten GmbH* (case 96/75), June 15, 1976, *Common Mkt. Rep.* (CCH) para. 8352 (1976); *EMI Records Ltd.* v. *CBS United Kingdom Ltd.* (case 51/75) June 15, 1976, *Common Mkt. Rep.* (CCH) para. 8350 (1976); and *Polydor Ltd.* v. *Harlequin Record Shops Ltd.* (case 270/80), February 9, 1982, *Common Mkt. Rep.* (CCH) para. 8806 (1982).

45. *Pronuptia de Paris GmbH* v. *Pronuptia de Paris Irmgard Schillgalis* (case 161/84) January 28, 1986, *Common Mkt. Rep.* (CCH) para. 14,245 (1986).

franchisors who can extend their markets without having to make prohibitive capital investments; (2) benefit franchisees who can gain important retailing know-how and access to goods that are effectively marketed and advertised; and (3) benefit the consumer who obtains quality assurances, the benefits of scale economies, and local vendors able to provide after-sale service.

Following on the reasoning of this decision, the Commission issued a block exemption for distribution and service franchise agreements, effective February 1989.[46] It continues to protect intrabrand competition to the following extent: franchisees may not be required to refuse to sell their products to other franchisees or retail customers who come into their exclusive territory from another territory to make a purchase. Other franchisees, however, may be prohibited from soliciting customers or setting up distribution operations outside their exclusive territory.

Despite the holding in Pronuptia, Barry Hawk has concluded that the EC's goal of market integration will continue to make "EEC competition policy toward vertical restraints radically different from U.S. antitrust policy."[47] This is the conventional view.[48] Hawk could be right, and the Commission may well continue to campaign broadly against intrabrand restraints justified by the long distance that still must be traveled to break artificial national market boundaries within the Community.

While easier politically, a rearguard campaign against exclusive dealerships will retard development of a single competitive market. Disallowing restrictions on transshipments, even when they achieve the benefits of broader and cheaper distributing found in the Pronuptia case will, for example, preclude Orangina from selling its soft drinks at a lower price in, say, Portugal and Greece, to develop consumer awareness there to a point enabling a single marketing strategy throughout the EC. Under existing EC doctrine, such low-price Orangina will find its way to France where it will undermine French distribution at normal markups. Therefore Orangina is likely to refrain from developing a single Com-

46. Regulation 4087/88, issued November 30, 1988, O.J. 1988 L359/46, Common Mkt. Rep. (CCH) para. 2767.

47. Barry E. Hawk, "The American Antitrust Revolution: Lessons for the EEC?" European Competition Law Review, vol. 9 (1988), p. 75.

48. See, for example, Bastiaan van der Esch, "EC Rules on Undistorted Competition and U.S. Antitrust Laws: The Limits of Compatibility," in Barry E. Hawk, ed., North American and Common Market Antitrust and Trade Laws (New York: Fordham Corporate Law Institute, 1989), pp. 18–29.

munity-wide market for its product. This outcome is properly criticized by Dan Oliver, the past chairman of the U.S. Federal Trade Commission.[49]

But several U.S. companies will find their interests served by trying to persuade European officials that some vertical restrictions can promote consumer welfare and the single market. U.S. franchisors, especially, have more experience than most European firms in establishing and maintaining large, efficient, cost-cutting distribution networks. Dan Oliver, however, goes too far in saying that Community *competition* policies may provide the means to make a "Fortress Europe" out of EC-1992. EC policy toward vertical restraints is likely to move eventually toward the U.S. norm because that norm encourages distributional efficiencies that promote a single market. But it will take time to change the conventional wisdom.

### Marketing and Consumerism

Europe is behind both the United States and Japan in appreciating the importance of marketing. There is less consumer testing and research, less follow-through on technological innovation, less sensitivity to what the consumer wants. Until recently, European consumers raised little objection to poor retail service, minimal retail price competition, unhealthy by-products like auto emission pollution, or cozy relationships between governmental officials and industry representatives. We are beginning to see change. How broadly, deeply, and quickly consumerism develops remains to be seen. Regional and cultural differences are important. There is more consumerism in the north than the south. It is nourished by a broad middle class with leisure time.

Assuming regulatory barriers are removed, one can predict more sophisticated marketing will inevitably come. In the consumer goods sectors, U.S. and Japanese companies will push the development of more extensive data bases of consumer preferences. Management consulting, polling, and advertising service firms will help companies develop regional and Community-wide marketing strategies. Clear brand identification, careful quality control, and aggressive trademark protection and promotion will all help create new consumer demand where it did not previously exist. Today's Europe-wide demand for Coca-Cola, Pepsi, Levi's, Reebok, and Nike products was not anticipated thirty years ago.

49. Daniel Oliver, "Antitrust as a 1992 Fortress," *Wall Street Journal*, April 24, 1989, p. A14.

This forecast does not mean that European tastes will homogenize into a uniform low common denominator of products and services—part of the horrified vision of Ortega y Gasset.[50] Again, drawing on recent U.S. experience, more knowledgeable and affluent consumers will generate more diversity of demand. Niche markets will emerge, mature, and subdivide.[51] New consumer demands will do as much as supply reconfigurations to restructure markets.

## Industrial Policy

Industrial policy is a concept with many connotations. It encompasses what the state does to help individual companies, industries, or regions to remain or become more competitive. The 1992 program explicitly declares that a paramount goal is to make European industry more competitive within the EC and in global markets. If the notion is that European firms will be strengthened, not by an industrial policy of state assistance, but merely by the bracing tonic of competitive markets themselves, then the goals of competition and a stronger EC industrial base are not in conflict.

While there has been relatively little discussion at this level of generality, many member state and EC officials probably favor substantial state intervention, especially through financial aid, to assist selected European firms in high-technology industries like telecommunications, semiconductors, and electronics, where dramatic economic growth is expected. They also want aid to lessen social dislocation in certain mature industries like coal, transport, and shipbuilding, where market forces alone could lead to surging unemployment and widespread social suffering in already depressed regions. More likely than not, industrial policy will conflict with the goal of competition.

### State Aid

Since the Treaty of Rome was adopted, the Commission, through the work of DG-4, has exercised responsibility for monitoring industrial policy grants by member state authorities. State aid that threatens to distort competition, by favoring certain enterprises or certain goods, violates Article 92 insofar as it affects inter-Community trade. Article 93

50. Jose Ortega y Gasset, *The Revolt of the Masses* (W.W. Norton, 1932).
51. For a reference to the importance of niche markets, see Tom Peters, "Tomorrow's Companies," *Economist*, March 4, 1989, p. 20.

gives the Commission the power to monitor member state aid and nullify any in violation. This power has been enforced with considerable vigor, and Sir Leon Brittan has stated on several occasions that he intends to increase this enforcement effort. In May 1989, for example, the Commission ruled that Finmeccanica had received approximately $425 million in illegal subsidies from the Italian government in connection with its sale of Alfa Romeo to Fiat. The Italian government was directed to obtain a refund. Similarly, in November 1989 the Commission put a stop to massive French assistance to Renault.[52]

State aid takes many forms: grants, tax reductions, tax deferrals, governmental equity participation, soft loans, and loan guarantees. In December 1988 the Commission published a white paper, a *First Survey on State Aids in the European Community.* It recognized that the Commission had not been receiving sufficient information about the full range of member state aid and, therefore, could not meet its monitoring and enforcement duties. According to the white paper, member states spend approximately ECU 100 billion annually on state subsidies. This figure represents 3 percent of EC gross domestic product, more than $2,000 per person engaged in manufacturing.[53] Most of this aid is provided to "crisis sectors," declining industries for which it is difficult even to contend that present anticompetitive effects may be outweighed by increased long-term competitiveness. The Commission has become more and more skeptical about the size and duration of crisis aid.

The Commission is uncertain also about the merit of aid to "growth sectors," aid to research and development programs, and across-the-board assistance. It suggests that aid to growth sectors may be appropriate when made on a Community-wide basis because then there is no effect on intra-EC trade.[54] Article 92 distinguishes between selective aid and aid that applies "uniformly across the economy," in a nondiscriminatory manner, such as broad-based charges to finance social benefits.[55] While recognizing that general aid may distort competition in violation of the Treaty of Rome (Articles 101 and 102), the Commission nonetheless

52. For the Fiat case, see *Wall Street Journal,* June 1, 1989, p. A26. For the Renault case, see "Commission Condemns France over Aid to Renault," *Common Market Reporter,* November 30, 1989, p. 5.

53. "Brussels Faces Tough Task in Controlling State Subsidies," *1992—The External Impact of European Unification* (Washington, June 1989), p. 5.

54. EC Commission, *First Survey on State Aids in the European Community* (Luxembourg, June 1985), p. 3.

55. Ibid., p. 5.

asserts that "it is not the aim of competition policy to try to remove fundamental differences between Member States' cost structures which contribute to the wider economic and social framework within which firms operate in each Member State. Indeed, to do so would undermine the basis for mutually beneficial trade."[56] What I take from this passage is that the Commission does not seek to remove broad-gauged state aids, even though they may alter the economic framework of production. However, relatively accessible state aid to induce foreign investment into the Community is likely to be phased out as a practice that discriminates against existing investment.

By giving the Commission explicit responsibility for curbing anticompetitive state aid, the EC constitution expresses, once again, a more deeply rooted legal commitment to a pro-competitive policy than U.S. law gives to U.S. antitrust authorities. Subsidies by U.S. federal and state authorities are legally protected state action, beyond the mandate of U.S. antitrust concern, whatever their impact on competition. By contrast, U.S. firms that find themselves the victims of discriminatory member state aid in EC markets should be able to enlist Commission assistance in securing its removal. But such firms will get little help *legally* attacking aid granted by Community authorities pursuant to the Treaty of Rome, especially where this aid is targeted to promote joint research and development, or even joint production in high-technology industries. Such aid would have to be opposed *politically*.

## Community Aid Targeted to Key Industries

There is a temptation, almost irresistible to many bureaucrats (and their political masters), to be entrepreneurs, to identify firms and industries that can be "turned around" by governmental assistance and made into profitable enterprises. Occasionally this temptation is resisted. Often it is not. Usually it does not work out well.[57] But hope persists in both Europe and the United States that "this time it will be done right."

56. Ibid., p. 7.
57. U.S. Commerce Secretary Mosbacher's plan to fund U.S. high-definition television (HDTV) development is a recent example of temptation resisted. See John Burgess and Evelyn Richards, "Commerce to Drop Role in HDTV," *Washington Post*, September 13, 1989, p. C1. On unsuccessful assistance, see, for example, recent claims that the U.S. government has cost taxpayers and IBM's U.S. competitors dearly in awarding federal computer contracts on a no-competitive-bid basis. Calvin Sims, "U.S. Agency Accused of Favoring I.B.M.," *New York Times*, September 19, 1989, p. D2. See also Mark Hunter, "France's Grand Computer Plan in Shambles," *Washington Post*, March 19, 1989, p. H8.

At present the Community is supporting some seventy joint research and development programs in high-technology industries. So far, virtually all appear to be open to participation by the European manufacturing and research subsidiaries of U.S. firms, on a nondiscriminatory basis, except perhaps for the JESSI project, to which IBM has been seeking access; the issue has not yet been resolved.[58] Even if most of these collaborative ventures do not exclude American firms doing business in Europe, they do exclude those who would export to European markets.

As this is written in early 1990, it is by no means certain that the Community will adopt more interventionist industrial policies for high-technology industry, or will be quicker to relax antitrust standards, than will the United States.[59] On both sides of the Atlantic, policy is being shaped in darkness: analysts know little about the likely competitive effects of large government-backed industry collaborations. Whatever those effects, it is widely suggested that U.S. and European high-technology firms should join forces in the semiconductor, computer, and electronics industries in an international collaboration to meet Japanese competition.[60] Within Europe industrial alliances seem even more attractive as a means of closing the technology gap vis-à-vis Japanese and U.S. firms.

Just because of the policy momentum for high-technology collaboration, DG-4 should assume greater responsibility for monitoring industrial targeting, and Commissioner Brittan should ensure that Commission policies are formed only after competition considerations have been taken into account. In the past, especially in the days of Viscount Etienne Davignon, there was powerful resistance to DG-4 playing a significant role in Commission industrial policy. Observers will learn if that changes in the new 1992 climate.

### Corporate Takeover Restrictions

A recent wave of hostile tender offers for publicly traded EC companies—for example, the successful acquisition of Plessey by an alliance

58. JESSI, the Joint European Submicron Silicon project, is expected to receive several billion dollars' worth of government assistance over the next several years to develop silicon process technology for very large scale integrated circuits.

59. For example, Sematech, the U.S. semiconductor industry's research corporation, which is expected to receive several hundred million dollars of congressional grants over the next several years, excludes all non-U.S.-owned firms from participation.

60. See, for example, Andrew Pollack, "U.S.-Europe Technology Union Urged," New York Times, July 24, 1989, p. D1.

between Siemens and General Electric Company of England, the unsuccessful attempt by Minorco to acquire Consolidated Gold Fields (which, once in play, was then acquired by the Hanson Trust), and the campaign by Sir James Goldsmith to acquire BAT—has alarmed many national and EC officials. The techniques of the hostile takeover were developed in the United States and enthusiastically exported by U.S. investment bankers, accountants, and lawyers. But, as these examples show, to date most hostile tender offers are occurring in England and do not involve American or Japanese companies. Last year, in value terms, 73 percent of takeovers in Europe were of British companies. Of the twenty-six hostile takeovers recorded, twenty-three were in the United Kingdom.[61] English companies are particularly vulnerable because the Takeover Panel of the London Stock Exchange forbids poison-pill takeover defenses in corporate charters, and English law and custom are not as hostile to takeovers as the laws and practices of many continental states.

A recent study by the accounting firm Coopers and Lybrand reportedly supports the case of the British government that major barriers exist to potential bidders in all EC states except the United Kingdom and, to a lesser extent, France. The British government intends to submit a report to the Commission that will draw conclusions similar to those of Coopers and Lybrand and demand takeover reforms throughout the Community.[62] Nevertheless, recent takeover activity could prompt EC adoption of certain potent anti-takeover devices that already exist under Dutch, German, and Italian law, to the detriment of potential purchasers.

National anti-takeover legislation and stock ownership arrangements vary widely among EC member states. In West Germany, for example, giant banks and insurance companies hold large blocks of voting stock in major German companies; this drastically limits their attractiveness as takeover targets. Dutch companies are protected by laws permitting special voting rights for large block shareholders, who can veto an unwanted offer. The British government retains sufficient stock interests in denationalized companies, plus controls on foreign ownership, to ensure against unwanted change in control. However, when Ford declared its intention to acquire Jaguar, the British government refrained from using its "golden shares" in Jaguar to block transfer of ownership of that prestigious company to the English subsidiary of an American parent.

61. Lucy Kellaway, "Brussels to Ease Takeover Barriers within Europe," *Financial Times*, November 24, 1989, p. 1.
62. Ibid.

Several EC draft directives on company law deal with the cross-border restructuring of public companies in the Community. Among other aims, they seek:

—to ensure early disclosure when a major (at least 10 percent) holding in a listed company is acquired or sold;[63]

—to reduce bureaucratic delays in governmental approvals for cross-border mergers;[64]

—to protect the rights of shareholders and creditors against precipitate action;[65]

—to require a person acquiring $33\frac{1}{3}$ percent of the voting rights of a public company to bid for all the securities in that company at a uniform price;[66]

—to give member states the authority to prevent foreign takeovers when the Commission has determined that reciprocal access is being denied to EC companies seeking to make foreign acquisitions.[67]

This last provision is not likely to be triggered against U.S. takeovers in Europe, unless the U.S. government unexpectedly begins to employ the 1988 Exon-Florio amendment (giving the president the authority to block foreign acquisitions of U.S. firms on national security grounds) in a free-wheeling fashion to block foreign acquisitions.[68] From a European vantage, however, the U.S. Department of Transportation's reservations about substantial KLM participation in a joint venture that acquired Northwest Airlines, and BA's proposed participation in a multiparty tender offer for United Airlines, were anticompetitive.

In the realm of public policy toward takeovers, many questions remain

63. Proposal for Eleventh Council Directive based on Treaty Article 54(3)(g) concerning disclosure requirements in respect of branches opened in a member state by certain types of companies governed by the law of another state (as amended), *Official Journal of the European Communities*, no. 89/C105/08 (Luxembourg, April 21, 1988), pp. 6–12 [hereafter *O.J. Eur. Comm.*].

64. Proposal for Tenth Directive based on Treaty Article 54(3)(g) concerning cross-border mergers of public limited companies, *O.J. Eur. Comm.*, no. 89/C23/08 (January 25, 1985), pp. 11–15.

65. Ibid.

66. Commission proposal for a Thirteenth Council Directive on Company Law concerning take-over and other general bids, *O.J. Eur. Comm.*, no. 89/C64/07 (March 14, 1989), pp. 8–14.

67. Ibid.

68. Personal communication to author. The Committee on Foreign Investment in the United States (CFIUS), chaired by the U.S. Treasury Department, has reviewed more than 280 acquisitions since Exon-Florio was enacted. In about six cases, the sponsors made modifications at the suggestion of CFIUS. So far, only one or two cases have been blocked.

to be answered. Is it anticompetitive to set regulatory standards that discourage *highly* leveraged buyouts? Is it anticompetitive to favor potential purchasers with a proven record of management experience over so-called corporate raiders and liquidators? These are competition policy issues for the 1990s in Europe and, some believe, in the United States too. If policy evolves in a parallel fashion on both sides of the Atlantic, accusations of de facto discrimination are less likely to arise. Such harmony is unlikely to exist, however, if decisions like one reportedly made recently by France's Defense Minister, Jean-Pierre Chevenement, become the norm. He justified rejecting advice from the French navy that France purchase U.S.-made F-18 fighters on the grounds that keeping France's aviation industry healthy is a reasonable national security consideration.[69]

## External Trade Policy

In the United States the question is asked whether 1992 will build a Europe of moats and drawbridges, if not a fortress. In Europe the question is whether the U.S. Omnibus Trade and Competitiveness Act of 1988 (1988 Trade Act) foreshadows future U.S. protectionism.[70] Each federation shares a fear of being victimized by the other. Each has responded to its own fear by creating the trade tools necessary to "reciprocate" if victimized. The United States established the so-called Section 301 remedy in the Trade Act of 1974 to counter unfair trade practices; the Community responded with the New Commercial Policy Instrument in 1984.[71] The United States raised the stakes with "Super 301" in the 1988 Trade Act. From such fears, perceptions, and retaliatory responses, mutual aggression is often provoked.

Reciprocity in international trade is used to mean even-handed concessions as a way to promote freer trade. More recently there have been some, on both sides of the Atlantic, who mean by reciprocity something akin to "an eye for an eye."[72] When retaliatory reciprocity is

69. Edward Cody, "French Turn Down U.S. F-18s," *Washington Post*, December 23, 1989, p. A16.
70. See, for example, Resolution of the European Parliament on Protectionism in Trade Relations between the European Community and the United States of America, *O.J. Eur. Comm.*, Doc. A2-89/88, no. C187 (July 18, 1988), pp. 238–43.
71. Council Regulation 2641/84 adopted September 17, 1984, *O.J. Eur. Comm.*, no. L252 (September 20, 1984), pp. 1–6.
72. See Keith A. J. Hay and B. Andrei Sulzenko, "U.S. Trade Policy and 'Reciprocity,'" *Journal of World Trade Law*, vol. 16 (December 1982), pp. 471–79.

justified as a means to promote international competitiveness and free trade, it recalls the 1960s' rhetoric about "killing people, if necessary, to liberate them." Retaliatory trade actions impose, at least in the short run, restraints on commerce. The empirical question is whether retaliatory threats and retaliatory actions lead to market opening or counterretaliation. If counterretaliation is the outcome, competition is harmed in the long run as well.

Retaliation is only one dimension where external trade policy may conflict with competition policy. There are many others, especially trade policy's preoccupation with producer welfare and competition policy's preoccupation with consumer welfare. A literature is emerging to debate whether antitrust and import trade laws are fundamentally and necessarily antithetical.[73] For reasons discussed elsewhere, they are currently in fundamental conflict, but this state of affairs is not inevitable.[74]

Unrestricted imports promote internal market competition. Restrictions on imports limit competition. Yet both the U.S. and EC governments have been willing to permit many more exceptions in their international than in their domestic competition policies. This disparity is justified politically: "safeguards" are a necessary safety valve in times of import surges and domestic economic distress, if free trade is to be preserved over time. Exceptions are also justified on the basis that there are few agreed international norms or enforcement tools for defining and curbing anticompetitive international trade practices. Dumping across international borders—a practice that attracts more trade restrictions than any other so-called unfair trade practice—would not even be an antitrust violation under existing laws in Europe, the United States, or Canada.[75]

In the United States antitrust enforcement and domestic competition

73. For example, compare Jacques H. J. Bourgeois, "Antitrust and Trade Policy: A Peaceful Coexistence? European Community Perspective," *International Business Lawyer*, vol. 16 (February 1989), pp. 58–67, and vol. 16 (March 1989), pp. 115–22 with A. Paul Victor, "Task Force Report on the Interface between International Trade Law and Policy and Competition Law and Policy," *Antitrust Law Journal*, vol. 56, no. 2 (1987), pp. 463–66.

74. Douglas E. Rosenthal, "Antitrust Implications of the Canada-United States Free Trade Agreement," *Antitrust Law Journal*, vol. 57, 1988, pp. 485–96. For a contrasting analysis, see Jacques H. J. Bourgeois, "Trade Measures, Competition Policy and the Consumer—An EC Perspective," paper delivered at Conference of the College of Europe on "The New Trends in EC and U.S. Trade Laws," Bruges, Belgium, September 14–16, 1989.

75. Mark R. Gillen and others, "Canadian and U.S. Antitrust Law—Areas of Overlap between Antitrust and Import Relief Laws," *Canada–United States Law Journal*, vol. 12 (1987), pp. 39–73.

policy have had little impact on trade policy throughout this century, save for a brief period after the Second World War when it appeared that a multilateral antitrust treaty, the Havana Charter, would be adopted as part of the international legal framework that led to the International Monetary Fund and the General Agreement on Tariffs and Trade.[76]

Likewise, there has been a de facto separation of spheres of influence between competition policy and trade policy within the EC Commission. DG-1 and DG-4 have operated with an implicit understanding that staying out of each other's hair is mutually advantageous. As markets become increasingly global and interdependent, however, this bargain becomes decreasingly attractive for DG-4.[77] Quotas, voluntary restraint agreements, and similar measures—in textiles, steel, autos, semiconductors, telecommunications, and other industries—exert significant anticompetitive effects within the EC. I agree with the authors of chapter 2, Carter Golembe and David Holland, that banking and securities deregulation should provide freer access to European markets than is currently available to providers of financial services in the United States. I accept the concerns of the author of chapter 4, Peter Cowhey, that local content rules, inclinations to control technological advances in the European market, and long-standing PTT resistance to open telecommunications markets in member states will make telecommunications a battlefield for trade and competition policy conflict in the years ahead. He rightly reminds us that Article 90(3) of the Treaty of Rome does give the Commission a tool to open markets even in the face of strong public utility opposition. The author of chapter 7, Joseph Greenwald, also is probably correct that some areas of potential conflict (for example, state aid) between the United States and the EC may be better addressed in a multilateral context.

The author of chapter 5, Kenneth Flamm, must also be right in anticipating continuing trade protection of EC firms in semiconductor

---

76. The official text of the ITO Charter is contained in U.N. Doc. E/Conf. 2/78, March 24, 1948, reprinted in U.N. Doc. ICITO/1/4 (1948), and in U.S. Dept. of State Pub. 3206, Commercial Policy Series 114 (1948). See also Douglas E. Rosenthal, "We Need More Old-Time Religion: A Response to Jim Rahl," *Northwestern Journal of International Law and Business,* vol. 10 (Spring, 1989).

77. One other commentator who has called for a more active role for competition policy in the trade policy process is John Temple-Lang. See John Temple-Lang, "Reconciling European Community Antitrust and Antidumping, Transport and Trade Safeguard Policies— Practical Problems," in Barry E. Hawk, ed., *North American and Common Market Antitrust and Trade Laws* (New York: Fordham Corporate Law Institute, 1989), pp. 7-1 to 7-90.

and related markets. However, Flamm's suggestion that private export-pricing restraints by Japanese semiconductor producers could be a feasible solution to incompatible protectionist demands from U.S. and EC trade authorities would raise serious potential antitrust problems under both U.S. and EC law. Anticompetitive trade restraints imposed by public authorities in a transparent manner are far preferable to a low visibility blend of administrative guidance and private collusion. If there is an informal understanding between Japanese industry and the U.S. and Japanese governments that foreign semiconductor manufacturers will be assured a 20 percent share of the Japanese market, one is faced with not only an antitrust violation under U.S. law but also what appears, ominously, as the beginning of a global semiconductor cartel. Such an understanding should be a matter of concern to both DG-4 and the Department of Justice.

One should keep an eye on Commissioner Brittan, and on DG-4 as it takes on a new director-general in January 1990. Will they seek a greater Commission role in promoting competition values in trade policy determination? Will more attention be given to the domestic competitive effects of import restraints in import relief trade cases? Evidence of accomplishment in this direction can help to calm American anxieties. It might even strengthen the hand of U.S. antitrust authorities in the U.S. trade policy process.

## Conclusions

European competition policy is more pro-competitive today than ever before. The commitment to deregulate and open markets is constitutionally imbedded; is strongly supported by the letter of antitrust law and policy and by officials who make, enforce, and adjudicate law and policy; and is welcomed by a majority of Community governments, important businesses, and Europeans at large. EC antitrust law is developing along the same lines as U.S. antitrust law in most significant respects. European markets are relatively less concentrated than U.S. markets, and there will be many further opportunities there for mergers and the formation of strategic alliances, providing U.S. companies with attractive opportunities for establishing and expanding their market presence in Europe. Even if the Commission's commitment to a pro-competitive policy waivers, private legal rights provide a measure of self-protection against anticompetitive practices, including those discriminating against U.S. firms. This is the optimistic scenario, and this is a time to be optimistic.

But there is also a basis for concern. The public commitment to competition can ebb as well as flow. Sustained recession, a surge in unemployment, a lack of confidence in the future, political polarization, the wrong signals from the United States, a fear of being overwhelmed by Japanese and American market leaders, if perceived to be doing relatively better in a deregulated market—all of these and more can lead to a weakening of competition policy.

Five items are particular causes for concern.

First, the resources provided to the Commission to enforce antitrust law in deregulated markets are inadequate.

Second, collusion is still an ingrained way of doing business in many European industrial and service sectors.

Third, bureaucratic and sectoral pressures for an aggressive industrial policy to promote winners in the global market may lead to anticompetitive effects.

Fourth, the national implementation of deregulatory directives has been sluggish, suggesting that the deregulatory process will be slower and more frail than the 1985 White Paper had hoped. And finally, insistence on intrabrand competition even where it does not promote consumer welfare may limit formation of a single market with effective interbrand competition.

Three of these concerns are troublesome aspects of U.S. competition policy as well. While the United States may be ahead of the Community in having acculturated American business to accept the norms of competition, and in recognizing that territorially exclusive distributorship networks can frequently promote consumer welfare, our federal antitrust agencies are also seriously understaffed, half their size of ten years ago when the U.S. economy was smaller and less concentrated. The pressures for a U.S. industrial policy are strong and likely to increase. A serious recession will not only erode competition values but will encourage larger and larger corporate bail-outs. While the U.S. market is already significantly deregulated, there are further opportunities for reform in government procurement, financial services, marine transportation, cargo delivery, and many other areas. But unlike Europe, there is little U.S. support for further reform, other than in financial services. The prospects for an optimistic European scenario will be enhanced if we Americans practice here what we would have the Community do there.

Relatively little competition policy coordination or consultation exists between U.S. and EC officials. Antitrust enforcers from the two jurisdictions meet a few times a year in the Restrictive Business Practices Committee of the Organization for Economic Cooperation and Development. There are also occasional, brief, informal contacts between heads of antitrust agencies. The usefulness of these meetings is limited by two circumstances. U.S. antitrust officials tend to believe they have little to learn from DG-4 expertise and experience, since they view U.S. antitrust law as manifestly better developed and more sophisticated than its European analogue. Even when there is some useful dialogue on antitrust policy, the respective antitrust officials do not play a significant role in many broader competition policy issues, such as industrial and trade policy.

It is time for U.S. antitrust officials to pay more respectful attention to EC antitrust law and policy. As demonstrated in this chapter, the European approach is similar to the American in analyzing antitrust issues, but the EC has a different menu of enforcement techniques. Furthermore, EC antitrust officials already play a larger role than their U.S. counterparts in the broad competition policy process—even if the DG-4 role is not as great as it might be. DG-4 officials are quite interested in U.S. developments and would be receptive to more meaningful coordination.

The need for coordination will increase as both U.S. and EC authorities assert their jurisdiction over complex transatlantic transactions. Even where two enforcement authorities apply the same basic concepts and employ the same methodologies of review, they will frequently weigh the evidence differently and reach conflicting conclusions. Even in the optimistic scenario, where U.S. and EC competition policy develop in parallel pro-competitive directions, conflicts will still arise in individual cases, as Minorco's attempted takeover of Consolidated Gold Fields shows.[78] There are as yet no ground rules for resolving such conflicts on a principled basis. Addressing this deficiency is sufficient justification for more dialogue. The best outcome would be parallel and coordinated evolution of competition policy and practice on a transatlantic basis.

---

78. In this case the U.S. courts in a private suit refused, on competition grounds, to permit a Luxembourg subsidiary of a South African company, Minorco, to acquire an English company, Consolidated Gold Fields, with important U.S. mining interests, after the transaction had been cleared by EC, British, and U.S. competition officials. *Consolidated Gold Fields, PLC* v. *Anglo American Corporation of South Africa*, 713 F. Supp. 1479 (S.D.N.Y.), *aff'd*, 871 F. 2d 252 (2d Cir.), *cert.denied*, 110 S. Ct. 29 (1989).

## APPENDIX 6–1. The New EC Merger Control Regulation, December 21, 1989

On December 21, 1989, the EC Council finally adopted a Regulation on the Control of Concentrations. It will enter into force in September 1990.

At that time all "concentrations" having a "Community dimension" will have to give notification to the EC Commission for clearance. Concentrations include mergers and acquisitions of a controlling interest in one or more companies (whether by purchase of shares or assets). Concentrations will be judged to have a Community dimension if the aggregate worldwide turnover of all corporate groups involved (excluding intra-group transactions) exceeds ECU 5 billion and the aggregate EC-wide turnover of each of at least two corporate groups involved exceeds ECU 250 million (unless each of the corporate groups achieves more than two-thirds of its aggregate EC-wide turnover within the same member state). Under certain circumstances, the Commission can, at the request of a member state, also apply the regulation to concentrations for which the aggregate worldwide turnover of the groups is less than ECU 5 billion. It is anticipated that between forty and fifty mergers will fall above the notification threshold in the first year. In four years the proper threshold level will be subject to review. It could be altered by a qualified majority Council vote.

A concentration with a Community dimension must give notification to the Commission one week after the execution of the agreement, the announcement of the public takeover or exchange bid, or the acquisition of a controlling interest, whichever occurs first. Intentional or negligent failure to notify can result in fines of up to ECU 50,000 on each company involved.

Subject to certain exceptions, the concentration may not be implemented before its notification, nor for a period of two weeks following the notification. Intentional or negligent implementation of the concentration in violation of this requirement can result in fines of up to 10 percent of the aggregate turnover of the corporate groups involved in the concentration. During the two-week period, the Commission can decide to extend the period during which the concentration cannot be implemented.

The Commission must declare a concentration to be incompatible with the Common Market if it creates or strengthens a dominant position with the result that effective competition will be significantly impeded. A concentration should be presumed to be compatible with the Common Market when the market share of the groups concerned does not exceed 25 percent of the relevant product market within the Common Market or a substantial part of it.

The Commission must adopt a formal decision within one month of the notification (subject to a possible extension of two weeks under certain circumstances), regardless of whether it decides that the concentration falls outside the scope of the regulation, does not raise serious doubts as to its compatibility with the Common Market, or decides to begin proceedings to determine the compatibility of the concentration with the Common Market.

Concentrations having a Community dimension are, in principle, to be reviewed solely by the EC Commission under the regulation and will no longer be subject to review under national merger control laws. An exception is provided, however, permitting the Commission to refer a case to a member state for review under its national law.

Chapter 7

# Negotiating Strategy

JOSEPH GREENWALD

THE UNITED STATES is depending heavily on the Uruguay Round of the General Agreement on Tariffs and Trade (GATT) negotiations to solve the problems raised by the Europe 1992 Program. This negotiating strategy is partly an attempt to restore the central role of GATT in the world trading system. It also reflects simple timing: the Uruguay Round is scheduled to finish at the end of 1990, well before the Europe 1992 deadline.

But the real world is not so neat. The internal market program began with the 1985 White Paper and, especially in controversial areas, is likely to stretch well beyond December 1992.[1] The GATT negotiations began with the Uruguay Round Declaration of 1986, and it is not yet clear what results will be achieved by December 1990.[2] The United States has already engaged in substantive bilateral talks with the European Community on such important matters as reciprocity in banking and mutual recognition in testing and certification.

It is surely right for the United States to press for a maximum Uruguay Round package, but it would be a mistake to put all the U.S. eggs in the GATT negotiating basket. The Community continues to move ahead on its single market program independently of the Uruguay Round. Indeed, if GATT meets its December 1990 deadline, there will be another disjunction: important Community measures will not be adopted until after GATT negotiations have drawn to a close.

Obviously, access to the single European market will not depend

Joseph Greenwald is an attorney in private practice and former U.S. Ambassador to the European Economic Communities.

1. EC Commission, *Completing the Internal Market: White Paper from the Commission to the European Council* (Luxembourg, 1985).

2. General Agreement on Tariffs and Trade, "Ministerial Declaration on the Uruguay Round," in *GATT: Basic Instruments and Selected Documents, 33d Supplement, Protocols, Decisions, Reports, 1985–1986 and Forty-second Session* (Geneva, June 1987), pp. 19–52.

entirely on deregulation within Europe or on government-to-government negotiations. Successful penetration of the EC market will largely depend on the competitiveness of American products and services and the ability of European firms to limit foreign entry through market dominance. But government negotiations will help set the stage for U.S. economic participation in the Community.

## The Negotiating Environment

To address tactics and strategy, it is necessary to understand the negotiating environment, some historical background, and the issues arising from the challenge of 1992.

### EC Attitudes

The return of self-confidence engendered by the Europe 1992 process has led the EC to be more contentious in disputes with its trading partners. European Commission officials say privately that, while the United States can push weak countries around, the Community can now stand up and slug it out with an aggressively protectionist United States.

Like the United States, the Community has adopted its own regulation envisaging retaliation for actions by countries that violate international trade rules.[3] The EC has also followed the U.S. pattern of aggressively using antidumping regulations to deter unfair trade practices.

Trade policy attitudes are also reflected in the priority given to multilateral negotiations in GATT and to the internal market program. Formally the Community supports the Uruguay Round to demonstrate its commitment to the open, global trading system and its intention not to use the 1992 program to construct a "Fortress Europe."[4] But the Commission's External Relations Directorate (DG-1) does not have adequate staff to keep up with the powerful Internal Market Directorate (DG-3). The Community has been participating actively in GATT negotiations in Geneva; the real conflict (if there is one) between the demands of the single market program and the priorities of GATT will arise in the

3. Council Regulation EEC 2641/84, *Official Journal of the European Community*, no. L252 (Luxembourg: EC Commission, September 20, 1984), p. 1 [hereafter *O.J. Eur. Comm.*]; and *Bulletin of the European Communities*, vol. 17, no. 9-1984 (Brussels, September 1984), point 2.2.5, p. 51.

4. EC Office of Press and Public Affairs, "1992: Europe—World Partner," *European Community News*, no. 28/88 (Washington, October 20, 1988), pp. 1–7.

second half of 1990, when the time comes to strike final deals in the Uruguay Round, somewhat before the dimensions of Europe 1992 are completely sorted out.

As with national governments, there are both liberal and protectionist tendencies within the European Community and the Commission. At the level of member states, Denmark, West Germany, the Netherlands, and the United Kingdom generally propound open market and deregulation policies, both within the EC and toward the outside world. In the past France has most often been on the restrictionist side. More recently both major political groupings in France have supported the European outlook of Commission President Jacques Delors (a Frenchman). President Delors has used his position primarily to further a vision of European monetary union, a strong "social dimension," and some central intervention.[5] The Mediterranean member states—Italy, Greece, Spain, and Portugal—tend to look at trade issues primarily in terms of agricultural protectionism (the Common Agricultural Policy) and regional benefits.

An important new factor in the EC decisionmaking process is the replacement of the requirement for unanimity by the qualified majority rule for most issues.[6] It generally takes three (two large and one small) or four (one large and three small) countries to block a directive. This means that a single member state can no longer prevent either protectionist actions or liberalization measures. On the other hand, it is still hard for the Community to take positive action because qualified majorities are hard to put together—though not quite as hard as unanimous agreement. U.S. negotiators must bear these tactical considerations in mind.

In organizational terms, Delors has increased the staff of the Commission's Secretariat-General, which reports directly to him, to the level of a sizable directorate-general. At the staff level, the Commission's Directorate-General for External Relations is naturally most concerned about the external impact of Europe 1992 measures. The External Relations Directorate is also responsible for backstopping the Uruguay Round and GATT. Other directorates-general, like Internal Market and

5. In December 1981 the French government used the summit meeting in Strasbourg, at the end of its EC Council presidency, to push through the "Social Charter" and a commitment in principle for a meeting on monetary union.

6. EC Commission, *Steps to European Unity—Community Progress to Date: A Chronology* (Luxembourg, March 1987). (See also chapter 1 in this volume.)

Industrial Affairs (DG-3), Regional Development (DG-16), or Employment, Education, and Social Affairs (DG-5), obviously have different preoccupations. The main problem for DG-1 has been the shortage of personnel to follow actions elsewhere in the Commission that might affect outside countries. For various reasons, including the vast increase in activity, the effectiveness of horizontal coordination within the Commission is not as good as it was before 1985.

A good deal of press coverage has been given to the conflict between the views of Prime Minister Margaret Thatcher on the future evolution of Europe and the views of President François Mitterrand and President Delors.[7] Will this difference affect the EC attitude in negotiations? Probably not. Although Thatcher has expressed reservations about sovereignty moving from national capitals to Brussels, her main concern seems to be the French-led drive for a significant "social dimension"— for example, labor union representation on company boards of directors— and the Europeanizing of government regulations. Because the erosion of national sovereignty is, in any event, likely to continue at both the European and wider international levels, Thatcher's arguments appear to be more political and rhetorical than substantive. For example, an important breakthrough affecting the status of the Commission occurred when, at the July 1989 economic summit in Paris, the Commission was given the task of coordinating Western aid to Poland and Hungary. This extension of the role of the Commission is presumably a development Thatcher did not welcome, but could not resist.

The economic climate over the next three years will clearly affect negotiations, both within the EC and outside. Stagnation or recession could slow the internal market program. More important for the United States is the possibility that poor European economic performance would give force to the argument that 1992 benefits should not be extended to outside countries until the member states have had time to absorb the deregulation and liberalization measures and the business cycle has turned up.

Even in the present relatively good economic situation the Commission has expressed concern over the failure of national legislatures and administrations to put into practice decisions made by the European

7. "Delors, the History Man," *Economist*, October 21, 1989, p. 50; *EuroMarket Digest*, vol. 11 (May 1989); and Wolfgang Hager, "Europe: Horizons 1992," *New York Times*, December 12, 1988, p. D16.

Council.[8] In fact, as history shows, European integration has not proceeded in a steady line. Public and governmental support for the process has waxed and waned over the past forty years. Even in the current atmosphere of enthusiasm for Europe 1992, national politicians and bureaucrats tend to drag their feet in putting Commission directives into effect. The first set of 1992 directives dealt with relatively easy issues like customs paperwork. The next set involves more difficult and sensitive areas like taxation, government procurement, and movement of people, where the sovereignty issue looms larger. For U.S. negotiators this means that even more attention and effort may be diverted from multilateral trade negotiations to internal market issues.

One development that may hasten the 1992 process is the breakdown of Communist rule in Eastern Europe. Member states may well be anxious to complete their own economic integration before turning to the economic absorption of Czechoslovakia, Hungary, East Germany, and other East European states.

Finally, the EC as a magnet phenomenon may affect the negotiating strategy. The European Free Trade Association (EFTA) countries (Nordics, Switzerland, and Austria) have enjoyed a special trading relationship with the Community since its inception.[9] The special relationship has come to be known as the European Economic Space. Within this space, the EFTA countries have grown increasingly dependent on their trade with the Community (see table 7-1). The 1992 program has caused them great concern.

To address this issue, President Delors invited the EFTA countries, in his January 17, 1989, speech to the European Parliament, to submit a proposal for safeguarding their interests.[10] This process moved further along when, at an EC-EFTA ministerial meeting in Brussels on December 19, 1989, agreement was reached to intensify negotiations toward completion of the European Economic Space. The only concrete step taken at that time was to require Community consultation with EFTA before

8. *Washington Post*, September 16, 1989; communication from the EC Commission, Brussels, September 7, 1989; and *Europe-1992: The Report on the Single European Market*, vol. 1 (September 1989), p. 325.

9. The Nordic EFTA countries are Sweden, Norway, Iceland, and Finland.

10. EC Commission, *The Commission's Programme for 1989: Address by Jacques Delors, President of the Commission, to the European Parliament and His Reply to the Debate* (Luxembourg, 1989); and *Europe-1992*, vol. 1 (February 16; March 15, 1989).

TABLE 7–1. Shares of European Community in EFTA Imports and Exports, 1959–88

| Country | EC imports from EFTA as percent of total | | | EFTA exports to EC as percent of total | | |
|---|---|---|---|---|---|---|
| | 1959 | 1972 | 1988 | 1959 | 1972 | 1988 |
| Austria | 57.1 | 57.9 | 68.1 | 49.1 | 38.7 | 63.8 |
| Finland | 31.6 | 27.5 | 43.2 | 26.1 | 20.9 | 43.1 |
| Iceland | 17.3 | 27.5 | 51.6 | 10.6 | 16.0 | 58.9 |
| Norway | 35.1 | 26.3 | 46.2 | 26.0 | 23.8 | 65.2 |
| Sweden | 41.2 | 33.3 | 55.9 | 31.0 | 25.8 | 52.1 |
| Switzerland | 13.8 | 24.5 | 71.3 | 15.5 | 22.9 | 56.0 |
| Denmark[a] | 36.8 | 33.6 | . . . | 31.7 | 22.7 | . . . |
| United Kingdom[a] | 13.8 | 24.5 | . . . | 15.5 | 22.9 | . . . |
| Portugal[a] | 39.0 | 31.8 | . . . | 22.7 | 20.5 | . . . |
| EFTA | 27.8 | 34.1 | 60.3 | 23.7 | 26.0 | 55.9 |

SOURCE: Secretariat of the European Free Trade Association, EFTA Trade, April 1984, December 1989.
a. Denmark, the United Kingdom, and Portugal left EFTA after 1972 to join the EC.

introducing product standards. Commissioner Frans Andriessen said the deadline for EC-EFTA negotiations would be the end of 1992.[11]

The United States began to react to the implications of a preferential EFTA arrangement in the fall of 1989. Since the outcome of the Delors initiative on EFTA was still unclear, the first step was a U.S. request for consultations with EFTA. A deal short of a complete free trade area between the EC and EFTA—in other words, full EC rights and obligations for EFTA countries—would raise the issue of discrimination against the United States. At this juncture, complete free trade (except in agriculture) seems the most probable outcome. However, the EFTA countries have been seeking some way to participate in the Community decisionmaking process. In January 1990 reports were that the Commission rejected the EFTA proposal for a body of EC and EFTA permanent representatives in Brussels that would parallel the work of the EC Committee of Permanent Representatives (COREPER) to prepare decisions for the EC Council of Ministers.

The European Space issue was further complicated in mid-1989 by developments in Eastern Europe and the Soviet Union. Particularly for Hungary, some ideas were floated about "association" with the EC, or membership in EFTA as a step toward linkage with the EC. In view of

11. Steven Greenhouse, "Broader Trade Accord Moves Closer in Europe," New York Times, December 20, 1989, p. D2.

the limited outcome of the EC-EFTA December 19, 1989, meeting, it seems likely that substantive negotiations with Eastern Europe will be deferred until after 1991. On the question of new members, the EC has announced that it will take no formal decisions before 1992.

Short of association with the EC, special treatment for the Soviet Union or Eastern European countries through trade-distorting bilateral agreements may raise problems for the United States. Western and Eastern European countries have traditionally negotiated trade agreements with provisions and commodity annexes of dubious legality under GATT. Currently, even after full accession to GATT and significant economic reforms, Hungary has been accorded a special, bilateral agreement with the EC. On December 18, 1989, in connection with Soviet Foreign Minister Eduard A. Shevardnadze's visit to NATO headquarters in Brussels, a first trade agreement was signed by the Community and the Soviet Union. The agreement covers cooperation in many areas, but the only concrete trade provision was the ending of EC quotas on Soviet products.[12] In light of recent developments in Eastern Europe, it is likely that the bilateral agreements will turn out to be simple agreements providing for liberalization of imports by the Community.

## U.S. Attitudes

The United States has also undergone significant policy and attitude changes in the second half of the 1980s. The first Reagan administration was ideologically free-trade-oriented and market-oriented. Although the executive branch imposed some extra-GATT restrictions, trade policy was driven mainly by private sector suits mounted under the unfair trade provisions of U.S. law.

The stage shifted in the second Reagan administration. Pressure from Congress after 1986 forced more frequent and aggressive use by the administration itself of unfair trade provisions of U.S. law. As the trade deficit grew and competitive pressures intensified, Congress became more and more involved in detailed, day-to-day trade policy decisions. It also put the administration on the defensive with a constant stream of protectionist legislation. Because "protectionism" was still a bad word, the accompanying rhetoric was "market opening." The congressional

12. Steven Greenhouse, "Community and Soviets in First Pact," *New York Times,* December 19, 1989, p. D1.

view was that only the U.S. market was truly open and that only the United States followed GATT rules; other countries dumped, subsidized, and used a multitude of other unfair practices to capture U.S. markets and to deny access to their own. Fair dealing in the international arena was merely a question of "reciprocity," which came to be defined as a level playing field according to U.S. specifications (that is, when the U.S. field was less tilted than the particular partner's field). The threat of retaliation was the way to level the field. GATT was tarred with the brush of ineffectualism when U.S. Trade Representative William Brock came back from a 1982 meeting that failed to initiate a new round of trade negotiations and gave the organization a grade of C minus.

The process of congressional intervention and executive resistance ended in a compromise called the Omnibus Trade and Competitiveness Act of 1988.[13] This legislation provided authority for U.S. participation in GATT negotiations and added to the array of bargaining chips in the hands of the U.S. negotiators. In terms of negotiating authority, it is unlikely that anything more is needed or—in terms of adding to positive offers that the U.S. Trade Representative (USTR) can make to other countries—is attainable.

On trade policy the United States is ambivalent. The public likes cheap, good-quality imports, but supports a tough line and, if necessary, import restrictions to preserve American jobs and firms. U.S. multinational companies still act globally in marketing and production, but no longer uncritically support free trade. U.S. agriculture wants open markets and no subsidies by others, but it is not yet clear whether the farm bloc is willing to abandon U.S. price supports and import restriction programs.

Another element in current U.S. trade policy is the issue of bilateralism or plurilateralism as against multilateralism. Do the agreements with Israel, Canada, and Mexico and the talk about other bilateral or regional arrangements mean that the United States is turning away from GATT and the global trading system? Are these agreements a bargaining tool to show that the United States has other options? Or are they a reflection of the world breaking into economic blocs, led by the enlarging EC? Even if the Uruguay Round is a clear success, this issue is likely to constitute background clutter for the next few years; it could become a central question if the Uruguay Round is a clear failure.

13. P.L. 100-418, 102 Stat. 1107.

These U.S. attitudes portend continued U.S.-Community trade frictions, with efforts on both sides to manage the disputes so they do not affect the political and security aspects of the Atlantic relationship or the multilateral GATT negotiations.[14] U.S. and EC positions also spell hard bargaining to put together a significant Uruguay Round package. The European Commission will have to bring along the member states and the U.S. administration will have to engage Congress and key business firms.

## Ganging Up with or against Japan?

In an increasingly interdependent world, developments outside the United States and Western Europe obviously affect negotiating strategy and tactics. North-South issues, including third-world debt, the environment, and the "graduation" of the newly industrialized economies into full GATT commitments, together with changes in Eastern Europe, the Soviet Union, and China, are all important. But the most important element is the role of Japan.

The growth of Japan's economic strength, perhaps more than U.S. competition, was the threat that helped propel the EC into its 1992 program. And Japan is the main target of many EC policies and programs. In frequent private conversations about the "building blocks" sometimes taken to be part of "Fortress Europe," EC representatives assure Americans that the measures are directed at Japan, not the United States. Even if the United States adopts an attitude of looking out only for itself in trade policy matters, EC assurances are not entirely comforting. The United States may be hit as well since it is difficult for the EC to discriminate overtly against Japan. The current jocular formulation is that the EC launches toward Tokyo a missile that lands in New York and explodes in Washington.

Yet just as the United States is relatively more comfortable with European trade policies and practices than with Japanese policies and practices, so the Europeans worry relatively less about American actions, even though U.S.-Community arguments may get more visibility and rhetoric. In other words, the American and European markets are

14. The GATT panel decision on EC soybean subsidies and its acceptance by the EC is a hopeful note in this connection. As pointed out in the press reports, the GATT dispute settlement process is rapidly gaining credibility. See, for example, Clyde H. Farnsworth, "Pact to End Soybean Subsidies," *New York Times*, December 21, 1989, D1.

considered more open than the Japanese market, and U.S. and European firms are more similar in terms of corporate culture. By the same token the Japanese are also considered more formidable opponents. The Europeans say they do not want to have their economy "hollowed out"—the manufacturing sector diminished—by Japanese competition, as happened to the United States.

As outsiders, Japan and the United States have many similar interests in how the Europe 1992 process evolves. But the United States has carefully avoided making common cause with the Japanese. One reason, already mentioned, is that the United States expects to get better treatment on some issues than Japan, almost without trying. Another reason is that the United States has been engaged in an almost never-ending series of trade disputes and negotiations with Japan. Until the late 1970s most of these disputes dealt with seemingly excessive Japanese competition in the U.S. market—textiles, apparel, and steel were early examples. Since the 1980s the trend has been toward complaints about closed Japanese markets, not only in such low-technology products as soda ash, lumber, and citrus, but most urgently in such high-technology areas as semiconductors, supercomputers, and satellites. In May 1989 the United States launched a Structural Impediments Initiative under the "Super 301" provision of the 1988 Trade Act to try to deal with so-called systemic barriers to trade.[15] The combination of this initiative, individual industry barriers, and the persistent bilateral U.S. trade deficit indicates that the United States will be in an adversarial posture toward Japan for some time to come. The United States does not want its efforts to open the Japanese market diverted or confused by U.S.-Community issues.

In Japan, on the other hand, there is some concern about being closed out of both the European and U.S. markets. After the Second World War Japan concentrated on the U.S. market because it was unified, open, and most easily penetrated, and because historical U.S.-Japanese ties paved the way. The Japanese knew little about Europe and paid little attention until the emergence of Europe's single market program. Now EC-Japanese trade frictions are mounting, and Japanese investment in Europe is increasing. The United States has, for political reasons, declined to join Community efforts in GATT to "gang up" on Japan, but the "Japan

---

15. Office of the U.S. Trade Representative, " 'Super 301' Trade Liberalization Priorities," Washington, May 25, 1989.

factor" will continue to be an important element of the negotiating climate.

## General Negotiating Strategy Issues

Before turning to specific substantive issues, I want to address four broad questions that are often raised in discussions of U.S. trade with the European Community.

First, will the debate about a federal Europe (the Delors vision), complete with its own central bank and monetary unit, as opposed to looser economic integration (the Thatcher vision) affect U.S. negotiating strategy?

Although the United States has consistently supported European integration, it has not tried—and should not try—to prescribe the steps or the final outcome. The United States should not get in the middle of the "what-kind-of-Europe" argument. The history of European integration has shown the wisdom of the post–World War II architect of European unification, Jean Monnet, who urged states to concentrate on specific actions and to avoid theoretical discussions about sovereignty.[16]

Second, will the debate in the United States about the virtues of bilateral or regional or managed trade (United States-Canada-Mexico; the semiconductor arrangement) as against open trade (multilateralism and GATT) affect the negotiating strategy?

This policy debate has effectively been put on hold until the end of 1990. Whether it then becomes a real issue will depend on perceptions of the outcome of the Uruguay Round, the effect of the Europe 1992 Program, and the ongoing negotiations with the Japanese. The option of a broad multilateral or plurilateral initiative after 1990 or 1992 should not be ruled out.

Third, is the United States no longer willing to pay an economic price for European integration?

This question contains more rhetoric than reality. It implies that the United States has willingly paid such a price in the past. In general, an integrated market has benefited the United States as well as Europe through greater growth and prosperity (see chapter 1). The Common Agricultural Policy (CAP) created the most problems, and the United

16. Pascal Fontaine, *Jean Monnet, A Grand Design for Europe* (Luxembourg: EC Commission, July 1988).

States never accepted the argument that the CAP was the cement that held the Community together. The United States has insisted that its trade and economic interests not suffer as a result of the construction of Europe. It may be, however, that U.S. attitudes toward Europe have shifted, that trade and industrial policy will be raised to the level of national security, and that the focus of U.S. diplomacy will be more narrowly concentrated on trade and investment issues.

Fourth, is there a conflict between the interests of U.S. multinational companies (primarily concerned about their investments in Europe) and those of small and medium-sized U.S. companies (primarily concerned about their exports to Europe)?

The U.S. negotiating strategy can, and should, accommodate the interests of all U.S. companies. Priority for market access need not be purchased at the expense of favorable treatment for companies already established in Europe.

For example, one issue of interest to companies exporting to Europe concerns product standards, testing, and certification. The bilateral framework agreed between Secretary of Commerce Robert Mosbacher and EC Commissioner Martin Bangemann in 1989 provides the basis for ensuring that EC standards, testing, and certification rules do not adversely affect U.S. exporters.[17] This concordance will proceed outside the GATT negotiations.

The distinction between export and investment interests is artificial. Studies since the 1960s have demonstrated that much of U.S. exporting is linked to investment abroad through intracompany transfers.[18]

In addition the export-investment distinction is not static. Many companies, regardless of size, begin exporting to a market and then invest to be closer to the market to serve it better. This means that, for the longer term, both exports and investment have to be part of the U.S. negotiating strategy. There can thus be a progression, depending on market development, from exports to investment, regardless of the size of the enterprise.

17. *1992—The External Impact of European Unification*, vol. 1 (June 2, 1989), pp. 10–11.

18. Aharoni Yair, *The Foreign Investment Decision Process* (Harvard University Press, 1966); and Peggy B. Musgrove, *United States Taxation of Foreign Investment Income: Issues and Arguments* (Harvard University Law School, 1969). See also William B. Reddaway, *Effects of U.K. Direct Investment Overseas: An Interim Report* (Cambridge University Press, 1967); and A. E. Safarian, *Foreign Ownership of Canadian Industry* (Toronto: McGraw-Hill Press, 1967).

## U.S. Negotiating Objectives and Channels

There are at least three approaches to negotiations over U.S. trade with Europe. The first is a global approach seeking to use the EC single market program and GATT negotiations to achieve further progress toward opening markets worldwide by reducing barriers to trade, services, and investment. The second is a more narrow, nationalist approach designed to deal primarily with issues of particular interest to the United States, giving priority where necessary to bilateral talks and solutions. The third is an Atlantic approach involving the negotiation of an exclusive U.S.-Community deal.

These approaches do not, of course, present a clear and simple choice. They may frequently overlap, and different negotiating strategies may be applied to different issues at different times.

## Global Approach

The broad U.S. interest in maintaining, deepening, and strengthening an open, multilateral trading system can be served by giving top priority to GATT. Thus the United States should use Europe 1992 problems as a platform for pursuing the greatest possible global liberalization in the Uruguay Round.

In most cases, this will mean seeking maximum access to the EC market in the context of reciprocal concessions from all participating countries. These concessions will range from the reduction of traditional tariff and nontariff barriers to the application of the principle of national treatment—according foreign firms the same rights and obligations as domestic firms—in areas, like services, where the Community is deregulating or moving toward the concept of mutual recognition.

The global approach might dictate a somewhat different set of priorities from those related strictly to the Uruguay Round and U.S. objectives in GATT. For example, agriculture has been high on the U.S. agenda in GATT. The United States has proposed a very ambitious plan for phasing out, or converting to tariffs, all trade-distorting subsidies and import restrictions. The Common Agricultural Policy is a major target in the agriculture negotiations. A maximum result in agriculture will go a long way toward rehabilitating GATT, benefiting U.S. trade, and reducing frictions between the United States and the Community. But it will have only a generalized, nonspecific impact on the Europe 1992 Program, which does not directly address the CAP. Pushing the Community to the wall on agriculture will not help much in the 1992 context.

On the other hand, both Europe 1992 directives and the Uruguay Round do cover phytosanitary and biotechnological regulations, important matters to U.S. farm exports. In this area, the existing international organizations are weak and slow moving. Improved, technically supported dispute resolution probably offers the best hope for the short term.

In any event, the main channel for the global approach would be GATT. Because of the current GATT and EC deadlines of 1990 and 1992, respectively, the global approach might require an extension of the Uruguay Round or some other form of continuing GATT negotiations. In addition, more specialized bodies could be used to support GATT efforts. For example, the Customs Cooperation Council (CCC) is a worldwide organization dealing with technical matters like tariff nomenclature and rules of origin. These subjects have recently become politicized, so core negotiations should take place in GATT, the more senior institution. But the CCC can provide useful technical support.

## National Approach

There is no sharp distinction between the global and the national approach. Much depends on the guidance and mind-set of the policymakers. U.S. Trade Representative Carla Hills has stated that the Uruguay Round has top priority. But this does not exclude strictly bilateral or unilateral actions.

To achieve the dual objective of avoiding damage to U.S. interests as a result of the 1992 program, while obtaining maximum benefit for U.S. companies, it will be necessary to supplement GATT negotiations with bilateral or plurilateral negotiations. For many important issues, it is unlikely that the Europe 1992 and GATT timing will mesh. At some stage in the GATT negotiations, the United States may thus face genuine trade-offs between primarily Europe 1992 issues and primarily GATT issues. The real question is whether the majority of important issues get dealt with issue-by-issue, on a bilateral basis, or whether bilateral talks will merely serve to round out the global approach.

## Regional Approach

There is a third option for U.S. negotiating objectives. It might be called a regional approach as opposed to the global or national approach. The United States might try to negotiate an EFTA-type deal with the

Community. It could be a formal, institutionalized, comprehensive trade and investment agreement, including dispute settlement provisions on the model of the U.S.-Canada Free Trade Agreement. With the striking developments in Eastern Europe, the Community might be amenable to a bilateral agreement that would go beyond trade and economic matters to include political and security issues. Such an approach would probably be resisted by those who feel NATO must be maintained. But it could appeal to those who are probing for a best "architecture."[19]

Another Atlantic approach might be that the United States could use the OECD to negotiate with the Community and other industrial nations on the single market principles of mutual recognition, deregulation, and liberalization. For both the national and regional approaches, the negotiating channel choices might be existing treaties of Friendship, Commerce, and Navigation, consultation arrangements, or new executive agreements or treaties. The OECD and ad hoc groups would provide a plurilateral channel.

## Specific Issues

Thus far, negotiations appear necessary in four major areas in the Europe 1992 Program: services; standards, testing, and certification; government procurement; and rules of origin and local content. In general, the directives issued by the Commission in these areas do not raise new barriers, such as tariffs or quotas, against the outside world. They mainly bestow benefits on member states through liberalization, deregulation, or harmonization. The objective of negotiations with the EC is to extend these benefits to the United States and to avoid the adoption of measures—for example, tighter standards or rules of origin—that effectively discriminate against outsiders.

### Tariffs

Traditional trade impediments, like tariff and nontariff barriers, will continue to affect the ability of U.S. companies—large, medium, and small—to take advantage of the single European market. The Uruguay Round offers a timely opportunity to attack the clear disadvantage facing outsiders: the application of the Community's Common External Tariff (CET) to foreign goods while European products circulate freely.

19. James A. Baker III, "A New Europe, A New Atlanticism: Architecture for a New Era," address to the Berlin Press Club, December 12, 1989.

Analysis done in connection with the GATT Dillon Round (1960–62) and Kennedy Round (1964–67) demonstrated that the main value for the United States of those negotiations was to be found in the reduction of the CET.[20] And this became the U.S. objective. To achieve maximum tariff reductions, the United States followed a formula approach rather than the classic request-and-offer negotiating technique.

The basic difference between the two tariff negotiating methods is whether the negotiations start from a maximum or a minimum position. Under the old request-and-offer system, negotiators initially offered small tariff cuts, increasing them in the process of negotiation until a reciprocal balance was struck. Under the formula approach used in the Kennedy Round, each participant agreed to a 50 percent across-the-board cut, subject to a list of exceptions. The negotiations then took place on exceptions lists. In the Tokyo Round, a similar formula approach was taken. In both cases, tariff reductions ended up in the 30–35 percent range compared with the 15–20 percent range achieved under the request-and-offer approach. It is fair to conclude that negotiating on exceptions from a high across-the-board rule leads to deeper cuts.

With this experience in mind, virtually all developed country participants in the Uruguay Round favor the use of a formula. Only the United States has retreated to the individual request-and-offer method.

There are probably two reasons for the U.S. decision. First, customs duties on industrial products are, on the average, so low that they are no longer important as trade barriers (see table 7-2). In fact, only a few U.S. industries, like forest products, where a 1 percent duty may be significant, urged the U.S. Trade Representative to make full use of the tariff negotiating authority granted in the 1988 Trade Act (see appendix 7-1). Second, many "sensitive" industries, like chemicals, argued to the U.S. Trade Representative and Congress that they had not increased exports as a result of previous tariff cuts by other countries, but that the U.S. market was effectively exploited by foreign competitors thanks to lower U.S. tariffs. These industries opposed the formula approach and asked to review the U.S. offer list, presumably with a view to limiting U.S. offers.

With this industry line-up, the administration opted for the easy way out. But there are strong arguments in favor of the formula and the maximalist approach. First, in the European single market context, it is

20. Ernest H. Preeg, *Traders and Diplomats: An Analysis of the Kennedy Round of Negotiations under the General Agreement on Tariffs and Trade* (Brookings, 1970).

TABLE 7–2.  U.S. and EC Tariffs by Industrial Sector, 1989

Percent ad valorem

| Sector | U.S. tariff[a] | EC tariff[b] |
|---|---|---|
| Textiles | 9.2 | 7.5 |
| Wearing apparel | 22.7 | 13.3 |
| Leather products | 4.2 | 2.8 |
| Footwear | 8.8 | 11.5 |
| Wood products | 1.7 | 2.4 |
| Furniture and fixtures | 4.1 | 5.6 |
| Paper and paper products | 2.4 | 7.0 |
| Printing and publishing | 0.7 | 1.9 |
| Chemicals | 2.4 | 7.9 |
| Rubber products | 2.5 | 3.5 |
| Nonmetal mineral products | 5.3 | 3.6 |
| Glass and glass products | 6.2 | 7.7 |
| Nonferrous metals | 0.7 | 2.8 |
| Metal products | 4.8 | 5.5 |
| Nonelectric machinery | 3.3 | 4.4 |
| Transportation equipment | 2.5 | 8.4 |
| Miscellaneous manufacturing | 4.2 | 5.0 |
| All industries[c] | 4.3 | 6.1 |

SOURCES: Data supplied by the Office of the U.S. Trade Representative and the U.S. Department of Commerce, Office of European Community Affairs; and EC Commission, *Official Journal of the European Communities*, no. L298 (October 31, 1988) [hereafter *O.J. Eur. Comm.*].

a. Calculated as the weighted average of tariff rates of U.S. imports within each sector.

b. Calculated as the simple average of member state tariff rates, where each member state rate is the weighted average rate, based on imports within each sector.

c. Calculated as the simple average of industrial sectors.

important to reduce the CET as much as possible. Second, the low average level of customs duties hides some significant tariff peaks (for illustrations, see table 7-3). Third, the negotiations must yield clear gains for the developing countries, along with progress on the "new items," for example, services and intellectual property, of concern mainly to the OECD countries. Reductions of duties on apparel, footwear, and processed raw materials, for example, are of great interest to the developing countries, whose support will be needed in other areas of the negotiations, such as services, where the United States hopes to deal with Europe 1992 problems.

For these reasons, the United States should position itself at the forefront of a drive for tariff reductions, rather than being the only country insisting on the outmoded and minimalist request-and-offer method. Both Japan and the EC have proposed substantial formula cuts.

In its first Uruguay Round submission, of July 1987, Japan made an "elimination proposal." The proposal was regarded as a throwaway gesture

TABLE 7-3.  U.S. and EC Tariff Profiles for Selected Products, 1989[a]

Percent

| Product | U.S. tariff | EC tariff |
|---|---|---|
| Textiles and apparel | | |
| Cotton woven fabrics, other, | | |
| containing 36 percent wool | 33.0 | 17.0 |
| Men's or boys' swimwear of | | |
| manmade fiber | 29.6 | 13.0 |
| Unglazed ceramic tiles | 20.0 | 8.0 |
| Footwear: soles and uppers of | | |
| rubber or plastic | 48.0 | 20.0 |
| Chemicals | | |
| Chlorine | Free | 11.0 |
| Vanadium oxide | 16.0 | 5.1 |
| Newsprint | Free | 4.9 |
| Automobiles | 2.5 | 10.0 |
| Dairy products | | |
| Ice cream | 20.0 | Variable |
| Blue-veined cheese | 20.0 | Variable |
| Soybean oil | 22.5 | 10.0 |

SOURCES: *O.J. Eur. Comm.*, no. L298 (October 31, 1988); and U.S. International Trade Commission, *Harmonized Tariff Schedules of the United States (1990)*, USITC publication 2232 (Washington, 1989).

a. These products have been chosen solely to show the tariff peaks within sectors of the U.S. and EC tariff schedules.

because no other industrial country was prepared to commit to removing all tariffs on industrial products, even over a long phasing period. In July 1989 the Japanese, "taking into account the views expressed by participants," submitted a revised paper with an automatic formula designed to achieve at least a 33 percent reduction of tariffs (see appendix 7-2). The EC also submitted, in July 1989, an elaborate "systematic approach" formula aimed primarily at lopping off high tariffs (see appendix 7-3).

In January 1990 the GATT negotiators reached a compromise: each country could choose its own tariff-reduction method, provided the result was an overall reduction of 30 percent in the nation's tariffs. If the Community and Japan will go along, the United States should announce an even more ambitious long-term objective before the close of the Uruguay Round: the staged elimination of tariffs by all developed countries on industrial products.[21]

21. Indeed, signs of a more forthcoming U.S. position appeared in a fall 1989 speech by U.S. Ambassador Carla Hills: "The United States challenges its trading partners to envision a future 'zero tariff' world. We stand ready today to work with others to achieve this in *key* sectors in the present round." "The Uruguay Round and U.S. Trade Policy: A Foundation for the Future," speech before the American Chamber of Commerce (U.K.) and the Royal Institute for International Affairs, London, September 14, 1989.

## Services

Tariffs, and even nontariff barriers on goods, are relatively easy to deal with compared with barriers to trade in services. But EC directives relating to financial services (banking, insurance, and securities), as well as the freeing of capital movements, are, for outsiders, among the most important aspects of the Europe 1992 Program. It is not surprising that the specter of Fortress Europe first appeared in connection with the Second Banking Directive.

The transatlantic debate was triggered in 1988 by then Commissioner Willy De Clercq's comments that the EC should extend the benefits of internal liberalization and deregulation to outside countries only if they offered "reciprocity" in return. Historically, reciprocity has meant the exchange of equivalent concessions (in terms of their trade-opening effects) at the margin. But in the 1980s the U.S. Congress turned the original notion of reciprocity around to mean mirror-image treatment sector-by-sector (as exemplified by Senator John C. Danforth's telecommunications amendment in the 1988 Trade Act).[22] Not surprisingly U.S. officials interpreted the EC position in the same sense. They reacted strongly because U.S. legislation (the Glass-Steagall Act) does not allow European banks the same scope of business in the United States as the EC directive allows banks in Europe.

The initial U.S. response was given in August 1988 by then Deputy Secretary of the Treasury Peter McPherson. He characterized "reciprocity" as bad and "national treatment" as good.[23] The exchanges on this issue continued until the spring of 1989 when a modified Article 7 on "Relations with Third Countries" proposed by European Commissioner Sir Leon Brittan was inserted in the draft Second Banking Directive, adopted by the European Council on July 10, 1989.

There are two main reasons why services are so difficult to deal with. First, trade in services—apart from some aspects of transportation and telecommunications—is not now subject to international rules. At U.S. initiative, this subject is on the agenda of the Uruguay Round. However, it is not easy to adapt GATT principles, designed for trade in goods, to trade in services.

22. P.L. 100-418, secs. 1101(b)(4), 1371–82, 102 Stat. 1107, 1121, 1216–24.

23. M. Peter McPherson, deputy secretary of the Treasury, "The European Community's International Market Program: An American Perspective," remarks to the Institute for International Economics, in *Treasury News* (Washington, August 4, 1988).

Second, services are inherently more complicated. In almost all cases, services are subject to regulatory regimes, and it is hard to separate the public policy aspects of these regimes from the protectionist aspects. For example, in most countries, banking and insurance are regulated by state or federal governments. The rules on entry and doing business in these sectors protect not only the public but often the established industry as well. Because of the intertwined nature of regulation, state ownership, and protection, and because the service sector is highly sensitive for many countries, agreement could be reached to include it in the GATT agenda only as a separate negotiating topic. One of the outstanding questions is whether any final code will be integrated into GATT or become a stand-alone agreement. The GATT committee spent two years struggling with basic concepts, including the definition of services to be covered. On October 23, 1989, the United States submitted its comprehensive services framework proposal in legal form (see appendix 7-3 for the conceptual outline). The proposal contemplates that specific sector provisions will be hammered out once the framework is agreed upon.

It is with services that reliance on the Uruguay Round to deal with Europe 1992 problems becomes most difficult. It is a question not only of finding satisfactory substantive solutions, but also of timing.

On both counts, the Second Banking Directive is apposite. The EC has moved well ahead of GATT negotiations and the directive includes a basic principle with respect to outside countries that may serve as the model for other EC financial services directives.[24] The principle adopted in the Second Banking Directive could be called "conditional national treatment."

The classic national treatment provision for goods, in its broadest formulation (Article III(4) of GATT), requires that "the products of the territory of any contracting party imported into the territory of any other contracting party shall be accorded treatment no less favorable than that accorded to like products of national origin in respect of all laws, regulations and requirements affecting their internal sale." The GATT standard calls for no less favorable treatment in terms of formal laws and regulations. It does not inquire into the "quality" of national treatment in terms of practical market access. The EC directive calls for negotiations whenever it appears that a third country is not "granting Community

---

24. At the moment, the "conditional national treatment" formula appears only in the Second Banking Directive. Other financial services directives still contain the earlier, more objectionable, "reciprocity" formula.

credit institutions effective market access comparable to that granted by the Community to credit institutions from that third country." The negotiating mandate would look "to obtaining comparable competitive opportunities for Community credit institutions." The banking directive language on "effective market access" and "comparable competitive opportunities" sounds very much like the "market-opening" provisions of the U.S. Trade Act of 1988 (especially Section 301).

It may be that, in the case of services, the GATT concept of national treatment is not appropriate. Perhaps the quality of national treatment must be examined on a case-by-case basis. Conditional national treatment might be the right answer. But it is not clear that the Second Banking Directive formula was carefully thought through, and the EC has not yet agreed to put the formula into other financial services directives. It was certainly not discussed in advance with the United States or other trading partners. To minimize the dangers and risks of unilateralism, some kind of multilateral surveillance of findings regarding the adequacy of national treatment should be added to GATT procedures.

Because there are no international rules covering services at the moment, the EC argues that it can adopt its own formula. It also points to the last paragraph of Title III of the Second Banking Directive, which states, "Measures taken pursuant to this Article shall comply with the Community's obligations under any international agreements, bilateral or multilateral, governing the taking-up and pursuit of the business of credit institutions."

Here the question of timing arises. Presumably, the Community would change the application of its directive, if necessary, to conform to any subsequent GATT agreement. But it is impossible, at this stage, to know whether a framework agreement on services will emerge from the Uruguay Round and what provisions it may contain on national treatment. It seems that specific sector agreements are not likely to be negotiated in GATT until after 1990. Therefore, this appears to be an area where bilateral negotiations should be pursued vigorously.

### Audiovisual Sector

Another service sector measure that became the subject of a U.S. demarche to the EC is the directive on "television without frontiers." Citing the need to preserve the richness and diversity of their cultural heritage, the European Council, on April 12, 1989, adopted a "common position" in favor of a requirement that, for cable and satellite television services to broadcast freely throughout Europe, they must "ensure, where practicable and by appropriate means, that broadcasters reserve for European works a majority proportion of their transmission time."[25]

This issue has been discussed for some time not only in the European Commission and the Council of Ministers, but also by the Council of Europe and the European Parliament. The Community member states are deeply split along liberal-protectionist lines. Some countries have raised EC constitutional questions. As the U.S.-Canada Free Trade Agreement negotiations revealed, cultural matters are very sensitive politically. In the view of cultural nationalists, television programming is not just another commodity to be bought and sold according to the highest ratings. In their view, it profoundly reflects and shapes the nation's politics, values, and art. After lengthy consideration, the directive on television without frontiers, which embraced the earlier Common Position, was adopted on October 3, 1989.[26]

As the major outside supplier of television programs, the United States reacted strongly and announced it would take the issue to GATT. The GATT rule (Article IV) on screen quotas would not appear to serve as a defense for restrictive measures. Article IV is a special provision adopted after the Second World War to help the European film industry recover. It allows screen quotas under certain conditions and, in the last subparagraph, states, "Screen quotas shall be subject to negotiation for their limitation, liberalization or elimination." Article IV(d) was clearly meant to be a transitional provision.

But GATT rules are unlikely to be decisive. In a dispute proceeding, GATT panelists may decide that GATT rules simply have no application to television programming. The Commission argues that because there is a great and growing demand for television material in Europe, the directive is not likely to have a restrictive impact. But this same argument was put forward about the Common Agricultural Policy twenty years ago, when the United States was assured that the Community would always be an importer of U.S. soybeans and feedstuff. In the long run, production of European programs will increase and, even with a rise in

25. EC Commission, Council Documents 5858/89, April 10, 1989, and 5858/89 COR, April 13, 1989.

26. EC Commission, *The Audio-Visual Media in the Single European Market* (Luxembourg, June 1988). See U.S. International Trade Commission, "Protectionist EC Directive on Broadcasting Angers the U.S.," *International Economic Review*, vol. 30 (November 1989).

U.S.-Community coproduction, U.S. television programming may be shut out of the European market. But the present formulation of the Commission directive is not likely to result in significant restrictions. The emerging issues will probably not be resolved in GATT, and the bilateral U.S.-Community channel will continue to be most appropriate.

## Standards, Testing, and Certification

After services and reciprocity, the issue that has caused most concern in the U.S. business community is the formulation of industrial standards and the mutual recognition of testing and certification of industrial products. This is an area of interest to all American companies—large, medium, or small, national or multinational. On this question, there is no apparent conflict between the interests of U.S. companies on the basis of size or structure.

In areas where a harmonized EC system is developed, U.S. companies will benefit from the development of a single standard and a Community-wide testing and certification system to replace twelve national standards and systems. But the U.S. objective, supported by the GATT standards code, is to ensure that the standards and systems do not become technical barriers to trade. Ideally, this means the adoption of internationally agreed upon standards and recognition and acceptance of testing and certification in the United States.

Because the international standards organizations are so weak, the ideal solution for this Europe 1992 problem is not going to be achieved in the foreseeable future. Furthermore, European standards organizations are more advanced and active than the U.S. national bodies. The same is true in the field of testing and certification, where the U.S. practice has been to rely on manufacturer self-certification, whereas the European practice is to depend on official laboratories. For these reasons, together with the complexity of the matter, standards issues will be with us for a long time.

They offer, even so, a good example of the use of the bilateral channel. On May 31, 1989, U.S. Secretary of Commerce Mosbacher and EC Vice President for Internal Market and Industrial Affairs Bangemann issued a joint communiqué dealing with standards, testing, and certification.[27] The agreement reflects the intention of the parties to cooperate in

27. See *1992—The External Impact of European Unification*, vol. 1 (June 2, 1989), pp. 10–11.

addressing U.S. company concerns by agreeing to discuss cooperation in ensuring openness and transparency in the mutual setting of standards and in the enhancement of international standard-setting; by agreeing that U.S. and EC imports should have equal access with domestically produced goods to testing and certification procedures; and by planning to go beyond access to testing procedures and explore mutual recognition of testing and certification done within each other's market.

On July 5, 1989, the Commission approved a Bangemann paper entitled "A Global Approach to Certification and Testing."[28] The Commission press release summarized the external implications as follows:

The introduction at the Community level of mutual recognition of methods and structure designed to establish conformity [with essential EC standards] will make the European market more readily accessible to products from non-Community countries which satisfy European quality criteria, since these products will no longer have to be subjected to national tests. By the same token, there is a legitimate case to be argued for negotiations between the Community and its external partners on the mutual recognition of testing, inspection and certification methods so as to ensure, for example, that products which have obtained the Community quality mark can have unhindered access to the markets of non-member countries.[29]

Although the standards, testing, and certification issue appears to be on the right track, the journey will be long and arduous, and there will be many glitches and disputes along the way.

Industrial standards can usually be addressed in a dispassionate manner since only commercial advantage or disadvantage is at stake. Much more emotional are environmental standards, pesticides, fertilizers, animal and plant health, and food and drug regulation. The beef hormone war was an early harbinger in this field—a U.S.-Community dispute in 1988–89 over EC rules that excluded beef produced with artificial hormones— followed by the milk hormone case. The question of sanitary and phytosanitary regulations is part of the agriculture negotiations in GATT, but things are moving very slowly. The existing international regimes

28. *Financial Times*, July 6, 1989, p. 2.

29. EC Commission, "The Single Market and Industrial Products Quality: Commission Proposes Confidence-Building Measures to the Twelve," Information Memo P-89-73, Brussels, July 5, 1989.

are weak and inadequate. This appears to be another area that requires U.S.-Community bilateral arrangements, including a special dispute-settlement mechanism.

## Government Procurement

A third important area of concern to U.S. industry is public procurement. According to the Cecchini report, public purchasing accounts for 15 percent of European GDP.[30] Recognizing the significance of such purchases, the GATT contracting parties negotiated an agreement on government procurement in the Tokyo Round (1973–79). It was subsequently improved and updated; the revised text entered into force on February 14, 1988.[31]

The GATT Agreement on Government Procurement (GATT procurement code) aims to secure greater international competition in the government procurement market. It contains detailed rules on the way in which tenders for contracts opened by entities listed in the Annexes to the code should be invited and awarded. The code is designed to make laws, regulations, procedures, and practices regarding government procurement more transparent and to ensure that they do not protect domestic products or suppliers or discriminate among foreign products or suppliers.

The European Commission also recognized the importance of public procurement in Europe. It first issued administrative directives on requiring open tendering in public supply and public works contracts. Then, taking up the finding of the Cecchini report that four sectors excluded from its first directives—telecommunications, energy, water, and transport—are costly both in terms of government spending and of a fragmented Community market, the Commission proposed directives that would open these sectors as well to EC-wide competition.[32]

---

30. Paolo Cecchini and others, *The European Challenge 1992: The Benefits of a Single Market* (Aldershot, Eng.: Wildwood House for the EC Commission, 1988), p. 16.

31. General Agreement on Tariffs and Trade, "Latest Amendments to the Agreement on Government Procurement Now Incorporated in Revised GATT Text," Press Release 1435, Geneva, May 24, 1988.

32. EC Commission, "Proposal for a Council Directive, Based on Articles 100a and 113 of the EEC Treaty, on the Procurement Procedures of Entities Providing Water, Energy and Transport Services," *Bulletin of the European Communities*, S6/88 (Brussels, October 11, 1988), pp. 79–98. See also U.S. International Trade Commission, *The Effects of Greater Economic Integration within the European Community on the United States*, USITC Publication 2204 (Washington, July 1989), chap. 4. For the Cecchini report findings,

The usefulness of the GATT procurement code depends, in large part, on the government entities covered, but efforts to expand the code have been stalled because of the lack of EC negotiating authority. With the Commission initiative on the four excluded sectors, the prospects for GATT code negotiations (which are independent of but related to the Uruguay Round) have brightened considerably.

The exceptional importance of open procurement in these excluded sectors is matched by the political difficulties. In all countries, governments will encounter strong resistance from domestic interests to bidding, on an equal basis, by nonnational suppliers—even within Europe's internal market. Because Council decisions in this area can now be made according to the new qualified majority requirement, that may make things easier. However, the balance between liberals and protectionists in the Community indicates that a blocking minority may still make approval of procurement directives difficult to obtain.

The goal of allowing bids from non-European countries will be even harder to achieve. Nevertheless, the Commission proposal does address the question of relations with third countries. It makes clear that "where an offer is made by a firm established in a Member State, the directives will apply to it even if the firm is a subsidiary or agent of a third country firm and the goods or services to be rendered under the offer have their origin entirely in that third country."[33]

To spur U.S.-Community negotiations on government procurement, the Commission proposal deliberately mirrors the U.S. Buy American legislation. Thus the basic Commission rule follows the U.S. 50 percent local content requirement. As in U.S. rules, all bidders must meet the local content requirement, but Community firms enjoy a 3 percent price preference (the margin in the United States is 6 percent).

The Community press announcement said that the requirement of local content could be adjusted through negotiations under GATT auspices offering equivalent treatment. Successful GATT negotiations would mean that goods and services from any code member would count toward satisfying the local content requirement. In addition, price preferences would be eliminated.

---

see EC Commission, *Research on the "Cost of Non-Europe," Basic Findings: Executive Summaries,* vol. 1 (Luxembourg, 1988), pp. 67–116.

33. EC Commission, *Communication from the Commission on a Community Regime for Procurement in the Excluded Sectors: Water, Energy, Transport and Telecommunications,* COM (88) 376 Final (Brussels, October 11, 1988), p. 104.

Although the original Commission position was that it must wait for Council action before negotiating in GATT, informal discussions have taken place without waiting for final Community action. In November 1989 the Commission reportedly proposed a broad package approach that would cover not only central government purchasing of the excluded sectors, but also state and local procurement. These reports indicate that the EC may be seeking some private sector commitments, for example, with respect to the regional Bell operating companies (RBOCs). Such a proposal would cause some difficulties for the United States. State, local, and private sector procurement commitments might have to be established on a voluntary footing, since the federal government may not have the political power to enforce mandatory commitments.

If the EC does, in fact, put forward such an ambitious proposal, the United States should accept it as a basis for negotiation. Some U.S. industry groups argue that America has already given more than it has gotten under the GATT procurement code, and that the code coverage should not be expanded. But since the United States is generally more open in government procurement matters than the EC member states, U.S. negotiators can use an ambitious proposal to good advantage. As far as RBOCs are concerned, they are already freely buying foreign telecommunications equipment.

Even if all the legal steps are taken to open public procurement both within the Community and with other signatories of the GATT code, the "systemic" problem remains. In nearly all countries, government purchasing agencies exhibit a built-in proclivity to "buy national," regardless of laws and regulations. In the case of Japan, this issue has been elevated to the level of a "structural impediment" by the United States under the "Super 301" of the 1988 Omnibus Trade Act. In the EC, success also depends on changing the attitude of the procurement agencies and their personnel.

## Rules of Origin

The fourth major area of concern to the American business community in the Europe 1992 Program—rules of origin—is perhaps the most difficult to understand and to cope with. While the problems appear to be technical, they can have important trade and investment consequences. At present, there is no good forum for negotiating the issues raised by rules of origin: for example, whether local content requirements are satisfied, whether import quotas apply, and whether antidumping duties are levied.

Rules of origin were, until recently, considered a specialized customs matter best left to experts. Although no international agreement exists, "substantial transformation" has historically been the generally applied rule to determine origin for customs purposes. Under this test, a product's origin is the country where it underwent its last substantial transformation. However, with the proliferation of customs unions, free trade areas, trade preferences for developing countries, discriminatory quotas, voluntary export restraint agreements, and the prospective opening of government procurement markets, rules of origin have taken on greater importance, and more differentiated and precise tests (sometimes "value-added" rules) have been applied. In part this reflects the fact that internationalization of production has made it harder to determine the origin of a product.

An early example of these problems was the modification of U.S. customs rules in the textile sector to avoid circumvention of country quotas (especially between China and Hong Kong) under the Multifiber Agreement. The United States defined more stringently the processing required to confer origin so that Chinese garments could not be transshipped to the United States through Hong Kong. Under the Generalized System of Preferences, the Caribbean Basin Initiative, and other preferential arrangements, a local value-added test for origin is used. In the U.S.-Canada Free Trade Agreement, the basic rule is substantial transformation, but more stringent rules apply when third-country materials are involved in the case of the textile, steel, and automotive sectors. These exceptions having been agreed, according to the U.S. press announcement, "at the request of private sector advisors," one may suspect that the motivation was protection.

The EC also has a multiplicity of rules of origin, provoking disputes from time to time. There is no formal local content requirement for a product to obtain EC origin; the test is substantial transformation unless some exception is agreed internationally or decreed by the European Commission Customs Union Service, which is responsible for origin matters.

The recent change in the origin rule for semiconductors has caused the greatest stir. In this case, the definition was changed from the last substantial transformation to the most substantial transformation (a diffusion process). Community users of semiconductors soon shifted their

sourcing patterns because they needed to meet local content requirements, either to maintain eligibility for government procurement or to
avoid antidumping duties. Even where local content is not formally
required by the Commission regulations, foreign companies do not want
to take a chance and so they err on the side of buying European
components. For U.S. suppliers of semiconductors and microprocessors,
this change has meant considerable investment in European plants to
avert a dramatic loss of business.[34] All in all, the seemingly technical
shift from "last" to "most" prompted a fairly dramatic migration of plant
capacity.

Thus far, the Europe 1992 rule-of-origin issue has caused problems in
connection with discriminatory import quotas (mainly affecting Japan),
circumvention of antidumping duties (mainly affecting Japan), and government procurement (with a major impact on the United States).

*Discriminatory import quotas.* Aside from country quotas applied
under the GATT textile arrangement and bilateral agreements, most of
the restrictions maintained by the individual member states are directed
against Japanese goods. Once the single market is fully in place, there
will be no way to control transshipment from a member state that
maintains restrictions to a member state that does not. National quotas
will have to be phased out or there will have to be a Community-wide
quota.

The internal Community debate over this issue has already been
joined. The French tried to preempt it by arguing that a Nissan car (the
Bluebird) produced in the United Kingdom with 70 percent local content
would not qualify as British and thus would not escape the French quota
on Japanese auto imports. France insisted that the local U.K. content
had to be raised to 80 or 90 percent. Britain contended that the Bluebird
already qualified as a British product. The French backed down. They
had no legal basis for their position, and they may have decided that a
conciliatory attitude might help attract Japanese investment to France.

As far as the Commission is concerned, it possesses the exclusive right
to authorize national protective measures under Article 115 of the Rome
treaty.[35] This article is directed to "the execution of measures of
commercial policy" taken by member states and gives the Commission

---

34. The mid-1989 announcement by Intel Corporation of its decision to set up a plant
in Ireland is concrete evidence of the "forced investment effect."

35. EC Commission, *Treaties Establishing the European Communities, Treaties Amending These Treaties: Single European Act* (Luxembourg, 1987), p. 316.

the right to "authorize . . . the necessary protective measures." With respect to the test case—discriminatory import quotas on Japanese cars and trucks—the Commission has stated that the national quotas must go and that there will be no Community quotas. Presumably this position will be upheld. Current discussion concerns the transitional phase-out period.

If this outcome actually emerges and is extended to the whole range of discriminatory restrictions against Japan, then a feared side effect of Community-wide quotas on products made in the United States by Japanese firms may disappear. An encouraging sign is found in paragraph 44 of the Commission's Fourth Progress Report on implementation of the White Paper program.[36] It states that there has been a substantial reduction in the recourse to monitoring measures (a drop from 1,800 in 1985 to 500 today) and market protection measures under Article 115, and it talks of the "final elimination of the need for such controls."

On the other hand, a failure in the Uruguay Round to deal with the problem of misuse or lack of use of GATT safeguard procedures (Article XIX) could lead, especially in a stagnant economic and trade situation, to the further proliferation of voluntary export restrictions (VERs). The Commission might then have more difficulty in exercising its authority under Article 115, or it could be impelled to adopt Community-wide VERs. The technical question would be whether VERs enforced by the exporting country, rather than the Community member states, would fall under Article 115. On this point, a decisive interpretation remains to be given by the European Court of Justice.

*Circumvention of antidumping duties.* In 1987 the EC imposed a duty on finished products assembled in the Community from parts imported from Japan in cases where a previous antidumping finding had been made against the finished product imported directly from Japan. The duty was intended to deter circumvention of the antidumping duty by the assembly of parts in the Community, and was colloquially referred to as the "screwdriver regulation." Most of the cases under this regulation have been resolved by "undertakings" that involve increased use of non-Japanese, mostly Community parts. The effect of this anticircumvention regulation on the United States is not clear. The United States adopted its own anticircumvention provision in the 1988 Trade Act. The EC

36. EC Commission, *Fourth Progress Report of the Commission to the Council and the European Parliament: Concerning the Implementation of the Commission's White Paper on the Completion of the Internal Market*, COM (89) 311 Final (Brussels, June 20, 1989).

regulation applies only to products assembled in the Community.[37] At the request of Japan, a panel has been established in GATT to consider the question of GATT consistency of the Community regulation.[38]

*Government procurement.* Until the EC-excluded sectors are covered by the GATT code (which may be a long time), a local content problem will persist for U.S. companies selling to European government agencies. U.S. firms established in Europe can probably make the necessary adjustments. But U.S. exporters will have to resort to the exception rules in national procurement regulations or to Community directives (when they are adopted). It seems unlikely that this matter will lend itself to bilateral resolution or to resolution in any forum other than GATT.

## Other Elements of the 1992 Program

The foregoing examination of specific issues covers many of the important directives, from the U.S. standpoint, in the 1992 program. Other chapters in this volume focus on particular industries and take up additional directives of sectoral significance. The chapter on competition addresses aspects, such as company law, that are included under the White Paper heading "The Creation of Suitable Conditions for Industrial Cooperation." Directives both on the free movement of workers and on the removal of border controls that were erected to enforce different value-added tax rates in different member states appear to raise few negotiating problems for the United States.

The abolition of physical frontiers deals mainly with simplification of formalities. The abolition of transshipment controls within the EC on strategic goods, however, is a matter for discussion and negotiation in the Coordinating Committee for Multilateral Export Controls (COCOM), the organization created to deal with strategic exports from OECD countries to Eastern Europe, the Soviet Union, and China. With the political revolution in Eastern Europe, the United States may be pushed to keep up with the more relaxed EC attitude toward high-technology trade, in general, including strategic goods trade. Relaxation will reduce the significance of this issue.

In one other area—intellectual property rights—the Commission proposals are of keen interest to the United States. However, EC and

---

37. Article 13(10) of Council Regulation EEC 2423/88, *O.J. Eur. Comm.*, no. L209 (Luxembourg, August 2, 1988).

38. The author of this chapter acted as chairman of the GATT dispute panel.

U.S. governments and business communities are generally in accord on matters relating to patents, trademarks, copyright, and other forms of intellectual property. They are working very closely together, for example, in the GATT intellectual property exercise. Another example of the close working relationship is the extensive exchange of views between U.S. and Community experts on the Green Paper on Copyrights circulated by the Commission.[39]

The issue of subsidies to trade and production is not technically part of the 1992 program. Rather, subsidies are subject to discipline under the basic EC treaties (see chapter 6). But the subject is also on the Uruguay Round agenda. The current discussion in Geneva clusters around a revived "traffic light" approach: an attempt to put subsidies into the green category (permitted), the red category (prohibited), and the yellow category (subject to discipline if the trade impact is great enough). At the moment, the EC is not enthusiastic for greater international discipline on subsidies, notwithstanding the rigorous discipline imposed by the Competition, Cartels, and State Aids Directorate (DG-4) on subsidies within the Community. However, the United States is pressing for renewed discipline, especially in light of problems in mature industries, such as steel, in high-technology industries, such as civilian aircraft, and in connection with the proliferation of research consortia, such as Sematech and JESSI. This issue will probably come to a head in mid- to late 1990. Even a successful conclusion of GATT talks will leave a great deal of follow-on work in terms of refining definitions and dispute resolution.

## Conclusions and Recommendations

Two basic conclusions emerge with respect to overall negotiating strategy between 1990 and 1992. First, at this stage, the United States is correct to stress the Uruguay Round as the main focus of efforts to shape the implementation of the Europe 1992 Program. A successful GATT negotiation will also further the broader objective of maintaining, widening, and strengthening the open world trading system. Second, the timing and likely outcome of the Uruguay Round will not allow the United States to put all its Europe 1992 eggs in the GATT basket.

39. EC Commission, *Green Paper on Copyright and the Challenge of Technology: Copyright Issues Requiring Immediate Action*, COM (88) 172 Final (Brussels, June 7, 1988). In Community parlance, green papers are technical expositions; white papers are policy declarations.

Implementation is already under way on important 1992 issues. Some problems are not likely to be resolved in the GATT context in timely fashion.

## Recommendations

From the analysis and conclusions, five recommendations can be offered.

First, the United States should revise key elements in its Uruguay Round negotiating strategy to reflect an aggressive open trade posture along the lines of the U.S. proposal on agriculture. The approach to tariff reductions is the clearest area where the United States needs a more assertive posture. On other subjects as well a more ambitious U.S. position will improve the chances of an outcome that will be balanced at the highest possible level of liberalization and GATT discipline. The objective would be to force the EC to implement its single market program in an outward-looking way, extending the benefits of internal liberalization in exchange for concessions from third parties or avoiding damage to outsiders.

Second, at the same time the United States should upgrade and intensify its bilateral consultations and negotiations with the European Commission, the member states, and the European Parliament. A key aspect of these talks should be the most effective way of handling the linkage between Europe 1992 and Uruguay Round issues. Within the U.S. executive branch, the interdepartmental structure should be staffed by people responsible for both sets of issues. Coordination should be improved between the U.S. missions in Brussels and Geneva. It should then be possible to work more closely with the Commission staff, which also needs to improve its coordination between the external relations (DG-1) and internal market (DG-3) divisions. Contacts with the member states and the European Parliament should be guided by the strategy and tactics worked out with the Commission.

Third, on some issues, like national treatment in services and rules of origin, the United States should initiate substantive negotiations as soon as possible, either bilaterally or plurilaterally (OECD or ad hoc), if it appears that GATT is not going to deal with the matter in an effective and timely manner.

Fourth, to avoid poisoning the atmosphere for these negotiations, the United States should use the maximum flexibility available in the market-opening provisions of the Omnibus Trade Act of 1988. Instead of constant threats of retaliation by U.S. market-closing measures, negotiations until the end of 1990 should concentrate on achieving the maximum reciprocal liberalization.

Fifth, toward the end of 1990, the United States will have to review its negotiating strategy in the light of the outcome of the Uruguay Round, the status of the implementation of the Europe 1992 Program, and overall U.S. economic policy. At that point, various options, including extension of GATT negotiations, bilateral agreements, or wider regional arrangements, will have to be considered.

If the single market yields the benefits forecast in the Cecchini report, the most attractive option might be to use the OECD and GATT to develop a program applying the principles of mutual recognition, deregulation, and liberalization to a wider geographical area. The applicability of the Cecchini report analysis to trade with non-EC countries was implicitly recognized by the authors. As Cecchini himself wrote, "If the fruits of the European home market are to be shared internationally, there must also be a fair share-out of the burdens of global economic responsibility, with market opening measures extended internationally on a firm basis of clear reciprocity."[40]

## U.S. Government Organization and Negotiating Tactics

To carry out these recommendations, changes should be made in U.S. government organization and operations. First, the Washington interdepartmental structure should be revamped. To show that the administration was on top of the Europe 1992 developments, a special working task force was set up in June 1988 under the chairmanship of the U.S. Trade Representative. The main purpose of this group was to follow EC activities related to the single market and to prepare a report on what issues should be addressed by the United States.[41]

Needed now is a higher-level group chaired by the USTR official responsible for both the Uruguay Round and Europe 1992. The function of this committee should be to develop negotiating positions for Geneva and Brussels. There will inevitably be questions of tactics having to do with trade-offs and timing to best achieve U.S. objectives in the two

---

40. Cecchini, *European Challenge 1992*, p. xx.

41. U.S. Government Interagency Task Force on the EC Internal Market, *Completion of the European Community Internal Market: An Initial Assessment of Certain Economic Policy Issues Raised by Aspects of the EC's Program*, Pub. Doc. 1288 (Washington, December 1988).

arenas. Only someone looking at both the Uruguay Round and Europe 1992 can effectively conduct a strategy linking the two.

Second, also on the Washington front, there should be a stronger and more concentrated effort to consult with and inform Congress. In recent years, congressional interest and involvement in trade policy, negotiations, and the EC has grown tremendously. This appetite is beyond the capability of one agency to satisfy. The USTR should handle the main trade policy committees (House Ways and Means and Senate Finance); the State Department should handle House Foreign Affairs and Senate Foreign Relations; the Commerce Department, House Energy and Commerce and Senate Commerce, Science, and Transportation; and the Labor Department, House Education and Labor and Senate Labor and Human Resources.

Briefings and consultations should take place not only when some action, position, or event warrants, but regularly. They should be offered almost weekly, with either staff or principals, even if the offer is frequently declined. The business community should be similarly informed and consulted, but many more channels and opportunities already exist for this task.

Third, tension is almost inevitable between Washington, the USTR representative in Geneva, and the U.S. mission in Brussels. Many decisions have to be taken in Washington, but input from the negotiating front is essential. Visits to Washington by the Geneva representative should be used not only for executive branch policy discussions, but also for congressional briefings. Rufus Yerxa, the current Geneva representative, has the advantage of extensive experience on Capitol Hill.

On the 1992 side, much of the work can most effectively be done in Europe. There must be close cooperation and coordination between the U.S. missions to the Community and those to GATT, and perhaps also those to the OECD. Periodic meetings should be held between the missions and U.S. ambassadors to the key European capitals to give them guidance. The cabinet-level U.S.-Community semiannual meetings, in Brussels and Washington, should be revived. They should be well-prepared, substantive sessions, lasting two days, rather than formal meetings on the margin of other occasions, like NATO meetings in Brussels.

At the mission in Brussels, influential European commissioners are emerging who generally take a liberal position on trade issues. The U.S. ambassador to the EC should work closely with these commissioners to establish a mutual early warning system for potential friction points. He or she should also work with them to find solutions acceptable to the United States that they can push in the Commission.

If the matter involves action by the Council of Ministers, the cooperating commissioners can inform the U.S. side of the member state positions, and the U.S. embassies in the key capitals can make the appropriate representations. The European Parliament, with its enhanced role under the Single European Act, should be factored into the orchestration of U.S. negotiating strategy.

APPENDIX 7–1. Trade Agreement Negotiating Authority (Section 1102) in the Omnibus Trade and Competitiveness Act of 1988

(a) Agreements Regarding Tariff Barriers.—

(1) Whenever the President determines that one or more existing duties or other import restrictions of any foreign country or the United States are unduly burdening and restricting the foreign trade of the United States and that the purposes, policies, and objectives of this title will be promoted thereby, the President—

(A) before June 1, 1993, may enter into trade agreements with foreign countries; and

(B) may, subject to paragraphs (2) through (5), proclaim—
(i) such modification or continuance of any existing duty,
(ii) such continuance of existing duty-free or excise treatment, or
(iii) such additional duties;

as he determines to be required or appropriate to carry out any such trade agreement.

(2) No proclamation may be made under subsection (a) that—

(A) reduces any rate of duty (other than a rate of duty that does not exceed 5 percent ad valorem on the date of enactment of this Act) to a rate which is less than 50 percent of the rate of such duty that applies on such date of enactment; or

(B) increases any rate of duty above the rate that applies on such date of enactment.

(3) (A) Except as provided in subparagraph (B), the aggregate reduction in the rate of duty on any article which is in effect on any day pursuant to a trade agreement entered into under paragraph (1) shall not exceed the aggregate reduction which would have been in effect on such day if a reduction of 3 percent ad valorem or a reduction of one-tenth of the total reduction, whichever is greater, had taken effect on the effective date of the first reduction proclaimed in paragraph (1) to carry out such agreement with respect to such article.

(B) No staging under subparagraph (A) is required with respect to a rate reduction that is proclaimed under paragraph (1) for an article of a kind that is not produced in the United States. The United States International Trade Commission shall advise the President of the identity of articles that may be exempted from staging under this subparagraph.

(4) If the President determines that such action will simplify the computation of reductions under paragraph (3), the President may round an annual reduction by the lesser of—

(A) the difference between the reduction without regard to this paragraph and the next lower whole number; or

(B) one-half of 1 percent ad valorem.

(5) No reduction in a rate of duty under a trade agreement entered into under subsection (a) on any article may take effect more than 10 years after the effective date of the first reduction under paragraph (1) that is proclaimed to carry out the trade agreement with respect to such article.

(6) A rate of duty reduction or increase that may not be proclaimed by reason of paragraph (2) may take effect only if a provision authorizing such reduction or increase is included within an implementing bill provided for under section 1103 and that bill is enacted into law.

(b) Agreements Regarding Nontariff Barriers—

(1) Whenever the President determines that any barrier to, or other distortion of, international trade—

(A) unduly burdens or restricts the foreign trade of the United States or adversely affects the United States economy; or

(B) the imposition of any such barrier or distortion is likely to result in such a burden, restriction, or effect; and that the purposes, policies, and objectives of this title will be promoted thereby, the President may, before June 1, 1993, enter into a trade agreement with foreign countries providing for—

(i) the reduction or elimination of such barrier or other distortion; or

(ii) the prohibition of, or limitations on the imposition of, such barrier or other distortion.

(2) A trade agreement may be entered into under this subsection only if such agreement makes progress in meeting the applicable objectives described in section 1101.

(c) Bilateral Agreements Regarding Tariff and Nontariff Barriers.—

(1) Before June 1, 1993, the President may enter into bilateral trade agreements with foreign countries that provide for the elimination or reduction of any duty imposed by the United States. A trade agreement entered into under this paragraph may also provide for the reduction or elimination of barriers to, or other distortions of, the international trade of the foreign country or the United States.

(2) Notwithstanding any other provision of law, no trade benefit shall be extended to any country by reason of the extension of any trade benefit to another country under a trade agreement entered into under paragraph (1) with such other country.

(3) A trade agreement may be entered into under paragraph (1) with any foreign country only if—

(A) the agreement makes progress in meeting the applicable objectives described in section 1101;

(B) such foreign country requests the negotiation of such an agreement; and

(C) the President, at least 60 days before the date notice is provided under section 1103(a)(1)(A)—

    (i) provides written notice of such negotiations to the Committee on Finance of the Senate and the Committee on Ways and Means of the House of Representatives, and

    (ii) consults with such committees regarding the negotiation of such agreement.

(4) The 60-day period of time described in paragraph (3)(B) shall be computed in accordance with section 1103(f).

(5) In any case in which there is an inconsistency between any provision of this Act and any bilateral free trade area agreement that entered into force and effect with respect to the United States before January 1, 1987, the provision shall not apply with respect to the foreign country that is party to that agreement.

(d) Consultation With Congress Before Agreements Entered Into.—

(1) Before the President enters into any trade agreement under subsection (b) or (c), the President shall consult with—

    (A) the Committee on Ways and Means of the House of Representatives and the Committee on Finance of the Senate; and

    (B) each other committee of the House and the Senate, and each joint committee of the Congress, which has jurisdiction over legislation involving subject matters which would be affected by the trade agreement.

(2) The consultation under paragraph (1) shall include—

    (A) the nature of the agreement;

    (B) how and to what extent the agreement will achieve the applicable purposes, policies, and objectives of this title; and

    (C) all matters relating to the implementation of the agreement under section 1103.

(3) If it is proposed to implement two or more trade agreements in a single implementing bill under section 1103, the consultation under paragraph (1) shall include the desirability and feasibility of such proposed implementation.

SOURCE: P.L. 100–418, 102 Stat. 1107, 1126–28.

APPENDIX 7–2. Excerpt from Japanese Tariff Proposal, as Made to the GATT Negotiating Group on Tariffs, July 1989

**Negotiating Group on Tariffs**
**Modalities for Tariff Negotiations**
**Submission by Japan**

The Government of Japan has been considering it desirable to aim at the reciprocal elimination of tariffs on industrial products by developed countries, as proposed in our first submission on July 1987 (MTN/GNG/NG1/W/8). Japan further made a supplementary submission in March 1988 (MTN/GNG/NG1/W/ 8/ Suppl. 1/Rev. 1), taking into account the views expressed by participants while still maintaining the *original aim of the elimination of industrial tariffs*.

Bearing in mind the aforementioned basic aim and in recognition of the need to achieve the targets as agreed at the Montreal Ministerial Meeting, such as "achieving lower and more uniform rates, including the reduction or eliminations of high tariffs, tariff peaks, tariff escalation and low tariffs, with a target amount for overall reductions at least as ambitious as that achieved by the formula participants in the Tokyo Round," Japan proposed the following as a generally applicable approach to tariff reduction, which will lead to the broadest possible participation.

1. The modality for the reduction of tariffs:
   The parameter "a" is chosen by each participant so as to achieve 33 percent or more tariff reductions.
   (1) Basic formula:
   $$Z = \frac{ax}{a + x}$$
   $x$ = tariff rate before reduction
   $Z$ = tariff rate after reduction

   (2) In principle, there will be no exceptions to the application of the above formula.

   (3) After the submission of the initial offer list based on the above formula has been made by the participants, the request/offer approach may be used to achieve tariff reductions deeper than the formula cut, including elimination of tariffs, as required.

2. The initial offer list should be submitted [by the end of January 1990] with the actual figure of parameter "a" that satisfies the above mentioned condition.

3. The formula mentioned in paragraph 1 is to be applied, in principle, to all participants. Developing countries will choose a figure of "a" as appropriate according to the general principles of the Punta del Este declaration and at the same time, will make efforts to increase the ratio of tariff bindings to the highest possible level.

SOURCE: *Inside U.S. Trade*, Special Report, August 4, 1989.

APPENDIX 7–3. Excerpt from EC Tariff Proposal, as Made to the GATT Negotiating Group on Tariffs, July 1989

**Submission by the European Communities**

1. In September 1986 the Ministers, meeting in special session of the Contracting Parties at Punta del Este, decided in particular that the negotiations should lead to improved market access by reducing and eliminating customs duties, quantitative restrictions and other non-tariff measures and obstacles.

2. In its submission of September 1987 (document MTN/GNG/NG1/W/11 of 28 September 1987) the Community deplored the discrepancy between the level of obligations currently assumed by the various contracting parties and the various participants and declared its readiness to examine with its trading partners procedures and methods aimed at reducing the discrepancy, in particular by means of tariff reductions accompanied by an undertaking by all contracting parties to bind their customs duties for products covered by Negotiating Group No. 1.

3. The Community clearly confirmed this readiness at the close of the meeting of the Trade Negotiations Committee on 8 April this year, when it stated in particular that "in the negotiating groups concerned with market access, the Community is prepared to play its full part, it being understood that there is a genuine commitment by others, in particular the more advanced developing countries to participate to the full."

**Market Access**

4. In order to respect the spirit of Punta del Este, negotiations on liberalization can be satisfactory only if they lead to a real, significant and stable improvement in access to the markets of all contracting parties.

   With this aim in mind, the European Community is proposing for all participants a co-ordinated negotiation linking tariff and non-tariff measures with the aim of achieving durable and effective improvements in market access. The Community considers it essential that all participate effectively in the negotiations and reserves the right to adjust its final offer if this condition is not met.

   In seeking through the process of negotiation the reduction or elimination of tariffs and non-tariff measures on the basis of mutual benefits the Community takes the view that at the end of the Uruguay Round all industrial tariffs should be bound by all participants using the methods outlined below and that similar techniques should be applied to the reduction and elimination of non-tariff measures. Such action will greatly increase the predictability and security of *international trade* to the benefit of all Contracting Parties. The Community does not intend to grant concessions nor give credit for tariff concessions nullified or impaired by non-tariff measures.

   The Community is in favour of a multilateral approach based on equity and fair burden sharing in order to meet the target laid down by Ministers at Punta del Este and Montreal.

**Customs Duties**

5. With more specific reference to customs duties, all the Ministers clearly expressed at Montreal their agreement that the negotiations should include the following elements:

   —Effective and positive participation of all partners to the negotiations subject in the case of the developing countries, to account being taken of individual development needs;

   —lower and more uniform rates of duty (both between different tariffs as well as within each tariff) by the reduction (or elimination) of high tariffs, tariff peaks, tariff escalation and low tariffs in order to achieve an overall result at least as ambitious as that achieved by participants in the Tokyo Round who applied the formula;

   —greater security in market access through the binding of rates resulting from the negotiations.

   The Community considers these conditions to be essential and will formulate its final offer according to their achievement.

6. With a view to effectively achieving the objectives agreed at Punta del Este and at Montreal, the Community proposes that the Group adopt the following systematic approach to customs duties:

   A. Industrialized and more advanced developing countries
      —base rate of 40% or higher reduction to a ceiling of 20%
      —base rate of less than 40% reduction on the following basis:
         —rates between 0% and 29%
            $$R = D + 20$$
      (where $R$ is the percentage reduction and $D$ the base rate of the customs duty);
         —rates between 30% and 40%
            $$R = 50$$
      (flat-rate reduction of 50%).

   B. Other developing countries (other than the least advanced)
      —base rate of more than 35%; reduction to a ceiling rate of 35%;
      —base rate of 35% or less; possibility of bilateral negotiations with a view to reducing and harmonizing rates of duty.

   **A and B:** both the new rates negotiated and any rates left unchanged should be bound.

   C. **Least advanced countries**

      Contribution within the limits of their capabilities, in accordance with Part 1.B, paragraph (vii) of the Punta del Este Declaration.

7. In addition to the proposed reductions, the Community does not exclude the elimination, by all participants, of base rates of 3% or less inasmuch as no compensation or credit is claimed therefore.

8. The other issues (staging, etc.) could be discussed within the group in the light of progress made as regards the proposed systematic approach.

9. The Community reserves its right to make further proposals at any further stage of the negotiations. It will also develop its approach on market access in the Negotiating Group on non-tariff measures.

SOURCE: *Inside U.S. Trade*, Special Report, August 4, 1989.

APPENDIX 7–4. U.S. Proposal for the Principles of Services Trade, October 24, 1989

**Summary**

On October 23, the United States introduced a comprehensive proposal on services in the Uruguay Round of multilateral trade negotiations. The U.S. text is the first proposal by any country that expresses in legal terms the obligations countries would assume under a services agreement.

The U.S. proposal seeks to open world services markets to the maximum extent possible. Under it, services providers would be free to locate in foreign countries and compete like local firms. They would face a fair, predictable environment for their services throughout the world.

**Elements of U.S. Proposal**

—Enable service firms to set up shop overseas and be treated like local firms.

—Restrict governments' ability to distort services trade through subsidies, regulations and state monopolies.

—Require that national laws and regulations governing services activities be openly administered.

**U.S. Services Proposal Objectives**

—Assure clear, open, fair, and non-restrictive rules for services.

—Increase market opportunities for U.S. services providers by removing foreign services trade barriers.

SOURCE: Office of the U.S. Trade Representative, *Fact Sheet* (Washington, October 24, 1989).

# Selected Bibliography

THE FOLLOWING sources deal with Europe 1992 in general. For reference material related to specific industries and policies, see the citations in each chapter.

## Books and Articles

Baldwin, Robert E., Carl B. Hamilton, and André Sapir. *Issues in US-EC Trade Relations.* National Bureau of Economic Research Conference Report. University of Chicago Press, 1988.

Buhart, Jacques, and Dennis Burton. *Legal Aspects of the Single European Market: A Working Guide to 1992.* Euromoney Special Report. Tonbridge, Eng., 1989.

Calingaert, Michael. *The 1992 Challenge from Europe: Development of the European Community's Internal Market.* NPA 237. Washington: National Planning Association, 1988.

"The Changing Map of Europe." *Harvard Business Review,* no. 3, May–June 1989.

Coffey, Peter, ed. *Main Economic Policy Areas of the EEC—Towards 1992: The Challenge to the Communities Economic Policies When the "Real" Common Market Is Created by the End of 1992.* International Studies in Economics and Econometrics, vol. 20, 2d rev. ed. Dordrecht, Neth.: Kluwer Academic Publishers, 1988.

Cooney, Stephen. *EC-92 and U.S. Industry: An NAM Report on the Major Issues for U.S. Manufacturers in the European Community's Internal Market Program.* National Association of Manufacturers, February 1989.

Davis, Evan, and others. "1992 Myths and Realities." Centre for Business Strategy, London Business School, 1989.

"Europe in 1992: Obstacles or Opportunities?" *International Business,* January 1989.

Ludlow, Peter. *Beyond 1992: Europe and Its Western Partners.* CEPS Paper 38. Brussels: Centre for European Policy Studies, 1989.

Meessen, Karl M. "Europe en Route to 1992: The Completion of the Internal Market and Its Impact on Non-Europeans." *International Lawyer,* vol. 23 (Summer 1989), pp. 359–71.

Siebert, Horst. "The Single European Market—A Schumpeterian Event?" Kiel Discussion Paper 157. Federal Republic of Germany: Kiel Institute of World Economics, November 1989.

"A Survey of Europe's Internal Market." *Economist*, July 9, 1989.

Treverton, Gregory F., ed. *Europe and America Beyond 2000*. Council of Foreign Relations, 1990.

U.S. Chamber of Commerce. *Europe 1992: A Practical Guide for American Business*. Washington, 1989.

Williams, Joan, Susanne Perry, and Alan Madian. *Europe-1992 Progress Report*. Washington: Lafayette Publications, October 1989.

Winter, Audrey, and others. *Europe without Frontiers: A Lawyer's Guide*. Washington: Bureau of National Affairs, 1989.

## European Community Publications

Cecchini, Paolo, and others. *The European Challenge 1992: The Benefits of a Single Market*. Aldershot, Eng.: Wildwood House for the EC Commission, 1988.

Emerson, Michael, and others. "The Economics of 1992: An Assessment of the Potential Economic Effects of Completing the Internal Market of the European Economy." *European Economy*, no. 35. Luxembourg: European Communities Directorate-General for Economic and Financial Affairs, March 1988.

European Communities Commission. *Completing the Internal Market: White Paper from the Commission to the European Council*. Luxembourg, 1985.

———. *Single European Act*. Bulletin of the European Communities, Supplement. Luxembourg, February 1986.

———. *Steps to European Unity—Community Progress to Date: A Chronology*. 6th ed. Luxembourg, 1987.

———. *Research on the "Cost of Non-Europe": Basic Findings*. Vols. 1–16. Luxembourg, 1988.

———. *Eighteenth Report on Competition Policy*. Luxembourg, 1989.

## U.S. Government Documents

Harrison, Glennon J. *European Community: Issues Raised by 1992 Integration*. Washington: Congressional Research Service, May 31, 1989.

———. *The European Community's 1992 Plan: An Overview of the Proposed "Single Market."* Washington: Congressional Research Service, September 21, 1989.

U.S. Congress. House Committee on Foreign Affairs. Subcommittee on International Economic Policy and Trade. *European Community's 1992 Economic Integration Plan*. 101 Cong. 1 sess. Government Printing Office, 1989.

———. Joint Economic Committee. "Bibliography on Europe 1992." In *Europe 1992: Long-Term Implications for the U.S. Economy*. Hearing. 101 Cong. 1 sess. Government Printing Office, April 26, 1989.

U.S. Department of Commerce. International Trade Administration. *EC 1992: A Commerce Department Analysis of European Community Directives.* Vols. 1, 2. Washington, May, September 1989.

U.S. General Accounting Office. *European Single Market Issues of Concern to U.S. Exporters.* Washington, February 1990.

U.S. Government Interagency Task Force on the EC Internal Market. *Completion of the European Community Internal Market: An Initial Assessment of Certain Economic Policy Issues Raised by Aspects of the EC's Program.* Pub. Doc. 1288. Washington, December 1988.

U.S. International Trade Commission. *The Effects of Greater Economic Integration within the European Community on the United States.* USITC Publication 2204. Washington, July 1989.

U.S. Trade Representative. Advisory Committee for Trade Policy and Negotiations. *Europe 1992.* Washington, November 1989.

## Guides and Newsletters

Arthur Andersen and Co. *1992: Guide for Clients.* Brussels, March 1989.

Bureau of National Affairs. *1992—The External Impact of European Unification: Biweekly News for Business and Government.* Washington.

Chadwyck-Healey Ltd. *European Access.* Cambridge.

KPMG. *The Company Guide for Business in Europe.* Edited by Clive Stanbrook. Melton Constable, Eng.: European Business Publications (Clement Publishers), 1989.

Lafayette Publications, Inc. *Europe-1992: The Report on the Single European Market.* Washington.

Shearson Lehman Hutton Inc. *International Strategies: European Unification Series.* New York.

# Index